Big Data Applications in Industry 4.0

Big Data Applications in Industry 4.0

Edited by
P. Kaliraj
T. Devi

CRC Press
Taylor & Francis Group
Boca Raton London New York

CRC Press is an imprint of the
Taylor & Francis Group, an **informa** business

AN AUERBACH BOOK

First Edition published 2022
by CRC Press
6000 Broken Sound Parkway NW, Suite 300, Boca Raton, FL 33487-2742

and by CRC Press
4 Park Square, Milton Park, Abingdon, Oxon, OX14 4RN

CRC Press is an imprint of Taylor & Francis Group, LLC

Library of Congress Cataloguing-in-Publication Data
A catalog record has been requested for this book.

ISBN: 978-1-032-00811-0 (hbk)
ISBN: 978-1-032-19179-9 (pbk)
ISBN: 978-1-003-17588-9 (ebk)

DOI: 10.1201/9781003175889

Typeset in Garamond
by MPS Limited, Dehradun

Prof. P. Kaliraj dedicates this book to
esteemed *Bharathiar University*,
his father *Mr. M. Perumal*,
mother *Mrs. P. Rathinammal*,
grand children *Prithika Karthikeyan*,
Kayan Karthikeyan,
Ayaan Prashanth and
Akira Prashanth.

Prof. T. Devi dedicates this book to
Department of Computer Applications
her mother *Mrs. A. Suseela*,
mother-in-law *Mrs. D. Singari*,
son *R. Surya* and,
grandson *V. Deera*

Contents

Preface

Industry 4.0 is the latest technological innovation in manufacturing with the goal to increase productivity in a flexible and efficient manner. This revolutionary transformation which is changing the way in which manufacturers operate is powered by various technology advances including artificial intelligence, Big Data analytics, internet-of-things, and cloud computing. Big Data analytics has been identified as one of the significant components of industry 4.0 as it provides valuable insights for the purpose of smart factory management. This scenario requires the data to be processed with advanced tools and technologies in order to provide relevant information. Big Data and Industry 4.0 have the potential to shape up the industrial process in terms of resource consumption, process optimization, automation, and much more. It can be inferred that it also plays a key role in achieving sustainable development. However, keeping pace with these technologies require an individual to be highly skilled and well knowledgeable in identifying and solving any real-time problem. Such problems can be as small as a minute shift in the data generated, which may affect their surroundings, even their lives later. The exponentially rising generation rate of data has made the Big Data analytics a challenging area of research.

The Big Data Analytics Market growth is forecasted to grow at a compound annual growth rate of 29.7% to $40.6 billion by 2023 as per Frost & Sullivan. The growth in the Big Data analytics market will accelerate the need for specialists in Big Data analytics. And with demand for talented professionals more than doubling in the last few years, there are limitless opportunities for professionals who want to work on the cutting edge of Big Data research and development.

The awareness and practice on Big Data and its applications, skill development to face Industry 4.0 and technological advanced infrastructure become the keys for successful development of future pillars of our Globe. Linking Big Data analytics, which is one of the tools of Industry 4.0 with arts and science education is the need of the hour. Today, the rate at which the transformation happening is very disruptive in nature and also exponential changes are being witnessed. Educational institutions have to be way ahead of the requirement and prepare their students to meet the new challenges to be created by Industry 4.0. Currently, educational institutions are at crossroads and do not know how to interweave the Industry 4.0 tools into the arts, science, social science and teacher education programmes in Universities. The book can aid in imparting the concepts and knowledge of Big Data among graduates studying in Higher Education Institutions as it highlights the fundamentals and research trends of big data. It also describes applications of big data in various sectors such as finance, education, social media, remote sensing, and healthcare. Currently, there are no books on big data and its applications that can be used in the curriculum of higher education. The proposed book has a huge scope to be included in the higher education curriculum. Hence, the demand for the book among graduates and higher education institutions will be present as long as the curriculum of higher education institutions focuses on the development of Industry 4.0 skills. The students, scholars, and teachers can be from Arts & Science Universities, Engineering Institutions, and Teacher Education Universities. Practitioners – Scientists, Engineers, and Statisticians who are interested in building Big Data applications or analytical models to solve real world problems can also use this book for reference.

This book covers the recent advancements that have emerged in the field of Big Data and its applications. The exponentially rising generation rate of data has made the Big Data analytics, a challenging area of research. The book introduces the concepts, advanced tools and technologies for representing, and processing Big Data. It also covers applications of Big Data in domains such as financial services sector, education, tribal health care, biomedical research, healthcare, logistics, and warehouse management. Students of every discipline must be familiar with this fast growing technology since their future job prospects will be influenced by this technology. This book can be used in courses offered by Higher Education Institutions which strive to equip their graduates with Industry 4.0 skills. It can be used by scientists, engineers, and statisticians who are interested in building Big Data applications to solve real world problems.

Chapter 1 entitled "*Data Science and Its Applications*" introduces Data Science and discusses its applications in the business today. This chapter explores the possible types of data available in the business today, the many types of data analytics methods accessible today and covers uses cases through its applications.

Chapter 2 entitled "*Industry 4.0: Data and Data Integration*" provides an overview of what Data Integration is, the different Data Integration solutions available, and the different methodologies of Data Integration. The chapter also discusses about various Data Integration service providers available in the market.

Chapter 3 entitled "*Forecasting Principles and Models: – An Overview*" gives the readers a clear understanding of the general framework of forecasting principles, applications, limitations, and procedures for the data pertaining to such fields along with three basic forecast models, namely, naïve, moving average, and exponential smoothing models highlighting their significance.

Chapter 4 entitled "*Breaking Technology Barriers in Diabetes and Industry 4.0*" explores the application of Big Data in diagnosing diabetes. Diabetes is a fertile area to implement the concepts of Industry 4.0 that would directly impact lives of millions of people in India and world-wide. Barriers in Diabetes technology and technical solutions to break the barriers are detailed in this chapter. Healthcare is a fertile area with huge potential for Big Data, precision medicine, artificial intelligence, data mining, development of prediction models, health apps, machine automation, closed-loop technologies, and noninvasive monitoring systems.

Chapter 5 entitled *"Role of Big Data Analytics in Industrial Revolution 4.0"* provides readers a complete understanding emphasizing the need for Big Data for Industry 4.0 transformation. The chapter provides a detailed roadmap of Data evolution and its related technological transformation in computing with a brief description of data related terminologies as an introduction.

Chapter 6 entitled *"Big Data Infrastructure and Analytics for Education 4.0"* examines the application of Industry 4.0 and Big Data in the field of education. This chapter outlines how Industry 4.0 is being applied in education and discusses various Big Data infrastructure and analytics to build effective online teaching and learning.

Chapter 7 entitled *"Text Analytics in Big Data Environments"* explains the background of text analytics and text analytics in Big Data domain. It also discusses how machine learning techniques are applied over the huge volume of data in Big Data environment, addresses the research challenges and issues of text analytics over the Big Data environment, and discusses the tools for text analytics.

Chapter 8 entitled *"Business Data Analytics: Applications and Research Trends"* discusses the overview of Education 4.0, Big Data Analytics and Business Analytics, and the impact of Big Data Analytics in Education 4.0 as well as Business Analytics. Research perspectives and directions in these domains are also projected in this chapter.

Chapter 9 entitled *"Role of Big Data Analytics in the Financial Service Sector"* summarizes the features, prospects, and significant role of Big Data in banking industry and also its advantages in the financial sector. The chapter tries to identify the various use cases of Big Data in banking, finance services and insurance (BFSI) areas, where this analytics is turning out to be paramount.

Chapter 10 entitled *"Role of Big Data Analytics in the Education Domain"* describes the use of Big Data Analytics in Education domain. This chapter discusses how to analyze the educational data to improve the quality of education. It further discusses how Big Data technology will be used to assess the student performance, evaluation strategies, preparation of question papers, online examinations, comparison of curriculum, open-source educational tools, and web-based learning.

Chapter 11 entitled *"Social Media Analytics"* discusses the social media platforms and step-by-step processes of analysing the data available through social media. It describes domains of social media analytics (SMA), various types of analysis, techniques and algorithms for analysis such as natural language processing (NLP), news analytics, opinion mining, scraping, and text analytics. It introduces the machine learning and deep learning algorithms, software tools that are available for social media analytics, and research challenges.

Chapter 12 entitled *"Robust Statistics: Methods and Applications"* is a study on the assumptions and limitations of classical statistical procedures. It explores various robust statistical procedures developed in recent past, by considering the measure of location and scale, in the area of data depth, regression and multivariate analysis. This chapter analyzes data using robust statistical methods along with conventional statistical procedures using robust statistical packages in R programming.

Chapter 13 entitled *"Big Data in Tribal Healthcare and Biomedical Research"* confers the process of Big Data approaches in socio-economic status and in genomic research (NGS and Metagenomics). The chapter aims at deliberating healthcare as a Big Data repository, its analytics, and challenges in data retrieval and reiterates the necessity of Big Data in tribal community healthcare.

Chapter 14 entitled *"PySpark toward Data Analytics"* explores Pyspark in detail. The chapter explores how PySpark overcomes the drawbacks of Apache Hadoop MapReduce and how it extends the MapReduce model for its interactive queries and stream processing.

Chapter 15 entitled *"How to Implement Data Lake for Large Enterprises"* focuses on implementation of the Data Lake (DL) in cloud and the significance of DL where the pre-existence of a Data Warehouse (DW) helps businesses to take decisions.

Chapter 16 entitled *"A Novel Application of Data Mining Techniques for Satellite Performance Analysis"* provides a brief knowledge on how data mining techniques can be used to analyze satellite performance.

Chapter 17 entitled *"Big Data Analytics: A Text Mining Perspective and Applications in Biomedicine and Healthcare"* provides an overview of the text mining perspective of Big Data analytics with an emphasis on applications in biomedicine and healthcare. The chapter illustrates phases and tasks of text mining in Big Data scope and provides a description of two application areas of biomedicine and healthcare where text mining using Big Data analytics is applied.

How to Use the Book?

The method and purpose of using this book depend on the role that you play in an educational institution or in an industry or depend on the focus of your interest. We propose five types of roles: student, software developer, teacher, member of Board of Studies, and researcher.

If you are a student: Students can use the book to get a basic understanding of Big Data, its tools, and applications. Students belonging to any of the arts, science and social science disciplines will find useful information from chapters on complete insight on Big Data, fundamentals and applications. This book will serve as a starting point for beginners. Students will benefit from the chapters on applications of Big Data and data analytics in *biomedicine, healthcare, education, social media, finance, and satellite performance analysis.*

If you are a software developer: Software developers can use the book to get a basic understanding of Big Data, its tools, and applications. Readers with software development background will find useful information from chapters on fundamentals and applications. They will benefit from the chapters on *data integration, data lakes based on cloud, robust statististical methods given in R programming* and *PySpark.* Software developers will find the data analytics tool *PySpark* very useful from configuring runtime options, running in standalone, interactive jobs, writing simple programs, streaming analysis, and machine learning packages for data analysis. Cloud-based data lakes can be built by software developers using the concepts and architecture given in the chapter on implementation of *Data Lake for large enterprises.*

If you are a teacher, the book is useful as a text for several different university-level, college-level undergraduate and postgraduate courses. Chapters on *forecasting principles and models,* and *robust statistical methods* will help in gaining the knowledge on the Statistical models and methods that form the base for data analytics. A graduate course on Big Data can use this book as a primary textbook. It is important to equip the learners with a basic understanding on Big Data, a tool of Industry 4.0. Chapter on *Big Data – A Complete Insight* provides the fundamentals of Big Data. To teach the applications of Big Data in various sectors, say Healthcare, teachers will find useful information from chapters on diabetes, biomedicine and healthcare. A course on Big Data for Science too could use the chapters on diabetes, biomedicine and healthcare, and satellite performance analysis. A course on Big Data and Education could use the chapters that deal with application of Big Data, data analytics in Education 4.0.

If you are a member of the Board of Studies: Innovating the education to align with Industry 4.0 requires that the curriculum be revisited. Universities are looking for methods of incorporating Industry 4.0 tools across various disciplines of Arts, Science, and Social Science Education. This book helps in incorporating Big Data across Science and Education. The book is useful while framing the syllabus for new course that cut across Big Data and disciplines of Arts or Science or Social Science Education. For example, syllabi for courses entitled Big Data in science, Big Data in healthcare, Big Data in medical biotechnology, Big Data in education may be framed using the chapters in the book. Industry infusion into curriculum is given much importance by involving more industry experts – R&D managers, product development managers, technical managers as special invitees in the Board of Studies. Chapters given by industrial experts in this book will be very helpful to infuse the application part of Big Data into the curriculum.

If you are a researcher: A crucial area where innovation is required is the research work carried out by universities and institutions so that innovative, creative, and useful products and services are made available to society through translational research. This book can serve as a comprehensive reference guide for researchers in the development of experimental Big Data applications. The chapters on *diabetes and Industry 4.0, Healthcare, biomedical research, Education 4.0, business data analytics, finance,* and *satellite performance analysis* provide researchers, scholars, and students with a list of important research questions to be addressed using Big Data.

*****

Acknowledgments

From Prof. P. Kaliraj

First and Foremost, I express my sincere gratitude to **Hon'ble Shri. Banwarilal Purohit,** Governor of Tamil Nadu, India who was instrumental in organising the conference on Innovating Education in the era of Industry 4.0 during Dec 14–15, 2019, in Ooty, which paved the way for further work in Industry 4.0 knowledge world.

My heartfelt thanks go to Hon'ble Chief Minister of Tamil Nadu, India and Hon'ble Minister for Higher Education, Government of Tamil Nadu. I thank Principal Secretary to Government, Higher Education Department, Government of Tamil Nadu.

I would like to express my thanks to Secretary to Governor, and Deputy Secretary to Governor, Universities Governor's Secretariat, Raj Bhavan, Chennai.

I thank my wife, Dr. Vanaja Kaliraj, and my son-in-law Mr. M. Karthikeyan, daughter Mrs. Ratna Priya Karthikeyan, son Dr. K. Siva Prashanth, daughter-in-law Dr. Ratna Priya Prashanth, grand children Prithika Karthikeyan, Kayan Karthikeyan, Ayaan Prashanth, and Akira Prashanth, and my family members for their support and being patient.

From Prof. T. Devi

I record my sincere thanks to **Prof. P. Kaliraj**, Hon'ble Vice-Chancellor of Bharathiar University, who identified the knowledge world gap when Professor searched for a book on Industry 4.0 and triggered the process of writing and editing books in the Industry 4.0 series. His continuous motivation during the lockdown period due to COVID-19, sensitisation and encouragement are unmatchable.

I express my profound thanks to the **Vice-Chancellor** and **Registrar** for the administrative support. Heartfelt thanks are due to the **authors of the chapters** for their contribution of chapters, continuous co-operation in improvising the chapters as and when requested and for timely communication. I thank all the expert members who served as reviewers for providing a quality and swift review.

We wish to thank **Mr. John Wyzalek, Senior Acquisitions Editor, Taylor & Francis/CRC Press**, who gave the reply mail in the first week of October 2020 mentioning that our proposal on Big Data book is **topical,** believed in this book's idea and helped us in realizing our dream.

Special thanks are due to Mr. Todd Perry, production editor, Taylor & Francis/CRC Press, Florida, for his excellent co-ordination and Mr. Manmohan Negi, Project Manager, MPS Ltd., for his untiring and swift support.

Thanks to Ms. Stephanie Kiefer, Editorial Assistant, Taylor & Francis/ CRC Press, for her efforts and communications during the project.

Thanks are due to **Dr. R. Rajeswari**, Associate Professor, Department of Computer Applications for her continuous support; **Sister Italia Joseph Maria** and **Ms. M. Lissa**, Project Assistants for providing earnest support.

Thanks to the faculty members **Prof. M. Punithavalli, Dr. T. Amudha, Dr. J. Satheeshkumar, Dr. V. Bhuvaneswari, Mr. S. Palanisamy, Dr. S. Gavaskar, Dr. R. Balu**, and **Dr. J. Ramsingh**.

Thanks to the Assistant technical officers **Mr. A. Elanchezian, Mr. A. Sivaraj, Mrs. B. Priyadarshini**, and office staff **Mr. A. Kalidas** of Department of Computer Applications of Bharathiar University, India.

Thanks are due to **Mrs. K. Kowsalya**, Assistant Registrar, **Mr. R. Karthick**, Assistant Section Officer, and **Mr. A. Prasanth** of office of the Vice-Chancellor and staff of the office of the Registrar of Bharathiar University, India.

Finally, I thank my husband Mr. D. Ravi, daughter Mrs. R. Deepiga, son Mr. R. Surya, son-in-law Mr. D. Vishnu Prakhash and grandson V. Deera and family members for their encouragement and support.

*****

Editors

Prof. P. Kaliraj, Hon'ble Vice-Chancellor, Bharathiar University, a Visionary and an Eminent Leader leading big academic teams is having more than three decades of teaching and research experience. He has held various renowned positions such as officiating Vice-Chancellor of Anna University, Head of Centre for Biotechnology of Anna University, Dean of faculty at A C College of Technology, and Member of the Syndicate for two decades at Anna University. Professor had research collaborations with the National Institute of Health in Maryland, United States, Glasgow University in Scotland, United Kingdom, and University of Illinois in Rockford, United States. University Grants Commission BSR Faculty Award and the Lifetime Achievement Award from the Biotechnology Research Society of India adorned the Professor. **42 scholars were gifted to receive the highest academic degree under his distinguished Guidance**. His remarkable **patent in the area of Filariasis is a boon in healthcare** and saving the lives of mankind. He is a Great Motivator and very good at sensitising the Faculty, Scholars and Students toward achieving Academic Excellence and Institutional Global Ranking. Professor is a recipient of **Life Time Achievement Award and Sir J.C. Bose Memorial Award** for his outstanding contribution in higher education research (e-mail: vc@buc.edu.in, pkaliraj@gmail.com).

Prof. T. Devi Ph.D. (UK), Professor, Centre for Research and Evaluation, Professor and Head, Department of Computer Applications, Bharathiar University, focuses on state-of-art technology that industries adopt in order to make the students ready for the future world. She is a **Gold Medalist** (1981–1984) from University of Madras and a **Commonwealth Scholar** (1994–1998) for her **Ph.D. from University of Warwick, United Kingdom**. She has three decades of teaching and research experience from Bharathiar University, Indian Institute of Foreign Trade, New Delhi and University of Warwick, United Kingdom. Professor is good in team building and setting goals and achieving. Her research interests include integrated data modeling and framework, meta-modeling, computer-assisted concurrent engineering, and speech processing. Professor had visited United Kingdom, Tanzania, and Singapore for academic collaborations. She has received various awards including **Commonwealth Scholarship**, **Best Alumni Award** from PSGR Krishnammal College for Women (PSGRKCW), Proficiency award from PSG College of Technology and awards from Bharathiar University for serving for BU-NIRF, Curriculum 4.0, and Roadmap 2030, and **guided 23 Ph.D. scholars**. Prof. T. Devi may be contacted at (e-mail: tdevi@buc.edu.in, tdevi5@gmail.com).

Contributors

V.G. Abilash
Department of Biomedical Sciences
Vellore Institute of Technology
Vellore, India

Paul Abraham
Data Science Evangelist
IT/ ITES Industry
Bangalore, India

N. Arul
Department of Zoology
Bharathiar University
Coimbatore, India

V. Balachandar
Department of Human Genetics
  and Molecular Biology
Bharathiar University
Coimbatore, India

Balu Bhasuran
DRDO-BU Center for Life Sciences
Bharathiar University
Coimbatore, India

V. Bhuvaneswari
Department of Computer
  Applications
Bharathiar University
Coimbatore, India

E. Chandra
Department of Computer Science
Bharathiar University
Coimbatore, India

Ragavendran Chandrasekaran
Senthil Nagar, Vandalur
Chennai, India

V. Dhivya
Department of Human Genetics
  and Molecular Biology
Bharathiar University
Coimbatore, India

Pavan Gundarapu
Data Integration solutions manager
Safran
Paris, France

R. Janani
Department of Computer Science
Bharathiar University
Coimbatore, India

Rathinaraja Jeyaraj
Kyungpook National University
Daegu, South Korea

N. Senthil Kumar
Department of Biotechnology
Mizoram University
Mizoram, India

C. Lalchhandama
Health and Family Welfare Department
Government of Mizoram
Mizoram, India

Gurusamy Murugesan
Department of Bioinformatics
Bharathiar University
Coimbatore, India

R. Muthukrishnan
Department of Statistics
Bharathiar University
Coimbatore, India

D. Napoleon
Department of Computer Science
Bharathiar University
Coimbatore, India

Jeyakumar Natarajan
Department of Bioinformatics
Bharathiar University
Coimbatore, India

Thavamani D. Palaniswami
Kovai Medical Center and Hospital
Coimbatore, India

V. Ramanujam
Bharathiar School of Management and
    Entrepreneur Development
Bharathiar University
Coimbatore, India

J. Ramsingh
Department of Computer Applications
Bharathiar University
Coimbatore, India

Lakshminarayanan S.
Department of Computer Applications
Bharathiar University
Coimbatore, India

Kannan S. A.
U R Rao Satellite Centre
Indian Space Research Organisation
Bangalore, India

S. Sharmila
Department of Computer Science
Bharathiar University
Coimbatore, India

C. Sivamathi
Department of Computer Science
Bharathiar University
Coimbatore, India

E. Suganya
Department of Computer Science
Bharathiar University
Coimbatore, India

Krishnan Swaminathan
Department of Endocrinology
Kovai Medical Center and Hospital
Coimbatore, India

R. Vijayaraghavan
Department of Statistics
Bharathiar University
Coimbatore, India

S. Vijayarani
Department of Computer Science
Bharathiar University
Coimbatore, India

Chapter 1

Data Science and Its Applications

Paul Abraham[1] and Lakshminarayanan S.[2]

[1]Doddabanaswadi, Bangalore, India
[2]Department of Computer Applications Bharathiar University, Coimbatore, India

Contents

DOI: 10.1201/9781003175889-1

This chapter starts with a brief introduction to data science and aims to cover *three industry segments and three business functions*, where and how data science is applied.

Objectives

The objective of this chapter is to introduce data science and discuss its applications in the business today. Data science is about solving business problems, and businesses must recognize this fact. It examines which questions need answers and where to find the related data to support business decisions. This chapter defines and introduces the field of data science, possible types of data available in the business today, the many types of data analytics methods available today and covers use cases through its application. Though data science is used in all walks of life, this chapter restricts only its text to the scope of business or commercial activity. Going a little deeper, this chapter aims to cover three industry segments and three business functions where data science is applied.

1.1 Introduction to Data Science

Businesses see an uprising in transactions, leading to creating a huge repository of data comprising these transactions. This creates a need for information, insight, and intelligence about the business. Managers in the businesses moved from making decisions out of experience or institution to fact-based, data-driven decisions. This was effectively done by understanding the business objectives and their operative nuances and building intelligence around them.

The last decade has seen a huge transformation in the businesses moving toward a digital era by automating their process flows. In this trend, most businesses have also been collecting and storing their data in digital formats, and now the time has come to analyze and bring some value from the collected data. The collected data now demands to be cleaned by removing noises or unwanted information before being processed (Foster Provost & Tm Fawcett, 2018) to bring out meaningful insights for the business. Significant advancements related to storage spaces, thereby reducing the hardware costs, faster processing, and software products capable of performing complex calculations have become a boon to the business wanting to have a data-driven culture for decision making.

1.1.1 Data Science: A Definition

The loose definition of data science is to analyze data of a business to be able to produce actionable insights and recommendations for the business (Affine Analytics, 2018). The simplicity or the complexity of the analysis also impacts the quality and accuracy of results. As businesses and the data they collect became sophisticated, the need for technological skills, math/stats skills, and the necessary business acumen to define and deliver a relevant business solution became more relevant.

Data science is the process of examining data sets to conclude the information they contain, increasingly with the aid of specialized systems and software, using techniques, scientific models, theories, and hypotheses. These three pillars have very much been the mainstay of data science ever since it started getting embraced by businesses over the past two decades and should continue to be even in the future (Figure 1.1): Computer Science & IT, Business Acumen and Methods, Models, & Process.

Data Science expressed like this in the above picture is an idea accepted in academia and industry. It's an intersection of programming, analytical, and business skills that allows extracting meaningful insights from data to benefit business growth. However, this is used in social research, scientific & space programs, government planning, and so on, but this chapter will focus on its application in the Business Industry.

	DATA SCIENCE MODEL DEFINITION
❶	Business Acumen in its purest form means running a Business Enterprise. Any business existing to sell its product or services for a profit incurring some cost and generally having the functions like HR, Supply Chain, Finance, Sales & marketing to support it

(Continued)

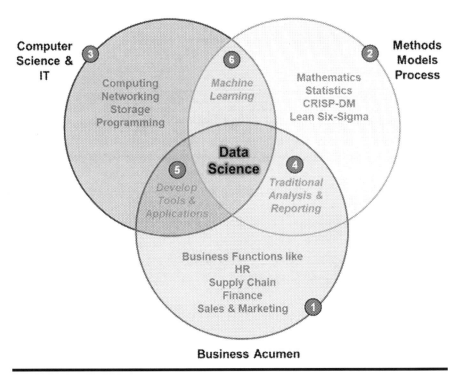

Figure 1.1 The Data Science model.

❷	Methods, Models, Process are defined as industry and academia proved practices that are the backbone to Data Science, including Mathematical models, theorems, Statistical methods, techniques, and process methodologies likes CRISP-DM, Six-Sigma, Lean, and so on
❸	Computer Science & IT practice is the full range of hardware, the software involved in providing computing for processing data, storage for storing and sharing data and networking for collecting and movement.
❹	When Business Acumen or Knowledge and Models methods process come together, it's classically called "traditional research." It involves using data collected in the business to make dashboards and reports to understand the business, plan for its future and make corrections if needed.
❺	Businesses take help from the Computer Science IT practice to help run business by building applications, web services, websites or plan IT-related strategies like going "digital" or adopting "cloud" based delivery of its products & services to serve their customers

(Continued)

❻	Machine learning is an idea to analyze data and automate the building of data models or algorithms. For example, medical diagnosis, image processing, prediction, classification, learning association, regression etc. Intelligent systems built on machine learning algorithms can learn from past experience or historical data.

1.1.2 Data in the Business

"In God we Trust, all others bring data"; this famous quote has been attributed to W. Edwards Deming. Deming was heavily involved in the economic reconstruction of post–World War 2 Japan. He proposed the philosophy to measure and analyze with data. This eventually helped in gaining increased performance in all areas of business. This philosophy is perfectly viable even today for any business or business situation. Leaving experience aside, many businesses seldom know about the performance of their business or, even more importantly, how they can improve it further.

In Industry 4.0, there is one key input or raw material playing the most critical role. This raw material is invisible and intangible in contrast to what we can see like oil, iron ore, or any physically visible components. It is nothing but "data," a special connection across a connected industry. With apt tools, techniques, and technology, companies can use data as their trump card. "Data are becoming the new raw material for business," says Craig Mundie, a senior advisor to the CEO at Microsoft and to the former American President Obama. Gone are the data when just rows and columns were data. Today everything is data.

An Industry pioneer was asked, "how do you deal with so much unstructured data that is generated through the social media, audio, chats, videos, emails, pictures, blogs posts?"; the pioneer believes that this data is rich in information and can be used to mine insights from it to be used to make a business decision. It's a challenge to work on such unstructured data because it calls for skillful hands to operate on it. People talk about or vent their feelings on social media. This means businesses can quickly gauge the sentiments among people for your business or brand. It just gives you an idea of what people out there are talking about you? Is there something valuable that you can use to make a course correction to your offer, brand, or business? In-store videos are used to generate heat maps to identify where people spend more time; this can be correlated with merchandise in those spaces, and now merchandise planning can be a lot more planned. A large tech giant is using product photographs to identify counterfeit products from real ones. Fraud detection is now possible. All of the above examples are big data analysis at work. So, there are a lot of possibilities to use unstructured data positively. How can unstructured data be paired with structured data to make it richer? How can this become a standard in the business are points to ponder over. This presents the business with immense opportunity to know what is happening in the business and react quickly to change and go faster to market.

Using data to prove some of the business decisions being taken gives confidence at different management levels to execute their plans, rather than depending on purely experience or trial measures. A data perspective provides structure and principles that give a framework to analyze any problems and implement a solution with confidence. Once industries develop data-analytical thinking, it clarifies the misconceptions and enriches the knowledge where they could apply these techniques in various domain topics.

1.1.3 Types of Data Analytics

For the given data collected and the business problems identified, numerous analysis methods can be identified. The below-mentioned four methods (Figure 1.2) can be considered to be generally accepted both by industry and academia alike.

The Analytics Advancement Model helps define, identify and illustrate what these types of analysis mean. In the above model, we can visualize four types of analysis possible and show them in terms of complexity of analysis and volume of analysis. Volume here means done often. There is no apparent relationship between volume and complexity.

Descriptive analysis is termed as the first step in any analytical problem-solving project. It is the simplest to perform in the analysis ladder of knowledge. As a foundational analysis, it aims to answer the question "what happened?" For example, a company selling breakfast cereals through descriptive analysis will find

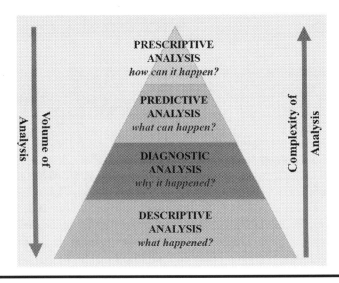

Figure 1.2 Analytics advancement model.

insight into its sales volume, units, value for a given geography and time period. With simple statistics like average sales, maximum sales, and minimum sales, the business can identify any trend, patterns, and seasonality in its sales. This will help understand what happened in its sales numbers.

The diagnostic analysis delves a little deeper to answer the question "why it happened?" and helps discover historical context through data. Continuing with the previous context, the question of "how effective was a promotional campaign based on the response in different geographies?" This type of analysis can help to identify causal relationships and anomalies in the data.

Predictive analysis is a little more complicated than the previous two discussed and answers "what can happen?" meaning looking into the future. The results from a predictive analysis should be treated as an estimate of the chance or probability of occurrence of that event. Widely used, a few examples are what the sales volume will be for the next time period? What is the propensity to buy for a new product release? Should I offer a loan to a particular applicant or no? This form of analysis uses knowledge and patterns from historical data to predict the future. In a world of uncertainty that businesses operate in, this is a very powerful tool to plan for the future.

The prescriptive analysis is almost the other end of the ladder, answering the question "how can it happen?" For example, businesses need the advice to understand the future course of action to take from all the available alternatives based on potential return and prescriptive analysis. For example, to achieve the outcome of a specific sale, it can suggest an alternative mix of investing in various types of promotions or media for advertising. This will be discussed more in-depth later with applications in supply chain, sales and marketing, and HR functions.

1.1.4 Use Cases in the Business

Businesses have come a long way in investing in groups that specialize only in data analytics. This group's only objective is to fuel the business with insights, decisions, and knowledge using data. Businesses have invested in a strong data science talent, data infrastructure, tools, frameworks & methodologies, and industry-proven techniques. Change is constant, and the data analytics group is no different. They also innovate for the future by learning from the data and business problems thereby contributing to the bigger picture.

The banking and retail industries were pioneers in the Data Analytics Era, as they were in the digital era. Still, other sectors like manufacturing, telecom & communications, hospitality, and more recently public sector and government are significantly catching up and starting to using data science techniques. Finance, sales & marketing, IT functions that have adopted data science are faster than other functions. Figure 1.3 illustrates the various use cases in the business for analytics for decision making.

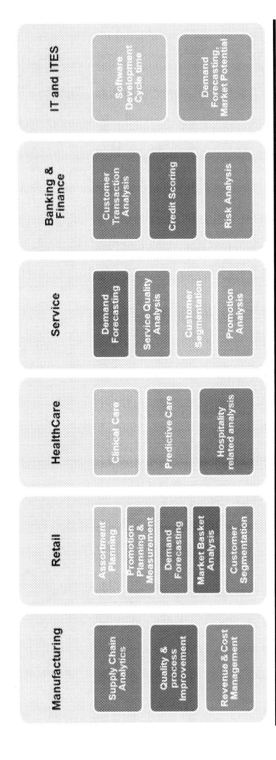

Figure 1.3 Industrywide application and its use cases (an illustration).

1.1.5 Data Analytics Process, Implementation and Measurement

The most important question to ask is how "data analytics" gets implemented in Industries? It all starts with a business problem. What are they? Industries collect a lot of data. What is the data telling? Are there commonalities that make eyebrows raise? Industries operate in an uncertain environment so decision-making is a challenge. Can industries forecast or predict the future? Be prepared! Be informed! is the key here. With limited resources like time, manpower, and material, how to get the best of them? Optimize! is the mantra. Industries cannot water all the roses in the garden, group points of data, help identify segments, make plans easier.

Solving a business problem using data science is a cycle of various tasks (Figure 1.4), namely:

- Always start with the question, "what is the business issue, problem to solve, goal to achieve, plan to support?"
- There is tons of data out there; gather the relevant data and prepare it for analysis.
- Explore the data, know what is data is saying as-is.
- Build a model to predict, associate, segment, and optimize as the case may be.
- Develop dashboard and visualize the results.
- Validate the findings with business and correct the findings if any.
- With the business teams, deploy the findings and measure results over time.

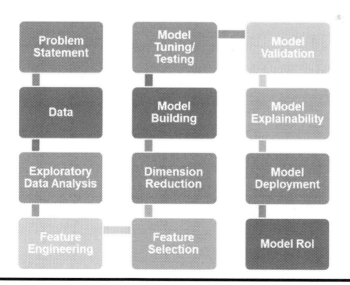

Figure 1.4   A typical data analytics process, implementation and measurement.

Data analytics is reshaped the way mankind historically was thinking of disaster response, business operations, media & entertainment, security and intelligence at all levels (Affine Analytics, 2021). The multitude of business exchanges, records, images, videos, sounds and signals are not simply being thought of as bits of data collected, marked, kept and retrieved, but as a possible wellspring of knowledge, which requires advanced analysis techniques that go from simple counts and aggregates to focus on finding relation and connected interpretations of the circumstance or situation present in the data.

The enormous collection of data, easily available hardware infrastructure, information management software, and advanced analytic capabilities have generated a celebrated moment in data analysis history. These connected trends mean that today mankind has the tremendous capacity and capability needed to analyze startling volume, variety, and velocity of data sets fast and cheaper than ever before. This body of knowledge is neither theoretical nor trivial. It represents a genuine attempt to leap forward and a fantastic opportunity to achieve big gains in efficiency, productivity, revenue, and profitability in any sphere. The business uses this to gain information, insight, and infer into its operations and thereby be ready to face the future with a bang!! Let us now look at how data analytics is used in various industries.

1.2 Data Science and Its Application in the Healthcare Industry

"Algorithm is the new doctor and data is the new drug," The "Healthcare Global Market Opportunities and Strategies to 2022" report (Business Wire, 2021) shows the Global Healthcare market at around $8.4 trillion in 2018, with a 7.3% compound annual growth rate (CAGR) since 2014, and estimates to grow at 8.9% CAGR to around $12 trillion by 2022.

One school of thought segments the healthcare market into largely healthcare service providers, pharmaceutical drugs manufacturing and distribution, medical equipment and supplies and veterinary care (Figure 1.5).

1.2.1 Data Types Generated in the Healthcare Sector

The move toward the adoption of technology in the healthcare sector has had a tremendously positive impact on the digitization of healthcare of both human health conditions and activities. This has created access to a large repository of knowledge and information. These milestones have presented various healthcare-related data through multiple resources (ETHealthWorld, 2019) like electronic health records (EHR), pharmaceutical research, healthcare digital platforms, medical imaging analysis, genomic sequencing, payer records, wearables and medical devices. Table 1.1 is an illustration of data sources in a general healthcare set-up.

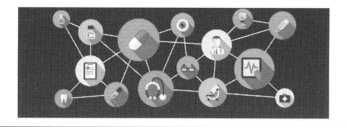

Figure 1.5   Analytics in the healthcare ecosystem.

Source: https://healthtechmagazine.net/article/2017/04/healthcare-analytics-point-providers-patients-need-most-care

1.2.2 Analytics Use Cases in Healthcare

Data analytics is widely used in the healthcare industry today. Predicting the outcomes for a patient, fund allocation effectiveness and diagnostic technique improvement are only examples of how data analytics is transforming healthcare. The pharmaceutical industry is also experiencing this transformation through advanced analytics like machine learning and artificial intelligence (AI & ML). Drug discovery, a time-consuming and complex task with many parameters, is significantly improved through AI & ML. Pharma companies have been using data analytics to gain insights into their market, sales, consumers, and future predictions.

Healthcare analytics is used differently by each of its stakeholders. They include healthcare practitioners, government, healthcare providers, pharmaceutical companies and patients (Figure 1.6). Here are some use cases where analytics is used or in potential use in the industry, discussed by the stakeholder roles.

The (ETHealthWorld, 2019) healthcare practitioners are interested in clinical analytics, which aids in personalizing treatment, monitoring health, consulting remotely, and utilizing predictive health analysis to make decisions. Healthcare practitioners include doctors, therapists, caregivers, radiologists, biologists, and so on.

- Caregivers can monitor medicine refills for discharged patients through comprehensive dashboards and alerts. Analyze daily parameters during admission to classify levels of abnormality and predicting the reoccurrence of a health problem. It can prioritize critical care.

- Using artificial intelligence in medical imaging can classify medical images based on their criticality, this can help Radiologists (Dr. Sunil Kumar Vuppala, 2020) spend better time with patients rather than on medical reports. This will improve workflow where radiology is a key service and reduce misdiagnosis due to fatigue or other reasons.

(Continued)

Table 1.1 Data Sources in a General Healthcare Set-Up

Data Source	Data Generated	Data Type
Electronic records of patient's health	Clinical results, patient medical history, medical test results and patient prescription and diagnosis	numerical, text
Clinical records	Laboratory results like blood reports, tests	numerical, text
Diagnostic or monitoring instruments	Wide gamut of images (like CT Scan, MRI, X-Ray) to numbers (like patient vital signs) to text report (diagnosis)	image, text, voice, video, numerical
Insurance claims/ billing	Information on treatment, the cost of those services, expected payment and level of service	text, numerical
Pharmacy	Information on the fulfillment of medication orders	text, numerical, image
Human resources and supply chain	List of people employed and the role they play in the institution; resource allocationStock, storage and utilization of medical supplies	text, numerical, image
Digital wearables	Data generated about human vitals and activities coming from digital wearables like smartwatch, healthcare bands	text, numerical, image
Clinical trials	Results of drug testing, trials performed on drugs	image, text, voice, video, numerical
Healthcare surveys/projects	Samples, clinical records, analysis, results and findings from focused healthcare surveys/ projects	text, numerical, image
Sales	Sales data of medical insurance, pharmaceuticals, hospital beds, consultations and so on	numerical

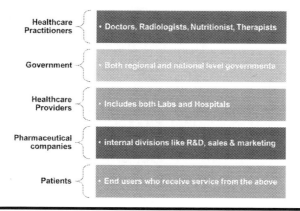

Figure 1.6   Stakeholders involved in healthcare.

> ■ Data analytics takes claims data, providers' electronic health records (EHRs) and any other piece of information available to help physicians become more aware of the patients they're treating. They need not wait for patients to tell everything. This can help doctors learning about high-risk patients.

Using (ETHealthWorld, 2019) the data of patients, the government can identify health patterns and trends and analyze needs in healthcare at various geographical levels in a population. It also helps the government to draft health policies, identify interventions, plan programs for specific demographics, and prepare and respond to healthcare emergencies.

■ Many health systems rely on government subsidies and support. Analytics help governments to have a clear picture of where the money is allocated and its reasons. Therefore, reducing the risk of resource wastage or unfair allocation of government subsidies.

■ Health research institutes under the government study to prevent the spread of infectious diseases. Studying drug data and clinical trial results, and correlating data from pharmaceutical manufacturers, physicians and patients to build a model. For example, if a pandemic disease appears in a given population, data analytics can help find answers to questions like: how the population could get affected? how quickly could it spread? Actions that the government should take regarding quarantining an affected area, and what steps would be needed to control the pandemic before it spreads across the geography?

■ Several governments also use data analytics to plan for population nutrition by promoting crops that help nutrition by season, region and prevalent health conditions of people.

For healthcare providers, like labs and hospitals, including insurance and claims processing companies' healthcare analytics entails mapping data into a form to better understand patients' health journey and know what contributes to improved healthcare outcomes.

- Analytics helps understand the historical admission and discharge rates of patients helping to analyze the staff efficiency and productivity while able to predict and handle the different volumes of patients at a time.

- Use data analytics to create consumer profiles, which will now allow the healthcare provider to send personalized messaging, improve retention and identify strategies meaningful for each individual. They use consumer behavioral patterns to draft impactful plans for care and keep their patients responsibly engaged through financial and clinical responsibilities.

- More than ever, it is now when predictive tools are in high demand with hospitals, which are looking to reduce variation in their order patterns and supply utilization.

- Hospitals are seeking to improve transition and deployment strategies of care coordination. Predictive analytics can warn the hospitals and other care providers when a patient's risk factors show a high probability of readmission, reducing financial burdens for the patient, hospitals and insurance companies alike.

- Assess hospital claims and prescription fulfillment data to identify the potential for fraud by using predictive analytics to determine and notify at-risk claims.

The pharmaceutical and life sciences companies' various internal divisions such as finance, supply chain, R&D, sales, and marketing are benefitting from advanced analytics, AI & ML and using it in the areas of drug discovery, market assessment, brand knowledge, customer outreach and engagement.

- Companies are currently using modeling to predict clinical outcomes, plan clinical trial designs, support the evidence of drug treatment effectiveness, optimize drug dosage, predict drug safety, and evaluate if any potential adverse event occurrence

---

- It is not easy to release a drug out without an in-depth and rigorous process of creating the drug. It has to go through elaborate clinical trials before it is finally approved. Every pharmaceutical company must strictly follow this process before releasing and administering the drug to the patients. The use of data analytics tools, techniques, methodologies and algorithms

---

(*Continued*)

companies can shorten the time to go to market for the drug. Data analytics has played a significant role in developing a super effective, highly productive and impactful R&D pipeline.

- Healthcare analysts in these companies scrub both structured and unstructured data, including data coming from social media, text messages and pair that with classical tabular data to generate useable insights and work toward bringing better health outcomes for all stakeholders involved in the process.

Health data can encourage patients to be very proactive and involved in their care process. This is in a different point of view from the classical approach where doctors have the control and make the decisions.

- Digitalized periodical health, clinical and personal nutrition reports give individuals access to their health at their fingertips. Many healthcare apps have made this possible and empowered individuals to be even more focused on their health.

- The patients who are suffering from high blood pressure, asthma, migraine or other severe health problems, doctors can observe their lifestyle and bring changes if necessary through the data collected via wearable health-tracking devices.

1.2.3 Future and Challenges

Though data analytics has evolved and major health advantages are reached, there remain several challenges. First, large amounts of data produced remain in various decentralized systems that are accessible easily. Another challenge to conquer is the opposition of healthcare professionals against technological changes fearing risk or replacement. Information systems in the healthcare industry as a whole were not designed with analytics in mind to "get the data out" from it is not easy. The IT community in the healthcare system has not standardized these systems or their performance indicators. Within a given clinical information system, they are free to define their own data structures and standards for treatments and often do. Sharing and exchanging data through standard data formats requires a strong regulation in place and increases interoperability, privacy protection, and healthcare data exchange. Healthcare for analytical and research purposes is not created equal, needing standardization and quality improvement. Finally, data may be in a clinical narrative, images, and diagnosis as text that is more difficult to mine, requiring specialized talent and algorithms to bring them to a usable format.

The above challenges are wonderfully captured in this future-looking quote by Dr. Devi Shetty – nicknamed the Henry Ford of heart surgery, a renowned cardiac surgeon and entrepreneur who believes developments such as computerized diagnoses and technicians doing the work of highly trained medics are just around the corner. He said, "*Five to 10 years down the line, it will become mandatory for doctors to take a second opinion from the software before reaching the final diagnosis. This software will make doctors more efficient.*"

In the midst of the above-mentioned challenges, the future is brighter. Personal care, self-monitoring is becoming more and more popular. Today, individuals have access to enormous valuable health information, and, as a result, they have personally become involved in seeking information and improving their health. Market statistics say there are around 400,000 health apps that monitor a variety of personal health data like blood pressure, heart rate, sleep patterns, calory consumption, physical activity, cholesterol levels, and blood glucose among other parameters. This self-monitoring behavior is only set to increase, become more accurate, and alter the way how healthcare will be delivered.

1.3 Data Science and Its Application in the Retail and Retail E-Commerce

Global retail sales are projected to reach around $30 trillion by 2023, with a flat growth rate of about 4.5%, while retail e-commerce is projected to grow to $6.54 trillion by 2023. By 2023, the share of retail e-commerce will account for 22% of total retail sales. In this section, we will look at both the retail and retail e-commerce industries together.

In the market today, being customer-centric is everything. It demands that businesses stay a step ahead of their customers. Retail data gives information and insights to the retailers needed to stay valuable, ahead, and competitive. Thus making the retailers more informed about their customers and their behavior, habits, needs, wants, and spending patterns (Figure 1.7). This will enable the retailers to create a strong innovative retail experience for their customers. Retail data can analyze its customer data and segment them based on spending, demographics and behavior thus knowing which products sell are popular and in demand. This will help to make decisions and plans for products to promote.

1.3.1 Data Types Generated in the Retail and Retail E-Commerce Sector

Retail data is collected in raw form from several sources. Sales data comes mainly from point of sale (POS) or transaction systems, and this is a key source of data. However, additionally rich and valuable data is also generated from inventory, operational, campaign management, customer relationship management (CRM), supply chain,

Figure 1.7   Analytics in the retail and e-commerce ecosystem.
Source: https://www.comtecinfo.com/rpa/predictive-retail-analytics-use/

and partner relationship management (PRM) systems (Table 1.2). When analyzing, for decision making in retail, generally all of them or multiple parts are considered together. Retail e-commerce data is available through click stream, order, shipment management systems, logistics, supply chain and vendor systems. E-commerce collects much richer demographic data as compared to a traditional retail-like phone, email, physical address, IP addresses, and so on (pwc publications, 2016).

1.3.2 Analytics Use Cases in Retail and Retail E-Commerce

In this hyper-connected, information-driven era, data and data analytics are occupying a pivotal role in measuring and tracking growth and steering strategies for sustainable, profitable growth in the sector. Advances in digitization are swift, and the resultant changes in the behaviors of the consumer have the retail business redefine its operating model and its value proposition. While brick and mortar or physical retail is still a large share of total retail; its online counterpart continues to exhibit accelerated growth. Leading retailers have merged both their online and physical divisions such that the same teams oversee merchandising, planning and marketing for their physical stores and online businesses. Customers who like to shop in physical stores can now browse products and place orders on mobile devices, which then they can pick up their ordered products from a designated collection point. Analytics is assisting retailers to improve their profitability by enabling data-driven decision making for both their in-store and digital operations alike. Retail analytics can be studied with the help of the framework given in Table 1.3.

Table 1.2 Data Details of Retail E-Commerce Sector

Data Source	Data Generated	Data Type
Customer data	General data – Demographic details like name, age, address, IP address, phone, email, family members; Loyalty program data – status, program number	numerical, text, image
Sales	Detailed attributes of a: Product – name, brand, level, category, bundle, manufacturer; Price – list price, discount, sale price, promotion; Geography – city, store; Measure – units, value, volume	numerical
Inventory	Incoming stock, stock in-store, stock out rate	image, text, numerical
Logistics, supply chain	Delivery schedule, shipment, transport carrier, packaging details	text, numerical
Clickstream (retail e-commerce)	Onsite traffic metrics, IP address, record of every single click on the website, login details	text, numerical, image
Human resources	List of staff who are assigned to various tasks/units of the firm and their role. Attendance, timesheets	text, numerical, image
Promotions	Type of promotion, promotion material, duration, location, level, sponsor, budget; Email engagement attributes; Social media engagement attributes	numerical, image, text
Pricing & discount	Unit price, vendor price, profit, sale price, trade price, discount rate, discount level	numerical
Store surveillance	Store videos collected for surveillance	text, numerical, image, video
Surveys, house panels	Customer satisfaction surveys, house panel to measure consumption	numerical, text

Table 1.3 Framework to Study Retail Analytics

Area of Application	Analytics Use Case
Sales and marketing	Sales and demand forecasting using time series modeling are always necessary to understand the future and plan for it in the present. This will help businesses to optimize stock purchase, plan staff and promotions using predictive modeling. Retail companies both offline and online businesses want the Customer Lifetime Value (CLV) to plan personalized communication for those customers. In the same manner, supplier value is also equally important and predicting that will allow promoting high valued suppliers
	Using text mining and natural language processing (NLP) firms conduct e-commerce review analytics to understand the sentiments of customers. Even customer satisfaction surveys or now social media posts/tweets can be a rich source to use for sentiment analysis
	Using advanced clustering techniques retail companies now can develop and measure micro segmentations from price, store, customer and product data and (Ramesh Ilangovan, 2017) create multiple what-if scenarios for various clusters. This process helps identify optimal clusters to help improve planning, decision-making, and execution.
	Attribution modeling helps retailers understand how to optimize their marketing spend based on how customers reach and navigate through their sites. Dynamic pricing has been a go-to methodology to push retail sales, especially in intensely competitive segments like electronics. Using internal factors like supply, sales goals, margins, etc. and external factors like traffic, conversion rate, popularity of the products, etc. to build optimized pricing models such as price elasticity and ensemble models, product prices increase or decrease based on market situations.
Merchandising	Using predictive and prescriptive analytics to improve merchandising, which product where and when within the store with respect to demand patterns can be identified. This means assortment varies from one store to another.
	Association rule mining and Recommender algorithms tell a retailer what customers are buying together. This will help retailers place such products, categories next to one another or in websites that offer those products as a bundle or recommend the next product as a pop-up. This helps in promotion planning and pricing. Deep learning techniques are used by online retailers to identify and stop

(*Continued*)

Table 1.3 (Continued)   Framework to Study Retail Analytics

Area of Application	Analytics Use Case
	fraudulent suppliers/sellers who sell defective, counterfeit products online which is an illegal activity.
Supply chain and logistics	In e-commerce business models, learning about returns is key because returns is a cost to the company. Using predictive analytics companies are now able to predict returns and also financially and logistically plan for it. Using optimization techniques, vehicle routing is planned for logistics and product delivery such that cost of transport is low and efficient reach to the location. This is sometimes absolutely required to meet delivery SLAs promised to the customer.
	Pricing optimization models are used to understand where and when to buy products from vendors. Today's retailers have a global model in sourcing and these pricing model allow them to get a good bargain on sourcing by combining it with demand forecasting data. Warehouse planning is another key decision and a backbone to the entire supply chain planning. Availability of space, distances to vendors, stores, closeness to highways, size of the warehouse are some key inputs into a warehousing optimization model.
Store operations	Using optimization techniques and location data companies can plan to optimize the mix of physical and online locations or to identify new store locations and plan franchise territories. Strong descriptive analytics resulting in a highly efficient dashboard for retail company management to understand store wise performance can help bring the right intervention for growth. There are thousands of stock-keeping units (sku) in a store both online or offline, optimization techniques are used to identify how much and what inventory to buy and stock or sell. Simple descriptive analysis dashboard to understand stock out scenarios and using predictive modeling be able to predict the stock-outs help in inventory planning for such items in store. Through IoT devices, cameras, and website navigation data is collected of customer movement with a store applicable both offline or online. This data is paired with advanced deep learning and computer vision analysis to optimize store layout, enhance merchandising, assess product performance, and improve customer experience.

1.3.3 Future and Challenges

New technologies (Datarade, 2020) like big data, artificial intelligence, machine learning, cloud infrastructure, new-age retail practices like 100% outsourced supply chain, e-commerce delivery, food-tech companies, mobile phone retail, QSRs and so on are on the move today. The most important question to be asked now is "why traditional companies have failed to keep pace with these modern developments?" Managers in these traditional companies continue to be doubtful about the claims made by these revolutionary technologies and often claims that they are greatly exaggerated. The knowledge of data analytics is often confined at most times to reporting and business intelligence. The few vendors of analytics who could have bridged this gap, in turn, lack business knowledge and understanding of challenges faced by retailers of today and are unconvinced about analytics application in their business beyond just tactics.

The party to retail business, "the customer" cannot (forbes, 2018) be seen as single community, but several communities across geographies are disparate in their habits and culture and expanding every day. The competition in the retail space is now not restricted to the neighborhood store, but many channels as mobile and web expand. Many me-too retailers imitate the more successful retailers, who were the early adopters of analytics, but only half-realizing its full benefits.

Finally, increasing conflict on pricing, discounts and range between traditional retail, e-commerce and modern retail is increasing pricing and margin pressure on companies as they juggle their volume growth ambitions with prices and margins, while trying to build their "Omni" presence across channels seldom realizing importance of each (Ramesh Ilangovan, 2017). While the end consumer may be benefitting in this conflict through lower prices, the pressure on margins across the value chain continues to grow. This makes us ask "Will analytics be the answer?"

1.4 Data Science and Its Application in the Banking, Financial Services and Insurance (BFSI) Sector

According to most of the studies conducted, out of the huge amounts (~2.5 quintillion [1018] bytes of data) of financial data collected nearly 85% of them were created in the last two years only. Further, with the continuous increase in the adoption of mobile technologies and IoT, **the scale of data was expected to grow exponentially** as stated above.

Due to the **increasing and changing customer expectations** and the **increased competition of Fintech players**, the financial services sector can simply not permit itself to leave those huge amounts of data unexploited (Joris Lochy, 2019). It is thus better for banks and insurers to leverage data science to maximize customer understanding and gain a competitive advantage (Figure 1.8).

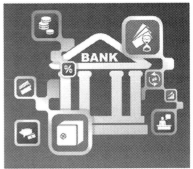

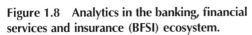

Figure 1.8 Analytics in the banking, financial services and insurance (BFSI) ecosystem.

Source: http://fusionanalyticsworld.com/ social-media-analytics-bfsi-part/

1.4.1 Data Types Generated in the BFSI Sector

Banks have huge amounts of data from customers in the form of their payments done online, customer profile data collected for KYC, deposits/withdrawals at ATMs, purchases at point-of-sales and others, but these all are not linked and hence at times not able to (Joris Lochy, 2019) utilize these rich data sets (Table 1.4). This while the financial services industry has been investing heavily for more than a decade in data collection and processing technologies (such as *data warehouses* and *business intelligence*) and is one of the forerunners in investments in data science areas.

1.4.2 Analytics Use Cases in BFSI

1. Identifying the change in customer behavior for personalized service:
    i. With digital usage, increasing more customer data is captured easily, which was not the case during the in-person nondigital era. These captured data points could be leveraged for building a personalized service that was present during the in-person connects.
    ii. Customers are comfortable using digital mediums for their bank transactions and purchases of stocks. Customers search using their mobile devices before buying any stock or products, and these footprints are also digitally captured. Now, the financial sectors are also reaching out to the customers via social media channels and selling their products/insurance premiums.
    iii. Now the stage has reached wherein the customers have expected more personalized and right information for their specific interest needs, than a generic recommendation. By integrating multiple data footprints of the specific customer along with like-minded customer data, this could be achieved.
2. Generate cross- and up-selling opportunities (Joris Lochy, 2019)

Table 1.4   Data Details of BFSI Sector

Data Source	Data Generated	Data Type
Customer data	General data – Demographic details like name, age, address, IP address, phone, email, family members Loyalty program data – status, program number	numerical, text, image
Product portfolio information	Credits, accounts, payments, securities, insurances...	Numerical, text
Clickstream (Banking site)	Onsite traffic metrics, IP address, record of every single click on the website, login details	text, numerical, image
Human resources	List of staff who are assigned to various tasks/ units of the firm and their role. Attendance, timesheets	text, numerical, image
Promotion details	Type of promotion, promotion material, duration, location, level, sponsor, budgetEmail engagement attributes Social media engagement attributes	numerical, image, text
Pricing & discount	Unit price, vendor price, profit, sale price, trade price, discount rate, discount level	numerical
ATM surveillance	ATM videos collected for surveillance	text, numerical, image, video

i. Through notifications, customer call agents or web ads, cross- and up-selling could be generated which is based on individual behavior of the customer.

ii. Customer is self-buying a bond on the stock market, this shows that it's a knowledgeable customer and would be open to the product: an up-selling opportunity for similar structured notes' basic info need not be explained.

iii. It is easier to understand about the customer that he does not have a home yet and is currently located at a house for sale, which helps to a selling opportunity for mortgage. These information could be obtained through the geo-location information and the public information or advertisements on the houses for sale.

    iv. Customer (Joris Lochy, 2019) modifies certain customer information (e.g. change of address due to move/relocation, change of civil status, e.g. following a wedding): selling opportunities for loans (e.g. mortgage, car loan) or insurances (home insurance, car insurance).

3. Helping with managing customer risks:

    i. *Cyber fraud prevention* can be addressed by continuously assessing the outliers or fraudulent transactions with restrictions and additional measures of security as required. These techniques would be useful for both physical money at branches as for the overall liquidity management of the bank/insurer.

    ii. Credit risk management improve the credit models at regular intervals based on customer patterns separately for private and corporate customers, thus having to improve credit scoring too. The models could help in deriving new rules, once the machine understands the data pattern, and this data can also be used to better manage the collateral of credits, thus also reducing credit risk for the bank.

    iii. Fraud detection for insurance: Many frauds happen during the claims of insurances; a good mechanism to identify these common fraudulent practices would help in managing the risks. Common past fraudulent data, sensor data, image of accident impact, etc. could help in guiding the adjudicator with the right estimate and reduce in insurance fraudulent claims.

1.4.3 Future and Challenges

New-age digital source data like the IoT data (e.g. sensors in home, equipments) in combination with the legacy old data sources (like transaction history, reports of companies) has a completely difficult task. Special care must be given to new data formats and data types because the underlying data structure changes may not be easily or readily updated on the trained models. The data privacy and intrusion, along with personalized services, are provided based on customer-specific data and their transactions, which is a fine line between being intrusive and helpful.

1.5 Statistical Methods and Analytics Techniques Used across Businesses

Statistical methods and analytics techniques help us systematically apply them to (Simran Kaur Arora, 2020) describe the data scope; modularize the data structure; condense the data representation; illustrate via images, tables and graphs and evaluate statistical inclinations and probability and to derive meaningful conclusions. These analytical procedures enable us to induce the underlying inference from data by eliminating the unnecessary chaos created by the rest of it.

These methods and techniques can be applied to analyze different styles of data like qualitative, quantitative, image, voice or speech, videos and text. Qualitative data mainly answers questions such as "why," "what" or "how." Each of these questions is addressed via quantitative techniques using scaling. Quantitative data is just numbers either point or with decimals. Now, data collection has evolved and so its analysis. Social media presents to us rich text-based data that is converted into numbers before analyzing. Images used for classification or recognition are converted into numbers based on color and pixels and then used for analysis. Video is nothing but multiple frames of pictures that are treated similar to images. Sounds and speech are converted into waves and frequency and that can, in turn, be converted into numbers before analysis.

There are numerous techniques to analyze data depending upon the business problem or question at hand, the type of data and the amount of data collected (Michael, J. A. Berry et al., 2011). Each of these techniques focuses on mining data, identifying meaningful information, deriving insights and transforming them into decision-making parameters.

In further sections, discussion will revolve around focused statistical methods and analytics techniques used in different functions of the business namely sales and marketing, HR and supply chain.

1.6 Statistical Methods and Analytics Techniques Used in Sales and Marketing

Sales and marketing are two business functions within an organization – they both lead generations and revenue along with creating an impact. The term sales refers to all activities that lead to the selling of goods and services. And marketing is the process of getting people interested in the goods and services being sold. Marketing informs and attracts leads and prospects to the business or product or service. Sales, on the other hand, works directly with prospects to reinforce the value of the company's solution to convert prospects into customers (Figure 1.9). The fundamental distinction between the two departments is that the marketing department's efforts cost the organization expenses, whereas the sales department generates revenue to the company.

1.6.1 Data Types Generated in Sales and Marketing Function

Sales data is usually information used to manage sales and key trends around the pipeline. The data may concern from market to opportunities and deals to the third party to actual sales performance. Marketing data as shown in Table 1.5 encompasses data collected from leads, spends for campaigns, advertising, branding and can be used to improve product development, promotion, sales, pricing, distribution and related strategies (Simran Kaur Arora, 2020).

Figure 1.9 Analytics in the sales and marketing ecosystem.

Source: https://talkinginfluence.com/2019/12/12/improve-influencer-analytics/

1.6.2 Statistical Methods and Analytical Techniques

As defined by SAS,

> Marketing analytics comprises the processes and technologies that enable marketers to evaluate the success of their marketing initiatives by measuring performance using important business metrics, such as ROI, marketing attribution and overall marketing effectiveness. In other words, it tells you how your marketing programs are performing.

Unlike marketing, sales have always been number-driven and now with the explosion of data and computational power; sales analytics has become central to any large sales organization. So, what is sales analytics? Sales analytics is the´process used to identify, model, understand and predict sales trends and sales results while helping in the understanding of these trends and finding improvement points. The best practice is to closely tie all activities to determine revenue outcomes and set objectives for your sales team.

Sales and marketing analytics are essential to unlocking commercially relevant insights, increasing revenue and profitability and improving brand perception. With the help of the right analytics, you can uncover new markets, new audience

Table 1.5   Data Details of Sales and Marketing

Data Source	Data Generated	Data Type
Market share/size	Mostly data from syndicated research studies or secondary sources of data collected by internal teams	numerical, text, image
Quote & config	All quotes given to customers/ channel partners during opportunity stages (before sale)	numerical, text
Campaign management	All sales and marketing related campaign data like budgets, programs, expenses, program details	image, text, numerical
Compensation	Both Channel Partner and Sales persons' compensation details like target, achievement variable pay	numerical
Partner relationship management (PRM)	All information about a contracted past, prospective and current partners. Also called Master data of channel partners. Should contain demographic and contact data. Often stored in PRM systems	text, numerical, image
Customer relationship management (CRM)	All information about a company's past, current and prospect customers. Also called Master data of customers. Should contain demographic and contact data. Often stored in CRM systems	text, numerical, image
Contracts	Lists of all contracts signed by the company with its partners and customers to be used for sales and marketing purpose	text, numerical, image

(Continued)

Table 1.5 (Continued)   Data Details of Sales and Marketing

Data Source	Data Generated	Data Type
Digital click stream	Data generated from the company's website, social media, software, knowledge management and campaign related web pages	text, numerical, image
Pipeline/opportunity/ deals	Mostly part of a CRM system will contain sales leads or opportunities	text, numerical
Third party	Data used to enrich data from internal transaction systems, mostly syndicated studies, surveys	text, numerical, image
Sales	Actual sales performance by product, customer, geography for a time-period and a measure like value, volume or unit. Should be available in the company's Order, Shipment and Revenue management ERP systems	numerical

niches, areas for future development and much more. Figure 1.10 shows the possible statistical methods and analytical techniques used in sales and marketing.

Sales and marketing analytics comprises analytics for each silo and at various levels including at a strategy level, sales function, marketing function, consumers and partners and not to leave out the sales representatives themselves.

1. Sales and marketing strategy – Analytics supporting sales and marketing strategy are today part of every analytics CoE. They are generally done at a corporate level and analysis provided at a geography, business unit, customer segment and sometimes product level too. It all starts with knowing the market size and of the most popular analytical techniques is TAM (total addressable market), which is a funnel-like analysis to identify and quantify the overall opportunity in the market that the business can address. In a more mature business generally White space analysis is done to bridge gaps with a new product, service release. Knowing your competitor and their strategies is like half the sale done. Win–Loss analysis using text mining from

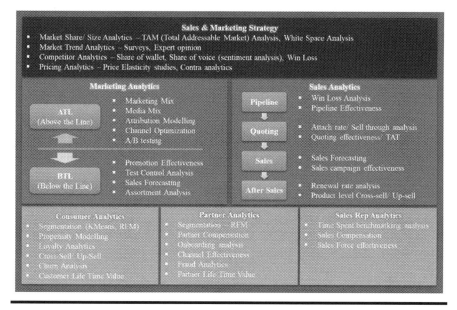

Figure 1.10 Statistical methods and analytical techniques used in sales and marketing.

salespersons' comments from CRM systems is a wealth of information in the hands of the business to plan a competitive attack. Price wars are everywhere, especially with the rise in e-commerce business. At what price will the customer stop buying? How elastic is my price for a product? Are questions answered from price elasticity analysis? Price-sensitive industries have a full pricing analytics team to feed business teams with decision-making insights.

2. Marketing analytics – Marketing analytics can be divided into analytics done on above the line (ATL) and below the line (BTL) activities. "ATL" meaning that the strategy is going to be deployed around a wider target audience, e.g. television, radio or billboards. ATL is most applicable when a product is directed at a broader spectrum of consumers. With so many options and limited resources where to focus most to maximize RoI question is answered using marketing mix modeling, sometimes media mix modeling thanks to the tech burst and the rich availability of media platforms today. While "BTL" strategies are going to target a specific group of potential consumers using tools like direct emailing or direct product demonstrations. Test control analysis, promotion effectiveness techniques drive the use of the right technique for the right product for the right audience.

3. Sales analytics – sales analytics can be understood using the sales towers starting with qualified leads called opportunities where win/loss analysis through ensemble techniques are used to predict which opportunity will win and optimization techniques used to identify where to spend time and

available funds. During quoting its always measuring and identifying opportunities for attaching meaning for every value of the main product sold what can be attached with that thereby increasing the overall bill value. A salesperson's time, funds and other resources are limited using which maximizing revenue is the key, so forecasting sales, possible trend and seasonality are very critical for businesses to better plan go to market strategies. Businesses use time series forecasting techniques or regression techniques for this depending on the criticality and data availability. After-sales predicting annuity sales like renewals in insurance, financial products or cross-sell/upsell possibilities is an important fuel for growth. The propensity to buy during a sales campaign offer will tell businesses to give offers for that work.

4. Consumer analytics – Many book articles combine customer analytics with sales or marketing analytics, but there is significant merit to call it out separately thanks to its drive and importance. Understanding consumer segments help in driving focused sales or marketing strategies. Unsupervised techniques are used to group customers and then profile them to understand them deeper followed by building targeted campaigns for them. Any product launch or upgrade that happens in the business is oftentimes followed with a propensity to buy a predictive model to target the highest-scoring consumers. This will help skim the market and realize quick sales. Acquire, build and retain consumers is the strategy of a growing business, so they focus on predicting customer lifetime value (CLV). CLV means loyalty to the business defined by purchase, repurchase and referral to other consumers. Another business question on why has a particular customer not purchasing is answered via churn analytics. Businesses need to know if a customer will churn and when are they likely to churn? Such that an intervention strategy or program could be designed to this target.

5. Partner analytics – With a significant share of businesses depending on the channel for their sales, partner-focused analytics are gaining importance. Businesses mine data from their PRM systems to segment their partners based on their value to the business using Recency, Frequency, Monetary technique or other unsupervised techniques like K Means. Onboarding a partner into the business requires a contract and legal clearances. With go-to-market pressures analytics teams often find analytics to their rescue to identify opportunities to reduce onboarding turnaround time (TAT) using simple descriptive statistic techniques. It is better to stop sales fraud before it occurs; predictive analytics techniques like logistic regression and artificial neural networks are used to predict if a sales deal is likely to turn into a fraud one.

6. Sales representative analytics – Businesses want their sales representatives to spend most of their time meeting customers and spend time in selling. Analytics teams in the sales operations often conduct time spent analysis to benchmark their sales representatives and their time spent on sales-related activities with that of the industry.

1.6.3 Future and Challenges

Over the years, as businesses expand into digitalization, the need for advanced targeting and tracking is becoming the main focus of sales and marketing initiatives. With the higher demand for efficient analytics solutions, the challenges started to rise.

The new technologies were typically deployed in isolations, and the result was a huge set of tools and platforms of a disconnected data environments. There were always be instability and mismatching results coming from the different platforms causing data discrepancies. At the end of the day, you will be facing the issue of which data source is the most reliable for analysis leading to decision making. Each business has its own technology stack and infrastructure therefore connecting internal company sales and marketing data with online data is sometimes one of the biggest challenges for marketers. Businesses should establish a strong privacy policy to address legal and ethical concerns for sales and marketing data, analytics and its implementation. Privacy laws like GDPR and other issues may affect some industries more strongly than others.

1.7 Statistical Methods and Analytics Techniques Used in Supply Chain Management

By the end of 2010, most of the companies had integrated all of their own and external resources available in the market. This integration has enabled their working pattern of a system for any quick response to the needs in the market. Creating a visualization dashboard to help in taking some quick decisions for ad hoc solutions has been made possible and such a system is referred to as supply chain management (SCM) system (Figure 1.11).

In this decade, the advancement in the supply chain field has been driven through implementing advanced analytics (data science) methods like time-series forecasting, route optimization techniques and hierarchical structuring. Business decision makers are now able to understand the fact on how data science is helping their companies to make the right decisions at the right time saving millions of dollars.

1.7.1 Data Types Used in the SCM

The supply chain is a great place to apply analytics for gaining a competitive advantage because of the uncertainty, complexity, varied data sources and the significant role it plays in the overall cost structure and profitability for almost any firm (Table 1.6).

Figure 1.11   Analytics in the supply chain management ecosystem.

Source: https://medium.com/o4s-io/how-supply-chain-analytics-can-transform-business-2fc9e16bc9ac

1.7.2 Analytics Use Cases in SCM

A supply chain management is a network of multiple businesses and relationships. Supply chain users need to be aware of the benefits given by the data analytics for their operations. Some of the key areas of SCM where data science plays a vital role are:

1. Demand prediction: Demand forecasting is essential in planning for sourcing, manufacturing, logistics, distribution and sales, which are is done in various forms in the past decade; with the advent of data science, it is becoming more effective and easier to handle these. In the current stages, firms are even starting to predict the demands for new products that are yet to be launched too this is helping in decisions like manufacturing, procurement planning and strategizing the OEMs. There is huge volatility in demand, which causes problems in the entire supply chain from supply planning, production and inventory control to shipping, hence it's challenging and equally important to forecast helping in planning at every level in the organizations, regions, stores, etc.

2. Optimal route identification: Route optimization is a very important factor, and it is more than just identifying the shortest route from point A (source) to point B (destination). For a perfect route optimization to handle the flow of supply chain and control it efficiently, the following are to be adhered to:

   i.   planning to be done to manage the entire fleet;
   ii. set processes and adherence to them;

Table 1.6   Data Details of SCM

Data Source	Data Generated	Data Type
Supplier provided data	General data – Demographic details like name, age, address, IP address, phone, email, family members Loyalty program data – status, program number,	numerical, text, image
Transactional sales data	Detailed attributes: Product – name, brand, level, category, bundle, vendor/ manufacturer Price – list price, discount, sale price, promotion Geography – city, store Measure – units, value, volume	numerical
Public open data	GPS tracking data - Vehicle info, route details Government data – Policy info, guidelines details	text, numerical
Third-party/OEM proprietary data	Incoming stock, stock in-store, stock out rate	numerical, text, image
Logistic data	Delivery schedule, shipment, transport carrier, packaging details	text, numerical

   iii. Real-time traffic information updates, helping to change the route directions;

   iv. Foresee and flexibility to handle any ad hoc situations.

Already many works have been proceeding in the above-mentioned area, and some have also reached advanced stages during this decade.

3. Space/inventory optimization: It's a trade-off between how many items to be stocked to handle the supply-demand effectively. Challenges faced in the decision could be out of stock, over dumped stocks, planning of space utilizations. A better understanding of the moving/non-moving items, cost benefits. With the right data points in hand, we could easily maximize the space utilization thereby improve productivity with an increase in profits.

4. Consignments track and trace: Each of the consignments is now attached with unique bar codes and using a proper RFID reader, complete info is

retrieved which could track and identify where the consignments are currently in transit. But just providing this info is just one stage, but currently, companies are using this and understanding better various stages in the complete SCM logistics cycle and optimizing the cycle time that is taking longer than expected.

1.7.3 Future and Challenges

To maintain the quality of customer service, the challenge is to adapt to a fast-changing environment and the delays during transit, probably due to unforeseen challenges. Finally, in the complete SCM cycle, data science is helping to understand and create transparency in the complete flow. This is also helping to set correct SLA and adhere to them to have increased inefficiency in the processes involved, thereby increasing customer satisfaction.

1.8 Statistical Methods and Analytics Techniques Used in Human Resource Management

In the current digital era, it is now evident that the HR team should use the available tools to aid in their core activities – whether it is talent acquisition, resource optimization, training & development or employee payments (Figure 1.12). Data science in HR is used for effective improvement in overall employee performance who have several open questions:

- How can we acquire the right talent? How can we decide which profiles are right for the job description?
- How can we identify the highly skilled people and retain them?
- How can we retain and engage our top talent?
- How can we leverage social network data for human resources operations?

1.8.1 Data Types Generated in Human Resource Management

HR analytics is the process of addressing a strategic HR concern using HR data (and business and external data if necessary), thereby identifying the HR issues and further preparing a subsequent action plan. Table 1.7 shows the data, data type and data source relevant to human resource management.

Figure 1.12   Analytics in the human resource management ecosystem.

Source: https://www.peoplematters.in/article/hr-analytics/workforce-analytics-how-mature-are-organizations-13135

Table 1.7   Data Details of Human Resource Management

Data Source	Data Generated	Data Type
Employee data	General data – Demographic details like name, age, address, IP address, phone, email, project details	numerical, text
Behavioral data	Detailed attributes, Performance details, previous ratings, payroll info	Numerical, text
Social media data	Social Engagement data, sentiment index data, campaigns data	text, numerical
Third-party/OEM proprietary data	In-premises camera video data	image, video

1.8.2 Analytics Use Cases in Human Resource Management

1. Employee profiling and segmentation
    i. All employees are not similar; their career planning/benefits should be on a case by case basis, hence there is a need to understand the exiting workforce better.

    ii. Understand the demographics, skills, educational background, experience and designation, and all these can be combined with information on each roles and responsibilities.

    iii. This would help in coming up with planned targeted programs for each segment profile and help in achieving better relationship and higher satisfaction from employees.

2. Employee attrition model

    i. Employee attrition is a major issue, as this has various other impacts like high financial costs, productivity losses, negative impact on customer service, loss of expertise, loss of business opportunities, job dissatisfaction of remaining employees and a bad image of the organization.

    ii. Devise a retention strategy for potential churners. To identify potential churners, we need a predictive model that can assist us with this.

    iii. The model can help in determining future possibilities and reducing employee turnover if desired. KPIs such as employee satisfaction, staff advocacy, etc. are helpful in this analysis.

3. No shows – post-offer roll out

    i. To estimate the employees joining probability, post-offer role out. A plan should be devised accordingly to reduce the no-show percentage.

    ii. Use the existing no-show data and accepted offers data across various skill set, job roles and experience to understand if there is any similar pattern or trend.

    iii. Once there are some identical patterns, we could validate and devise a proper mitigation plan to help reduce the no-shows.

4. Employee sentiment analysis

    i. Healthy presence on social media platforms via running campaigns, posting ideas, shouting achievements and initiatives increases the social HR brand for employees to follow and employers to measure.

    ii. Social identification for potential candidates and understanding resource profile. Empowering with an additional information.

    iii. Helps to define and manage social engagement with employees, accurately measuring sentiment and understanding each employee's social sentiment index.

1.8.3 Future and Challenges

Being transparent is better, and one way to achieve this is to have the correct data in front during discussions. Please make sure everyone in the organization knows and understands it. This would help during the challenging times and bringing in a positive organizational culture too. It is always advisable to start small and grow with the challenges to handle along the way – have conversations with employees, record their responses, add managers in the loop, involve various functions, make a plan, share it with everybody and commit to it. HR analytics will help you monitor and improve employee engagement, employee retention, employee wellness, employee productivity, employee experience and work culture.

References

Affine Analytics. (2021). The Evolution of Data Analytics – Then, Now and Later. Retrieved Oct 15, 2021 from https://www.affineanalytics.com/blog/the-evolution-of-data-analytics-then-now-and-later/

Bridgei2i. (2021). Interview with BRIDGEi2i CEO and Co-Founder, Prithvijit Roy in conversation with Neeraj Krishnamoorthy. Retrieved Oct 15, 2021 from https://bridgei2i.com/interview-with-bridgei2i-ceo-prithvijit-roy/

Business Wire. (2021). The "Healthcare Global Market Opportunities And Strategies To 2022". Retrieved Oct 15, 2021 from https://www.businesswire.com/news/home/201 90625005862/en/11.9-Trillion-Global-Healthcare-Market-Key-Opportunities

Driving Retail Growth by Leveraging Analytics, PWC Publications 2016. Retrieved from https://www.pwc.in/assets/pdfs/publications/2016/profitable-growth-for-retail-businesses-online.pdf

Enabling various types of Healthcare Data to build Top 10 DL applications Dr. Sunil Kumar Vuppala Apr 5. Retrieved from https://medium.com/@sunil.vuppala/enabling-various-types-of-healthcare-data-to-build-top-10-dl-applications-f5c6f45eddba

ETHealthWorld. (2019). Healthcare Analytics: How Data Is Transforming the Healthcare Landscape in India, ETHealthWorld July 19, 2019. Retrieved from https://health.economictimes.indiatimes.com/news/health-it/healthcare-analytics-how-data-is-transforming-the-healthcare-landscape-in-india/70288906

Foster Provost & Tm Fawcett. (2018). *Data science for business*. Newton, MA: O'REILLY.

Gartner. (2018). *Analytics*. Retrieved from Gartner: https://www.gartner.com/it-glossary/analytics/

Healthcare Analytics Point Providers to Patients that Need the Most Care by Juliet Van Wagenen. Retrieved from https://healthtechmagazine.net/article/2017/04/healthcare-analytics-point-providers-patients-need-most-care

How Retailers Can Make The Most of Their Data, Hugo Moreno Contributor, Thought Leaders Contributor Group, Leadership Strategy, Jun 28, 2018. Retrieved from https://www.forbes.com/sites/forbesinsights/2018/06/28/how-retailers-can-make-the-most-of-their-data/#4bead88d453c

How Supply Chain Analytics can Transform Business? By O4S Team. Retrieved from https://medium.com/o4s-io/how-supply-chain-analytics-can-transform-business-2fc9e16bc9ac

Ilangovan, R. (2017). Retail Analytics Trends — 2017 and beyond Ramesh Ilangovan May 15, 2017. Retrieved from https://towardsdatascience.com/retail-analytics-trends-201 7-and-beyond-374bc6627cb0

Linoff, G.S., and Berry, M.J.A. (2011). *Data mining techniques*. New York: Wiley Publishing, Inc.

Lochy, J. (2019). Big Data in the Financial Services Industry - From Data to Insights, Sep 2019. Retrieved from https://www.finextra.com/blogposting/17847/big-data-in-the-financial-services-industry---from-data-to-insights

Predictive Retail Analytics – Why Should You Use It? by Chandra Gogineni. Retrieved from https://www.comtecinfo.com/rpa/predictive-retail-analytics-use/

Search Data Management Tech Target Data Analytics (DA) by Margaret Rouse. Retrieved from https://searchdatamanagement.techtarget.com/definition/data-analytics

Social Media Analytics – BFSI by Kalyan Banga. Retrieved from http://fusionanalyticsworld.com/social-media-analytics-bfsi-part/

Six Ways to Improve Your Influencer Marketing Analytics by Kayla Matthews. Retrieved from https://talkinginfluence.com/2019/12/12/improve-influencer-analytics/

The Ultimate Guide to Retail & Commerce Data 2020, Datarade. Retrieved from https://datarade.ai/data-categories/retail-commerce-data/guide

Types of Analytics in Human Resource Management. Retrieved from https://talentedge.com/articles/analytics-hr-management/

What is Data Analysis? Methods, Techniques & Tools; Posted in Data Analytics by Simran Kaur Arora Apr, 2020. Retrieved from https://hackr.io/blog/what-is-data-analysis-methods-techniques-tools

Workforce Analytics: How Mature are Organizations? Retrieved from https://www.peoplematters.in/article/hr-analytics/workforce-analytics-how-mature-are-organizations-13135

Chapter 2

Industry 4.0: Data and Data Integration

Pavan Gundarapu

Data Integration Solutions Manager, Safran, France

Contents

DOI: 10.1201/9781003175889-2

Objectives

The decision is made after the **information** is analyzed. **Information** is prepared after the **data** is transformed. This line perfectly portrays the importance of data to any data-driven decision making. This chapter discusses the invisible work that is carried under the hood; all this work is what we call data integration. Data integration helps to process the raw data to polished data that will enable us to make the right decisions at the right moment. This chapter provides an overview of what data integration is, the different data integration solutions available, then we will go through different methodologies of data integration. Finally, we will discuss various data integration service providers available in the market.

2.1 Introduction

The fourth industrial revolution or Industry 4.0 is a digital manufacturing enterprise that is interconnected and also analyzes, communicates and further utilizes the information to initiate intelligent action into the real world: Physical-to-digital-to-physical (PDP) loop (Mark Cotteleer, 2020). The continuous flow of information along with cyclical streams and actions between the real world and digital worlds will indeed allow real-time access to information and intelligence (Mark Cotteleer, 2020). This allows deriving some meaningful insights. Thereby data becomes the heart of any disruptive revolutions like Industry 4.0. So, let's understand what is data, and why it is important? Data is a collection of facts, such as numbers, words, observations, or descriptions of things that is further translated into the language that computers can understand.

Data in its initial state is frequently referred to as raw data or atomic data. Data only becomes information suitable for making decisions once it has been processed and analyzed. We can compare the process of transformation by taking a real-life example that happens daily in our kitchen. You wish to prepare a dish (information); to do that you get the recipe from your grandmother or your mother or even from the internet. Once the recipe (recipe is the set transformation rules) is ready, you buy the vegetables (raw data) that is in their raw format. We sort the vegetables (data sorting), clean the vegetables (data cleansing), cut the vegetables and cook the dish and add the condiments according to the recipe (data transformation rules). Now the dish is ready to be consumed. It can be served directly out of the pan or presented to the consumer in a visually appealing way (data visualization). The extent to which a set of data is informative to someone depends on how well the recipe is followed.

Now that you are comfortable with what the data is, let's dive a bit deeper to understand how we transform the data into information. We call this process a data integration. Data integration is a process where data from multiple sources are combined into a single and unified view. Also, integration begins with the extraction process and includes steps such as data cleansing, mapping and transformation (Pearlman, 2019).

2.2 Data Integration

"You can have data without information, but you cannot have information without data" (Keys, 2020). Atomic data or raw data does not have meaning unless this has been prepared and processed and made available as information to the end-user that will help to make the right decisions at the right time. For any company, information is power: the more you know, the more effective you will be to take strategic decisions that will determine your next direction and come up with an effective game plan. In today's data-driven culture, you must have high-quality data to achieve success. An effective way to get high-quality data is by integrating data by connecting to all heterogeneous data sources available and make accessible in one centralized location.

In Figure 2.1 to the left are heterogeneous structured data sources (the list is not exhaustive), then extract, transform, and load (ETL) is used to transfer the data to a staging area (usually a database), then ETL is again used to transform the data and load it into a data warehouse. As you can see, the data is prepared and is ready to be consumed using any analytics tool. This is a typical data warehouse architecture. ETL is a short form for extract, transform, and load and is the process of extracting data from different sources, transforming it into a different structure or format, and loading it into a target.

2.3 Data Integration Solutions

In this data-driven world, you hear quite often the terms ETL, ELT – extract, load and transform, and even custom code to answer specific demands. We will unfold

Figure 2.1 Data integration schema.

custom code data integration and then discuss the pros and cons of this solution. Then, we will delve into the ETL and ELT and how they are different.

2.3.1 Custom Code

What exactly is custom code? This will be easier if we begin with a metaphor. Imagine the code is a car: Tesla Model S. You might say to yourself; I want the Tesla Model S all-electric five-door liftback sedan. So, I will put the car together, build the electric engine with an 85 kWh battery, then add electric powertrain, add dual-drive all-wheel drive, install all the electronics, get it entirely road-legal and become responsible for driving it and maintaining it too. In other words, the custom code is flexible to make changes. It leverages in-database processing. But you are solely responsible for fixing the issues. The custom code is time consuming and complicated to create, maintain and change.

2.3.2 ETL

ETL is an integration approach that pulls data from different sources, transforms it into defined formats and styles and then loads it into a relational database or a data warehouse, or a simple delimited file. Data in its "raw" form is typically not sufficient to get a business's envisioned goals. Before it can be used, the data has to undergo a few sets of steps called ETL (McDaniel, ETL Architecture, 2019). The steps included are the following:

2.3.2.1 Extract

First, data is extracted from various heterogeneous or homogeneous data sources based on different validation rules (Figure 2.2). This process allows the staging of the data coming from various sources that are critical for the subsequent processes (Transform). A data source refers to the location where the data is originated from (McDaniel, Data Source, 2019). A data source may often be a database or a flat file and sometimes live measures from devices (IoT devices) or data from the web (McDaniel, Data Source, 2019). Example of a data source in a manufacturing unit: when a manufacturing unit receives an order from the customer, you need to verify if your items are in stock. You get this information from the inventory database of the ERP. The inventory tables are the data sources in this case, which are accessed through ERP. Data can also be transported with the help of various network protocols, such as hypertext transfer protocol, file transfer protocol, or application programming interfaces that are provided by either websites, networked applications, and other services (McDaniel, Data Source, 2019). There are additional protocols for transporting data from sources to targets, especially on the web, include SOAP, REST, NFS, and SMB (McDaniel, Data Source, 2019).

Figure 2.2   ETL → Extract.

Data sources can be hosted on-premises, or on the cloud, or even as software as a service. There could be a mix of on-premises and cloud or on-premises and software as service or three of them.

- On-premises:
  The data is typically backed by a local transactional database installed in data centers inside the firewall.
  The company has full access to the data; this gives complete visibility and control.
- Cloud:
  The data is typically backed by a cloud database. The data resides outside of the company. Cloud offers fewer options than on-premises.
- Software as a service:
  Data is available via API.
  The data is outside of the company's firewall. The company has very little control over the handling of data.

The common data-source format includes:

- Relational databases
- Flat files
- XML
- JSON
- Web services
- Cloud data warehouse
- Cloud data lake

An essential part of extraction includes the validation of data. It is important to confirm if the data drawn from various sources possess the right or required values. If the job fails, the data is rejected completely or partly. The rejected data may be further reported back to the source for further analysis either to detect or to resolve the faulty records.

2.3.2.2 Transform

The data is transformed to achieve the intended results (Figure 2.3). The transformation process involves steps like eliminating inaccuracies or missing data to safeguard data integrity, or converting the required data from one format to another (McDaniel, ETL Architecture, 2019). The data is prepared for loading into the target by applying the set of rules or functions to the extracted data (ETL, 2020).

Transformation prepares the data for analysis. Find below some common types of transformation:

Basic transformation:

- Data cleaning: Fix or remove anomalies discovered. Examples: Assigning 0 to null values, data formatting.
- Format conversion: Data type conversions like date time conversions, integer conversions, character set conversion.
- Deduplication: Identifying and eliminating duplicate records.
- Advanced transformations:
- Applying business rules: usually derives new calculated values – for example supplier on-time delivery metric derived from the promised date and delivery date (this rule may change from company to company).
- Filtering: Choosing only certain rows or columns.
- Joins: Joining the data coming from multiple data sources.
- Splitting: Splitting the data, for example splitting the full name column to a first name and last name.

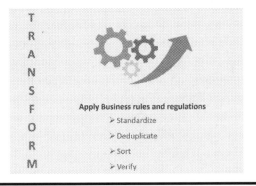

Figure 2.3   ETL → Transform.

- Data validation: Validation of data. For example a telephone number if does not respect certain patterns then rejects the value for processing.
- Aggregation: Aggregate or group the data from multiple databases.

2.3.2.3 Load

The load phase inserts the data into the end target (Figure 2.4). The target can be a simple delimited file, a transactional database, or a data warehouse. Depending on the requirements of the project in a company, the load process differs. If it is a data warehouse project, the updated process can be an incremental load or a full load. Well-designed data warehouse projects usually opt for incremental loads that can have a huge impact on performance and load times, and these changes from the source can be reflected in the data warehouse in near real-time. The data loads can be scheduled to run on an hourly, daily, weekly, monthly or even yearly basis (ETL, 2020).

2.3.3 ELT

ELT is the variant of ETL. The difference between ETL and ELT is the order of the events. In ETL, we apply the data transformation while the data is being moved. Whereas in ELT, the transformation occurs after it has been moved.

So why and how ETL and ELT are different. Let us try to understand a bit of the history behind both processes. ETL became popular in the companies when the companies tried to integrate data from databases, files into a data warehouse. The database infrastructure and technology were not well equipped to handle the volumes of data. So, ETL came with a proprietary engine to support the transformation.

But, in today's world, the traditional relational database management systems are now far more superior, and the robust capabilities of massive parallel processing allow to use of a large number of computer processors to simultaneously perform certain computations in parallel, and of course big data technologies.

ETL, significant effort is required to manage this data for increasing data volumes. ETL tools are sometimes a black box as the code that executes cannot be viewed or modified. The transformation part can be pushed down to, or manual

Figure 2.4   ETL → Load.

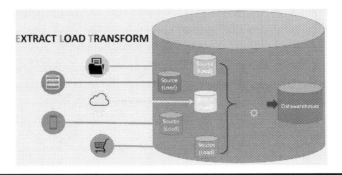

Figure 2.5   ELT → Extract, load and transform.

SQL overrides can be used as techniques to optimize the ETL, then why do we need the transformation server.

This is where ELT comes into the picture. The data from different sources is directly loaded into the target and the transformations are done by the robust capabilities of the database engine (Figure 2.5). ELT is very much recommended when you have high processing power like that of spark and robust capabilities of teradata.

Advantages of ELT:

■ No need for the target data to be unloaded in another server for a lookup to capture delta. Delta means only the changes that have not yet been applied to the data warehouse, which usually comprises new, updated data and purged data. Most of the time capturing delta is a cumbersome process; in the ETL lookup process, this is done in the transformation server. But it has its cons; when the ETL does a lookup, it has to get the data from the target that then stores in a cache to perform the lookups that can have performance impacts. In the ELT process as the data resides in the same server, a simple join is enough.
■ Cost-effective and scalable.
■ No blackbox as in ETL. For the end-user, the code is visible that increases transparency.

2.4 Data Integration Methodologies

Data integration has different methods to load the data into the target. Defining the right data integration methodology is crucial in any data integration project. Many factors influence the choice of a method. It can be the destination into which you are loading the data – data warehouse used for analytics, transactional database or it could be the cost of the project, the volume of data to be transferred,

and so on. To choose the right methodology, you need to have a clear understanding of different existing methods.

2.4.1 Bulk Loading

Bulk loading is the method of loading data in large chunks into a database system
in a relatively small amount of time. At each run, the data from the target is purged
and the full dataset is loaded.

When you use bulk load, the integration process bypasses the database log
therefore the transactional integrity can be an issue. Bypassing the logs means no
need to write to the log and therefore huge gain in performance. But if you do not
write to the database log, the target database does not perform a rollback, where
you may not be able to perform recovery operations in case of failures. This option
should be considered with caution, if you only need speed and are not worried
about transactional integrity, this could be the best option. Usually, this is the least
efficient option, but it is very simple to manage.

2.4.2 Daily Differentials

Bulk loading does the full load of the data means, purge the target data and insert
the full data from the source. Data integration jobs can be scheduled through some
orchestration tools provided by the data integration solution or can be scheduled
using the operating system–specific orchestration tools, for example Windows has
Windows Task Scheduler and even third-party tools like Control-M, Dollar
Universe, IBM Workload Automation, etc. Usually, the schedules are planned
according to the business needs usually hourly loads, daily loads, weekly loads,
monthly, or even yearly loads. This completely depends upon the frequency of data
source updates and the business requirements. When you do bulk loading as the
data gets truncated every time and loaded fully, the process consumes a lot of
system resources and time. This is not ideal if you are processing heavy volumes of
data. Imagine, if the process takes 6 hours to load terabytes of data and the job fails
after running 5 hours, the process must run again, and you need to wait until 6
hours assuming the job does not fail. In such scenarios, daily differentials or incremental loads help resolve these issues.

Incremental data load refers to the changes that occurred to the source
system since the last integration of data. Every change should be reflected in the
target systems. There are different methods to detect the changes. This is usually
done through date timestamps available in the data source systems. In few cases,
you need to rely on the database log system if the date timestamps are not
available or even deploying change data capture systems on the source databases.
Change dta capture is an approach to determine and track the data changes
inserts, updates, and deletes that are further used to load to the target systems
(Figure 2.6).

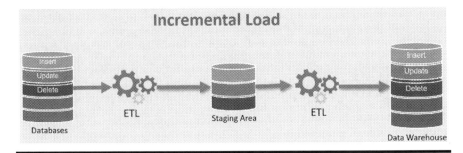

Figure 2.6 Incremental load.

Advantages:

- Speed: Incremental loads are very fast as they process only the changes.
- Frequency: Incremental loads can be planned more frequently as they can run faster, for example hourly or even every 1 minute that will be near real-time.
- History: No need to remove the history as in full load. The history is preserved.
- Availability: The availability of data can be near real-time.

Disadvantages:

- Requires a change data capture mechanism on the source systems to identify the changes.

2.4.3 *Insert Only*

Inserts only new data to the target based on the date range (Figure 2.7). This eliminates the need of deploying change data capture to the source systems.

Changes to data from previous periods require the deletion of all data for the given date range. This simplifies the data processing as we extract data by date range. Depending upon the date range and volume of data, this could or could not be a time-consuming process.

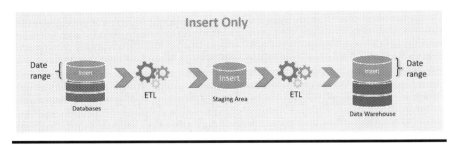

Figure 2.7 Insert only.

2.4.4 Database Replication

Replication of a database is the process of storing the same data in multiple locations. This is usually a master–slave relationship between the original and the copies. When there are changes made in the master database, those changes are logged and then rippled to the slaves. The slave then confirms the reception of the updates.

Database replication can be divided into two types:

Asynchronous replication: Asynchronous replication refers to writing data to the master database first and then, based on the implementation method, binds data to be replicated to the memory or the disk-based log. The data is then copied in real-time or even at planned intervals to the slaves.

Synchronous replication: Replication takes place simultaneously to the master database and the slave databases. As such master and the slaves will always remain synchronized.

Database replication improves the availability and accessibility of the data. Data replication is used sometimes for the disaster recovery plan. A disaster recovery plan is a process to have a database up and running and overcoming the data loss. Replication allows restoring the databases in case of failure.

Database replication generally runs in near real-time. The replicated data is often used as an operational data store that serves as a data source for data warehouse systems or this can be used as a transactional database for doing some reporting or simply for recovery and backup purposes. Identifying the changes requires a change data capture mechanism. The schemas must match between source and destination that imposes some strict change request policies on the source database systems. Whenever there is a change in the schema, this needs to be informed and changes need to be propagated to the target.

2.4.5 Batch Processing

Batch processing, as the name indicates, happens in blocks of data or batches. This method is used to process high volumes of data and through repetitive data jobs (Figure 2.8). For example to calculate monthly balance data, you must process millions of data from General Ledger coming from an ERP (enterprise resource planning) or flat files. Another example would be processing the inventory data from the inventory database to calculate obsolescence. Obsolescence is the inventory that has not been used for a long period and is also not anticipated to be sold soon (Tuovila, 2019). Calculating key performance indicators for obsolescence can help the industry save millions of dollars. The above two examples can be processed in batches that could be planned daily, weekly, or monthly.

There are several advantages to using batch processing for enterprise data management (Pearlman, Batch Processing, 2019). Batch processing can be carried

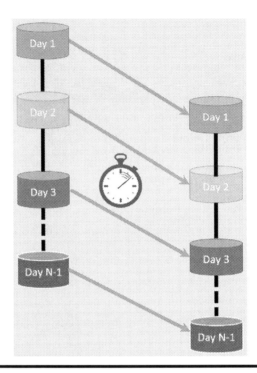

Figure 2.8   Example of a daily batch processing.

out while computing or when other resources are available instantly usually when there is no activity (Pearlman, Batch Processing, 2019). They can also run offline to reduce stress on the processors depending on the architecture (Pearlman, Batch Processing, 2019). Errors are reduced; thanks to batch processing that automates maximum components of a job processing and decreases user interaction (Pearlman, Batch Processing, 2019). Precision and accurateness are enhanced to produce a higher degree of data quality (Pearlman, Batch Processing, 2019).

2.4.6 Streaming

Streaming is an unbounded continuous flow of records in real-time; when put in other words, this is the method of sending the data continuously in contrary to batches. So, there is no "start" or "finish" to this process. This is beneficial when the data from the data sources is sent in small chunks in the continuous flow as the data is generated. Data can come from multiple data sources simultaneously. Data streaming applies to most of the industry segments like aerospace, retail, manufacturing, educational systems, financial institutions, gaming companies, and so on. Gaming companies collect the streaming data from the players to analyze all the interactions with the games, for example games they are playing the most and the accessories they are trying to buy in the games and so on to propose some discounts and engage them to play more. Video streaming companies like Netflix and Amazon prime collect real-time data to improve the user experience through recommendation engines. Sensors used in the machinery in manufacturing units can be streamed to analyze the data in real-time to avoid any downtime in the manufacturing process and detect any potential defects in advance to take necessary action.

Data streaming is also used during catastrophes caused by nature or by a human. Examples of natural catastrophes include hurricanes or earthquakes and human catastrophes like COVID-19. Data streaming helps the government to identify the most vulnerable communities to take preventive measures as soon as possible. Data is collected from social media to react and track COVID-19's global impact. Geo-localization data streams help people to predict the dynamic of COVID-19 spread that helps people to avoid crowded areas.

2.5 Service Providers

Companies like Microsoft, Amazon, Oracle, IBM, Informatica, and Talend (Figure 2.9) are well-known actors in the data integration domain. Apache Software Foundation has also developed different tools. Meanwhile, many startups are evolving and giving tough competition to the big companies. As there are hundreds of data integration service providers, choosing a service provider depends

Figure 2.9   Data integration service providers.

upon many factors like the connectors they provide, features, ease of use, and the price. As the need for digital transformation in companies is increasing, companies are adopting new digital technologies by changing the prevailing business procedures, user experience, and culture to meet constantly changing business requirements. Multiple technologies lead to multiple and heterogeneous data sources. Having the right connectors to connect to the data sources can surely have an impact on the choice of the service provider. Price could be another factor; nowadays many companies are moving toward open-source tools due to their cost-effective pricing models.

2.6 Brief on Each Software

Microsoft:

A. Microsoft SQL Server Integration Services (SSIS) is a platform for data integration (Microsoft, 2020).
B. Microsoft's Azure Data Factory is a service built for all data integration needs and skill levels on Microsoft Azure (cloud platform).

Talend:

A. Talend Data Integration: Data integration software can be used to link, access, and convert any data on the cloud or on-premises (Talend, 2020).
B. Talend Real-Time Big Data: Talend real-time big data can be used to work with Spark Streaming. You can also turn all your batch data pipelines into real-time (Real-time big data, 2020).

Informatica:
Informatica PowerCenter is a data integration technology.
Apache:

A. Apache Spark refers to an analytics engine for large-scale data processing (Apachespark, 2020).
B. Apache Kafka is a distributed publish–subscribe messaging system that integrates applications and data streams (Kafka, 2020).
C. Apache Flink is a data streaming flow engine that allows the distributed computation over data streams (Flink, 2020).

SAP:

SAP data services is an ETL tool capable of extracting data from a wide range of data sources regardless of system or supplier.

Matillion:

> Matillion is one of the data integration tools for cloud data warehouses. It is mainly used to integrate data based on ELT solutions on the cloud solutions like Amazon Redshift, Google Big Query, and Snowflake that enables companies to accomplish the new levels of speed, scale, speed, and also savings (Matillion, 2020).

2.7 Conclusion

Data integration as a strategy is the first step toward transforming the raw data into a piece of valuable information. This is crucial to any industry to make data-driven decision-making. We saw what data Integration is and different data integration solutions like custom code, ETL, and ELT. We also saw different data integration methodologies like batch mode, incremental mode, database replication, batch processing, and streaming. Data integration is evolving by adapting to new strategies like cloud, hybrid platforms, and new ever-growing data sources. Some data integration tools have embraced the DevOps methodology by enabling the possibility to use version control tools and CI/CD (continuous integration/continuous deployment) to automate the deployment process. This helps teams to increase flexibility and agility.

References

Apachespark. (2020). Retrieved from spark: https://spark.apache.org/

ETL. (2020, April 16). Retrieved from Extract, transform, load: https://en.wikipedia.org/wiki/Extract,_transform,_load

Flink. (2020). Retrieved from apache Flink: https://flink.apache.org/

kafka. (2020). Retrieved from kafka: https://kafka.apache.org/

Keys, D. (2020, April 25). *Daniel Keys Moran quotes.* Retrieved from BrainyQuote.com: https://www.brainyquote.com/quotes/daniel_keys_moran_230911

Mark Cotteleer, B.S. (2020). *Forces of change: Industry 4.0.* Retrieved from https://www2.deloitte.com/us/en/insights/focus/industry-4-0/overview.html

matillion. (2020). Retrieved from matillion: https://www.matillion.com/

McDaniel, S. (2019, October 2). *Data source.* Retrieved from talend.com: https://www.talend.com/resources/data-source/

McDaniel, S. (2019, September 16). *ETL architecture.* Retrieved from talend.com: https://www.talend.com/resources/etl-architecture/

Microsoft. (2020). *SSIS.* Retrieved from Microsoft: https://docs.microsoft.com/en-us/sql/integration-services/sql-server-integration-services?view=sql-server-ver15

Pearlman, S. (2019, March 14). *Batch processing.* Retrieved from talend.com: https://www.talend.com/resources/batch-processing/

Pearlman, S. (2019, September 3). Retrieved from https://www.talend.com/resources/what-is-data-integration/

Real-time big data. (2020). Retrieved from Talend: https://www.talend.com/products/big-data/real-time-big-data/

Talend. (2020). Retrieved from talend.com: https://www.talend.com/products/data-integration/

Tuovila, A. (2019, May 24). *ObsoleteInventory*. Retrieved from investopedia.com: https://www.investopedia.com/terms/o/obsoleteinventory.asp

Chapter 3

Forecasting Principles and Models: An Overview

R. Vijayaraghavan

Professor and Head, Department of Statistics, Bharathiar University, Coimbatore, India

Contents

DOI: 10.1201/9781003175889-3

3.1 Introduction

Statistical methods or simply statistics are playing a progressively more imperative role practically in all phases of human endeavor. Statistics, formerly, has dealt with affairs of the state. The influence/growth of statistics has now spread over many fields that include agriculture, biology, business, chemistry, communications, economics, education, electronics, insurance, medicine, physics, political science, psychology, sociology, and copious other fields of science and engineering. The complex nature of societal, environmental, biological, economic, business, and management problems is required to be addressed by adopting scientifically formulated strategies and methods. The framework of statistical methods that comprises many such scientific methods provides ways and means of arriving at solutions to various problems that exist or arise in all the domains of complex society and environment.

Statistics, in general, deals with data pertaining to the problem under study and concerns what could be studied from the available data. It can be classified into two, namely, (1) descriptive statistics and (2) inferential statistics. Descriptive statistics are the statistical methods that can be used to summarize or describe a collection and analysis of data in the diversified fields of science, which include humanities and social sciences, physical sciences and life sciences, and to model data pattern for determining randomness and uncertainty in the observations. Inferential statistics deal with the practice of using the models to draw valid conclusions or inferences about the population under consideration.

The descriptive statistics and the application of inferential statistics constitute a major area, called, applied statistics. A framework for understanding the properties and scope of methods used in applications is provided by theoretical statistics. The statistical concepts and tools framed in theoretical and applied statistics are, in general, applied to various problems that would exist in almost every area of human activity where statistical data are involved. Statistical modeling is one of the various important concepts in the theory of statistics that plays a vital role by providing insightful evaluation and assessment of the available information.

Regression, econometric, and time-series (forecast) models are among the various types of statistical models which have wider applications in business, economic, and management problems. These models are vitally used by business decision-makers and government policymakers to perform quantitative analyses and business and economic forecasts. The objective of this chapter is to present a brief account of the general framework of forecasting principles, limitations, and procedures that are applied in the fields of business, commerce, economics, and management. The basic forecast models for time series data, such as naïve, moving average, and exponential smoothing models are provided highlighting their significance.

3.2 Meaning of Forecasting

In more formal terms, forecasting is defined as a process of predicting or estimating the future based on past and present data and provides information about the potential future events and their consequences for the organization. Forecasting uses many statistical techniques. As a statistical planning tool, it permits the policymakers, managements, and organizations to envisage the future behavior or activity based effectively on the historical or past data. Uncertainty may prevail even when the right decisions could be made by them with their ability to predict future trends. Forecasting can be used as a mechanism to steer such decisions.

It is imperative for many sectors or organizations, which may be large or small, private or public, to meet the demands of future conditions with imperfect knowledge. Such situations certainly warrant the use of forecasting either explicitly or implicitly. Though the complications and uncertainty of the future may not be reduced much by forecasts, the insightful information provided by forecasting trends could increase the confidence of the sectors or organizations to make strategic decisions. For further details on the principles of forecasting, one may refer to Hoshmand (2010) and Hanke and Wichern (2014).

3.3 Applications of Forecasting

As pointed out earlier, the concept of forecasting has applications in various fields where forecasts of future conditions are extensively useful for policymakers, managements, and organizations to derive policy decisions and managerial decisions. A brief account of forecasting applications pertaining to four different fields, such as (1) business, (2) supply chain management, (3) epidemiology, and (4) weather, is presented in the following subsections.

3.3.1 Business Forecasting

In the contemporary world of competition in the business and managerial environment, every organization or enterprise functions in an atmosphere of uncertainty. The policy decisions that are likely to be taken in an uncertain or ambiguous environment that exists in an organization will affect its future activities.

Hence, a proper mechanism is required to deal with such a situation of uncertainty while making decisions with the available information drawn from the business organization or enterprise.

Business forecasting is an essential and powerful statistical tool that provides management and business enterprises with important information that will facilitate decision making in the presence of uncertainty. Forecasts in business and trade would always be helpful for business communities to identify the challenges in marketing and sales, responses to changes in the demand-supply ratio, unpredictable stock prices, market volatility, economic recession, economic slowdown, foreign exchange, etc. The past data on these aspects are made use of to forecast future trends, which would help policymakers or managers to plan or fix the targets for the future.

3.3.2 Forecasting in Supply Chain Management

Supply chain management is an activity of sourcing the goods, commodities, raw materials or components by a firm or an enterprise or a supplier to manufacture a product or render service and delivering the product or service to customers at a satisfactory level. To improve the effective performance of any supply chain, a firm or an enterprise or a supplier needs to concentrate on the information about the demand put in for the product, the stock of the product in the inventory and the associated price of the commodity.

Excess stock in the inventory when demand is less would affect a firm or supplier dearly as the cost of storage and maintenance of stock would high. When there is lesser stock and the demand for the product is high, a firm or supplier would lose their market as the customers may approach other firms or suppliers where the stock maintenance is better. Hence, the need for forecasting is arising in supply chain management focusing on the customer's demand for the product, the supplier's or firm's capability of supplying the product or service and the associated cost of the product. The concept of forecasting in supply chain management consists of three aspects: (1) supply forecasting, (2) demand forecasting, and (3) price forecasting.

Supply forecasting, which is based on the data about production, supplier's capacity of producing the products or services and of maintaining the stock, helps to determine how much raw materials should be ordered and stored for manufacturing or production, how much should be produced, stored, and delivered to customers. Demand forecasting makes use of the data relating to the customer's choices and requirements for a specific period, say day, week, month, and year. This would help in predicting the purchasing behavior of the customer and their requirements in the future period of time. Price forecasting utilizes the information relating to demand and supply of the products and costs or prices of the products, raw materials, commodities that are associated with environmental and economic factors and are greatly influenced by the changes in such factors.

3.3.3 Epidemiological Forecasting

One of the important challenges in medical and health sciences is to address the problem of uncertainty in the prevalence of infectious diseases, such as dengue, chikungunya, corona, etc., which inflict a burden on society. Epidemiological forecasting is an emerging area of research in applied statistics that includes bioinformatics and computational biology and helps to understand the processes that drive epidemic trajectory and to forecast future trends and prevalence of the pandemic. This makes use of observable epidemiological information arising from the early stages of an outbreak.

3.3.4 Weather Forecasting

In meteorology, weather forecasting is the task of predicting the conditions of the atmosphere for a location and time based on the data about the current state of the atmosphere such as temperature, humidity, and wind with the utilization of the advancements made in science and technology. It is a systematic procedure, which consists of the collection of observable meteorological or atmospheric data, analysis of data adopting largely statistical principles and methods, and extrapolation of the derived results to determine the future state of the atmosphere. Weather forecasting has many potential applications in various fields which include agriculture, aviation, navigation, trade, etc.

Short-term and long-term weather forecasts are more often considered for effective planning of planting and harvesting of agricultural products. In the air aviation sector, forecasts made based on atmospheric conditions are much helpful for planning and operating flights in the prevalence of strong winds. Marine weather forecasting and ocean ship routing forecasting are the integral parts of weather forecasting, which develop stochastic models based on past weather conditions over the earth's oceans. The marine forecast models are used for finding optimum shipping routes that would minimize the lost time, damage to ships, and fuel cost and consumption, and cost in seas where waves run high. The forecasts made through models often facilitate the proper planning of shipping routes and effective operation of shipping vessels in the routes.

3.4 Limitations of Forecasting

Forecasting methods do have some limitations besides several advantages. They are generally based on certain assumptions; the uncertainty of occurrence of events in the future; lack of skill and knowledge among individuals involved in the process of forecasting and economic factors such as time, cost, and labor. A few of the limitations are listed below:

■ Assumptions imposed in forecasting studies are both deterministic and probabilistic. In a deterministic case, it is assumed that the values of the dependent variables are completely determined by the parameters of the model, whereas in a probabilistic case, assumptions about the probability distributions and the correlation of variables are imposed. While deterministic models have the advantage of often being amenable to mathematical analysis, where verification of imposed condition is not required, it is a prerequisite under a probabilistic approach that the imposed assumptions are to be verified before applying the model for forecasts.

■ Prejudices and human judgments, which are largely based on the history of events that occurred, are considered sometimes for forecasts or predictions. As they do not have any scientific bases in general and are made without scientific analyses, such forecasts or predictions would often lead to wrong results and conclusions.

■ As forecasting is a scientific and systematic approach largely based on stochastic variables and the distributional assumptions, trained and skilled personnel, who have adequate knowledge are to be involved in the process of forecasting.

■ Economic considerations in terms of time, cost and labor are to be given attention in the forecasting activity. As the process involves in itself huge data, most of time series nature, which may be qualitative and quantitative, the time, labor, and cost involved in the collection, classification and manipulation of data are high, which indicates that forecasting is an expensive and a time-consuming exercise.

■ The environmental, atmospheric, economic, and market conditions are quite dynamic. They influence the process of forecasting, whatsoever the field, and have a severe impact on forecasts, thereby accurate forecasting may not be realized eventually.

■ Forecasts are viewed as estimates. 100% accuracy of forecasts may not be realized even if the process of forecasting is carefully planned. The forecast accuracy depends on adopting the proper criteria for choosing a suitable forecasting method.

■ Forecasting methods do not provide proper results if the data presented for analysis are distorted by nonperiodic events.

■ As the process of forecasting involves large data, it may not be possible to determine the relationship between past and future events.

3.5 Types of Forecasting Procedures

Forecasting procedures can be classified according to whether they are used for short-term, medium-term or long-term forecasts. For instance, in a business environment, short-term forecasts, which are made for periods of less than one year, with a normal range between 1 and 3 months, are required to fix production planning and control, to set cash requirements for a shorter period and to make adjustments within the organizations to tackle the short-term fluctuations. Medium-term and long-term forecasts, which are related largely to resource implications, respectively, focus on minor and major intended decisions within the organizations.

While medium-term forecasts are made normally for 12 months duration, long-term forecasts are done for a period of 2 or more years. While long-term forecasts are necessary for an organization to set its strategic plans for the long run, short-term forecasts are used by first-line and middle managements to fix their strategies instantaneously in order to meet up the demands of future and medium-term forecasts help the organizations to address the start-up financial pitfalls and build the financial resources.

Forecasting procedures, in general, fall under two categories, namely, (i) qualitative approach and (ii) quantitative approach, which are outlined along with their objectives.

3.5.1 Qualitative Approach

Qualitative methods of forecasting include the experience, knowledge, instincts and intuitive judgment of managements or executives or experts, the opinions of individuals, surveys, salesforce composites and the Delphi method. When opinions or prejudices are expressed by experienced experts, executives or managements based on the expertise that has been developed over time on a particular work or activity, a group of experts or managers interact and collectively develop a forecast. Opinion, market, and field surveys are the approaches that can be adopted to decide on choices or preferences of consumer or stakeholder and to assess the expected demand in future.

While a group of stakeholders or customers are involved in the discussion and express their views about the products, it might be possible to measure their interests and choices in the products, which an organization is intended to produce in the future. The participation of the customers who give feedback and the experts who utilize their expertise on the products in a group discussion might help derive demand forecasting. Salesforce composite is another qualitative method by which future demand for the products or services can be projected.

For instance, sales in a region can be estimated by sales managers or sales executives by this method making use of the information about the quantity that is expected to be sold by a sales manager in that region. This method helps an organization to frame the production planning and control and to fix the target levels such as how much goods are to be produced within a specified period, how much demand for the product would be expected in the future and how much raw materials would be needed for production.

The Delphi method is the structured, systematic, and interactive forecasting tool involving a panel of experts in business organizations or establishments, who have a methodical knowledge of their businesses, services, and products, can envisage the future trends in the market and focus on the principle that they must reach out with a compromise or consensus agreement among themselves to derive the forecasts with greater accuracy. The experts involved in the Delphi method consider a series of questions in the form of a questionnaire and solution and ultimately arrive at the best responses by consensus agreement.

One of the serious limitations of such methods is that they are employed when historical information or data are inadequate or sparse. The forecasts that would result from these approaches may not be much accurate and consistent as the opinions and judgments of individuals often introduce uncertainties and biases in the results. However, they are fast, less expensive, and flexible and do provide good results when experienced and trained forecasters are involved in the forecasting process.

3.5.2 Quantitative Approach

Quantitative methods of forecasting are systematic and objective procedures that include time series and regression or causal methodologies. Such methods do not need information from subjective judgments or opinions, and hence they are not influenced by bias. They develop statistical models based on historical data to forecast market conditions and trends. Examples for historical data include yield of the crop in a region over a period, sales turnover realized by a firm, amount of rainfall in the region, etc. Time series models are such statistical models that forecast future values of a variable based on the historical observation of that variable assuming time as an independent variable.

These models are built considering data patterns, such as trend, seasonal, cyclical, irregular, and stationary, and attempt to predict the future based upon the underlying patterns contained within the data. More often, time-series data may exhibit a pattern showing a relationship between the value in one time period and the value in previous periods. Such a pattern is termed an auto-correlated pattern and the data exhibiting the pattern is called auto-correlated data. Time series models of auto-correlated data are termed autoregressive models. The autoregressive methodology consists of various forecast procedures, which include moving averages, exponential smoothing and Box–Jenkins models.

Regression or causal models are developed under the assumption that the variable being forecasted is related to other variables in the environment. Such models attempt to project future trends based upon the theoretical relationships existing between variables. One may decide on fitting a regression model when the objective is to forecast long-term trends. If the interest of the business establishment or management is to make a short-term forecast, the moving average, exponential, and Box–Jenkins models can be used. An integrated approach utilizing the qualitative and quantitative methods for making long-term forecasts is also found a place in the forecasting procedures.

3.6 Process of Forecasting

It is clear from the earlier sections that the past experiences or occurrences of events are required to forecast or predict the future and forecasting requires the proper description of data generated by historical events or data. The process of forecasting, in general, involves the following steps:

1. Problem identification
2. Collection of data
3. Description and manipulation of data
4. Analysis of data, model construction, and evaluation
5. Model implementation, forecast evaluation, and model performance

3.6.1 Problem Identification

Problem identification is an important step in the forecasting process, wherein the intended objectives of the forecast model are specified. The information about how the forecasting model will be helpful for a stakeholder or firm or enterprise, to whom the forecasts are estimated and how the forecasts will be used for decision making or future planning of activities of the firm or enterprise are required for formulating the forecasting problem.

3.6.2 Collection of Data

Appropriate data relating to the problem defined are collected. Statistical data based on qualitative and quantitative approaches are gathered. The forecasting problems largely make use of the historical data. When quantitative information is seldom available, it may be required to redefine the problems and adopt the judgmental or qualitative forecasting procedures. In some problems, old data may not be much useful due to the abrupt changes, for instance, in economic and environmental conditions. In such situations, the recent data would be used.

3.6.3 Description and Manipulation of Data

Data description is a very significant step in statistical data analysis. By this, we mean exploring the information contained in the entire data set has been gathered for studying the problem. For instance, the relationship existing between explanatory and response (forecast) variables can be explored by describing the data. Exploratory data analysis is a preliminary analysis, which is required to be performed to assess the data patterns exhibited by the data and can be considered as a part of data description. The presence or absence of outliers, trend and seasonality, and cyclic and irregular variations in the data is assessed by this analysis.

Data manipulation is a form of cleaning the data and is adopted after checking the appropriateness of data for the defined problem. Sometimes, there may be cases of inadequate data, missing of specific information, presence of irrelevant information, etc. In such cases, cleaning of data is initiated to make the data more appropriate for use.

3.6.4 Analysis of Data, Model Construction, and Evaluation

Following the exploratory data analysis, the main analysis consists of constructing the forecast model. The historical data gathered and manipulated or cleaned and the strength of the relationships between explanatory and response (forecast) variables are considered to fit a suitable forecast model for the data. Though it is possible to fit more than one forecast model for a given data set, a unique model is always desirable. The forecast models are generally constructed based on a set of implicit and explicit assumptions, and each model is defined with one or more unknown parameters, which would describe the statistical properties and would be estimated using the historical data.

When more than one forecast models exist, the principle of a minimum of forecasting error is adopted. Accordingly, a forecast model is considered to be an appropriate model when the forecasting error corresponding to that model is a minimum when compared to the other models. Once a model is identified or fitted to the data, it is always necessary to check the validity of the model before using the model for forecasts. This can be evaluated by the verification of assumptions about randomness, the probability distribution of the random errors, diagnostic checking and residual analysis, etc.

3.6.5 Model Implementation, Forecast Evaluation, and Model Performance

The forecast model, which contains the estimated values of the parameters, so chosen after verification of the assumptions, diagnostic checking, and residual analysis is used for generating forecasts. The performance of the model is assessed by comparing the actual historical data and forecasts for the recent past data and determining the forecasting error. By performing a detailed analysis of the forecasting, magnitude, and patterns of errors can be found that would be helpful to reconstruct the forecast models.

3.7 Basic Forecasting Models

Forecasting models are statistical models that are constructed based on data patterns of historical data. They are of many types, which include regression and Box–Jenkins models. The three basic forecast models, such as naïve, averaging, and exponential smoothing methods, are described in this section.

3.7.1 Naïve Forecast Model

The naïve forecast method is an estimating device in which the real data of the previous period are used as the forecast of the current period without adjusting them or attempting to establish causal factors. In other words, the actual values in the previous period are simply used as the forecasts for the present period, and the present values are used as the forecasts for the subsequent future period. The forecasts obtained by the naïve approach are considered as the estimates that depend on the most recently available information. It is used only for comparison with the forecasts generated by sophisticated or advanced techniques.

The naïve forecast model is useful for a quick forecast when the data pattern is such that there is no great deal of a change between one time period and another. It is suitable when the past data pattern exhibits slow changes. A specific naïve model is defined under the assumption that the recent period is the indicator of the future period. It is denoted by

$$\hat{Y}_{t+1} = Y_t,$$

where $\hat{Y}_{t+1}$ is the forecast made at the time t for time $t + 1$.

It is to be noted that the forecast value at any period is set equal to the value observed in the immediately preceding period. When the time series data exhibit a trend, say the data values increase or decrease continuously over time, the forecast for the next period should be made taking into account the difference between the data point at the recent past period (Y_t) and the previous period (Y_{t-1}). Thus, the forecast equation, in this case, would be defined by

$$\hat{Y}_{t+1} = Y_t + (Y_t - Y_{t-1}).$$

3.7.2 Forecasting with Averaging Models

Averaging models are the techniques that can be used when the management is interested to make forecasts of daily, weekly or monthly production; inventory; sales, and so on. Such models are specifically useful for eliminating randomness in the data. While naïve forecast model uses recent past observations and discards all other observations in a time series, the averaging models take into account an entire time-series data along with the random fluctuations exhibited by them. Thus, averaging models are considered as an improvement over naïve models and are treated as smoothing models since the short-run fluctuations in the data are smoothened by averaging the observations.

Averaging methods are of two types, namely, simple averages and moving averages. The method of simple averages consists of computing the average of the entire time series data and using it as a forecast. On the other hand, the method of moving averages considers as much historical data as needed for finding moving averages for a specified span.

3.7.2.1 Simple Averages

Consider time series data Y_1, Y_2, ..., Y_t for t time points. The simple average of these data points is used as a forecast for the next period $t + 1$. Thus, the forecast of time $t + 1$ is defined by

$$\hat{Y}_{t+1} = \frac{1}{t} \sum_{i:1}^{t} Y_i.$$

When an observation at a time $t + 1$ is known, the forecast for the next period $t + 2$ is made by using the following equation:

$$\hat{Y}_{t+2} = \frac{t\hat{Y}_{t+1} + Y_{t+1}}{t + 1}.$$

3.7.2.2 Moving Averages

In situations where the recent observations are more important than farther data points of a time series, the method of moving averages can be used as an approach for forecasting. In this method, initially, the number of data points is specified and the mean for the data is computed; when a new data point becomes available, a new mean is computed by dropping the oldest data point and by including the newest observation. Given time series data for t periods, the forecast for the period $t + 1$ is obtained by the moving average defined by

$$\hat{Y}_{t+1} = \frac{1}{n} \sum_{i:1}^{n} Y_{t-i+1},$$

where $\hat{Y}_{t+1}$ is the forecast value for time $t + 1$, Y_t is the actual value at the time t, and n is the number of terms in the moving average.

It can be noted that the moving average for period t is the average of the n most recent observations and equal weights are assigned to each observation. A prerequisite for adopting the method of moving averages is that the forecaster should choose the number of periods, n, in a moving average. A moving average is said to be of order n when it is computed with n number of periods or the data points and is denoted by $MA(n)$.

3.7.3 Exponential Smoothing Models

Exponential smoothing is another forecasting approach that is based on the assumption that the time series data are stationary. It is useful in situations where the data do not exhibit the pattern of an upward or downward trend, and where the most recent observations play an important role in making a forecast. In this method, the estimates are revised continuously when recent information becomes available and smoothing of data is done in an exponentially decreasing fashion. It works on the principle that the most recent observation is assigned with the largest weight, the next most recent one is assigned with less weight, and so forth with the oldest observation receiving the least weight.

Given a time series data Y_1, Y_2, ..., Y_t for t periods, in exponential smoothing approach, the forecast for time $t + 1$ is defined as a weighted sum of the new observation at a time t and the old forecast for time t, and smoothing (averaging) of past values of the series is done in an exponential (i.e., decreasing) fashion. Accordingly, when the most recent observation, Y_t, receives the weight α $(0 < \alpha < 1)$, the observations Y_{t-1}, Y_{t-2}, ... should be assigned with weights α $(\alpha - 1)$, α $(\alpha - 1)^2$, ..., respectively. Thus, the exponential smoothing equation is defined by

$$\hat{Y}_{t+1} = \alpha Y_t + (1 - \alpha)\hat{Y}_t,$$

where $\hat{Y}_{t+1}$ is the forecast (smoothed) value for time $t + 1$, Y_t is the actual value at the time t, $\hat{Y}_{t-1}$ is the forecast value at the time $t - 1$, and α is the smoothing constant lying between 0 and 1.

It is to be noted that from the smoothing equation, the new forecast value depends on three factors, namely, the recent past value, the recent forecast value, and the smoothing constant. In the exponential smoothing approach of forecasting, the choice of the value of the smoothing constant (α) is very significant. A smaller value of α to the most recent time series value may be desirable when the data pattern exhibits erratic and random behavior, which must be smoothened. A larger value α may be quite appropriate when a quick response to changing behavior is desirable.

However, arbitrariness should be avoided in choosing the values of α. Alternatively, it is advocated that, for estimating α, an iterative method that minimizes the mean squared error (MSE), defined by $MSE = \frac{1}{n}\sum(Y_t - \hat{Y}_t)^2$, could be employed. The iterative method of estimating α suggests that forecasts for different values α in the range (0, 1), say 0.1, 0.2, ..., 0.9 and the corresponding mean squared errors may be computed, and the value of α that produces the smallest error may be chosen as the optimum value for use in the forecasting equation.

3.8 Software Tools for Forecasting

In the present era of the digital world, due to technological advancements and revolution, the generation of data sets under various dimensions for diverse problems becomes an effortless task than that existed earlier. The present situation also appears to be conducive for the storage, prevention, and management of data. Data generation is possible by observing the experimental results and by drawing information from past records and documents. It is always essential to consider the information contained in the stored data sets for further treatments or transformation to address the problems relating to society, environment, industry, management, business, health, etc. The data sets, which are amenable for statistical treatments, are analyzed employing appropriate methodology, the choice of which would depend on the objectives of the problems formulated, and proper interpretations and inferences are drawn from the analysis.

Advanced analytical methods of mathematics and statistics are applied for constructing both deterministic and probabilistic models, and the analyses of experimental or simulated data are performed for the intended purposes using sophisticated mathematical/statistical software. In the problem of forecasting, time series data sets are used for making predictions and forecasts by constructing forecast models based on certain scientific principles. The data sets, in practice, may be either large or small, and the computations involved in the analyses of data are complex. Thus, the analyses of time series data for forecasting are plausible only by the application of statistical software or by executing or running well-written computer codes in programming languages. While high-level and sophisticated software has been developed for application in various studies of forecasting problems, programming languages such as R or RStudio, Python, and C or C++ are also vitally used for computation of statistical measures required for the construction of forecast models by writing appropriate codes. A brief account of the features of such programming languages and important statistical software, which have potential application in forecasting studies, is presented in Table 3.1.

3.9 Conclusions

Forecasting is a process of predicting the future based on historical and present data. Forecasts resulted from appropriate forecasting approaches are generally used by policymakers in the government and private sectors that include management, business, industry, health, and environment and other commercial establishments for making strategic decisions in the existence of uncertainty of future. They enhance the confidence level of the people involved in decision making and management to formulate vital decisions. The contents presented in this chapter provide an outline of the basic principles, applications, processes, and methods of forecasting. Three basic forecasting modeling approaches, namely, naïve,

Table 3.1 Programming Languages and Software Tools for Time Series Forecasting

Tools	Features
R or RStudio	**R** is a programming language, available in open source, referenced in ORMS (Oberwalfach References on Mathematical Software) and works in Linux, Windows and Mac platform. As an integrated development platform for R, RStudio is widely used for time series forecasting and all other statistical computations.
Python	Developed as a high-level programming language, it has the data manipulating tool called Pandas that has libraries to handle time series data for forecasting.
ITSM	It stands for '**Interactive Time Series Modeling**' and is developed as an interactive Windows based menu-driven software exclusively for time series modeling and forecasting.
NCSS Software	It contains a wide range of statistical tools for time series and forecasting besides a varied collection of tools for statistical computation and graphs.
RATS	It refers to '**Regression Analysis of Time Series**' and is referenced in ORMS. It is the statistical software which performs effective and comprehensive analyses of data in the studies of econometrics and time series.
XLSTAT	It is a user-friendly software for computing statistical measures based on smoothing methods for time series data and other advanced forecasting methods for making business and sales predictions for the future period. Data simulation is possible using this software to determine forecasts.
SPSS	It is an abbreviation of '**Statistical Package for Social Sciences**'. It is one of the comprehensive and state of the art software used by many researchers in social sciences and sciences for analyzing data for forecasts and predictions.
SAS	It is the short form of '**Statistical Analysis System**'. It helps to handle and analyze large database and allows flexibility in writing specific codes to perform complex statistical analysis.
MINITAB	It is handy statistical software, mostly used by entrepreneur, business tycoons, managers for making forecasts on business trends, revenue, sales, production, etc. Many text

(Continued)

Table 3.1 *(Continued)* Programming Languages and Software Tools for Time Series Forecasting

Tools	Features
	books on Quantitative Methods, Business Forecasting, Business Statistics, etc., illustrate the case studies through MINITAB solutions.
GLEaMviz	Abbreviated for **Global Epidemic and Mobility**, it is a user-friendly and a sophisticated software system extensively used for developing epidemic and embedded forecasting models. It also helps to simulate epidemic conditions.
Delft-FEWS	Developed as flood forecasting and warning system, it is used as software to link data with stochastic environmental models for making forecasts on environmental conditions.
Agromet-Shell	Developed as a software tool, it helps to construct crop forecasting models and to evaluate climatic conditions.

averaging, and exponential smoothing are described with their significance. The introductory material presented, here, will be found useful to practitioners and researchers who work in the disciplines of commerce, economics, management and other areas as well. The literature in the applications of forecasting provides ample resources on the construction of various forecast models, which include regression models and Box–Jenkins models, for time series data. The interested researchers can learn forecasting methods through practically oriented texts that demonstrate the construction and application of forecasting models with the use of sophisticated statistical software such as MINITAB.

References

Hanke, J. E., & Wichern, D. (2014). *Business forecasting* (9th ed.). Essex, UK: Pearson Education Limited.

Hoshmand, A. R. (2010). *Business forecasting – A practical approach* (2nd ed.). New York: Routledge Publications.

Chapter 4

Breaking Technology Barriers in Diabetes and Industry 4.0

Krishnan Swaminathan[1]
and Thavamani D. Palaniswami[2]

[1]*Consultant Endocrinologist & President, KMCH Research Foundation,
Coimbatore, India*
[2]*Vice Chairman & Joint Managing Director, KMCH, Coimbatore, India*

Contents

4.1 Brief Introduction to Diabetes

4.1.1 The Epidemic of Diabetes

Diabetes is in epidemic proportions currently and has been declared as one of the largest global health emergencies of the 21st century. An estimated 422 million (8.5%) adults were living with diabetes in 2014, compared to 108 million (4.7%) in 1980 worldwide (WHO, 2016). Besides, 318 million (6.7%) adults are having glucose intolerance, which puts them at high risk of developing diabetes in the future. WHO projects diabetes prevalence to expand from the current level to 592 million (12%) in 2035 (Forouhi and Wareham, 2014). Diabetes is not only a metabolic disorder but also a vascular disease associated with long-term damage to various organs, especially the eyes, kidneys, nerves, heart and blood vessels. Such complications are the major cause of morbidity and mortality worldwide. Besides the impact on individuals, diabetes imposes a huge obstacle to the sustainable economic development of all countries due to health care costs and productivity loss (IDF, 2015).

4.1.2 Burden of Type 1 Diabetes in India

Type 1 diabetes predominantly affects children between 1 and 18 years of age. This is a result of friendly fire by our immune cells against our pancreatic insulin-producing cells leading to absolute insulin deficiency. Children present with increased thirst, pass a lot of urine and lose weight but if not treated early, present with a dangerous emergency termed "Diabetic Ketoacidosis" and die. Such children need life-long insulin four times a day or an insulin pump, a smart gadget that gives insulin without the need for pricking four times a day. Contrary to popular belief, India has an estimated 97,700 children with type 1 diabetes (Kumar, 2015; Das, 2015). There is a trend of increasing incidence at a rate of 3–5% every year in India. Our country accounts for most of the children with type 1 diabetes in South East Asia. The prevalence of type 1 diabetes in India is variable. Studies have shown a prevalence of 10.2/100,000 children in Karnal, Haryana, with a higher prevalence in the urban population at a staggering 31.9/100,000 in Karnal city. The incidence of type 1 diabetes based on the Karnataka state registry showed 3.7/100,000 in boys and 4/100,000 in girls over 13 years of data collection (Kumar et al., 2008). The incidence of type 1 diabetes over 4 years in Chennai was 10.5/100,000/year with a peak age of 10–12 years (Ramachandran et al., 1996). A study conducted on 92,047 students in Uttarakhand, Madhya Pradesh and Rajasthan showed a prevalence of type 1 diabetes in around 1.5% of school children. An estimated 18,000 children under the age of 15 years were newly diagnosed with type 1 diabetes in these three regions (Kumar, 2015). The prevalence of type 1 diabetes in the South East Asian region is 111,500, predominantly from India. The bottom line is that type 1 diabetes is not an uncommon disorder, prevalent in around 1% of school-going children in India, causing enormous strain on children and their families. At our center at the Kovai Medical Center & Hospital alone, we have more than 500 children with type 1 diabetes, mostly from the poor socio-economic strata and the numbers are increasing exponentially every week.

4.1.3 Burden of Type 2 Diabetes in India

The overall prevalence of type 2 diabetes in 15 states of India in a recently completed landmark study was 7.3% (Anjana et al., 2017), but this may be an underestimate. India is a nation within a nation with huge regional differences in diabetes rates. For example, in Tamilnadu state, the overall prevalence for diabetes was 10.4% with urban accounting for 13.7% and rural 7.8% of the population. This translated to 4.8 million individuals in Tamilnadu state alone with diabetes. Extrapolated to the whole nation, this translated to 62.4 million subjects with diabetes as of 2011. The overall prevalence for prediabetes in all the 15 states was 10.3% with a wide variation of 6% in Mizoram to 14% in Tripura. In Tamilnadu state, the prevalence of prediabetes was 9.8% among the urban population and 7.3% in rural areas. This translates to 3.9 million subjects with prediabetes as of 2011. Extrapolated to the whole country, this translates to 77.2 million with prediabetes in India. One could easily add a further 10 million since 2011 for current estimates at 2020. Our own epidemiological work in and around Coimbatore, Erode districts present a much bleaker picture of diabetes with prevalence rates of 16% and 25% of diabetes in rural & urban areas of our districts (Swaminathan et al., 2017).

4.1.4 Burden of Type 1, Type 2 Diabetes and Prediabetes in India: So, What?

Diabetes is a "vascular disease" and not a metabolic disorder alone. India leads the world in the number of patients with diabetes and has the infamous tag of being referred to as the "Diabetes Capital of the world." Currently, it would not be an exaggeration to practically define diabetes as a "state of premature cardiovascular death associated with chronic hyperglycemia and in the absence of effective treatment to control glucose levels, will lead to heart attacks, strokes, blindness, kidney failure, and foot amputations." In fact, there is good evidence for terming diabetes as a "coronary risk equivalent." Studies have shown that diabetic patients without a previous heart attack have the same high risk of getting a heart attack as someone without diabetes who already had a previous heart attack (Haffner et al., 1998). Poorly controlled diabetes is a major risk factor for end-stage kidney disease (ESRD) needing dialysis and renal transplants in India. More than 1 lakh patients enter the renal replacement therapy annually in India but due to extremely scarce resources, only 10% of this population receive renal replacement therapy (Kher, 2002; Jha, 2004; Sakhuja and Sud, 2003). Poorly controlled diabetes is a leading cause of foot amputations in India. Foot ulcerations occur in 25% of patients with diabetes and approximately 15% of such foot ulcerations result in amputations (Singh et al., 2005). With this background, we are now witnessing a huge explosion in the diabetes epidemic that can have potentially catastrophic consequences for the healthcare of our nation. One hospital admission with diabetes-related complications will drain the family of all their resources, especially from the, lower socioeconomic backgrounds, as 70% of Indian urban and rural households visit only private sector providers over public services (Das et al., 2012). Prediabetes is the prelude to diabetes. Colloquially, this is termed "borderline diabetes." Intuitively, one would underestimate prediabetes, as this is not yet full-blown diabetes. However, even many physicians are unaware that prediabetes is also associated with the same set of comorbidities like heart attacks and strokes, very similar to diabetes (Tabák et al., 2012). Indians also have one of the highest conversion rates from prediabetes to diabetes. Data from follow-up of patients over 10 years from the Chennai Urban Study (CURES Study) indicates a conversion rate of prediabetes to diabetes in the order of 60% (Anjana et al., 2015). Taken together based on the above discussions, Indians have one of the highest incidence rates for diabetes with the rapid conversion from prediabetes to diabetes.

The pressing need of the hour is to slow down and reverse this diabetes and prediabetes epidemic and its complications in our population. The challenge is that people with diabetes need personalized care that addresses their specific needs rather than general solutions. Digital tools and solutions, capturing data that can allow for seamless tracking and analysis, indigenous technologies like non-invasive glucose monitoring and insulin pump technologies, use of Artificial Intelligence and supporting algorithms will revolutionize the management of diabetes in the years to come. It is therefore high time we embrace the concepts of Industry 4.0 to make a difference to our population, not only in terms of diabetes but also all health problems. One hospital admission prevented, one life saved, one rupee reduced, all go a long way in improving the physical and economic health of our nation. Our focus is to explore the ideas behind Industry 4.0 and how it can be utilized in making the lives of people with diabetes better.

4.2 "Big Data" Concept

4.2.1 "Big Data": Definition and Concepts

"Big Data" refers to a large data set having the 5 Vs, Volume, Value, Velocity, Veracity and Variety (Rumbold et al., 2020). Volume refers to the amount of data;

Value refers to the worth of the data; Velocity refers to the speed at which the data can be processed; Veracity denotes the reliability and accuracy of the data and Variety refers to the numeric, nominal and ordinal varieties of the data. While all the five Vs are not absolute for Big Data analytics, the baseline requirement is the need for special technologies and techniques to analyze a complex dataset. The main utility in Big Data concepts is the ability to improve healthcare dramatically and at the same time do this cost effectively. Such innovations rely on Big Data concepts.

4.2.2 Big Data and Diabetes

Diabetes is a fertile ground for Big Data as there are several sources of data during routine management of diabetes. Such data sets include electronic health records, the patient held data in various apps in their mobile phones, glucometers that are smart in storing all the information, insulin pump delivery systems, and continuous glucose monitoring sensors and digital images from retinal screening.

4.2.3 Big Data, Predictive Analysis and Diabetes

This will be one of the holy grails in diabetes management for the future. Imagine a patient sitting in front of us with a clinical situation needing some important decision-making about a medication or a procedure. In this context, we wish to make the best choice possible. Instead of relying on trial and error or gut feelings, it would help immensely if we had information from thousands of similar patients just with a click of the button, that would aid us in suggesting the appropriate treatment. In a nutshell, "Big Data" is all about having information on millions of our patients in our database compiled from various sources, run them through advanced algorithms and analytics to reveal underlying patterns that aid in decision making. This would also be an excellent tool for research, leading us to new areas of therapeutics that we may have never thought about.

4.2.4 Case Study in Big Data

While in no way is our database big enough, our case study highlights the importance of analyzing predictive patterns that opens new avenues for clinical decision making, novel research and preventive medicine. We were collecting data on rural and urban populations in Tamilnadu state looking at variables including age, sex, smoking, alcohol, family history of illness, anthropometry, diabetes status, blood pressures, exposure to pesticides and fertilizers to name a few. On analyzing the data, we found that farmers mixing and spraying pesticides had a higher prevalence of diabetes compared to those who were staying at home or were not involved in agricultural practices (Swaminathan and Thangavel, 2015). Till then, anecdotally we were seeing a lot of farmers present with florid diabetes and its complications at a younger age with no significant risk factors for diabetes. The pattern of results from this study raised a vital research question as to whether non-traditional risk factors like pesticides and heavy metals in fertilizers could be an additional cause of diabetes in a farming population. Based on this research question, we focused on a completely rural farming village where we found a staggeringly high prevalence rate of diabetes at around 17% (Swaminathan et al., 2017). Further exploration of our research hypothesis by assessing the serum pesticides and urine heavy metals indicated the possible role of such environmental endocrine disruptors in diabetes and heart disease in rural farming populations (Velmurugan et al., 2018; Velmurugan et al., 2020). A larger analysis of 106,111 subjects by our study group from 61 districts of Tamilnadu state showed a twofold higher prevalence of diabetes in farming subjects than in nonfarming subjects (15% vs. 8.7%, unpublished data), again raising the hypothesis as to whether endocrine disruptors have a role in rural diabetes. Overall, pattern recognition and predictive analysis from our database was the seed for exploring new areas of diabetes pathophysiology, raising vital questions on nontraditional risk factors like arsenic in fertilizers and pesticides in the development of diabetes and heart disease. If such a small database can lead to such phenomenal research questions, what would it mean to have data on our nearly 70 million diabetic patients in India linked together for "Big Data and Predictive Analysis"?

4.3 Recent Technological Advances in Diabetes Management

4.3.1 Closed-Loop Insulin Pump Systems

We recently had a 23-year-old bright girl with type 1 diabetes on four times a day insulin injection for 5 years. She was married for 3 years and had two miscarriages despite best efforts to control her diabetes with multiple daily injections per day and seven times finger prick glucose monitoring. She had extremely brittle diabetes with erratic fluctuations of glucose levels that were difficult to predict. She also suffered from recurrent low glucose that led to seizures. She was fed up, exhausted and depressed with her diabetes and came to us to know what else can be done for her diabetes to lead a happy healthy life and go through a normal pregnancy. She was started on an insulin pump, which is a smart device the size of a pager, that can continuously pump insulin smartly without the need for injections. This patient went through a normal third pregnancy on an insulin pump and delivered a healthy baby at term!

This is one example of the thousands of patients we have in our database. The above-mentioned patient would also benefit from a closed-loop insulin pump, otherwise termed as "Artificial pancreas," with a continuous sensor that records the blood glucose levels and transmits them to the insulin pump (Akturk et al., 2020).

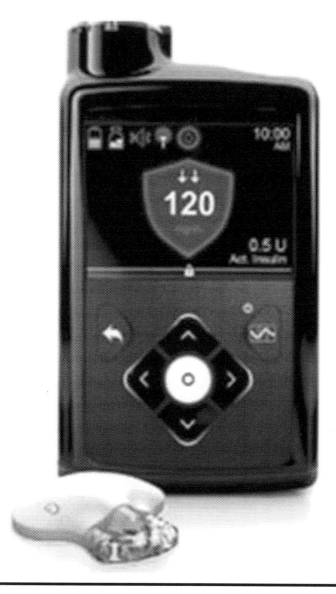

Figure 4.1   A closed-loop insulin pump, which can automatically adjust the doses of insulin based on glucose levels transmitted by a sensor continuously.

Such technology is available in Western countries and yet to be available in India at the time of writing. The closed-loop insulin pump (Figure 4.1) has built-in al-gorithms to adjust the rate of insulin delivery depending on the glucose levels and can automatically switch off when the glucose levels are trending on the lower side.

The closed-loop insulin pump can automatically adjust the doses of insulin based on glucose levels transmitted by a sensor continuously.

In the type 2 diabetes segments, the future would be the "patch pumps," which directly adhere to the patient's skin and requires no tubings. This patch pump will be small enough to fit the size of the palm and would have adjustable rates for basal and bolus insulins. Industry 4.0 would be a great opportunity to advance technology in this area of insulin drug delivery by automated closed-loop systems that can smartly adjust the dose of insulin based on trends in glucose levels and completely take away the need for insulin injections by syringes and needles.

4.3.2 Glucose Monitoring Sensors

Glucose monitoring sensors are another huge area where Industry 4.0 has a role. In India, we still measure finger-prick capillary glucose now and then to record glucose levels or go to labs once a month for blood glucose checks. However, such monitoring may become obsolete as we do not have an insight into glucose fluctuations that happen minute by minute. For example, a patient's glucose level can be 150 mgs/dl in the morning but can shoot up to 500 mgs/dl in the evening. If one were to check the morning glucose alone, we can miss the high levels later in the day. Continuous glucose monitoring sensors or ambulatory glucose profiles have completely revolutionized the way we assess glucose levels. An example of an ambulatory glucose profile (Figure 4.2) in one of the patients showing low glucose

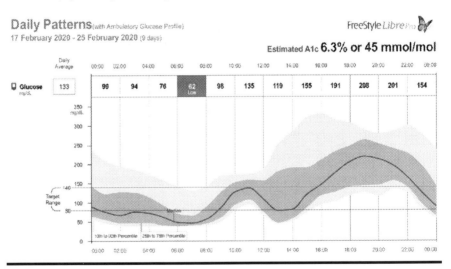

Figure 4.2 An example of ambulatory glucose profile in one of our patients showing low glucoses between 6 and 8 am and high glucose later in the afternoon. This would have been missed if blood glucose were checked on pre- and post-breakfast. The report is by using an Abbott FreeStyle Libre system that records interstitial glucoses for up to 14 days.

between 6 and 8 am and high glucose later in the afternoon. This would have been missed if blood glucose were checked on pre-breakfast and post-breakfast. The report is by using an Abbott FreeStyle Libre system that records interstitial glucose for up to 14 days.

Using advanced wire enzyme technology, this 2-week sensor requires no calibration in between by the patient and can be downloaded within seconds by getting a reader close to the sensor. Such graphs are extremely helpful to the clinician both for evaluation and intervention. Work is going on ever since the continuous glucose monitoring system has an implantable sensor that can be used for 90 days. The implantation site is a transmitter that transmits the data to a mobile application.

4.3.3 Smartwatches for Noninvasive Glucose Monitoring

The science is ripe for concepts of Industry 4.0 in diabetes technologies including smartwatches with integrated sensors to detect glucose levels, easy and personalized interface with motivational messages and diagrams, graphs that show daily, weekly and monthly glucose data at the touch of a button.

4.3.4 Deep Machine Learning for Diabetic Retinopathy Screening

Diabetic retinopathy is a leading cause of blindness amongst working-age people worldwide. A meta-analysis of the worldwide population for 20 years showed that nearly 1 million people were blind due to diabetes and another 3.7 million visually impaired due to diabetic retinopathy (Leasher et al., 2016). In a country like India, we have no protocol-based screening programmes to detect diabetic retinopathy. Very often, the eye disease is detected so late that by the time an ophthalmologist is consulted, the damage has been done and blindness has set in. In view of the huge increase in diabetes and a lack of ophthalmologists in relation to the burden of disease, computer-based analysis of retinal images by an automated system would pick up patients in immediate need of an ophthalmologist consult to save vision.

IDx-DR is an AI-based algorithm for the detection of diabetic retinopathy in the consulting rooms of nonophthalmologists. The patients walk into their diabetologist or general practitioner's office. The device, a smartphone, is linked to a retinal camera that has no need for dilating eye drops. The captured images are sent to a cloud-based server that utilizes special software and a "deep learning" algorithm to detect changes in diabetic retinopathy. The software then provides two sets of results, either an all-clear and rescreen annually or changes detected that need an ophthalmological consult (Padhy et al., 2019).

For a country like India, such AI technology will be a game changer in creating a workflow for all diabetic patients so that eye disease can be picked up early and unnecessary visits to specialists can be avoided as well. Diabetic retinopathy is just the tip of the iceberg in the role of AI technology in diabetes. Machine learning from millions of continuous glucose monitoring data that gives a guide to the correct insulin dose, algorithms to predict the rise and fall of glucose levels, robots with "artificial empathy" that can chat with patients at their homes, precision medicine in identifying clusters of patients who are prone to develop complications or insulin deficiency are some of the major applications for AI in diabetes in the future (Unnikrishnan, 2019; Hamet and Tremblay, 2017).

4.4 Barriers in Diabetes Technology

There is a great saying in medicine and in life, "No side effects = No effects." As we advance in technology and go for more automation, there are significant disadvantages that we need to take into account. First, in an area like medicine, personal touch and face-to-face communication are still so relevant as it was hundreds of years ago. Automation and AI may significantly impact the doctor–patient relationship. It is also possible that society can become more socially depersonalized. Data security is a huge area of concern. Computers and machines can be easily hacked into, and data were stolen or changed that can have a hugely detrimental effect on the patient's wellbeing. There are plenty of coronas for computer systems as well which even the best antivirus may be impotent to stop. More worrying would be the ability of hackers to change the insulin infusion rates in insulin pump technologies, for example, that would have an immediate impact on the patient. This also comes with huge medico-legal implications for the doctor, hospital and the companies involved in the products. Gadgets also can deskill people that decision-making during technology failures will be compromised. Finally, the cost of technology can be significant. We do not want technology to serve the rich alone. The advances should break socioeconomic barriers and help the poor as well.

4.5 Technical Solutions to Break the Barriers

We believe that the onus is on all the stakeholders including governmental, private and NGO partners to break technical and socioeconomic barriers for diabetes technologies to make a successful impact on every single citizen of this country. Some of our suggestions are as follows:

■ Computerization and Electronic Health Records should be made a priority for all Central, State Governmental and private institutions by the Health Ministry as a policy decision. While we are in no way underestimating the challenge, if this is successful, this would pave the way for Big Data analysis that would help the Health Ministry to target valuable resources to the deserving segments of the country.

- ■ "Make in India" and "Made in India" should become a reality rather than a slogan. With esteemed institutions like the Indian Institute of Technology and the Indian Institute of Sciences, a big push should be made for an industry–institute partnership to develop indigenous technologies like insulin pumps, ambulatory glucose profile sensors, smart noninvasive glucose watches and AI for retinopathy screening at a fraction of cost that we pay for imported technologies.

- ■ With an estimated 67% of the Indian population still living in villages, a concerted attempt should be made to ensure penetration of telemedicine from major regional centers to every single village in India. This can be done by employing trained nurses or physician assistants to do the bulk of the work, thereby reducing the costs of employing doctors and at the same time, ensure high-quality care for the rural underprivileged.

4.6 Summary

To summarize, the concepts of Industry 4.0 are in line with the current trend of diabetes management worldwide. Diabetes is a fertile area with huge potential for Big Data, precision medicine, Artificial Intelligence, data mining, development of prediction models, health apps, machine automation, closed-loop insulin pump technologies and noninvasive glucose monitoring systems. While there are cautions and roadblocks ahead with any advances in technology, there is a great saying in Tamil, "There is no fault in older concepts being replaced with newer concepts, everything changes with time." Technology with a great touch of humanity is our dream. We wish to finish this chapter with a saying from our visionary President Dr. Abdul Kalam, "Dreams are not the ones you get in sleep but prevent you from going to sleep in the first place." We dream of a day when India is a leader in Industry 4.0 in terms of diabetes care, especially for the underprivileged sections of our society. We dream of a day when there are no more patients who suffer for want of the best treatment and technology. We are very optimistic about realizing our dreams in the next two decades.

References

Akturk, H. K., Giordano, D., Champakanath, A., et al. (2020, Apr). Long-term real-life glycaemic outcomes with a hybrid closed-loop system compared with sensor-augmented pump therapy in patients with type 1 diabetes. *Diabetes Obes Metab*, *22*(4), 583–589.

Anjana, R. M., Deepa, M., Pradeepa, R., et al. (2017, Aug). ICMR–INDIAB Collaborative Study Group. Prevalence of diabetes and prediabetes in 15 states of India: Results from the ICMR-INDIAB population-based cross-sectional study. *Lancet Diabetes Endocrinol*, 5(8), 585–596.

Anjana, R. M., Shanthi Rani, C. S., Deepa, M., et al. (2015, Aug). Incidence of diabetes and prediabetes and predictors of progression among Asian Indians: 10-year follow-up of the Chennai Urban Rural Epidemiology Study (CURES). *Diabetes Care*, 38(8), 1441–1448.

Das, A. K. (2015, Apr). Type 1 diabetes in India: Overall insights. *Indian J Endocrinol Metab*, 19(Suppl 1), S31–S33.

Das, J., Holla, A., Das, V., Mohanan, M., Tabak, D., & Chan, B. (2012). In urban and rural India: A standardized patient study showed low levels of provider training and huge quality gaps. *Health Aff Millwood*, 31, 2774–2784.

Forouhi, N. G., & Wareham, N. J. (2014). Epidemiology of diabetes. *Medicine (Abingdon)*, 42, 698–702.

Haffner, S. M., Lehto, S., Rönnemaa, T., Pyörälä, K., & Laakso, M. (1998, Jul 23). Mortality from coronary heart disease in subjects with type 2 diabetes and in non-diabetic subjects with and without prior myocardial infarction. *N Engl J Med*, 339(4), 229–234.

Hamet, P., & Tremblay, J. (2017, Apr). Artificial intelligence in medicine. *Metabolism*, 69S, S36–S40.

IDF. International Diabetes Federation. (2015). IDF Diabetes Atlas Seventh edition. https://www.diabetesatlas.org/upload/resources/previous/files/7/IDF%20Diabetes%20Atlas%207th.pdf, ISBN: 978-2-930229-81-2

Jha, V. (2004). End-stage renal care in developing countries: The India experience. *Ren Fail*, 26(3), 201–208. doi:10.1081/JDI-120039516

Kher, V. (2002). End-stage renal disease in developing countries. *Kidney Int*, 62(1), 350–362. doi:10.1046/j.1523-1755.2002

Kumar, K. M. (2015, Apr). Incidence trends for childhood type 1 diabetes in India. *Indian J Endocrinol Metab*, 19(Suppl 1), S34–S35.

Kumar, P., Krishna, P., Reddy, S. C., et al. (2008, Nov). Incidence of type 1 diabetes mellitus and associated complications among children and young adults: Results from Karnataka Diabetes Registry 1995–2008. *J Indian Med Assoc*, 106(11), 708–711.

Leasher, J. L., Bourne, R. R., Flaxman, S. R., et al. (2016, Sep). Global estimates on the number of people blind or visually impaired by diabetic retinopathy: A meta-analysis from 1990 to 2010. *Diabetes Care*, 39(9), 1643–1649.

Padhy, S. K., Takkar, B., Chawla, R., & Kumar, A. (2019). Artificial intelligence in diabetic retinopathy: A natural step to the future. *Indian J Ophthalmol*, 67(7), 1004–1009. doi:10.4103/ijo.IJO_1989_18

Ramachandran, A., Snehalatha, C., & Krishnaswamy, C. V. (1996, Oct). Incidence of IDDM in children in urban population in southern India. Madras IDDM Registry Group Madras, South India. *Diabetes Res Clin Pract*, 34(2), 79–82.

Rumbold, J. M. M., O'Kane, M., Philip, N., & Pierscionek, B. K. (2020, Feb). Big Data and diabetes: The applications of Big Data for diabetes care now and in the future. *Diabet Med*, 37(2), 187–193.

Sakhuja, V., & Sud, K. (2003). End-stage renal disease in India and Pakistan: Burden of disease and management issues. *Kidney Int Suppl*, 83(83), S115–S118.

Singh, N., Armstrong, D. G., & Lipsky, B. A. (2005, Jan 12). Preventing foot ulcers in patients with diabetes. *JAMA, 293*(2):217–228.

Swaminathan, K., & Thangavel, G. (2015). Pesticides and human diabetes: A pilot project to explore a possible link. *Practical Diabetes, 32*(3), 111–113.

Swaminathan, K., Veerasekar, G., Kuppusamy, S., et al. (2017, Jan–Feb). Noncommunicable disease in rural India: Are we seriously underestimating the risk? The Nallampatti non-communicable disease study. *Indian J Endocrinol Metab, 21*(1), 90–95.

Tabák, A. G., Herder, C., Rathmann, W., Brunner, E. J., & Kivimäki, M. (2012). Prediabetes: A high-risk state for diabetes development. *Lancet, 379*, 2279–2290.

Unnikrishnan, A. G. (2019, Sep–Oct). Artificial intelligence in health care: Focus on diabetes management. *Indian J Endocrinol Metab, 23*(5), 503–506.

Velmurugan, G., Swaminathan, K., Sundaresan, M. et al. (2020). Association of co-accumulation of arsenic and organophosphate insecticides with diabetes and atherosclerosis in a rural agricultural community: KMCH-NNCD-I study. *Acta Diabetol, 57*(10), 1159–1168.

WHO. World Health Organization. (2016). Global report on diabetes. https://apps.who.int/iris/bitstream/handle/10665/204871/9789241565257_eng.pdf ISBN 978 92 4 156525 7 France

Chapter 5

Role of Big Data Analytics in Industrial Revolution 4.0

V. Bhuvaneswari

Associate Professor, Department of Computer Applications, Bharathiar University, Coimbatore, India

Contents

DOI: 10.1201/9781003175889-5

Objectives

The chapter Big Data Analytics provides readers a complete understanding emphasizing the need for Big Data for Industry 4.0 transformation. The chapter provides a detailed roadmap of data evolution and its related technological transformation in computing with a brief description of data-related terminologies as an introduction. Big Data components are presented relating to data characteristics, architectures with a comparative view on existing systems, and Big Data. The requirement of Big Data as a technology, platform, and a tool is explained with specific applications for implementing Big Data in various technologies such as IoT, Artificial Intelligence, and machine learning. The need for Big Data is presented for the current technological trends with leading IT reports. Big Data–specific Industry 4.0 applications are discussed for social benefits and industries for domains of healthcare, logistics, and warehouse management. Industry-specific skillset technological stack required is also detailed with job opportunities.

5.1 Big Data Analytics

Around the globe, the word data has gained more attention where Big Data and data analytics are viewed as important technological components. This chapter provides a comprehensive view to the users to understand the need for Big Data and data analytics. Basic understanding of the evolution of data to Big Data is essential as the data has become a driving factor in the business domains. The sections discussed below provide a detailed note on data evolution.

5.1.1 Data: Terminologies

Data: It is a collection of raw facts.

Information: Processed data with appropriate inputs is called Information.

Database: Database is defined as a collection of interrelated items represented in structured notation.

DBMS: Data Base Management System (DBMS) is a software that is used to store, manage, and maintain related information in a systematic approach. Databases are used for transaction processing (OLTP). Examples: Banks, Hospitals, Insurance, and Government.

Data Warehouse: Data warehouse is defined as a large multidimensional data model to store past summarized data. Data warehouse is a data store and defined as "Subject Oriented, Non-Volatile, Time-Varying and Integrated, Past summarized Information" used for analytical processing (OLAP).

Subject Oriented: Data is organized across a specific purpose. Data warehouse for student admission will not be suitable for analyzing student skillset.

Time-Varying: Data warehouse stores organization past historic summarized data where every instance is recorded with time to extract hidden knowledge.

Non-Volatile: Data warehouse stores organization past historic summarized data in terms of minimum, maximum, average, count, etc. and hence not modified often.

Integrated: Data warehouse data is integrated from various related sources of databases that is important for the aggregation of summarized results.

Data Mining: Data mining is a technique used to find hidden information and extract knowledge from such as a database or a very large data store data warehouse. It is also used as a technique to find associations and relationships among data attributes as patterns. Data mining is used to perform tasks of verification and validation. Data mining is generally defined as an approach to find implicit, previously unknown, hidden patterns from past historic data.

5.1.2 Data Evolution: A Look-Back

Early 1960 computers were used to store data electronically and some processing is carried out by collecting similar jobs together in batches that involves simple calculations in mainframe systems. The increased usage of computers required an easy tool to store and retrieve data and during 1980, the database has emerged as a tool for storing and retrieving information in an easily accessible way for decision making. The database is viewed as a collection of related information maintained in DBMS in a structured tabular format as rows and columns. Desktop applications like management information systems and decision support systems are developed to retrieve business outcomes to the top-level managers and placed in personal computers. The next technological development happened with the evolution of the Internet during late 1990 with advancements in mobile communications. Internet technology has broken the barriers of communications allowing the users to stay connected across geographical boundaries in 24 × 7 environments allowing computer processing in a distributed environment. The distributed applications transformed in bigger perspectives in service industries as web applications like enterprise resource planning, customer relationship management in banks, and telecommunications, which is evident from systems implemented in public transportation such as railways and airlines. All these business transactions generated huge data are stored in a database. Knowledge management system like data mining and business intelligence was developed to gather the hidden information stored in the past transactions of business stored in data warehouses of the organization. In 2010, social media platforms emerged as a great technological innovation that changed the dynamism of the digital globe.

Social media platforms Twitter, Facebook, and Instagram initially emerged as chatterbox platforms for an individual to get connected virtually to share their views and opinions. Social media platforms have grown tremendously in recent years where billions of users stay connected 24 × 7 generating large data streaming in form of texts, audio, video, and images accounting for 90% of world data. In the current data era data, the fuel is represented in three formats such as structured, unstructured, and semi-structured in various domains as given in Table 5.1 leading data viewed as volume, velocity, and variety.

Table 5.1 Data Formats Viewed as Volume, Velocity, and Variety

Data Formats	Domains	Data Sources	Size
Structured data	Business transaction data	Databases Bank, Hospitals, Smart Cities	KB to GB
Unstructured data	Social media streaming data as text, audio, video, images	Whatsapp Chats, Facebook likes, Tweets, Instagram	MB to PB
Semi-structured data	Metadata from databases, machine-generated data	IoT devices – SMART Meters	KB to MB

5.1.2.1 Transformation: Data to Big Data

Social media platform deposits have a huge volume of data ranging from peta-bytes to zettabytes, which is more than the physical universe. Social media is used in business as a tool to promote products offering a recommendation of products to users based on the surfing patterns and collect user reviews to understand user requirements and data in social media holds information related to product views, likes, feedback rating, sentiments, and emotions. Business organizations started leveraging unstructured data pool with business structured to gather business insights that evolved a large volume of data transforming to Big Data. The data as a whole with a huge volume streaming nature and variety of formats is called Big Data.

Example: Let us have a view of simple of how we generate Big Data as discussed above. Every individual household digital transaction gets reflected in the database. The transactions related to electricity bill, water charges, insurance of individual, vehicles, financial transaction in banks related to loans, cash withdrawal and deposits in ATM, credit cards, purchase of provisions, and accessories as a whole discussed accounts only to 4–8 transactions as an average for one single family as large data. These data are represented only in a structured format and get processed in various business domains that hold a value component represented in terms of profit and loss. On the other hand, when we look in the data deposited to social media platforms concerning likes of particular products, movie reviews, photo uploaded and chats vary a minimum of 5–10 data every day by an individual leaving out the metadata stored by digital mobile applications about individual surfers respect to their demographics. These data are higher and voluminous than the business data generated every day generating complex data formats as Big Data.

5.1.2.2 Data Formats and Sources: Data Growth

Data has progressed from kilobytes to zettabytes from 1930 to 2010. The units of measurement can be understood easily as tabulated below in Table 5.2.

5.1.3 Big Data: A Comprehensive View

The term Big Data not only stands for volume of data but also is implied as a tool and platform. This section helps the readers to get a complete view of Big Data definitions.

Big Data is

1. A complete subject with tools, techniques, and frameworks.
2. Technology that deals with a large and complex dataset that are varied in data format and structures does not fit into the memory.

Table 5.2   Data Growth and Data Units of Measurement

Size Units (b = Bits B = Bytes)	Units	Storage
1930 onwards		
1 bit = 0 or 1		
1 Byte = 8 bits		Memory chips
1 KiloBytes (KB) = 1024 bytes	1000^1 bytes	Floppy disk
1990 Onwards		
1 MegaByte (MB) = 1,048,576 bytes	1000^2 bytes	CD drives
1 GigaByte (GB) = 1,073,741,824 bytes	1000^3 bytes	DVD, Flash drives
2010 Onwards		
1 TeraByte (TB) = 1,099,511,627,776 bytes	1000^4 bytes	External hard dISK, Cloud storage
I PetaByte (PB) = 1,125,899,906,842,624 bytes	1000^5 bytes	CLOUD storage such as *Google drive, Drop box*
1 ExaByte (EB) 1,000,000,000,000,000,000 bytes	1000^6 bytes	
1 ZettaBytes (ZB) = 1,000,000,000,000,000,000,000 bytes	1000^7 bytes	
1 YottaByte (YB) = 1,000,000,000,000,000,000,000,000 bytes	1000^8 bytes	

3. Not about the huge volume of data; provide an opportunity to find new insight into the existing data and guidelines to capture and analyze future data.

5.1.3.1 Definition

Big Data is defined as a tool and platform that is used to store, process, and analyze data to identify business insights that were not possible due to the limitation of the traditional data processing and management technologies. Big Data is also viewed as a technology for processing huge datasets in distributed scalable platforms.

Data that cannot be stored and processed in commodity hardware and greater than one terabyte is called Big Data. The existing commodity hardware size of computing is only one terabyte where processing and storage of data are limited.

5.1.3.2 Data Analysis

The term analytics is found to be a twin word found along with Big Data. Analytics has gained attention in the world of digitization. Data analysis is traditionally used as an approach to understanding the data in disciplines of statistics, economics, and other social sciences. Understanding the key ingredients of data analysis and data analytics is important in data science and Big Data analytics.

5.1.3.2.1 Data Analysis

Data analysis stands for human activities aimed at gaining some insight into a dataset. Data analysis primarily focuses on understanding the hints of the data for a specific occurrence that is based on the previous know-how. Data analysis does not require any special data processing. For example, a trader can rely on his or her experience to open or close a trading position. Data analytics tools such as Excel, R, and SAS are used to validate and analyses data to gather insights based on known assumptions using statistical approaches and advanced mathematical models.

5.1.3.2.2 Data Analytics

Data analytics requires huge processing of data to gather automating insights from a dataset through queries and data aggregation procedures to identify and represent various dependencies between variables or features in the dataset. Computational approaches are essential to extract the hidden insights in the dataset based on data analysis. Techniques of data mining and machine learning models are used to predict and evaluate the insights.

5.1.3.3 Big Data vs. Statistics vs. Data Mining

Big Data analytics is an all-around approach where computational approaches are used to process and gather insights from a large volume of data silos.

Statistical approaches are based on theoretical concepts and used widely in data analysis in domains of marketing, census, and quality control. Statistical techniques are generally suitable for the analysis of small datasets for well-defined problems to understand data. Analysis of larger datasets in statistics is done using sampling approaches. Data sampling has a limitation of larger bias and variance. Example:

Prediction of opinion during election polls, many of the times, provide a different result due to the sampling nature.

Data mining uses scientific approaches to gather patterns from datasets. Data mining techniques extract hidden knowledge for prediction and decision making based on data associations and relations. Data mining techniques are very efficient in processing larger datasets but require high computational costs for executing larger datasets. Data mining provides optimized business solutions but ends up with the limitation of processing only transactional data (structured data).

Big Data analytics overcome the limitation existing in the statistical approach and data mining. Big Data analytics process a huge volume of data of structured, unstructured, and semi-structured in large-scale computing environments with optimal costs. Big Data analytics provides insights not only from transactional data but also integrated behavioral insights for planned business decisions.

5.1.3.3.1 Data Science

Data Science is an umbrella that integrates multiple disciplines and fields for data analytics and analysis. Data Science as an outer layer that holds all the technologies discussed (Figure 5.1). Section 5.1 has presented a detailed description of various data-related terminologies as the terms co-occur often in the domain of Big Data analytics.

5.2 Big Data Components

Term data that denotes a slice of information has transformed into science evolving a new discipline data science. This section discusses the components of Big Data focusing on data characteristics, processing architectures, and

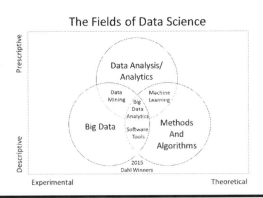

Figure 5.1 Fields of data science.

applications of Big Data. Data was not referred to in earlier data technologies with any specific characteristics. The term Big Data is a homonym with multiple dimensions viewed as a tool, technology, and platform, and hence when refer to data is characterized by different V's specified as Big Data characteristics.

5.2.1 Big Data Characteristics

Big Data is characterized by 6 V's describing volume, velocity, variety, veracity, validity, virality, and value.

Volume: The first V in Big Data refers to the content of data storage denoting the volume of data stored in TB, PB.

Velocity: The second V refers to the live streaming nature of data generated during chats, transaction, and smart devices.

Variety: The third V denotes the different data types generated in various domains of the computing environment. Examples: audio files, video files, image, text, databases.

Veracity: The fourth V denotes the veracity of the inconsistent data patterns available in the dataset.

Validity: The fifth V denotes the validity of data that is essential in business to identify the validity of data patterns for planning business strategies.

Virality: The sixth V denotes the virality aspect of data that is generally used to measure the reach of data.

Value: The seventh V is denoted to represent the value component in the data that is essential to be known which is important in business outcomes that leads to success or failure.

The first 3 V's volume, velocity, and veracity are essential for data analytics to validate transactional and OLAP systems. V's variety, validity, virality, and value are crucial to identify predictable outcomes based on behavioral analysis of data patterns in the social media domain.

Example: The characteristics of Big Data V's for the coronavirus pandemic is mapped below.

Volume: Huge volume of data is evolved every hour related to a patient affected, illness conditions, precaution measures, diagnosis, and hospital facilities.

Velocity: The information about people affected and the ill effects of COVID-19 is streaming in nature which is evolving dynamically.

Variety: Huge volume of data related to COVID 19 is accumulated as structured data in patient database, demographics of citizens, clinical diagnosis, travel data, genomic studies, and drug targets. Unstructured data for COVID-19 is voluminous in social media platforms of Twitter, Facebook, and WhatsApp to share preventive measures in the form of text, audio, video, and related chats.

Veracity and Virality: The information of preventive cure mechanism mentioned in social media platforms are inconsistent and viral leading to uncertainty among people.

Validity and Value: Measuring the validity and the value of the content available in the digital globe for the pandemic has become a challenge.

5.2.1.1 Big Data Myths

There exist various Big Data myths such as

1. Big Data is only a massive volume of data
2. Big Data is only HADOOP
3. Big Data refers only to unstructured data
4. Big Data is only for processing data from social media

Big Data is beyond massive volume of data with other characteristics that process all data formats and suitable for all business domains.

5.2.2 Big Data Processing: Architecture

The characteristics of Big Data are complex to be processed in traditional computing environments due to limited storage and processing. The existing computing environments are discussed to understand how Big Data as a platform overcomes these limitations processing framework.

Generally, the following steps are required to process data in processing architectures:

1. Splitting of data for processing in small sizes
2. Moving data from secondary storage, memory to processing nodes
3. Replication of data for multiple access
4. Investment in resources when data size increases
5. System designed to support only structured data

5.2.2.1 Traditional vs. Big Data Framework

Distributed Processing: Multiple computers are connected across the geographical location to share computer processing and storage.

Parallel Processing: Multiple computers are connected where multiple processors execute multiple tasks.

Distributed and parallel processing architectures are used in technologies of grid computing and parallel computing in existing computing environments. Traditional system involves high cost for the investment of resources whenever data increases leading to vertical scaling. Big Data computing environment overcomes these limitations using horizontal scaling.

Vertical Scaling: In vertical scaling, the computing nodes and servers have to be increased proportionally when data size increases that leads to high investment costs

Horizontal Scaling: In horizontal scaling, the existing resources are pooled together to create the required computing nodes without high investment cost.

Big Data has emerged as a platform to process and store huge volumes of data through horizontal scaling by using the existing resources. Big Data platforms is based on distributed architectures HDFS devised by yahoo and Map Reduce Programming model of Google named Hadoop a new distributed parallel data processing architecture. Big Data processing architectures support a variety of data storage through SQL and NoSQL databases.

HDFS: It is a distributed file system where data is shared across various nodes to enable parallel processing for the huge volume of data.

MapReduce: It is a framework used for performing parallel computation based on the programming model.

NoSQL Databases: Non-relational databases are called NoSQL that does not require predefined structures to store data. NoSQL databases are used to store distributed data in large volume in different formats.

A comparative view of the architecture is given in Table 5.3.

Table 5.3 A Comparative View of the Architecture

Traditional Approach	Big Data Approach
Computing Frameworks are based on Distributed and Parallel Processing Architectures	Computing Frameworks is aligned with Distributed and Parallel Processing Architectures connecting multiple frameworks
Data Storage has a Master-Slave architecture. Data for processing is moved to Data Nodes where processing nodes are static (High-Performance Computing Clusters)	Data Storage has a Master-Slave architecture.Parallel Processing Logic MapReduce is moved to the data nodes `where data remains static by distributing data to multiple nodes (HADOOP) which enables massive data processing possible
Support only Structured Data – RDBMS	Support Data Storage of both SQL and NoSQL
Vertical Scaling	Horizontal Scaling
Hardware-based Parallel Processing nodes	Software-based Parallel Processing MapReduce

5.2.3 Big Data–Related Technologies

Big Data technology has a huge benefit and a significant tool for data analytics. The need for using Big Data is essential for industries to understand their business data associations through the all-around approach. Big Data analytics with other related technologies delivers a seamless view of all data points. Organizations use Big Data for the following applications.

360° View: Business organizations leverage data from structured business transaction databases, unstructured data as recommendations, opinions, chats from social media platforms, semi-structured data from IoT devices connected with smart applications and machines. The data integrated from all these sources account for huge data in a variety of formats and inconsistencies. Big Data platforms are required to analyze the integrated huge volume of data in 360° view to gather insights into their business functionalities by identifying association and correlation of all data points.

Example: E-commerce companies such as Amazon and Flipkart use Big Data analytics to have a 360° view of the data points associated with their business domains in warehouse management, location-specific product delivery. Insurance firms need a 360° view of their customers related to policy preference, payment options, etc.

Customer Relationship Management: Digital users record their opinions and reviews related to products, movies, and likes on social media platforms. Understanding customer requirements is important in business for any business organization for strategic planning in domains such as marketing, product recommendations, health care services, etc. Big Data analytics is an important tool that overcomes the limitation of existing approaches by processing massive volumes of data.

Operational Analysis: Big Data platforms are used to understand the data insight hidden in the past transactions database and data warehouses. Operational analysis helps the organizations to leverage the value component of their business driven to know about their whereabouts for performance analysis and effective budget planning.

Data Warehouse Augmentation: In the current scenario, business functionalities require integration of related unstructured data sources with the existing structured data warehouses to predict future outcomes. The traditional system has the limitation and complexities in handling various data formats where Big Data as a platform provides a framework to integrate various related tools by setting up an ecosystem.

Risk and Security Analysis: Big Data analytics is an important technology that provides solutions to identify the risk and security issues in data that evolved and generated during the long business process. Big Data analytics is essential to identify cyber risks and security issues for business organizations. For example, banking and financial enterprises need to identify loyal and fraudulent transactions in credit card payments and loan reimbursement. Organizations need to find the security attacks prevailing during transaction flow, behavioral analytics of smart devices.

5.2.4 Big Data: Industry 4.0 Applications

Manufacturing industries are toward automation where IoT becomes an important technology where sensors are placed with physical systems to enable smartness communicating to computing environments.

1. Amazon uses robots to pick the products from the warehouse. The warehouse environment parameters temperature, light, and load of devices are captured using sensors that are stored in cloud storage across boundaries. Amazon uses machine learning and Artificial Intelligence to predict the warehouse stock, loading and unloading leading to smart factories.
2. Shipping and logistic companies use automated cranes for shipping products and when added weather data automatic organization of logistics is scheduled using AI and ML to organize their Manufacturing
3. African gold mine found ways to capture more data from its sensors and identified unsuspected fluctuations in oxygen levels during leaching, a key process using AI that increased yield by 3.7%, worth up to $20 million annually.

The advancements of hardware technologies have widely gained attention in the data era. These technologies are not only used by industries for business but also used to solve the problems of society. Big Data has evolved as an important framework for the above for mentioned technologies for processing huge volumes of data. This section provides a detailed look at these technologies and the essentials of Big Data integration.

5.3 Big Data & Industry 4.0

During Industry 3.0 transformation, computers have been introduced and business processes were automated running on the fuel data. Industry 4.0 is the optimization of Industry 3.0 where communications are seen across networks between machines and decide without human intervention using technologies of machine learning and Artificial Intelligence. The cyber-physical systems along with the IoT and Internet of systems leads to Smart Factories the Industrial Revolution Industry 4.0

The technologies of Industry 4.0 leading to Smart Factories include Artificial Intelligence, Machine Learning, Mobile Communication, Internet of Things (IoT), Internet of Machines (IoM), Cyber Security, Robotics, Cloud Computing, Edge Computing, and Big Data constituting Cyber-Physical Systems. Industry 4.0 technologies are slowly on the rise and used in many applications. All automated functionalities are based on the core fuel data where Big Data analytics is seamlessly essential for Industry 4.0.

5.3.1 Big Data Analytics: Essentials

Growth of IoT Networks: The IoT enables Intelligence across products and there is found to be a tremendous increase in the usage of sensors in manufacturing industries. McKinney states that 25% of business organizations started deploying IoT networks with an estimate that sensors increase to 43 billion in 2023. Consumer-based manufacturing industries will generate tremendous data which will help then enterprise to understand customer loyalty and increase sales. IoT devices around the globe will generate huge volumes of data and require massive storage and processing.

5.3.2 Data Migration to Cloud

Small and medium enterprises are currently moving their data to cloud environments to scale business to a larger level with optimized cost as cloud services ensure scalability, performance, mobility, and disaster recovery.

1. 70% of enterprises have at least one application or portion of their infrastructure in the cloud
2. 30% of IT investment was towards cloud
3. 69% of the enterprise is moving their data applications (ERP) to cloud

5.3.3 Predictive Analytics

Predictive analytics is a technique based on machine learning that is used to predict future outcomes based on past historic data. Enterprises have started using predictive analytics at a larger scale after the broadening of Big Data analytics. Google has recently announced a novel prediction algorithm to identify heart risks using retinal images based on deep learning models.

5.3.4 Artificial Intelligence

Artificial Intelligence is a branch of computer science that is used to build smart intelligence to machines either using hardware (robots) or software (process automation) that requires human intelligence. AI has larger scope and applications in the areas of unmanned vehicles, robotics for both society and nation security. AI applications are used by enterprises as virtual assistance as chatbots offering expertise in medical diagnosis, insurance, finance, media, and journalism.

Any applications using the Industry 4.0 technology stack mentioned generate huge volumes of data and have to integrate with existing past historic data of business enterprises. Big Data analytics will be an influential chain to assemble these technology stacks to process and store these tremendous volumes of data.

5.4 Big Data Use Cases

Big Data has gained attention and become an important component in the technology stack to process huge volumes of data deposits available in business data warehouses; social media data in various sectors; and domains of marketing, finance, education, banking, insurance, e-commerce, and healthcare.

5.4.1 Big Data Use Case: Social Good

5.4.1.1 An Epidemic: Preventive Care Management

Automated alerting systems are essential during epidemics and pandemic for efficient preventive care. The prevention of individuals getting affected is very complex due to the movement of individuals to various locations. The pandemic COVID-19 has become a serious threat across the globe that has affected millions of individuals. Preventing the spread of the pandemic requires the integration of multiple heterogeneous data of individuals concerning their vital signs, demographics, travel history, previous medical history, and tracking of affected individuals. As the pandemic is caused due to a viral infection integration of data related to the genomic profile of COVID-19, research literature, the study of existing drug targets also has to be mapped to identify and provide correct therapeutic for individuals affected.

Pandemic management also requires managing infrastructure data related to hospitals, services, equipment, functionality, and transportations of essential commodities to individuals. The entire data has to be integrated that leads to the tremendous volume of data. The countries that are not digitized with healthcare domains face challenges in controlling pandemic. Technological intervention is required in all stages of pandemic management from tracking individuals, treatment, and providing safe services to individual care.

Big Data analytics is used to gather insights and analyze the effects of COVID-19 in many countries. China has used Big Data platforms for diagnosis, tracking the movement of people affected with COVID-19 for preventive care. Big Data analytics is also used as a security measure to prevent spread by analyzing facial images without a mask in crowdsourcing environments alerting the police. Artificial Intelligence–based chatbots are developed by WHO to identify the spread of pandemic concerning locations to provide accurate data and Robots are deployed to distribute Masks, hand cleansers [Kerala]. Deep Learning models are used to study genomic profiles in the process of drug discovery where Big Data analytics plays a vital role. Automated technology in the forthcoming years will help in building effective preventive care for handling these kinds of pandemics and epidemics.

5.4.1.2 Natural Resource Management: Oil and Gas

Big Data analytics has evolved as an important technology in managing natural resources water, soil, minerals, and timbers. Natural resource management requires the processing and assembling of heterogeneous data from conventional sources equipment's databases, RFID tags, documents in the form of unstructured representation. Big Data provides the required infrastructure to process this wealth of data to gain measurable insights.

Data in the oil industry evolve rapidly at a faster rate where Big Data analytics is a need in processing large volumes of data not only for improving efficiency but also for better decision making. Big Data analytics is used in identifying drilling locations, check the working of machines assembled through data populated from sensors saving 100 million dollars of the cost, time, and effort required. Sensors are used to identify hydrocarbon remains under deep oil wells transmitting data through fiber optic cables for effective utilization of manpower, identifying leakage (Analytics Magazine. 2012; Wire, 2014).

5.4.1.3 Agriculture

Big Data analytics in agriculture has gained attention in recent years. To manage cultivation, agriculturalists depended upon their sole tacit knowledge and used traditional approaches as new methodologies could not be reached up. The current technologies cloud computing, IoT, and AI will transform agriculture into smart farming. The massive volume of data related to the weather forecast, crop details, water management, and pest management is available to farmers and shared through cloud platforms as services through mobile phones. Mobile devices have become inevitable in agriculture which benefited large farmers for data sharing and facilitated Big Data analytics. The spatial and farm information of farmers is made available to agricultural researchers for analyzing large fields through research. IoT sensors and drones used in farming will measure soil conditions, water availability, and pest infections to push notifications on areas of improvement. Big Data analytics with agricultural networking of farmers with recent technologies will help small farmers to reach potential benefits (Brennan, 2019).

5.4.2 Big Data: Industry Use Case

5.4.2.1 Warehouse Management and Supply Chain

Big Data analytics is used to gather insights from a huge volume of data from various related data sources by Amazon for efficient delivery of products, customer purchase prediction, and personalized recommendations. Amazon uses predictive modeling to understand the preference of customer purchases based on the online surfing patterns which are also used to map the nearest warehouse location for faster delivery and warehouse stock management.

5.4.2.2 Automobile Industry

Autonomic vehicle and the smart vehicle has made Big Data as an important technology that leads to the data-centric automotive industry. Smart vehicles are embedded with IoT components with AI-based techniques to provide a smart driving experience through assistance related to traffic, fuel efficiency, acceleration, battery, and other automobile governing factors. The data collected are further used by automobile manufacturing for designing customer-specific requirements leading to safety delivering smart transportation systems. Big Data analytics is used for automobile financing to understand customer's financial history and preferences based on demographics to design financial plans that meet customer-specific needs. Big Data analytics is also used to predict the demand for vehicles and used for market segmentation based on the data collected from social media platforms. Big Data analytics will help automobile industries to improve the road performance of vehicles and retain customers (Sas, 2020).

5.4.2.3 Pharmaceuticals

McKinsey Global Institute states that Big Data analytic strategies in pharmaceutical R&D, the clinical trial will bring in a lot of innovations and improvements in new tools for physicians, consumers, insurers, and other regulators. Big Data is essential as a huge volume of data is generated in healthcare and pharmaceutical from varied sources of R&D, care-givers, and retailers. Integrating and analyzing these data will help pharma companies in identifying new drug targets and medicines. Predictive modelling using machine learning techniques on molecular and clinical data will increase the probability of identifying the biological targets for new drugs. Big Data analytics is significant for identifying patients for enrolling in clinical trials through the integration of varied data sources for real-time monitoring, avoiding adverse events and unnecessary delays. Smarter devices embedded with biosensors for patient diagnosis data gathered in real time will be voluminous and help pharma industries to facilitate R&D, evaluate drug effectiveness and predict drug sales. Examples of such devices include smart pills that can release drugs and relay patient data, as well as smart bottles that help track usage (Cattell et al., 2013).

5.4.2.4 Sports Analytics

Data is a prime concern for managing sports-related activities. Big Data applications have emerged as important for sports analytics using machine learning and Artificial Intelligence techniques to guide players, athletes, organizations, and fans. Sports integrate various entities coaches, players, front offices, playgrounds, fitness devices, health, and diet. Data is also generated in streaming fashion from team event-based games like cricket, hockey, basketball, and badminton and lost in no matter of time. Big Data analytics platform is essential to integrate data generated from various sources in various formats like referee comments, audio, video to leverage analytics to guide players and athletes. Wearable devices are used by athletes to monitor their patterns of playing during training. Coaches rely on training data of athletes to train for the Olympic Games to identify the challenges they undergo during endurance training. Big Data analytics will leverage understanding fan preferences and behaviors posted in social media to nourish your high-value fans with more personalized and relevant communications and promotions. Retain and boost revenue from season-ticket holders and new fans.

IoT in sports will become an essential component embedded in wearable devices like shirts, caps where data from the device identify the top performers and provides real-time stats on each player, such as speed, heart rate, and acceleration, fatigue, and hydration levels. Bryan Colangelo, former general manager and president of the Toronto Raptors, says teams should hire data analytics specialists in front offices to handle the data transmitted from new technologies and devices (Ayers et al., 2018).

5.5 Big Data Roles

Data being the fuel in driving Industry 4.0, the various skills and roles have evolved. This section provides an overview of skills and responsibilities (Woodie, 2015; Team Machine Learning, 2017).

5.5.1 Data Scientist

Data scientist is responsible for scrubbing data to bring out deep insights into data.
Skills: Expert in CS, mathematics, statistics.

1. Work on open-ended research problems
2. Problem Solving and Innovative thinking
3. Knowledge of Hadoop, SPARK, SQL, NoSQL, Machine Learning Models.

5.5.2 Big Data Engineer

Big Data engineering is responsible for data ingestion, data transformation, and managing administering infrastructure and storage of data for optimizing performance. The roles of a Big Data engineer requires the following:

Skills: Strong skills in programming and software engineering.

1. Deep knowledge in data warehousing.
2. Expertise in Hadoop, NoSQL, and SQL technologies.

5.5.3 Machine Learning Engineer

Machine learning engineers should be proficient in mathematics and statistics. They are responsible for building data architecture for the data.

Skills: Strong programming language expertise, Cloud architectures.

5.5.4 Data Analyst

A data analyst views the data from one source and has deep insight into the data based on the organization's guidance.

Skills: Competency skills in the understanding of statistics (Berger-de Leon et al., 2018; Imanuel, 2014; UBS, 2015). Knowledge in SQL and data analytics tools, visualization, programming.

5.5.5 Business Analyst

Business analyst is domain experts who transfer business knowledge for IT transformation to fill in the industry gap (Table 5.4).

Skills: Strong skill in business analysis, statistics knowledge of data visualization tools, DBMS.

5.5.6 Statisticians

Statisticians are required to analyze and find patterns and relationship in data.

Skills: Strong skills in statistics, intermediate level programming expertise, machine learning models, visualization, DBMS.

Table 5.4 Role-Based Skills

	Programming	Databases	Visualization Tools	Frameworks/ Technologies	Other Skills
Data Scientist	PythonJavaScala	SQLNoSQL		Web servicesAWS	Domain ExpertiseCommunicatio-n Skills
Data Analyst	R, Python, SAS	SQL, NoSQL	C3j	Data MiningText Analytics	Communication Skills
Business Analyst	R, Python	SQL	TableauPower BI	Data MiningData Warehouse	Business ExpertCommunication Skills
Big Data Architect/ Engineer	Python, ScalaJava	NoSQLMongoDBCassandra		HADOOP, SPARK, FLUME, PIG, HIVE, SAS	
Machine Learning Engineer	PythonJavaScala	SQLNoSQL		Web servicesAWS, Algorithms, Data Structures	Business Expertise
Statisticians	PythonR	SQLNoSQL		Data MiningText Analytics	Business Expertise

References

Analytics Magazine. (2012). How Big Data is Changing the oil & gas industry – Analytics Magazine.analytics-magazine.org. Retrieved April 11, 2020, from http://analytics-magazine.org/how-big-data-is-changing-the-oil-a-gas-industry/

Ayers, R., Panova, E., Deen, K., Panova, E., Deen, K., Panova, E., Deen, K., & Panova, E. (2018). How Big Data Is Revolutionizing Sports - Dataconomy. *Dataconomy*. Retrieved April 12, 2020, from https://dataconomy.com/2018/01/big-data-revolutionizing-favorite-sports-teams/

Berger-de Leon, M., Reinbacher, T., & Wee, D. (2018). *The IoT as a growth driver*. McKinsey & Company. Retrieved April 04, 2020, from https://www.mckinsey.com/business-functions/mckinsey-digital/our-insights/the-iot-as-a-growth-driver

Brennan, E. (2019). A new global agriculture: Using Big Data to bring farmers together. foodtank.com. Retrieved April 11, 2020, from https://foodtank.com/news/2019/04/a-new-global-agriculture-using-big-data-to-bring-farmerstogether/?gclid=CjwKCAjwvtX0BRAFEiwAGWJyZGgIcE6i5Hpv MT-lI5uv7AoH7QqBaAXzEhE8WcYOhfstLqI-CiyfexoC3UwQAvD_BwE

Cattell, J., Chilukuri, S., & Levy, M. (2013). *How Big Data can revolutionize pharmaceutical R&D*. McKinsey & Company. Retrieved April 20, 2020, from https://www.mckinsey.com/industries/pharmaceuticals-and-medical-products/our-insights/how-big-data-can-revolutionize-pharmaceutical-r-and-d

Imanuel. (2014). Pat research: B2B reviews, buying guides & best practices. *What is predictive analytics?*. Retrieved April 05, 2020, from https://www.predictiveanalyticstoday.com/what-is-predictive-analytics/

SAS. (2020). Big Data in real life: The impact of analytics on car manufacturing. sas.com. Retrieved April 13, 2020, from https://www.sas.com/en_au/insights/articles/analytics/impact-of-analytics-on-car-manufacturing.html

Team Machine Learning. (2017). 8 different job roles in data science Big Data industry. *HackerEarth Blog*. Retrieved April 09, 2020, from https://www.hackerearth.com/blog/developers/8-different-job-roles-data-science-big-data-industry/

UBS. (2015). The evolution of artificial intelligence. AI's Coming Of Age. ubs.com. Retrieved April 10, 2020, from https://www.ubs.com/microsites/artificial-intelligence/en/ai-coming-age.html

Wire, B. (2014). Research and markets: Big Data in extraction and natural resource industries report: Mining, water, timber, oil and gas markets 2014–2019. *Business Wire*. Retrieved April 08, 2020, from https://www.businesswire.com/news/home/20140707005873/en/Research-Markets-Big-Data-Extraction-Natural-Resource

Woodie, A. (2015). 9 must-have skills to land top Big Data jobs in 2015. *Datanami*. Retrieved April 08, 2020, from https://www.datanami.com/2015/01/07/9-must-skills-land-top-big-data-jobs 2015/

Chapter 6

Big Data Infrastructure and Analytics for Education 4.0

Chandra Eswaran[1] and Rathinaraja Jeyaraj[2]

[1]Professor and Head, Department of Computer Science, Bharathiar University, Coimbatore, India
[2]Post-Doctoral Researcher, Kyungpook National University, Daegu, South Korea

Contents

DOI: 10.1201/9781003175889-6

6.1 Introduction

The applications of Industry 4.0 in education have been growing since the last decade. The history of the industrial revolution is dated back to the 17th century. The very first revolution (Industry 1.0) took place when natural sources such as water, coal, and steam were used as fuels to improve the production process and transportation using machines in industries. Since then, it is in a growing phase to enhance the quality of our life. Now, Industry 5.0 emerged due to advancements in Information Technology. Every industrial revolution transformed people living aspects smart. Education is not an exception. Although conventional classroom teaching is more effective, it is not an efficient way to reach students globally. Industry 4.0 is successfully being employed in classrooms to improve the quality of education. However, Industry 5.0 is far ahead to align and automate teaching and learning on Internet completely. Data-center infrastructure and data analytics are important to establish and manage using cloud services or on premise to make this successful. This chapter outlines how Industry 4.0 is being applied in education and discusses various Big Data infrastructure and analytics to build effective online teaching and learning.

6.2 Industrial Revolutions

Revolution in the manufacturing industry is shaping all aspects of human life. Technological advancements and innovations lead to improvements in industrial production and transportation. At present, the industrial revolution has reached version 5.0, taking advantage of the cyber physical system (CPS), Internet of Things (IoT), and cloud computing. The history of industrial development is dated back to the 17th century. The first revolution (Industry 1.0) took place when natural power sources such as water, coal, and steam were used as fuels to improve production processes and transportation in the industry using machines. Since then, it is in a growing phase to make human life better. The second industrial (Industry 2.0) revolution happened in the 18th century when electricity replaced those natural fuel resources and simplified manufacturing and transportation. This vastly increased productivity and was marked as a technological revolution. Industry 3.0 emerged when computers came into existence in the 1970s. As computers were huge in size and expensive, it was not quickly adapted by industries. However, it laid the foundation for using computers in industries to ease the human effort to improve productivity. In the last decade, the industry's advancements continued with smart machines that communicate with each other and trigger actions without human intervention with IoT-enabled environment and cloud computing. It is called Industry 4.0. By then, Industry 5.0 emerged due to advancements in Information Technology applying human cognitive skills (Artificial Intelligence) to simplify the whole production process. With the successful application of Industry 5.0, almost everything in the industry will be automated to eliminate human assistance in the production process. Today, it is impossible without computers to automate and remotely operate machines in industries. Every industry revolution transform has been transforming human's living aspects to be smart, and education is not an exception.

6.3 Advantages of Industry 4.0 in Education

Industry 4.0 is mainly focusing on interconnecting industrial machines and computers to improve efficiency and productivity. The application of Industry 4.0 in the field of education has been growing since last decade. While Industry 4.0 is nowadays being applied in education, Industry 5.0 also has taken a step forward due to the technological innovations in Information Technology. It transforms machines and computers to mimic human intelligence to automate the whole production process. Is it possible to apply in the field of education to improve the quality of education? Although conventional classroom teaching is more effective, it is not an efficient way for remote teaching. So, universities wanted to reap the benefit of Industry 4.0 to improve online and offline teaching. To advance education on Internet, the smart classroom is essential to connect students virtually. World has witnessed and successfully achieve this during COVID-19 pandemic. Almost, it is more than 10 months since the global lock-down was announced, business people, software engineers, students, etc. take up their duties virtually via tools such as MSTeams, Google Meet, Web-ex, etc. While Industry 4.0 is widely on practice, Industry 5.0 is far ahead to align and automate teaching and learning on Internet completely. Industry 4.0 is deployed with advanced equipment and technologies to observe smart classroom environment and students. To have nice experience with smart classroom, students must use camera in their phone/laptop for interactive environment. This helps the host to observe student's attention on the class delivered. The advantages of applying Industry 4.0 in education are listed below.

- Interaction between students and teachers becomes more transparent, which establishes trust and bond.
- Students can promptly attend classes even if they are not in right place but having right gadget.
- Participants can discuss each other outside the syllabus and exchange information.
- Teachers can handle students globally to clarify doubts with elegant presentation.
- Google, Microsoft, etc., provide cloud services to prepare presentations, documents, audio/video tutorials, labs, quizzes, etc. and periodically maintain information online.
- Content can be presented, and session can be recorded and watched anytime.
- Gadgets can be used for taking notes from classes to save learning time. So, students need not carry notebooks.
- Learning is more dynamic with online classrooms as recorded classes are available 24/7. So, missed sessions can be retaken multiple times until the concept is clearer and understandable.
- Smart classes are more environmental friendly as it eliminates the use of papers for printouts/photocopies.
- Traditional classroom teachings require a lot to spend on stationaries like pen, book, etc. Such expenses can be minimized using gadgets, which require onetime investment and can be used during the entire study period.
- Students can focus more on practical workouts than writing theory-based assignments and exams. Moreover, hundreds of written assignments and exams tire professors to spend time for evaluating them.
- Online forums can bring more valuable discussions on a topic of interest to show different perspectives of attendees.
- Natural disasters or any other crises like the COVID-19 pandemic cannot stop one from learning from online classrooms unlike traditional education.

Physically disabled students can continue their education being in the home. Similarly, students with learning disabilities like lack of visualization can learn from animated video lectures. This is one of significant features of classroom. Let us have a detailed view on this. Implementing a smart classroom model could have a huge impact on the learning of students with disabilities in general and more specifically students with learning disabilities, speech and language impairments, visual impairments, and hearing impairments. Many of the smart features of smart classroom are the exact areas where students with these disabilities have documented weaknesses. Most noted are deficiencies with learning, inferring, and self-organizing. Thus, the smart classroom should be considered when working with students with all these disabilities. Where traditional classrooms do not specifically address the levels of smartness unless specific lessons focus on them, the implementation of smart classrooms would be suggested to meet the difficulties students with learning disabilities encounter. Among the many great things about assistive technology (AT) today is how easy it can be for schools, teachers, and parents to get their hands on. For one thing, traditional AT has merged with consumer technologies. The application of assisted learning technology is a massive step forward in the effort to achieve inclusion for students with special needs also, implementing assistive technologies in the classroom gives students of all abilities a voice in their education.

Even though these advantages emphasize smart teaching's goodness, there are constraints and challenges to be addressed to bring this out more successful and simplified. Moreover, it provides more jobs and research opportunities to improve the teaching and learning experience online.

6.4 System for Smart Education

Adoption of the latest technologies such as cloud computing, Internet of Things (IoT), Big Data infrastructure and analytics, and Artificial Intelligence (AI) (Buyya et al., 2009) helps to reap technological benefits while transforming Industry 4.0 smart. Figure 6.1 shows how these technologies are employed in different sectors, especially in the education system. There are many standard frameworks for the education system to deploy Industry 4.0 into academic sectors. A standardized model is shown in Figure 6.1, in which four layers are included. The first layer is stakeholders who are part of the online education system and interact with each other. To make stakeholders interact with each other online, a dashboard is included in the second layer. Dashboard must be easy to interact and self-descriptive. The third layer comprises the gadgets and tools to observe environment around stakeholders and store in a centralized storage environment. Last layer includes the backend system installed with latest technologies for storing huge data and processing. These layers are further discussed in detail from top to down (Figure 6.1).

6.4.1 Stakeholders

Stakeholders in the smart education system are students, teachers, education management, and any other who participate in the smart classroom. They use IoT devices to interact each other. Students and teachers play a major role while education management hosts this service being an intermediate between them. Teachers have more responsibilities compared to students and education management in terms of interaction in the smart education system. So, functions like student's attention and attendance in the smart classroom should be automated to ease the workload of teachers. For instance, based on the attendee's facial expression, it is easy to determine whether the class is boring or interesting. Teachers performance is also obtained from

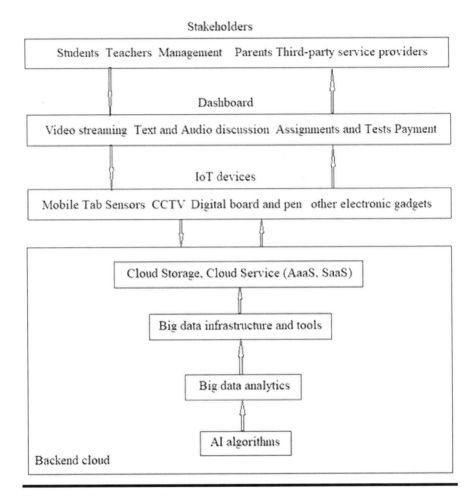

Figure 6.1 Smart education system.

the dashboard displayed to the students. To achieve this, artificial intelligence algorithms are implemented and given as a service for teachers to monitor students. Education management takes on only administrative services to track students' performance and bridges all the smart education system stakeholders.

6.4.2 Dashboard

It is a user interface to collect input from student's gadgets and let access to the smart classroom services. All the services for students, teachers, and management are hosted in cloud infrastructure to consume them as service 24×7. Stakeholders are given credentials to obtain the access to resources hosted in cloud environment. All the administrative activities are simplified such that one can pay tuition fee and receive degree certificates online. So, it is just an input/output environment for all the stakeholders in smart classroom.

6.4.3 *Internet of Things*

Connecting electronic devices, typically over Internet and communicating with each other to deliver instructions in education is called e-learning (Paul and Jeyaraj, 2019). It is unavoidable in the education system as technology is ubiquitous to everyone with Internet and mobile phones. So, the application of IoT in educational institutions means a lot. Connecting every object such as physical (phone, tab, sensor, reader, scanner) and virtual (processes, applications, software) objects over the Internet is called Internet of Things (IoT). These objects have unique identifiable address to communicate and exchange information each other. In order to bring academic institute under online-based action and employ Industry 4.0, we deploy IoT around the campus and classrooms. Therefore, one can be virtually present in the classroom as if physically attending the classes. To enable IoT environment faster, 5G-enabled devices and network are used. Technologies such as mmWave, mMiMO, ZigBee, dynamic spectrum access, Bluetooth low energy, etc. are used in the latest IoT environment. 5G leads to a successive path for augmented and virtual reality in today's digital education system. So, IoT plays a vital role in smart education.

6.4.4 *Cloud Computing*

Deploying the latest industrial evolution into all spheres of human life became possible with ubiquitous storage and computation on the Internet. Offering such resources over the Internet on a pay-per-use basis is called cloud computing (Yang et al., 2014). As the IoT environment abundantly streams data, there is a need for the infrastructure to store and process. While traditional on-premise data-centre is confined due to significant limitations, cloud data-centre offers resources on demand geographically. Cloud service providers like Google, Amazon, Microsoft, etc. play a vital role in offering resources competitively. Cloud services are of different types: Application as a Service (AaaS), Software as a Service (SaaS), Platform as a Service (PaaS), and Infrastructure as a Service (IaaS). Today, almost anything that is possible with computer is offered as a service, which is called Everything as a Service (XaaS). So, one can hire any type of service from cloud at any time regardless of the location. Sometimes, on-premise data centre is transformed to host services like real cloud service providers. There are different types of cloud deployment models (Diaz et al., 2016) to transform on-premise data-centre to private cloud environment: public cloud, private cloud, hybrid cloud, multi-cloud, federated cloud, etc. These deployment models differ based on capital expenditure and the type of services required to host. With the help of these cloud deployment model, huge data observed from IoT environment is locally stored. All the gadgets and IoT devices used by stakeholders are connected to cloud computing to get seamless service. Nowadays, fog computing and edge computing get more attention than cloud computing. When public cloud is used, it takes more bandwidth and time to transfer data to the centralized repository. Sometimes, devices require quick response for decision making. At this moment, accessing public cloud may not be time efficient. Therefore, cloud-like services are extended to the devices (router/switch/any other device capable of offering service) deployed near the edge devices in IoT environment. It is called fog computing. Sometimes, decision must be taken on time. So, algorithm is executed in edge devices and decision is made in few seconds. It is called edge computing.

6.4.5 AI in Smart Education

Let us discuss a use case on application of Artificial Intelligence (AI) in university environment. Chatbot is a natural language processing application to converse with people for question and answering. To boost student admission, chatbot (Becky) was used in Leeds Beckett University. Becky interacted with prospective students to clear doubts by providing necessary information. Similarly, another chatbot (Ada) was used by Bolton College to answer student queries about university services and the life in campus. Ada is being upgraded to interact with faculties and staffs to support management.

The role of AI in education is the emerging popular field globally. AI has received greater attention in recent years especially in education sector. AI enabled smart education are expected to grow by 43%. Increasing growth rate in computational power and big digital data in education has led to the advancement in AI technologies. Most of the research study is focused on analysis of searching patterns from the collected data for developing models and make prediction for student/teacher interaction, administrative decision support.

Extending Industry 4.0 in education opens a lot of research opportunities while applying AI based methods to mimic human cognitive skills to software system for smart classrooms. AI is an end goal instead of pointing a specific algorithm. Any algorithm that mimics human cognitive skills to solve a problem is called AI algorithm. For example, to play chess game with computer, it must run machine learning and optimization algorithms. Machine learning algorithm learns from the player moves over time and produces an approximate/predicted value for the next move on behalf of computer. While there are hundreds of moves for the next step, a single move with an optimal value is selected using optimization algorithms. Therefore, to achieve a human-kind skill, different algorithms are deployed together. So, there is no specific algorithms to be called as AI algorithm. This type of algorithm is used in many ways to transform education to be smart. For instance, observing facial expression of participants, one can determine whether students are sleepy or reluctant in the classroom. However, AI algorithms are resource and time constraint. In addition, such algorithms take more time as computation is deeper and extensive. That is the reason, edge devices are not suitable and for running such algorithms for decision making. Therefore, fog computing is enormously welcome to break this barrier. Therefore, cloud service providers offer more specific resources to AI-based methods to solve real-world problems.

Artificial Intelligence today has integrated IT into education for intensive technology usage, innovative integration, and service optimization in smart education growth. Applying AI on Big Data becomes more complex when dealing with natural language processing, image processing, voice processing, etc. using deep learning methods. Intelligent adaptive environment will take the future towards hand-free computing education. Single text application will be replaced with text-, audio-, video-, and images-based teaching aids. The intelligent adaptive system can stimulate human teaching method by applying AI technologies for teaching, learning, testing, assessment and exercise, and event handling. Intelligent adaptive teaching platform are user friendly to students by collecting students learning data for planning and scheduling their loop of learning procedure. This is achieved by applying Big Data analysis and personalized recommendations.

6.4.6 Augmented Reality

In the present situation, almost every student owns smartphones and is active 30% of the time a day to play games, chat friends, watch videos, browse Internet, etc. Moreover, students are actively connected to Internet and available any time. Education 4.0 takes this opportunity to achieve smart education. Live telecasting remote objects locally with the help of camera is called augmented reality (AR). Extending the combination of AR and smartphones into Education 4.0 has become possible. Despite it is expensive to adopt, it brings up a realistic learning experience, especially in medical and engineering fields. Moreover, it would be beneficial to teach in primary schools as it can boost the students learning power. However, there are many challenges to adopt AR into education with the help of smartphones. More specifically, finance is a barrier in every educational institution to deploy AR system. It is sure that AR will improve education when more research in AR is invested.

6.5 Big Data Infrastructure for Smart Education

As per International Data Corporation (IDC), Big Data is expected to grow up to $46 billion by 2020. The growth rate of Big Data is 23% in the period of 2014–2019. Hadoop (Dean and Ghemawat, 2004) has grown 58% in the period 2013 and 2020. Big Data technology is a supporting backbone for digital learning smart educational model. The rapid growth of information communication and technological tools leads education industry into innovative way to access information and knowledge in education. Instructors/learners mostly rely on YouTube in accessing education related videos using smart devices deployed in the IoT environment. Data is collected in large amount from IoT environment and other gadgets used by stakeholders in the smart education system environment. A typical Big Data infrastructure and the components used are shown in Figure 6.2. In user environment, all stakeholders interact with cloud using gadget and other IoT devices that generate raw data. Data could be structured or unstructured or semi-structure data. Dashboard is used to display the analysis to stakeholders in understandable way. To support smart education system, infrastructure for data storage and processing in cloud environment is required. Components included in the Big Data infrastructure (Figure 6.2) are discussed in detail.

6.5.1 Database and Distributed File System

Before processing huge amount of data, it must be stored in a distributed environment. There are two possible choices to store based on the nature of data. If data is structured or semi structured, there are NoSQL databases to store them in multiple computers in a cluster. Typical NoSQL databases are HBase, Cassandra, etc. There are graph databases as well to store graph data. These databases provide

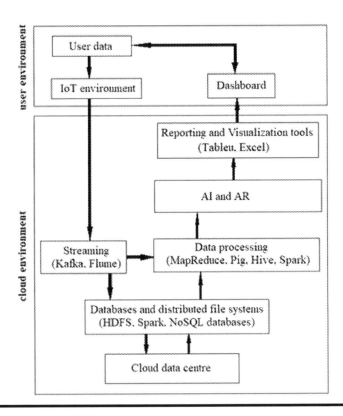

Figure 6.2 Big Data infrastructure.

many analytical functions that can be launched to extract pattern or trend. If data is to be stored as files, then Hadoop Distributed File System (HDFS) is used. Apache HDFS is a distributed file system and an open-source version of Google File System. HDFS breaks huge data into small chunks and stored in multiple computers. Files like images, videos, etc. can be stored in HDFS as it performs just file copy. There are no pre-defined functions available to process in HDFS. Therefore, we must write user-defined functions with the help of library tools available to implement our logics.

6.5.2 Stream Processing

Data is streamed from devices in IoT environment. Processing data as it arrives to the computer is called stream processing. Algorithm for stream processing must be resource and time efficient to produce timely results. There are many stream processing tools such as Strom, Kafka, Flume, Flink, Spark, etc. for this purpose. Some stream processing tools execute algorithms on stream data while some tools are just used to stream collected data to the processing system. Once data is streamed into cloud environment, it should be stored in a database or distributed file system. If data is structured and stored in big structured table, then there are many NoSQL databases. If data should be stored as files, HDFS stores huge data in more than one computer in a distributed way. HDFS is mainly used by many Big Data processing engines such as Hadoop and Spark. Apache Strom is used to perform real-time, iterative, and interactive processing. It performs mini batch processing like MapReduce but on real-time. LinkedIn created Samza for stream processing to handle various streaming applications. Samza handles huge number of messages and offers file system persistence. Apache Kafka is a distributed message broker to obtain data from various devices and files from other storages.

6.5.3 Batch Processing

Collecting and storing data into storage before processing on time is called batch processing. A set of jobs is included in a batch and executed periodically. Once a batch is submitted, it gets executed upon getting enough resources. Batch processing is not interactive and iterative to provide real-time response. Both Hadoop and Spark are the best batch processing framework that provides a set of tools for various purposes. For machine learning, there is a precoded library that can be used for specific purposes. Hadoop provides Mahout and Spark provides MLBase to achieve machine learning functionality. Spark is built to overcome certain limitations of MapReduce. Many reports claim that Spark is 10 times faster than MapReduce at the disk level and 100 times faster than MapReduce at the memory level. To exploit this performance, one should be ready to invest for high-performing RAM. In short, Spark is a better option if we work on real-time applications and machine learning algorithms, but a little bit costlier. Hadoop is a better option for applications which is not time-bound. To conclude, MapReduce will coexist with Spark for a long period as Spark uses HDFS and YARN tools from Hadoop. So, Spark needs to come a long way to replace Hadoop.

6.5.4 Data Visualization

Visualizing huge data is a challenge as it cannot fit into a single computer. It is also difficult to combine the graph generated in different computers. But, there are visualization tools to perform this more elegantly and produce nice, graphical visuals easily. Tableu, D3, and Qlikview are some of the notable Big Data visualization tools that have different options to plot graphs and charts efficiently.

6.5.5 Data Processing Model

MapReduce is a data-parallel batch processing model that comprises a set of map and reduce tasks. Aggregation-related applications such as counting and ranking are typical use cases of MapReduce. A graph processing model contains a set of vertices and edges. Graph data is divided and loaded into multiple nodes and processed in parallel. It involves significant computational dependencies (not as much as BSP) and multiple iterations to converge. But, it does not require any global synchronization. Some of the graph processing tools are Pregel, Giraph, Graphlab, Graphchi, and Powergraph.

6.6 Big Data Analysis for Smart Education

Big Data has become the prominent application in smart education (Paul and Jeyaraj, 2019). Big Data acts as a core physical platform for storage and computation of data for data analysis and processing. With Big Data analysis, the collected data is pooled together and organized into patterns that are finally fed into smart applications. Big Data analysis has a greater role in education. Data science has a greater impact and an essential element in the collaboration of modern science and scientific discovery. The data processing and knowledge discovery vary from business to industrial needs. Data must be structured in different fashion for various purposes. Moreover, every problem needs enough data to extract adequate quality of solution for an undefined problem. Data science therefore used to produce favorable solution for easy decision making. The role of data science in smart education has a greater impact in social and technological development. Use of Big Data, Internet of things, NFC and RFID, etc. has a greater transformation for advanced form of modern education by building global network infrastructure, computing data center, and IoT-based sensing system in a multidimensional scenario for smart education system. This is performed by integrating learning analytics initiated from different channels that provide enough and valuable information in design and development of smart learning.

Big Data analysis consists of a sequence of steps: capture, store, manage, process, perform analytics, visualize/interpret, and understand. These steps are performed to determine undiscovered hidden patterns, relationship, trend, association, and other useful and actionable details for decision making. The following are the components integrated for the operation of data analysis.

Data capturing – It records data in different format like structured/unstructured. It is done by devices like digital sensors, digital camera, barcode readers, etc.

Data storage – The captured data is stored in structured/unstructured format using NoSQL databases or distributed file systems.

Managing data – plays a major role in rearranging/deleting stored data based on the availability of storage space and storing data in the future in dig data HDFS is used to read/write data from/to the disk.

Processing data – Various concepts are used in processing of Big Data in different style. Tools like Spark, Pig, Hive, and MapReduce are used for processing data in different fashion such as batch processing, stream processing, iterative/ interactive processing, etc.

Performing analytics – Analytical tools such as statistics, probability, data mining, machine learning, optimization, mathematics, etc. are used to extract information from Big Data.

Visualization/interpretation – Extracted information is presented to the end users using tools like Excel, D3, Tableau, etc.

Understanding data – From the information presented, the audience/analyst arrives to a conclusion, called as decision making.

6.6.1 Data Science

Data science deals with entity observation, performing analytics, and understanding from it regardless of discipline. Data science employs tools like statistics, probability, mathematics, distributed computing, data mining and machine learning, optimization algorithm, etc. in different phase of data analysis. Data scientist is a domain expert who finds appropriate algorithm for a specific problem. Data scientists should have a wide knowledge in both engineering and analytical discipline. A data scientist will focus on the right problems that have more value to an origination than on addressing business problems.

6.6.2 Data Analyst

The main difference between a data scientist and data analyst is that data scientist develops data analytical tools such as Mahout and MLBase libraries, whereas data analyst develops reports by using those tools. For example, in the business perspective, data scientists' role and responsibilities include identifying trends and challenges using Big Data analytics. This is done using various techniques that result from multiple data sources, namely data mining, data aggregation, and statistical analysis. Many statistical tools, data mining tools and machine learning libraries are available: R, MATLAB®, Weka, SAS, SPSS, etc.

6.6.3 Big Data Analytics

Applying logic to extract information from Big Data is called Big Data analytics, which is what data science covers elaborately. Data analytics differ concerning different types of data and the level of intelligence required. An algorithm designed for social media applications (audio/video dataset) may not be suitable for healthcare datasets (highly interlinked text dataset). Similarly, the level of intelligence required to extract from dataset also differs across applications. For instance, the intelligence required for playing chess is higher than other scientific applications like weather simulation, etc. Considering this, let us discuss different Big Data applications and its information extraction by applying data analytics. For instance, if data analytics is applied in text data, it is called text analytics, and so on.

6.6.4 Text Analytics

Text analytics helps to extract information from unstructured text data. It is applied to social network data such as tweets, Facebook comments, chats, emails, blogs, online forums, survey responses, corporate documents, news, call-center logs, etc. Understanding the semantics of text is called computational linguistics, also known as Natural Language Processing (NLP). This is also called text mining. Text analytics generate meaningful summaries and insights from large text dataset to help businesses for evidence-based decision-making. Example: movie success/failure prediction from comments, stock market prediction from financial news. There are different text analytics applications: information extraction, text summarization, question answering, and opinion mining.

6.6.5 Text Summarization

Generating a summary of one or multiple documents is called text summarization. The generated summary must be able to deliver useful and important information from original texts and documents. Applications include scientific journals, news articles, advertisements, emails, and blogs. Text summarization employs two methods: extractive and abstractive methods. In extractive summarization, a summary (usually sentences) is generated from the given dataset. Summary of the result is a subset of the original document. Extractive summarization need not deliver any meaning and understanding of the original text and documents. Abstractive summarization helps to extract semantic information from the text. Texts present in the resulting summary need not necessarily be a subset of the original documents. Advanced NLP methods are mostly used to extract abstractive summary from the original text. However, extractive systems are more comfortable to adopt, especially for Big Data.

6.6.6 *Question Answering (QA)*

Questions raised in natural language can be answered using these techniques. Many commercial QA systems are faster and answer meaningfully. Example: Apple Siri and IBM Watson. Healthcare, marketing, finance, education, etc. are some of the application areas of QA systems. QA systems highly rely on NLP techniques like abstractive summarization.

There are three categories in QA techniques:

■ Information retrieval-based approach
■ Knowledge-based approach
■ Hybrid approach

Information retrieval-based QA systems has three subcomponents.

Question processing – It determines the type and focus of the question and predicts the answer type. It also finds the tenses of question and answer.

Document processing – Based on the question type and focus from question processing, relevant prewritten texts are retrieved from a set of existing documents.

Answer processing – There can be many relevant passages for a question type. Some of the more suitable answers, called candidate answers, from those relevant passages, are selected.

Knowledge-based QA systems generate a syntactical form from the question, using which structured resources are queried. Typical application areas are transportation, tourism, medicine, etc. where very less pre-written documents are available. Apple Siri QA system exploits the knowledge-based approach. In hybrid QA systems, rather than analyzing questions semantically, candidate answers are extracted using information retrieval methods. IBM Watson uses this approach.

6.6.7 *Sentiment Analysis (Opinion Mining)*

Everybody has started to use smartphones. People share their opinions toward entities such as products, organizations, events, individuals, etc. in social media. It is a good source of data to find what group of people think about a particular entity. Some of the application areas are marketing, finance, political, and social events. There are three ways to perform sentiment analysis: document-level, sentence-level, and aspect-based.

6.6.8 *Audio Analytics*

Extracting information from unstructured audio data is called audio analytics. Applying this to human speech recognition is called speech analytics. Some of the application areas are call-center, healthcare, etc. where millions of recorded calls are analyzed for threat detection, improving customer satisfaction, finding customer behavior, identifying service issues, etc. Live calls also can be analyzed and given feedback in real time. Also, automated call center use interactive voice response platforms to identify and handle frustrated callers.

6.6.9 Video Analytics

The process of extracting information from video data is called video analytics or video content analysis. It is done on prerecorded videos and real-time video. Increasing usage of CCTV produces abundant video data that requires information on real time. Prerecorded videos in video sharing community (YouTube, Netflix) are analyzed to improve customer experience by suggesting interesting videos. Massive amount of video data takes more time process and comes up with a decision. Example: one second of a high-definition video is equivalent to over 2,000 pages of text in terms of size. How about processing huge videos and categorizing them into different titles on YouTube?

Video indexing can be done using meta-data of the video, soundtrack, or transcripts. RDBMS is used to store meta-data and search the videos based on data. Video analytics is done in two different places: centralized processing, or edge processing. Captured video data from CCTV/sensors is stored in a centralized data center. Data from edge devices is compressed before sending over the Internet as public bandwidth is costly. Therefore, we lose some data before we process; this affects the accuracy in the outcome. In edge processing, analytics is applied in the device, which generates video data. So, the entire video data is processed without losing tiny content. However, processing in the edge devices itself is costlier than central processing approach as it needs more power and takes more time.

6.6.10 Social Media Analytics

Social media such as Facebook, Twitter, blogs, etc. is an effective way of communication medium at present, and people contribute huge data nowadays by sharing their feedback, views/thoughts, reviews, emotions, etc. as for comments. Different opinions on different entities help to identify what people estimate about that particular entity. The research on social media analytics broadly covers several disciplines, including bio-informatics, psychology, sociology, and anthropology. Marketing has been the primary application of social media analytics in recent years. User-generated content (texts, images, videos, and bookmarks), relationships and interactions between the network entities (people, organizations, and products) are the primary sources of information in social media. Social media analytics can be classified into two groups: content-based analytics and social network analysis.

Content-based analytics – It focuses on the data posted by users on social media platforms. It is possible to perform text analytics, audio analytics, video analytics, etc. from such social media data, which is often voluminous, unstructured, noisy, and dynamic.

Social Network Analysis (SNA) is also called structure-based analytics and deals with mapping relationships and flows between the entities (denoted as nodes in the graph). Nodes in the network denote people and groups while the links denote the relationships or flow between the nodes. SNA helps predict the links (line prediction) among nodes and predict communities or hubs (nodes having many connections). Example: How many degrees of distance are you from MS Dhoni on Facebook? SNA has also been applied in various applications such as anthropology, bioinformatics (protein structure evaluation), communication studies, economics, geography, history, information science, organizational studies, social psychology, etc. Analysis of networks consisting of millions of connected nodes is computationally costly. However, social computing is a hot cake at present in the Internet-based companies. Processing high dimensional data was already a tough task in current scientific research. Early, we did dimensionality reduction (using PCA, LLE, etc.) with less loss of information as possible. Remember, Big Data should not be restricted in minimizing dimension.

6.7 Conclusion

Application of Industry 4.0 in the education system is inevitable in the future. Educators are keen to deploy Industry 4.0 in academic sectors to ease teaching and learning. To enable a smart education system, IoT-enabled environment is essential to observe the smart classroom. Cloud computing is used to offer storage and computation as a service online. Artificial intelligence and augmented reality certainly can transform the teaching system as human-like soon. Despite it benefits a lot, classical classroom teaching will also remain and coexist with the latest technologies.

References

Buyya, R., Yeo, C. S., Venugopal, S., Broberg, J., & Brandic, I. (2009). Cloud computing and emerging IT platforms: Vision, hype, and reality for delivering computing as the 5th utility. *Future Generation Computer Systems*, *25*(6), 599–616.

Dean, J., & Ghemawat, S. (2004). Mapreduce: Simplified data processing on large clusters. 6th ACM Conference on Symposium on Operating Systems Design Implementation.

Díaz, M., Martín, C., & Rubio, B. (2016). State-of-the-art, challenges, and open issues in the integration of Internet of things and cloud computing. *Journal of Network and Computer Applications*, *67*, 99–117.

Paul, A., & Jeyaraj, R. (2019). Internet of Things: A primer. *Human Behavior and Emerging Technologies*, *1*(1), 37–47.

Yang, X., et al. (2014). Cloud computing in e-Science: Research challenges and opportunities. *The Journal of Supercomputing*, *70*(1), 408–464.

Chapter 7

Text Analytics in Big Data Environments

R. Janani and S. Vijayarani

Department of Computer Applications, Bharathiar University, Coimbatore, India

Contents

DOI: 10.1201/9781003175889-7

Objectives

Text analytics is used to analyze the large volume of natural text, and it discovers lexical or linguistic patterns from the unstructured documents. The techniques of machine learning and natural language processing are used to elucidate the information overload problem. Preprocess the documents, storage of intermediate representations and analysis of represented documents, and visualization of results are the significant steps in text analytics. It is the confluence of different areas such as statistics, computational linguistics, and Artificial Intelligence. Big Data is a concept designating a tremendous amount of information within the system of structured, semi-structured, and unstructured. Text analytics in the Big Data domain is a scheme of taking out and producing advantageous data and insights from structured and unstructured data, making knowledge management more efficient via its categorization, visualization, and analysis. Hence, text analytics is necessary to analyze the massive volume of unstructured data. Text analytics becomes essential for the different domains such as healthcare, social media, education, telecommunications, industrial automation, aerospace, defense, weather forecasting, and so many. In future industry revolution 4.0, text data analytics would be an essential task and produce optimal results. The key aim of this chapter is as follows:

- This chapter explains the background of text analytics and the need for text analytics.
- It also discusses the various text analysis techniques.
- It also addresses the research challenges and issues of text analytics.
- The tools for text analytics are also discussed in this chapter.

7.1 Introduction

Text analytics, i.e. analyzing text information, is the method of originating unique inferences from the unstructured textual data previously unknown. It is the confluence of various research fields like data mining, database, artificial intelligence, library science, information science, computational linguistics, statistics, etc.; it is a combination of humanistic and computational technologies.

Text analytics is an emerging field, hence text data is gaining more importance. The unstructured text data is establishing in informal settings like news blogs, web pages, e-mails, online chats, social media, etc. Data mining techniques can handle the structured data while text mining concerns semi-structured or unstructured data. It consists of various technologies for analyzing the semi-structured and unstructured data (Sebastiani, 2002). The main motive of text analytics is to convert the text into numeric and derive the hidden knowledge from them.

Big Data is a concept designating a tremendous amount of information and is typically structured, unstructured, and semi-structured. Though the amount of information is not significant, it is extremely important what organizations do with the data (Bifet, 2013). Every digital process and every sharing of social media produces Big Data. Text analytics in a Big Data environment is the evolution of analyzing huge quantities of unstructured or semi-structured data to evaluate hidden patterns, industry dynamics, unknown associations, consumer preferences, and some other useful purposes. Data defines the raw fact for information until it is sorted, organized, and analyzed. The technology was developed and used in all facets of lifestyles, increasing the need for larger information to be stored and processed. As a result, various structures were built that involves cloud storage that assists enormous documents. Even though large statistics are responsible for data collection and processing, the cloud attempts a secure, open, and accessible platform for large statistical configurations (Cloud Security Alliance, 2013).

7.1.1 Need for Text Analytics

The amount of text data is increasing rapidly every second. Text is being important in various domains such as healthcare, social media, education, telecommunications, industrial automation, defense, weather forecasting, internet of things, and aerospace. Machines and humans produce and consume plenty of unstructured and semi-structured data in all those domains. Hence, there is a need to analyze the enormous dimensions of unstructured or semi-structured data.

- Text analytics is great support for organizations handling the huge volume of text data because the methods and techniques of text analytics can identify and determine the relevant insights from the text contents.
- It enables better decision-making and automates the process.
- Therefore, text analytics is significant because of its scalability, ease of understanding, real-time analysis, and consistent criteria.

7.2 Text Analytics: Big Data Environment

The way to perform text analytics process in Big Data platform is shown in Figure 7.1.

7.2.1 Text Data Collection

In text analytics, the input considered for analysis should be good and reasonable. Because of this reason, high-quality data is collected and used for further analysis tasks. Generally, the data used for text analysis is in semi-structured format or

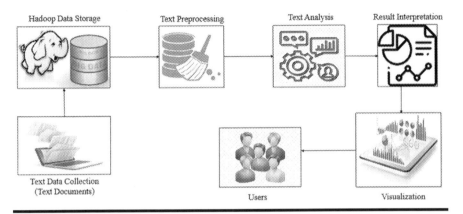

Figure 7.1 Big Data architecture for text analytics.

unstructured format (Talib et al., 2016). The unstructured data is raw data that contains text or multimedia content. This unstructured data can be generated and used by the human or machine. Such unstructured data can be obtained from news blogs, articles, e-mail, social media data, and web pages. Data based on web pages are becoming more prevalent in the applications of text analytics because of its availability, low cost, and accessibility. The important quality dimensions of text data are accuracy, relevancy, completeness, security, and ease of operation as represented in Figure 7.2.

- **Accuracy:** It refers to the degree to which an event or object represented accurately reflects the data.
- **Relevancy:** The degree to which information is provided in the same format and is relevant to past data.
- **Completeness:** When it meets standards of comprehensiveness, data is deemed complete.
- **Timeliness:** Is the data properly available when it is needed?
- **Interpretability:** The data definition like symbols, languages, and units are clear.
- **Accessibility:** The information is easily and quickly accessible.
- **Ease of Operation**: The data can be easily operated and maintained.
- **Security:** The information is maintained with its security.

7.2.1.1 Data Collection Methods

Some of the important methods of data collection (Kabir, 2016) are listed as follows:

- **Questionnaires:** To collect information from respondents, a questionnaire or form or survey is a study method comprising of a set of queries and other prompts.

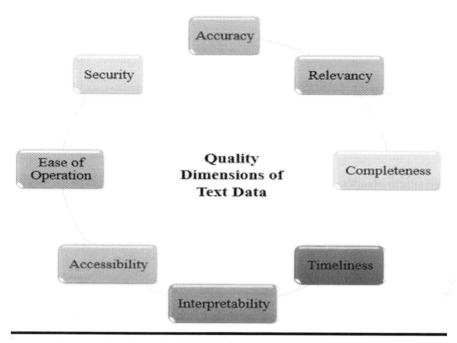

Figure 7.2 Quality dimensions of text data.

- **Interviews:** Conducting an interview requires asking questions and obtaining feedback from the participants. There are several ways of interviews, like individual meetings, face-to-face meetings, and group discussions.
- **Direct Observations:** Normally, observation is an organized method to gather data by perceiving people in usual circumstances. Direct observation is significant because it provides real-time information about the way to conduct the study. The drawback of direct observation is, it can be vulnerable to bias and imprecision because people act differently when they are observed by someone.
- **Case studies:** Comprehensive examinations of a particular individual, organization, incident, or society are case studies. Data is typically obtained from several sources and using a range of various approaches.
- **Surveys:** Surveys offer a way to quantify the attributes, knowledge of services, attitudes or beliefs, and community needs. To track improvements over time, repeating surveys at regular intervals can help.

7.2.2 Data Storage

Nowadays, text analytics has been extensively used by a variety of new technologies. Hence, the size of text data is increasing exponentially in digital form. The Hadoop Distributed File System (HDFS) is used to store the vast amount of unstructured data collected from various sources. It is designed for operating on commodity hardware because it is a distributed file system. HDFS provides excessive quality of access to the stored data (Hadoop, 2015). So, managing a large amount of data is very useful in this storage. This distributed file system will serve as an interface for master slaves. Two major nodes are used in this architecture, name node, and data node.

Name node is liable for managing HDFS file metadata. This metadata contains different HDFS file information such as file name, file permissions, file length, blocks, etc. Its responsibilities are implementing various namespace processes such as opening, closing, renaming the files or folders. Whenever a file is stored in HDFS, it is broken down into blocks (Hadoop, 2015). The block size is 64 MB, by default. For quicker data transfers, these blocks are repeated and processed around the various data nodes. Name node maintains a data node mapping of the blocks. Data nodes are used to read and write requests from clients with the HDFS file system. These are also responsible for making block replicas and testing whether or not the blocks are compromised. It leads the beep messages to the name node in the form of block mappings.

7.2.3 Text Preprocessing

A document consists of many characters and the characters are combined to form the terms or words. These terms are the main factor for the text analytics process. The collection of terms is often called a dictionary or vocabulary. Text preprocessing is a prerequisite in correctly interpreting the documents (Isa et al., 2008). Preprocessing of text documents have the primary goal of reducing storage space and query processing time (Mirończuk & Protasiewicz, 2018). Normally, preprocessing methods depends on natural language processing (NLP). The significant stages included in text preprocessing are tokenization, standardization, removal of stop word, and stemming. It removes the unnecessary information from the raw text data in each stage.

Tokenization: Tokenization is the procedure of cutting text information into tokens, which can be words, phrases, symbols, or any other recognizable elements. The token list is used as input for more analysis along with text mining or parsing. Both computer science and linguistics support Tokenization, where it practices the part of the lexical analysis (Feldman & Sanger, 2007). The tokenization process usually happens at the term level. But, defining what is meant by a "term" is often tough.

Standardization: This is the process of converting the text into lower case letters. Then the numbers, punctuation, and symbols are eliminated in this process. Some documents can have extra spaces and these extra spaces also deleted in this step. This process will prevent the possibility of the occurrence of the same word with different dimensions. For example, the text terms, "Data" and "data" is considered as the similar word (Anandarajan & Nolan, 2019).

Stop word Removal: Stop word is a common word that is cleaned out before handling natural language text (Silva & Ribeiro, 2003). In the English language, "and, the, are, is, to" are the most common stop words. A group of stop words is recognized as a stop list. These stop words have no value in the text analytics process. There are several stop word list is existed and it includes different languages and methods.

Stemming: Stemming reduces the fluctuated text words to base words, root words, and stem words. Stemming involves dropping a word suffix to eliminate vocabulary dimensions (Porter, 2001; Lovins, 1968). Words with a common origin hold a related meaning. The words would then be grouped into a symbol. There are exemptions to the root of words with a similar meaning. However, the extra decrease in length also costs the price of a few words mistakenly categorized (Manning et al., 2008).

7.2.4 Text Analysis

Text analysis is the automated process of originating trivial knowledge and facts from a massive amount of text documents. In this stage, typical data mining techniques are combined with the text mining process to discover interesting and important patterns from the huge volume of unstructured documents. The process of text analytics is shown in Figure 7.3.

7.2.4.1 Text Classification

Text classification (TC) (Agarwal & Mittal, 2014) is also termed as the text categorization. It is the process of allocating the text documents into one or more categories or no group at all based on their contents. A category emphasizes the relation between both the information or knowledge subjects and objects. It involves defining

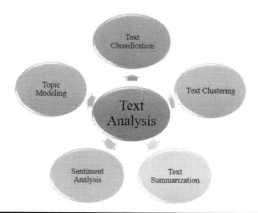

Figure 7.3 Text analysis.

a document's recurring motifs by putting it in a predefined collection of topics. Once the document is classified, a computer system will usually view the document as a "word bag" (Joulin et al., 2016). As with information extraction, it does not try to process the real information. Comparatively, the classification procedure is used to count the words that occur in the document, and the relevant topics addressed by the document are defined from the counts. This usually relies on a thesaurus for which subjects are predefined, and relationships are described by the quest for specific words, narrow terms, synonyms, and related terms. This can be used in a variety of application domains. Most businesses and industry sectors have customer service or need to be forced to answer their customer's questions on a variety of topics.

In natural language processing, text classification is a routine job with a broad range of applications that are related to sentiment analysis, intent detection, spam detection, and topic labeling. Text classification plays a significant role in multiple information management systems because of the massive progress of unstructured text data on the web. The text being an exceedingly rich source of information and the extraction of knowledge would be a time-consuming and complex task. Hence, text classification is utilized for structuring the text document, which enhances the decision making and the automation processes. Preprocessing and dimensionality reduction are vital steps in text classification because the high dimensional text serves as the important challenge in text classification (Nigam et al., 2000). This in turn enhances the speed and the accuracy of the classification. Dimensionality reduction tasks are categorized into two subtasks. They are feature extraction and feature selection. Feature selection and extraction are used to rise the precision, scalability, and efficiency of the text classification by constructing a vector space.

At this point, the amount of knowledge available on the internet is growing drastically (Ikonomakis et al., 2005). As a result, the classifier is used to automatically detect the text documents in order to determine the appropriate category for an unstructured document. Automatic text classification highly depends on machine learning algorithms. It automatically creates the classifier by acquiring the characteristics of the categories from a predetermined collection of similar documents (Sebastiani, 2002). Spam filtering, e-mail routing, topic tracking, sentiment analysis, and web page classification are all examples of text classification.

Text classification can be performed in a manual and automatic way of classification. In the manual approach, a human annotator infers the text content and categorizes the text documents based on the content (Krippendorff, 2012). This approach yields superior results; the major drawback of this approach is that it requires more time and too expensive. To automate the system, the advanced techniques like natural language processing and machine learning were introduced. In automated systems, the approaches are grouped into three categories: machine learning-based system, rule-based system, and hybrid system.

- **Rule-Based System** – These are used to categorize the text into structured sets by utilizing the linguistics rules. These rules train the system to utilize

Table 7.1 Classification Algorithms

	Algorithms	*Descriptions*
Text classification	Rule-based system	Based on the linguistics rules. Requires deep knowledge. Time-consuming. Difficult to maintain.
	Machine learning-based system	Rely on the past insights. Does not require more training data. Easy to maintain. Accurate predictions.
	Hybrid system	Grouping of rule-based and the machine learning. It is used to fine-tuned by the addition of the specific rules.

the semantically and syntactically related components in the text to identify the relevant classes that are related to the context. Every rule must know the knowledge about the categories as well as the predicted category (Sebastiani, 2002).

■ **Machine Learning System** – In this approach, text classification is performed by learning which helps to categorize the text documents based on the previous perceptions (Mirończuk & Protasiewicz, 2018). Machine Learning algorithms will learn by analyzing the training data and to find out what type of relationships exist among the text. Text classification based on machine learning algorithms is especially more precise than the rule-based system. Naive Bayes, Linear Regression, Decision Trees, Random Forest, Support Vector Machine, and Neural Networks (Debortoli et al., 2016) are some of the prominent machine learning algorithms.

■ **Hybrid System** – The hybrid system is the combination of both the machine learning system and rule-based which improve the efficiency of the text classification system. It can be efficiently modeled by accumulating detailed rules for conflicting tags.

Table 7.1 gives the details about the types of text classification algorithms.

7.2.4.2 Text Clustering

Text clustering is a method of segregating a collection of documents in typical groups established on the correspondence of the text. The cluster community which includes the shapeless format also deals with the similar format (Abraham et al., 2006). It was commonly used to efficiently search, organize, compile, summarize, and retrieve massive quantities of text documents (Abraham et al., 2006). Primitively, the clustering of documents is used to boost the quality of the knowledge recovery program. Text clustering is a competent way of finding a single document nearest neighbor within the sets of records. The clustering technique is now used to surf a document set and to standardize the results provided by the search engines based on the query which is given by the users.

Text clustering is often used to identify the relevant dimensions and to meaningfully denote the dimensions (Abraham et al., 2006). The documents in the knowledge discovery system are defined as multifaceted high-dimensional documents. Broad document clustering applications are automated topic extraction, a grouping of documents, and the retrieval of information. Nonetheless, a number of significant research has been performed in the field of text clustering, which necessitates the fortitude to improve and enhance the accuracy of the text clustering method.

The hypothesis of text clustering is the related documents seem to be more similar than the nonrelated documents. This is an automated process of grouping the relevant documents into a single group related to the document's content without any predefined training or taxonomies. Topic extraction, fast information retrieval or filtering, and automatic document organization are applications of text clustering.

Text clustering may be used in various chores such as grouping the similar documents, such as news, feedback, tweets, customer analysis, and identifying the meaningful instincts from the documents (Zhang et al., 2010). Text clustering is categorized into different types, such as hierarchical, agglomerative, and flat clustering algorithms.

- **Hierarchical Clustering** – It consists of a single link, group average, ward's method and the complete linkage (Xu & Wunsch, 2005). Hierarchical-based algorithm utilizes the process of aggregation or division to frame the document into clusters in a hierarchical structure. These types of clustering are more suitable for surfing the applications. Though they seem to be promising in clustering text providing in-depth information for a comprehensive analysis, it often endures efficiency complications.
- **Flat Clustering** – This algorithm will make the flat group of clusters without any specific structures (Manning et al., 2008). The algorithm is established by utilizing the k-means and the variants, which are more efficient and produce a substantial amount of information that are required.

Apart from the categories mentioned above, many more algorithms belong to distribution models, density models, subspace models, graph and signed graph models, and neural models also available. Each algorithmic model for the clustering in the text differs only by understanding what constitutes the cluster and the efficient way of finding the clusters (Mohammed et al., 2015).

The initial step in the process of text clustering is parsing, which converts the text documents into smaller units (words and phrases) known as tokenization.

Popularly used tokenization models are bag of words and the N-gram. The next step proceeds with the minimization of the inflected words known as stemming and grouping of the inflected words into a single term known as the lemmatization, the following step removes the stop words, punctuation's, and computes term frequencies in the document.

Finally, clusters, which are the variety of the documents based on the features, were generated (Abraham et al., 2006). The cluster models' efficiency is evaluated by the various performance metrics such as cluster purity, recall, precision, etc. The single difference that separates the text clustering and the classification is the former is processed in an unsupervised manner and the latter is processed in a supervised manner.

7.2.4.3 Text Summarization

Text summarization refers to the procedure of shortening the huge volume of documents. Text summarization aims to create a concise and smooth overview of documents and is achieved in two different ways: extraction-based and abstraction-based summarization (Gaikwad & Mahender, 2016). The method of extractive text summarization involves dragging and merging key phrases from the source document to produce a summary.

The extraction is performed in accordance with the given metric without changing the text. The abstractive summarization involves the portions of the source document being paraphrased or shortened. Once abstraction is implemented in deep learning problems for text summarization, the grammar contradictions of the extractive approach can be resolved. The abstract text analysis algorithms create new sentences and phrases that excerpt the most beneficial information from the original text (Tas & Kiyani, 2007).

7.2.4.4 Sentimental Analysis

Sentiment analysis is used to clarify the document that holds the emotions that can be either positive or negative. There are several uses for sentiment analysis, particularly for businesses. It benefits companies to evaluate community opinion on the product, the impact of ads, or the responses to product releases (Liu, 2012). There are two significant methods to sentiment analysis: lexicon or dictionary and learning or corpus. The method to the lexicon assigns a polarity to terms from a dictionary generated in advance. The dictionary describes a word with its polarity. When the lexicon includes a similar term or sentence that looks in the text, it returns its polarity value. On the other hand, the learning-based approach creates an automated sentiment classifier for a formerly annotated document with sentiments. From here, a trained is applied to the unknown data to discover the sentiments (Nasukawa & Yi, 2003).

7.2.4.5 Topic Modeling

Topic modeling is also known as probabilistic topic modeling, which is the unsupervised method to automatically understand the topical information from the unstructured text documents. The topics in topic modeling are defined as the distribution of probability over the terms of the specific document. It can either be a single or multiple membership model, in which the documents belong to a single topic or a mixture of multiple topics respectively. Topic modeling is based on various methods such as dynamic topic modeling, LDA-based topic modeling, supervised topic modeling, correlated topic modeling, and structural topic modeling (Blei, 2012).

- **LDA Topic Modeling:** Latent Dirichlet Allocation (LDA) is a procreative probabilistic model underlying two assumptions: a distributional and a statistical hypothesis. This method aims to map the documents into a collection of topics that covers the distribution of the words in the document. In this, the documents are exchangeable and the document topics are independent (Blei et al., 2003).
- **Correlated Topic Modeling:** This model is the hierarchical model, which correlates the latent topics. This is the extended version of LDA, which does not satisfy the assumption of topic independence while it is the mixture model. This approach determines the more flexible model than LDA. It measures the normal distribution and structural covariance among the topics (Blei & Lafferty, 2007).
- **Dynamic Topic Modeling:** This category of model incorporates LDA, which models the document topics in sequential order. It involves data splitting and creating time-dependent groups based on the month or year. This method uses the logistic-based normal distribution (Blei & Lafferty, 2006).
- **Supervised Topic Modeling:** It uses the labeled documents for topic modeling, which is similar to the text classification. The class variables are associated with each document, and the variable is the response to topic modeling. To estimate the model, the variation expectation-maximization model is employed (Anandarajan & Nolan, 2019).
- **Structural Topic Modeling:** It is the semi-automated process to model the topics. It incorporates the Metadata and covariant in the text analysis. This task is useful for open-ended text documents. To estimate the model, the selected topics and covariates are compared (Anandarajan & Nolan, 2019).

7.2.5 Result Interpretation

The retrieved results are interpreted and it is important to the users to get the knowledge. To interpret the extracted knowledge from the unstructured documents, various efficient visualization techniques and tools are available.

7.2.6 Visualization

Pictorial presentation of information and data is termed as data visualization. Data visualization tools offer a reachable mode to perceive and recognize the movements, patterns, and outliers in data with the usage of visualization elements such as graphs, charts, and maps. In the Big Data period, the tools and skills are more significant for analyzing the vast quantities of information and making decisions (Keim et al., 2013). It is also another form of visual art. There are many types of data visualization available like graphs, charts, maps, tables, infographics, etc. Some of the distinct methods for data visualization are bar chart, bubble chart, Gantt chart, heat map, histogram, word cloud, scatter plot, text table, timelines, etc. (Wang et al., 2015). There are various visualization tools such as Google data studio, Tableau, and looker are avilable to process the text results. Some of the sample charts for text analytics are depicted in Figure 7.4.

7.3 Applications of Text Analytics

Text analytics has gained significant prominences, and it is used in various industries for various purposes like healthcare, education, industry, social media, etc. Some of the applications are (Kim et al., 2014):

- **Social Media:** Social media data is unstructured data, which is used to track several fragments of information that are shared online. Text analytics are applied to social media platforms to find deeper visions.
- **Banking:** With the massive quantities of information flowing through banks, new and creative ways of processing Big Data are being found. It is most critical that the consumers are thoroughly understood and their joy enhanced around the same time. Reducing the risk of fraud activities of also ensuring regulatory enforcement is equally paramount. Big Data provides huge insights, which additionally includes innovative technology from financial institutions.
- **Education and Research:** Educators equipped with data-driven knowledge could greatly influence the program, students, and curriculum for the institution and colleges. By analyzing Big Data, they can identify students' risk, ensure adequate growth for teachers, and introduce a better framework for evaluating and supporting education administration. Apart from this, there are many research areas that are using text analytics like, clinical text mining, IoT, speech to text analytics, bioinformatics, etc.
- **Healthcare:** When Big Data concerns healthcare, in some situations, it needs to be done efficiently, easily, and reliably, with adequate clarity to meet the strict regulations of the industry. By using Big Data efficiently, healthcare professionals can discover unseen perceptions that enhance patient care.

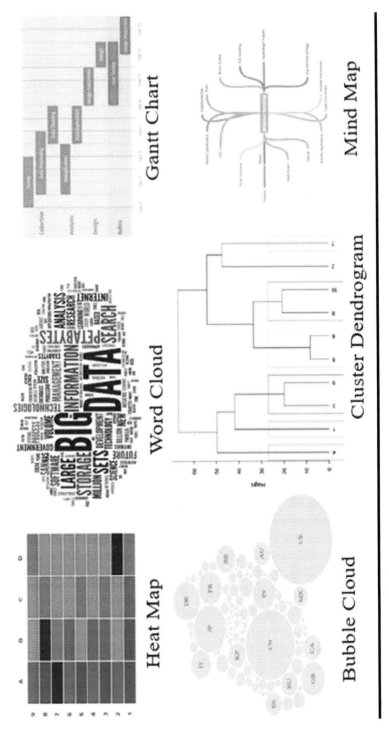

Figure 7.4 Text visualization.

- **E-Mail Filtering:** To clean the spam of e-mail, these analytics are helpful. Different approaches are used to reduce spam that is the virus entry point.
- **Manufacturing:** Equipped with an understanding that Big Data can have, industrialists will at the same time achieve the highest quality and production while reducing risk and waste. Many companies are operating in a culture focused on analytics, which means they can fix the manufacturing deficiencies earlier and become more involved in the business verdicts.
- **Business Intelligence:** The creation of customer relationships is crucial to the retail enterprise, and they can exploit, i.e. to handle Big Data. Merchants requisite to consider the top publicizing methods for consumers, the most successful approach is to handle sales, and perhaps the most efficient method of doing business that has lapsed.
- **Fraud Detection:** Text analytics has helped to expose the allegations of fraud, benefiting the insurance industry in general. Companies can now process the claims at a much faster rate without using text mining to fall back on false claims.

7.4 Issues and Research Challenges in Text Analytics

Text analytics in a Big Data environment has a lot of research challenges and issues as follows:

- **Data Collection:** Data collection is significant in a Big Data environment. Because Big Data consist of six V's. Hence, data collection is based on volume, variety, velocity, variety, value, veracity, and variability (Granello & Wheaton, 2004).
- **Data Storage:** Big Data being enormous and composite. Automated storage tiering (AST) is a feature of the storing software that dynamically transfers data amid different disks. Furthermore, AST is not concerned with device protection, where the data is put. Thus it raises another data storage security problem (Pipino et al., 2002).
- **Data Cleaning:** Nevertheless, the cleaning of unstructured text data, primarily high frequency broadcast real-time data, presents various problems and challenges to the research (Rahm & Do, 2000).
- **Data Aggregation:** This process task involves the collection and incorporation of clean data derived from massive unstructured data. Big Data regularly groups the various online events such as retweets, Tweets, Facebook likes and microblogging (Edwards & Fenwick, 2016). Aggregated data may contain some deficiencies, and they should be rectified before proceeding further.
- **Data Modeling:** After the data is collected, cleaned, stored, processed, and implemented, Big Data processing and modeling can come in. Traditional

data analysis and modeling techniques address the complexity of schema-enabled data relationships. As Big Data is habitually heterogeneous, noisy, dynamic in nature, and unreliable, these criteria do not put on in this context to schema-less databases, nonrelational.

- **Visualization:** Visualization techniques are used to depict the data in a conceptual manner. It also provides efficient and interactive information using graphical illustrations. These are used to represent different sizes of data effectively which in turn reduces the data scalability issues. Visualization is becoming increasingly necessary considering the scale of the data involved.
- **Data Privacy and Security:** Once the resource for Big Data is developed, the data must remain protected, ownership and IP issues set on, and consumers should provided with various access stages.

7.5 Tools for Text Analytics

There are many tools and software available in the market for text analytics. Some of them are listed below (PAT Research).

- **DiscoverText:** This software provides a competent basis for extensive data analytics. This tool can integrate the data from various sources. The main features of this tool are, it classifies the documents via automatic and manual, it also ascribes the memos to the datasets, documents, etc.
- **Google Cloud Natural Language API:** It offers the more powerful machine learning algorithms for text analytics. The main features of this API are syntax analysis, sentiment analysis, text analysis, and content classification.
- **IBM SPSS:** It surveys the unstructured text and transforms them into a quantitative model. The main features are automated categorization, data management, and effective visualization.
- **Meaning Cloud:** This tool is used to extract meaningful insights from unstructured data like social media, documents, and articles. The main features are text classification, language identification, topic modeling, and summarization.
- **Microsoft Azure:** It detects the topics, key phrases, and sentiments from the unstructured text content. The main features are its in-built machine learning techniques and nonrequirement of training data.
- **SAS Text Miner:** It determines the information from the collection of documents automatically. The features are that it consists of high-performance text analysis, automatic Boolean regulation, and multiple language support.
- **Startifyd:** It consists of machine/deep learning and natural language processing algorithms. It analyzes both structured and unstructured data and has the customized widgets and interactive dashboards.

- **Bitext:** It has grammar-based methods for sentiment analysis, and it supports more than 20 languages. The main features are entity extraction, topic extraction, and linguistic approaches.
- **Smart Logic:** It is a content intelligence platform for text analytics. It derives human intelligence from the collection of documents. It consists of enhanced information discovery, sentiment analysis, and process automation.
- **Word Stat:** It is the powerful content analysis and text analysis to handle a vast size of unstructured data. It relates the unstructured data with structured data for analysis.

7.6 Conclusion

At present, the data in organizations are increasing exponentially. Due to its large volume and fast arrival nature, conventional data mining methods cannot deal with Big Data. The most difficult aspect of Big Data is not about collecting but about handling Big Data. The collected data is unstructured form, and it must be pre-processed before analyzing the data. After preprocessing, these data can be used for several forms of analysis. Yet because of its features, the conventional methods struggle to accommodate and control Big Data. The development of new technologies and algorithms is required to manage text in a Big Data world. This study explored text processing, principles, process flow, research problems, and text analytics functionalities in the Big Data context. Different tools used for text analytics are also discussed in this chapter.

References

Abraham, A., Das, S., & Konar, A. (2006, July). Document clustering using differential evolution. In 2006 IEEE International Conference on Evolutionary Computation (1784–1791). IEEE.

Agarwal, B., & Mittal, N. (2014). Text classification using machine learning methods-a survey. In Proceedings of the Second International Conference on Soft Computing for Problem Solving (SocProS 2012), December 28–30, 2012 (701–709). Springer, New Delhi.

Anandarajan, M., & Nolan, T. (2019). Practical text analytics. Maximizing the value of text data. In *Advances in Analytics and Data Science*, Vol. 2, p. 285. New York: Springer.

Bifet, A. (2013). Mining Big Data in real time. *Informatica, 37*, 15–20.

Blei, D. M. (2012). Probabilistic topic models. *Communications of the ACM, 55*(4), 77–84.

Blei, D. M., & Lafferty, J. D. (2006). Dynamic topic models. In Proceedings of the 23rd International Conference on Machine Learning (113–120). ACM.

Blei, D. M., & Lafferty, J. D. (2007). A correlated topic model of science. *The Annals of Applied Statistics, 1*(1), 17–35.

Blei, D. M., Ng, A. Y., & Jordan, M. I. (2003). Latent Dirichlet allocation. *Journal of Machine Learning Research, 3*, 993–1022.

Cloud Security Alliance. (2013). *Big Data analytics for security intelligence.* Retrieved from www.cloudsecurityalliance.org/research/big-data62

Debortoli, S., Müller, O., Junglas, I., & vomBrocke, J. (2016). Text mining for information systems researchers: An annotated topic modeling tutorial. *Communications of the Association for Information Systems, 39*(1), 7.

Edwards, R., & Fenwick, T. (2016). Digital analytics in professional work and learning. *Studies in Continuing Education, 38*(2), 213–227.

Feldman, R., & Sanger, J. (2007). *The text mining handbook: Advanced approaches in analyzingunstructured data.* Cambridge: Cambridge University Press.

Gaikwad, D. K., & Mahender, C. N. (2016). A review paper on text summarization. *International Journal of Advanced Research in Computer and Communication Engineering, 5*(3), 154–160.

Granello, D. H., & Wheaton, J. E. (2004). Online data collection: Strategies for research. *Journal of Counseling & Development, 82*(4), 387–393.

Hadoop. (2015). *Apache Software Foundation (ASF).* Retrieved December 18, 2015, from http://hadoop.apache.org

Ikonomakis, M., Kotsiantis, S., & Tampakas, V. (2005). Text classification using machine learning techniques. *WSEAS Transactions on Computers, 4*(8), 966–974.

Isa, D., Lee, L. H., Kallimani, V. P., & Rajkumar, R. (2008). Text document pre-processing with the Bayes formula for classification using the support vector machine. *IEEE Transactions on Knowledge and Data Engineering, 20*(9), 1264–1272.

Joulin, A., Grave, E., Bojanowski, P., & Mikolov, T. (2016). *Bag of tricks for efficient text classification.* arXiv preprint arXiv:1607.01759.

Kabir, S. M. S. (2016). *Basic guidelines for research.* Chittagong: Book Zone Publication. Chapter 9.

Keim, D., Qu, H., & Ma, K. L. (2013). Big-data visualization. *IEEE Computer Graphics and Applications, 33*(4), 20–21.

Kim, G. H., Trimi, S., & Chung, J. H. (2014). Big-data applications in the government sector. *Communications of the ACM, 57*(3), 78–85.

Krippendorff, K. (2012). *Content analysis: An introduction to its methodology.* Thousand Oaks: Sage.

Liu, B. (2012). Sentiment analysis and opinion mining. *Synthesis Lectures on Human Language Technologies, 5*(1), 1–167.

Lovins, J. B. (1968). Development of a stemming algorithm. *Mechanical Translation and Computational Linguistics, 11*(1–2), 22–31.

Manning, C. D., Schütze, H., & Raghavan, P. (2008). *Introduction to information retrieval.* Cambridge: Cambridge University Press.

Mirończuk, M. M., & Protasiewicz, J. (2018). A recent overview of the state-of-the-art elements of text classification. *Expert Systems with Applications, 106*, 36–54.

Mohammed, A. J., Yusof, Y., & Husni, H. (2015). Document clustering based on firefly algorithm. *Journal of Computer Science, 11*(3), 453–465.

Nasukawa, T., & Yi, J. (2003). Sentiment analysis: Capturing favorability using natur-allanguage processing. In Proceedings of the 2nd International Conference on Knowledge Capture (70–77). ACM.

Nigam, K., McCallum, A. K., Thrun, S., & Mitchell, T. (2000). Text classification from labeled and unlabeled documents using EM. *Machine Learning, 39*(2–3), 103–134.

PAT Research. Retrieved from https://www.predictiveanalyticstoday.com/top-software-for-text-analysis-text-mining-text-analytics/

Pipino, L. L., Lee, Y. W., & Wang, R. Y. (2002). Data quality assessment. *Communications of the ACM, 45*(4), 211–218.

Porter, M. F. (2001). Snowball: A language for stemming algorithms. Retrieved from http://snowball.tartarus.org/texts/introduction.html

Rahm, E., & Do, H. H. (2000). Data cleaning: Problems and current approaches. *IEEE Data Engineering Bulletin, 23*(4), 3–13.

Sebastiani, F. (2002). Machine learning in automated text categorization. *ACM Computing Surveys (CSUR), 34*(1), 1–47.

Silva, C., & Ribeiro, B. (2003, July). The importance of stop word removal on recall values in text categorization. In Proceedings of the International Joint Conference on Neural Networks, 2003 (Vol. 3, 1661–1666). IEEE.

Talib, R., Hanif, M. K., Ayesha, S., & Fatima, F. (2016). Text mining: Techniques, applications and issues. *International Journal of Advanced Computer Science & Applications, 1*(7), 414–418.

Tas, O., & Kiyani, F. (2007). A survey automatic text summarization. *Press Academia Procedia, 5*(1), 205–213.

Wang, L., Wang, G., & Alexander, C. A. (2015). Big data and visualization: Methods, challenges and technology progress. *Digital Technologies, 1*(1), 33–38.

Xu, R., & Wunsch, D. (2005). Survey of clustering algorithms. *IEEE Transactions on Neural Networks, 16*(3), 645–678.

Zhang, W., Yoshida, T., Tang, X., & Wang, Q. (2010). Text clustering using frequent itemsets. *Knowledge-Based Systems, 23*(5), 379–388.

Chapter 8

Business Data Analytics: Applications and Research Trends

S. Sharmila and S. Vijayarani

Department of Computer Science, Bharathiar University, Coimbatore, India

Contents

DOI: 10.1201/9781003175889-8

Objectives

In the current digital world, data analytics has become more vital to get deeper insights into data to infer unexplored knowledge. Particularly, data analytics is very much essential for the business domain that helps business organizations to increase their growth. In business data analytics, a set of algorithms are incorporated to analyze the past and present business data, to obtain the hidden knowledge that can lead to making better decisions. Education 4.0 focuses on the schemes to learn and it aligns with the rising fourth revolution among the industries. The mass infiltration of data that are generated through the user paved the way for Big Data analytics that impacts everyday lives. The process of decision making is enriched with the help of analytics. Tremendous benefits have been witnessed in recent years due to the use of Big Data. To business, technology is to keep the customer and the company closer. The new trend of business firms embarking on the projects of Big Data shows the massive development in the world of business. The interesting aspect of business analytics is to facilitate better customer services and to generate new products. Understanding the necessities of the customers and devising modern methods to satisfy them are exceptional fields that have helped to enhance the quality of new services. This chapter is about an overview of Education 4.0, Big Data analytics and business analytics, and the impact of Big Data analytics on Education 4.0 as well as business analytics. Some of the research perspectives in these domains are also projected.

8.1 Big Data Analytics and Business Analytics: An Introduction

The data are generated through internet usage and the size of the data is also grown exponentially. The generated data consist of both structured and unstructured data. The proliferation in the growth of the data needs advanced approaches to store, capture, and process the data that lead to the initiation of Big Data technology. Various researches and implementations based on Big Data have been conducted over a decade by researchers. This revolution is due to the increased areas of applications in the education system, decision making in business, healthcare industry, and other network optimization approaches.

Business analytics (BA) is the exploration and iteration of business organization data with an accent on statistical examination. Data-driven decisions are made with the assistance of business analytics and companies use analytics that is committed to judgment on the decisions. To attain deep insight into this area and impel the same in business planning, analytics has to be performed on the past business performance that refers to a continuous practice on iterative examination, numerical analysis, technologies, predictive modeling, and skills. New insights were framed based on the observation of business data and statistical methods.

Business intelligence (BI) focuses on a set of metrics that are used in measuring the previous performance and regulation on business planning and it is associated with management science. Business intelligence is a contrast factor of business analytics. Automated and human decisions are attained from the result of analytics. Big Data and business analytics are the recent trends that are optimistically attracting the business world. Development in the industry made data analytics and business analytics the most needed factors. Revolution in technology is termed as 4.0, and the relevant teaching concepts are stated as Education 4.0.

The development of Industry 4.0 has motivated the expansion of Big Data analytics, cloud computing, Internet of Things (IoT), business analytics, and Artificial Intelligence. The correlation between Industry 4.0 and the modern education system has insisted the educational institutions make education meet the modern industrial requirements. The education pattern and the curriculum have been framed based on the current needs, and it educates students with skills of technology, science, statistics, mathematics, artificial intelligence skills, and engineering. Recently, the approaches like Big Data analytics and business analytics have been developed to process the massive size of the data that are created by various business groups. Consequently, each business organization necessitates rapid insights into the ever-rising volume of transactional data. Analytics on the real-time data assists to look at the previous data and foresee the prospects of the future. The main intention behind Big Data is to attain effectiveness in business operations, proliferation in the economy, and enriching the standard of the society (Grover et al., 2018; Chahal et al., 2019).

The remaining sections of this chapter are organized as follows: Section 2 discusses the digital revolution of education 4.0. Section 3 presents a conceptual framework of Big Data for industry 4.0, while Section 4 explores the business analytics in Big Data. Section 5 sketches the key applications and the sources of data for Big Data and business analytics. Section 6 discusses the challenges of Big Data in business analytics. And in Section 7, various research insights are discussed.

8.2 Digital Revolution of Education 4.0

The fourth industrial revolution has brought many alterations in education. The invasion of the industrial revolution has made education extra versatile and has disciplined many digital physical frames as well as interaction among human–machines. Introducing a creative education system 4.0 has improved the education and skills for future learning. Augmented reality, virtual reality, and virtual classrooms have made several advancements in education. The usage of internet technology in education has resulted in the enormous growth of data.

8.2.1 Education 4.0

The chief intention behind Education 4.0 is to endorse the intelligence skills and smart observational as well as thinking behaviour of the students. The curriculum development in education is designed based on advanced technologies, tools, and other resources. Education 4.0 permits learners to utilize internet technology and other online educational information. It helps in promoting the business activity through the business skill development based on education system initiation among the students.

8.2.2 Requirement of Education 4.0 in Industry

The development in modern research has illustrated that education maintains pace with the environment of the learner and supports them with maintainable as well as secure prospects. Education 4.0 incorporates unique technology and a customizable education system. The revolutionized education system has introduced several learning tools, teaching aids, and learning management software that uplifts the standard of students to promote the growth of the industry.

8.2.3 Benefits of Education 4.0 for Business Sector

Education 4.0 is also applicable for noneducators such as administrators and other business professionals. It mainly focuses on the optimum use and utilization of technological resources and the relevant tools. The business decisions were taken based on the initiation of business knowledge in the curriculum of the students. It produces the education system in a well-ordered way and generates better financial outcomes. By minimizing the incompetent costs of administration, it is applicable to attain the savings that all educational institutions still need. Second, administration can transmit to an additional proficient place of work and can employ a more valuable business model. Figure 8.1 outlines the evolution of the education system. Whereas Education 1.0 encourages practice memorization done through centuries. Later Education 2.0 encouraged learning through the internet. Education 3.0 enhances the consumption of knowledge and labour. Finally, Education 4.0 encourages all three versions as well as incite students to create.

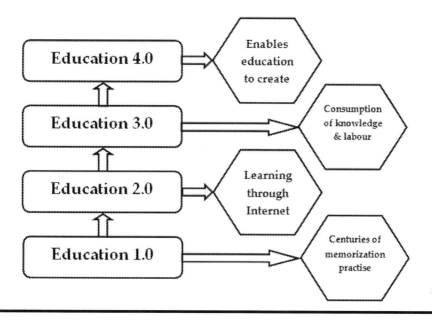

Figure 8.1   Growth of education system.

8.2.4 *Influence of Industrial Revolution 4.0 on Higher Education*

Higher education in the fourth industrial revolution (HE 4.0) is a vibrant door, rational, and openness that alters the consideration of the public and improves the standard of human living. The HE 4.0 has been activated by blending all the three former versions that have been modified by the working atmosphere in the midpoint of the administrative centers. The blend of machines and humans minimizes the partitioning of sociological disciplines and humanizing the machines that are being practiced among science and innovation. Revolution in education has made several advancements in the teaching methods and enrichment in the contents. In this kind of education system, the availability of books, teaching contents, and other information is displayed through the internet. Numerous alterations have been made for future teaching approaches (Teaching tools 2012). Figure 8.2 shows the impact of the industrial revolution on Education 4.0.

8.3 Conceptual Framework of Big Data for Industry 4.0

The architecture of the conceptual framework is composed of four modules such as the design of the Big Data application, input data streams for pre-processing, distributed infrastructure and results. Figure 8.3 explains the conceptual framework of Big Data for industry 4.0.

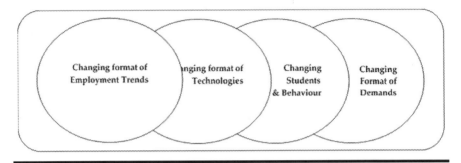

Figure 8.2   Impact of industrial revolution on Education 4.0.

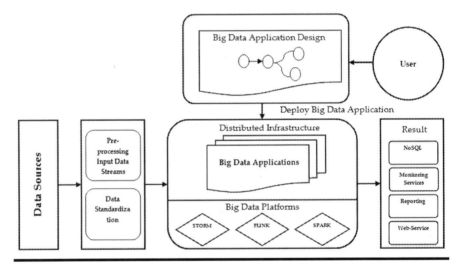

Figure 8.3   Conceptual framework of Big Data.

8.3.1 *Big Data Application Design*

This module helps the system engineers to extend their own Big Data applications with the availability of visual editors. The developed applications are signified as directed graphs and the vertices help in denoting the data mining and machine learning methods as well as the construction of programmes. The generation of data takes place at the programming nodes and similar standards are used in handling the data from a variety of sources that is shown in Figure 8.4. The obtained data sources are integrated with varied programming nodes. Figure 8.4 explains the Big Data analytics programming model, and Figure 8.5 displays the outline of the Big Data analytics and business analytics in the Hadoop framework.

With the help of programming nodes, application logic is generated without taking the internal data and interfaces. A huge number of data sources were

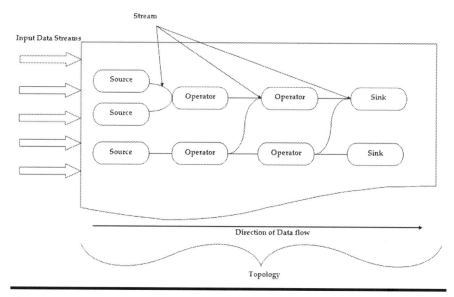

Figure 8.4   Big Data analytics programming model.

accumulated with the platform to reclaim the related information of varied features of a factory. The heterogeneity of the data results from disparate data formats. Therefore, the format of the data is a significant challenge in utilizing Big Data analytics in Industry 4.0.

8.3.2 Preprocessing Input Data Streams

This module is employed to change data into a general format that is used for further data processing. Pre-processing is developed based on data standardization that explains a general standard for obtaining unstructured, semi-structured, and structured data from numerous numbers and varied resources. To maintain the Big Data use cases, the instilled application requires rapid and scalable infrastructures. Preprocessing module plays a central role in the Big Data framework.

8.3.3 Distributed Infrastructure

The main phase of the Big Data platform is developed on a distributed infrastructure. Automatics deployment of the application is carried on the distributed infrastructure that is a user-defined application. Depending on the use cases, the necessity for processing varies and it relies on the nature of the data. It supports multiple platforms of Big Data, namely Flink, Spark, and Storm. The design of the framework depends on the nature of the data format. Use cases and logic perform a major role in designing the framework.

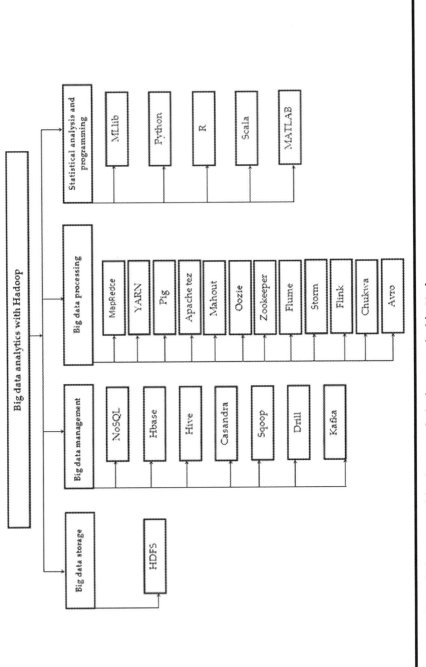

Figure 8.5   Outline of Big Data and business analytical process inside Hadoop.

8.3.4 Distribution of Results

Different kinds of forms are designed based on the interest of the parties and the results are forwarded to the relevant forms. The channel of every distribution is explained as a programming node in the visual editors. Users are permitted to select more than one channel of distribution to retrieve the results. In this way, some kind of production issues will be forwarded to the relevant staff. The manufacturing process is improved with this kind of framework and the data-driven decisions are enriched. Delivery of the output to the peripheral entities through web services for data visualization or supervising purposes is facilitated with this framework (Gokalp et al., 2016). Table 8.1 explains some of the tools that are used in Big Data analytics and their features are illustrated.

8.4 Business Analytics

To analyze the past transactions in a structured database management system (DBMS) business intelligence and business analytics were used. The arrival of Big Data and Big Data analytic approaches offer chances of attaining reasonable insights into the data with the assistance of tools and processes. The implementation of the analytical process is observed in text analytics, structured data analytics, network analytics, web analytics, and mobile analytics. Due to the velocity and volume of the data, data analytical tools are used that identify the foreseen future and make novel discoveries. In business, the data related to business demand for business analytics and intelligence.

Moreover, prominent business analytic approaches have been employed over the business data and business-oriented applications reported by a wide range of industries and business firms. In most of the developed countries, they have attained success in the business with the incorporation of the Big Data analytic and business analytic approaches, and the developing countries have also been exercising the same method. Business analytics is the prioritized Information Technology in business firms that is identified by the international data corporation (IDC). The identification through various researches spotted the business practice and many of the business firms use traditional approaches for handling the data that is stored over the spreadsheet. Business analytics have shown sensible growth in many business firms. Nonetheless, it is widely applied in the business units or within the departments.

Besides, business firms are in exploration of analytics which principally assists in enriching the bottom line, minimizing the costs, and some handling factors that raise risks. Meanwhile, business organizations have faced the arrival of business analytics with fear of meeting the feasibility, consistency, data accuracy, and even access of data. Most of the business firms lack in skills to execute the analytics and some of the business organizations have used the analytic process,

Table 8.1 Big Analytics Tools and Their Features

S. No.	Tool	Feature	Inference	Reference
1.	Hadoop Distributed File System (HDFS)	Employed for storing enormous volume of data. It is highly scalable and fault-resistant.	The data is written in many files after reading from the storage. It is an inexpensive system for storing huge data.	(Tom, 2012)
2.	NoSQL	The process of querying, managing and storing the data.	It offers elasticity and supports multiple hosts. It reduces computational complexity.	(Tom, 2012)
3.	Hbase	View of data in column orientation is attained.	It supports the aggregation operation	[Apache Hbase]
4.	Cassandra	Developed for Facebook and a large volume of data is analyzed.	It supports high throughput and immediate response time.	[Apache Cassandra]
5.	Apache Hive	It acts like a SQL interface. It performs operations, namely querying and summarization	The indexing approach is used for managing and writing huge data.	[Apache Hive]
6.	Sqoop	It facilitates the importing and exporting of data.	It minimizes the processing time and offers offloading computation	[Apache Sqoop]
7.	YARN	It acts as an operating system for Hadoop 2.0. It performs allocation of resources and scheduling of the relevant job.	Availability is offered and effective utilization of the resource is achieved by YARN.	[Apache YARN]

(Continued)

Table 8.1 (Continued) Big Analytics Tools and Their Features

S. No.	Tool	Feature	Inference	Reference
8.	Mahout	A huge array of processing schemes is introduced.	It facilitates distributed mining	[Apache Mahout]
9.	Oozie	It acts as a coordination tool for the parallel job in the Hadoop Cluster.	It permits workflow and offers web service API	[Apache Ooozie]
10.	Apache Tez	A directed acyclic graph is used to state the performance of data and defines workflow.	A simplified interface facilitates quick data processing.	[Apache Tez]
11.	Flink	It handles batch and streaming process	Fault endurance mechanism is offered by snapshot and offers single runtime background.	[Apache Flink]
12.	Flume	It retrieves the data from in and out of Hadoop	Transmission of huge streaming data to the HDFS is attained.	[Apache Flume]
13.	R Programming	It is an open-source programming language. Vector-based operations are performed. Complex data handling, analysis of those data, and visualization of data are attained with R Programming.	It provides support for the operations like data reading, writing, removing noise, machine learning, etc.	[The R Project for Statistical Computing]

(Continued)

Table 8.1 (Continued) Big Analytics Tools and Their Features

S. No.	Tool	Feature	Inference	Reference
14.	Python Programming	It offers a huge number of open-source packages and natural language processing as well as machine learning.	It supports multiple platforms for data processing, user-friendly, flexible, and object-oriented approach.	[Python Programming]
15.	Scala Programming	It supports multifaceted applications and Big Data processing. It manages all the processes through Apache Spark. Java Virtual Machine (JVM) is needed for the development of a complicated application.	It is inherently immutable	[The R Project for Statistical Computing]
16.	Pig	It supports the representation of data flow.	It makes the mining process easy by eliminating the complicated MapReduce approach	[Apache Pig]
17.	Sqoop	Large datasets are imported and exported	It minimizes the processing time and computational offloading	[Apache Sqoop]
18.	Apache Spark	Machine learning and real-time processing	It provides effective reading and writing operation	[Apache Spark]

(Continued)

Table 8.1 (Continued)   Big Analytics Tools and Their Features

S. No.	Tool	Feature	Inference	Reference
19.	MapReduce	It supports Job management and helps to schedule the resources and batch processing	It is cost-effective and highly scalable	[Apache MapReduce]
20.	Storm	It performs online real-time data processing	It offers non- complicated operations	[Apache Storm]
21.	Zookeeper	Roust synchronization process is accomplished	It provides serialization, and availability, and reduces the inconsistency	[Apache Zookeeper]
22.	Chukwa	It monitors the distributed system	It offers the features of visualization	[Apache Chukwa]
23.	Avro	Data reduction and query processing are initiated	It offers enhancement in query processing	[Apache Avro]
24.	MLib	It offers interoperability	MLlib is fault- resistant and reusable	[Apache MLib]

but they have failed to use the outcomes. Business organizations have used "analytics culture" to benefit from the advantages of their analytics in the investments. Therefore, establishing the bridge among the gap of the business group to utilize the Big Data and business analytics in their business data is essential for proficiency in making decisions and enhancing success rate in the business. These teams comprise Big Data analysts, business experts, Hadoop operators, Big Data architectures, and engineers. Figure 8.6 illustrates the Big Data analytics for business analytics.

8.4.1 Business Analytics vs. Business Intelligence

8.4.1.1 Business Analytics (BA)

Recent researches have shown that business analytics is more proficient than the normal analytical process. It explores business data with an accent on statistical examination and performs an iterative operation. Data-driven decisions are carried out with the help of business analytics that the companies incorporate the analytics which is committed in judgment on the decisions. To attain deep insight into business planning, analytics has to be performed on the past business performance that refers to a continuous practice on iterative examination, numerical analysis, technologies, predictive modeling, and skills. New insights have been framed based on the observation of business data and statistical methods.

Business analytics uses the blend of descriptive, diagnostic, predictive, and prescriptive analytics. Descriptive analytics explains the occurrence of the data, diagnostic explains the reason for the occurrence, predictive explains future occurrence and prescriptive explains the future occurrence. Analyzed data is retrieved from the data of business reports, business databases, and cloud data. Business analytics performs the operations of reporting the outcomes regarding the business intelligence.

8.4.1.2 Business Intelligence (BI)

Business intelligence focuses on reporting and querying the business data. It also includes the report of data from an approach called business analytics (BA). Moreover, business intelligence responds to the questions such as what is occurring now and where, and also what business steps are required based on the former incident. Business intelligence (BI) focuses on a set of metrics that are used in measuring the previous performance and regulation on business planning and it is associated with management science. Business intelligence is a contrast factor of business analytics. Automated and human decisions are attained from the result of analytics. Big Data and business analytics are the recent trends that optimistically attract the business world. Development in the industry has made data analytics and business analytics the most needed factors. Revolution in the technology is termed 4.0 and the relevant teaching concepts are stated as Education 4.0 shown in Figure 8.6.

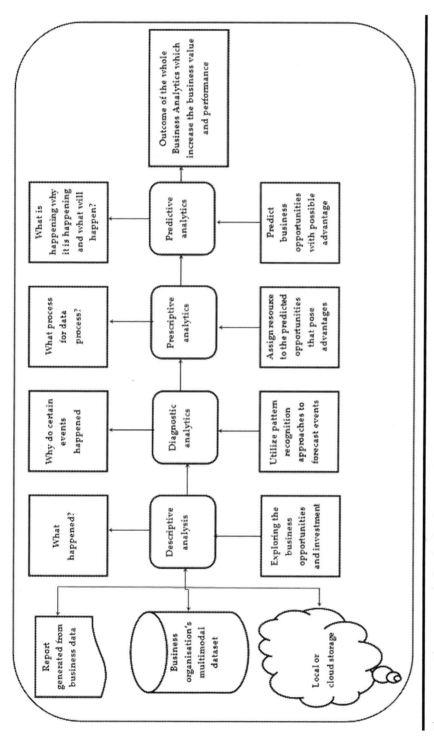

Figure 8.6 Big Data analytics for business analytics.

8.5 Applications of Big Data and Business Analytics

Numerous areas of industry and business firms have gained needed data from the process of analytics through the technology called Big Data analytics. Proficient decision-making and effective data processing from the generated data are achieved by analytical process (Hashem et al., 2015; Wang et al., 2016). The key application areas of Big Data and business analytics are elucidated in Table 8.2.

8.6 Challenges of Big Data and Business Analytics

The data generated from various resources is turned to be Big Data that is not equal to good data. The data may come with imperfect data that is due to the concert of the imperfect world. Some of these issues are outlined below.

8.6.1 Uncertainty of Data Management

Due to the varied structure of data, they are generated across the world by various sources. Numerous challenges are raised while storing and managing the data.

8.6.2 Talent Gap

Big Data analysts lack in skills to handle the available Big Data–based technologies in the market. Apart from the aspects of Big Data management, the distinctive expertise has also gathered knowledge via the usage of tools and it is incorporated as a model of programming.

8.6.3 Synchronising the Data Sources

The needed data is imported into the Big Data infrastructure that has migrated from a variety of resources. Different transmission rates of the data may relay out of the synchronization. It is a major issue in Big Data.

8.6.4 Issues with Data Integration

As the count of data consumers increases, the necessity to maintain the growing collection of various instantaneous usages of users also increases. The increase of requirement spikes at any time in reaction to varied characteristics of the processing cycle of business. Integration of data and assuring the availability of data at the right time to the consumers of data is a huge issue.

Table 8.2 Key Data Sources and Applications of Big Data and Business Analytics

S.No.	Applications	Data Sources	Characteristics	Reference
1.	Healthcare	Health history of patients, Electronic Health Record (EHR), Medical images, Patients data.	Supports enriched monitoring of health, Analysis of patient immune system, a recommendation system for elderly patients	(Wang et al., 2016; Wyber et al., 2015; Khatib et al., 2016)
2.	Network Optimization	Weblog, data of geolocation, sensor data, network user information, Network signal information	Supports Proficient network signaling, identification of variation in network, and managing the network.	(Dobre et al., 2014; De Domenico et al., 2015)
3.	Travel Estimation	GPS data, Call Data Record (CDR), location data, personal information satellite imagery	Offers data for complicated routes, tracking location, military operation-based recommendation, identification of disease, and emergency condition.	(Dong et al., 2015; Lokanathan et al., 2016; Douglass et al., 2015; Lima 2016)
4.	User Behaviour Modelling	Log data, product review, blog post, social media data, and tweets	Proficient service recommendation	(Finger et al., 2016)
5.	Human Mobility Modelling	GPS, Location data.	Supports transportation planning and preserves global movement pattern to facilitate disease containment	(Zhan et al., 2014; Salehan & Kim, 2016; Chatzimilioudis et al., 2012)
6.	Suggestion of services	Reviews provided by the customer, location data,	Enriches product buying using customer and potential of products	(Chatzimilioudis et al., 2012)

(Continued)

Table 8.2 (Continued) Key Data Sources and Applications of Big Data and Business Analytics

S.No.	Applications	Data Sources	Characteristics	Reference
		electing the product, buying behavior data		
7.	Energy Consumption Analysis	Gas status, location data, consumption pattern, and data of meter and usage history.	Endorses green energy, attains proficiency through the utilization of energy, prediction, and conservation	(Hashem et al., 2015)
8.	Crowdsourcing and Sensing	Sensor-based sensing data such as accelerometer, magnetometer, gyroscopes, pulse rate, other data sources such as online Questionnaire and survey.	Approaches for huge compilation of data	(Yang et al., 2017)
9.	Educational Progression	Information regarding personal, Enrolment, examination, allocation, and contents data.	Spots the student enrolment and rate of failures after the completion of a specific course or session	(Mohammadi et al., 2018; Ochoa et al., 2017)
10.	Financial Groups	Reports related to financial, blog post, news related to the stock, social media, and regular annual meeting related information	Offers a system for the identification of fraud activity; stirs decision-making for mitigates the circumstances regarding laundering of money.	(Bhadani & Jothimani, 2016)

8.7 Open Research Directions

A tremendous amount of benefit has been attained by the use of Big Data and related tools. For a business class, this technology has made a close relationship between a company and the customer. The data generated in today's world is huge and the variations of the data are also high. The researchers are developing various algorithms for offering security mechanism which assures the dynamic security features for the heterogeneous kind of the data (Ochoa et al., 2017). To analyze the data of various kinds, algorithms and relevant frameworks are developed. Moreover, other approaches in Big Data are aggregation and data cleaning. In the process of recent exploration of mobile big data, the method of data is examined for behavioral analysis, advertising the target, identification of crime regions with the hotspot significance, and supervision of disaster occurrences (Xu et al., 2016).

The distinguished Industry 4.0 period applied sciences as huge data, synthetic intelligence, augmented reality, MR, and VR have a necessary role in schooling except for different areas. Big Data evaluation is one of the revolutionary science tendencies in the Education 4.0 era. Big statistics are consisted of data received from the traces of one-of-a-kind sorts of digital environments and offer a chance to analyze in accordance with the requirements.to consider information as huge data, it is anticipated that it will consist of five factors recognized as the 5V model: variety, velocity, volume, accuracy, and value. Big records evaluation has created new challenges and opportunities in schooling as nicely as many different fields.in mastering processes, it is viable to use large facts with the possibilities provided via learning analytics.

Learning analytics is described as collecting, measuring analyzing, and reporting information about beginners to apprehend and enhance getting to know environments. The foundation of the innovative and productive training strategy of training four is primarily based on personalized learning in personalized learning, the content material has introduced the use of the most terrific learning methods and techniques to optimize gaining knowledge of experiences based totally o the evaluation of students educational active, among different fabulous technological know-how developments and progressive applications, data analytics will be of precise significance for the education of college student with private learning difficulties. The synergy created by the way of studying analytics and synthetic brain permits the evaluation of performance, figuring out the relationship between materials, teachers, and programs, figuring capacity and needs, and creating instructional content material at exceptional stages of difficulty. It is of great importance to growing a gaining knowledge of application in line with the person mastering desires of this technology and to spotlight challenging issues. Student overall performance reviews received through gaining knowledge of analytics will additionally assist instructors to higher appreciate their students. In this manner, the will power of students will be made strong.

In the close to future, the mixture of synthetic genius and smart structures is expected to enable laptop packages to predict pupil responses and assist instructors to diagram their own customized, adaptive tutoring systems. The greater computers become acquainted with learner behaviors, the greater computerized character assignment, grading, and creation of new content material is anticipated in the close to future learning and MOOC training. A growing quantity of statistics is viewed to be necessary for phrases of analyzing learner behaviors in online gaining knowledge of environments and growing mastering environments appropriate to the person profile. The use of large records evaluation and synthetic genius in educational processes is predicted to be automatic in the future with the aid of structuring courses, asserting and educational assets, and the use of dynamic algorithms in accordance with scholar stages

Deep learning-based approaches are automatically needed data illustration schemes for the analysis of huge data and are mostly employed in the fields of natural language processing, image classification, human activity recognition and medical diagnosis with electronic gadgets, and other information related to the cyber-physical system. Several deep-learning approaches have been developed for the estimation of data models of various variations. The Big Data area needs further research in data fusion for the well-organized examination of data. The assimilation of heterogeneous or homogenous data raises the reliability, generalizability and robustness of Big Data analytics algorithms. Areas that need to be researched in the future are Internet of Things (IoT)–related application with the incorporation of a cyber-physical system, assessments infusion for the improved generality and multiplicity and to handle the heterogeneous kind of data and recognizing the connotation of the modality of data (Nweke et al., 2018; Nweke et al., 2019).

8.8 Conclusion

Big Data applications and tools are used for analyzing the huge data that are generated from various resources. These tools were developed by various companies, namely Google, LinkedIn, Twitter, and Yahoo that are all open source tools. The developed tools have shown a low level of complexity that has made the researchers and programmers make use of them for data analysis. Big Data–based domain, and data flow models can eliminate the issues by permitting the programmers to continuously design new approaches that can use the most of real-time data. In business groups, individuals can rapidly establish small programs to explore whether there is any competence or issues with quality in the production and processing of services. These approaches are significant steps toward the Industry and Education Vision 4.0.

References

Apache Avro. Retrieved April 12, 2020, from https://avro.apache.org/
Apache Cassandra. Retrieved April 12, 2020, from http://cassandra.apache.org/

Apache Chukwa. Retrieved April 12, 2020, from https://chukwa.apache.org/

Apache Flink. Retrieved April 12, 2020, from https://flink.apache.org/

Apache Flume. Retrieved April 12, 2020, from https://flume.apache.org/

Apache HBase. Retrieved April 12, 2020, from http://hbase.apache.org/

Apache Hive. Retrieved April 12, 2020, from http://hive.apache.org/

Apache Oozie Workflow Scheduler for Hadoop. Retrieved April 12, 2020, from http://oozie.apache.org/

Apache Pig. Retrieved April 12, 2020, from http://pig.apache.org/

Apache Spark. Retrieved April 12, 2020, from https://spark.apache.org/

Apache Sqoop. Retrieved April 12, 2020, from http://sqoop.apache.org/

Apache Storm. Retrieved April 12, 2020, from https://storm.apache.org/

Apache Tez. Retrieved April 12, 2020, from http://tez.apache.org/

Apache Zookeeper. Retrieved April 12, 2020, from https://zookeeper.apache.org/

Bhadani, A. K., & Jothimani, D. (2016). *Big data: Challenges, opportunities, and realities. Effective big data management and opportunities for implementation* (pp. 1–24). Hershey, PA: IGI Global.

Bloomberg Businessweek Research Services, The current state of business analytics: Where do we go from here? Retrieved April 12, 2020, from https://www.sas.com sources/asset/busanalyticssstudy_wp_08232011.pdf

Chahal, H., Jyoti, J., & Wirtz, J. (2019). Business analytics: Concept and applications. In *Understanding the role of business analytics* (pp. 1–8). Singapore: Springer.

Chatzimilioudis, G., et al. (2012). Crowdsourcing with smartphones. *IEEE Internet Computing, 16*(5), 36–44.

Davenport, T. (2014). *Big data at work: Dispelling the myths, uncovering the opportunities.* Boston, MA: Harvard Business Review Press.

Davenport, T., & Harris, J. (2017). *Competing on analytics: Updated, with a new introduction: The new science of winning.* Boston, MA: Harvard Business Press.

Davenport, T. H., Barth, P., & Bean, R. (2012).How "big data" is different. *MIT Sloan Management Review, 54*(1), 43–46.

De Domenico, M., Lima, A., González, M. C., & Arenas, A. (2015). Personalized routing for multitudes in smart cities. *EPJ Data Science, 4*(1), 1.

Dobre, C., & Xhafa, F. (2014). Intelligent services for big data science. *Future Generation Computer Systems, 37*, 267–281.

Dong, H., et al. (2015). Traffic zone division based on big data from mobile phone base stations. *Transportation Research Part C: Emerging Technologies, 58*, 278–291.

Douglass, R. W., et al. (2015). High resolution population estimates from telecommunications data. *EPJ Data Science, 4*(1), 4.

Finger, F., et al. (2016). Mobile phone data highlights the role of mass gatherings in the spreading of cholera outbreaks. *Proceedings of the National Academy of Sciences, 113*(23), 6421–6426.

Gokalp, M., et al. (2016). Big data for industry 4.0: A conceptual framework. 2016 International Conference on Computational Science and Computational Intelligence (CSCI). IEEE.

Grover, V., et al. (2018). Creating strategic business value from big data analytics: A research framework. *Journal of Management Information Systems, 35*(2), 388–423.

Hashem, Ibrahim AbakerTargio, et al. (2015). The rise of "big data" on cloud computing: Review and open research issues. *Information Systems, 47*, 98–115.

IDC. *Big data big opportunities*. Retrieved April 12, 2020, from http://www.emc.com/microsites/cio/articles/big-databig-opportunities/LCIA-Big Data Opportunities -Value.pdf

Jackson, T. W., & Lockwood, S. (2018). *Business analytics: A contemporary approach.* London: Macmillan International Higher Education.

Khatib, E.J., Barco, R., Munoz, P., La Bandera, I. D., & Serrano, I. (2016). Self-healing in mobile networks with big data. *IEEE Communications Magazine, 54*(1), 114–120.

LaValle, S., et al. (2010). Analytics: The new path to value. *MIT Sloan Management Review, 52*(1), 1–25.

LaValle, S., et al. (2011). Big data, analytics and the path from insights to value. *MIT Sloan Management review, 52*(2), 21–32.

Lim, E.-P., Chen, H., & Chen, G. (2013). Business intelligence and analytics: Research directions. *ACM Transactions on Management Information Systems (TMIS), 3*(4), 1–10.

Lima, A. (2016). *Digital traces of human mobility and interaction: Models and applications.* Dissertation, University of Birmingham.

Lokanathan, S., et al. (2016). The potential of mobile network big data as a tool in Colombo's transportation and urban planning. *Information Technologies & International Development, 12*(2), 63.

Mahout. Retrieved April 12, 2020, from http://mahout.apache.org/

MLLib. Retrieved April 12, 2020, from https://spark.apache.org/mllib/

Mohammadi, M., et al. (2018). Deep learning for IoT big data and streaming analytics: A survey. *IEEE Communications Surveys & Tutorials, 20*(4), 2923–2960.

Nweke, H. F., et al. (2018). Deep learning algorithms for human activity recognition using mobile and wearable sensor networks: State of the art and research challenges. *Expert Systems with Applications, 105*, 233–261.

Nweke, H. F., et al. (2019). Data fusion and multiple classifier systems for human activity detection and health monitoring: Review and open research directions. *Information Fusion, 46*, 147–170.

Ochoa, S. F., Fortino, G., & Di Fatta, G. (2017). Cyber-physical systems, internet of things and big data. *Future Generation Computer Systems, 75*, 82–84.

Python Programming. Retrieved April 12, 2020, from https://www.python.org/

Salehan, M., & Kim, D. J. (2016). Predicting the performance of online consumer reviews: A sentiment mining approach to big data analytics. *Decision Support Systems, 81*, 30–40.

Stubbs, E. (2011). *The value of business analytics.* Hoboken, NJ: John Wiley & Sons.

Teaching tools (edudemic). (2012). *10 incredible powerful tools of the future.* Retrieved from https://educationprospector.wordpress.com/2012/08/18/teaching-toolsedudemic.

The R Project for Statistical Computing. Retrieved April 12, 2020, from http://www.r-project.org/

Tom, W. (2012). Mobile big data fault-tolerant processing for ehealth network. *IEEE Network, 30*(1), 36–42. Hadoop: The definitive guide (p. 36). Newton, MA: O'Reilly Media, Inc.

Wang, K., Shao, Y., Shu, L., Zhu, C., & Zhang, Y. (2016). Mobile big data fault-tolerant processing for ehealth networks. *IEEE Network, 30*(1), 36–42.

Watson, H.J. (2009). Tutorial: Business intelligence – Past, present, and future. *Communications of the Association for Information Systems, 25*(1), 39.

Wyber, R., Vaillancourt, S., Perry, W., Mannava, P., Folaranmi, T., & Celi, L.A. (2015). Big data in global health: Improving health in low-and middle-income countries. *Bulletin of the World Health Organization, 93*, 203–208.

Xu, Z., et al. (2016). Crowdsourcing based description of urban emergency events using social media big data. *IEEE Transactions on Cloud Computing, 8*(2), 387–397.

Yang, T.-Y., et al. (2017). Behavior-based grade prediction for MOOCs via time series neural networks. *IEEE Journal of Selected Topics in Signal Processing, 11*(5), 716–728.

Zhan, X., Ukkusuri, S. V., & Zhu, F. (2014). Inferring urban land use using large-scale social media check-in data. *Networks and Spatial Economics, 14*(3–4), 647–667.

Chapter 9

Role of Big Data Analytics in the Financial Service Sector

V. Ramanujam[1,3] and D. Napoleon[2,3]

[1]*Associate Professor, Bharathiar School of Management and Entrepreneur Development, Bharathiar University, Coimbatore, India*
[2]*Assistant Professor, Department of Computer Science, School of Computer Science and Engineering, Bharathiar University, Coimbatore, India*
[3]*Corresponding author*

Contents

DOI: 10.1201/9781003175889-9

Objectives

This chapter aims to focus on:

1. To understand the meaningful data that have been gathering for decades, the Big Data movement occurring in and around the 21st century has found a resonance with banking firms.
2. To understand the Big Data effect and usage of Big Data in the financial or service or banking industry.
3. To understand the feature, prospects, leverage, and significant role in the banking industry and also Big Data's advantages in the financial sector.
4. To recognize the various scenarios in big data in the banking, financial services, and insurance industries, where analytics is becoming increasingly important and the potential benefits of new-age technologies.

9.1 Introduction

The first wave of the industrial revolution upheaval happened from the 17th century to the mid of 18th century. This industrialization the manufacturing yard goods began the shift of manufacture starting from homes to industrial units. Steam power and the cotton gin played a significant function in this period. The next revolution insurgency began in an assembly line on permitted knowledge specialization, represented by the Ford engine mechanical production system in the 20th century. The third industrial revolution accompanied the quality control system through the Japanese approach and media transmission innovation utilization. Industry 4.0 (European) or fourth industrial revolution is the utilization of Artificial Intelligence, robotics, inventive plan, and rapid figuring ability to upset creation, appropriation, and utilization. Monetary economics is contributory to a genuine financial system, and the motivation is to provide genuine manufacturing. The early fund was about the account of exchange and governments to take part in the war. Finance 3.0 was the period of monetary-related derivatives, in which multipart subordinates turned out to be hazy to the point that financial specialists and regulators acknowledged that they became what called "weapons of mass demolition."

The basic meaning of Industry 4.0 is the gradient of new technologies such as Artificial Intelligence, cloud computing, and the Internet of Things (IoT). IoT implies that digital physical frameworks could connect among one another to deliver appropriate information and exchange in a dispersed production system. Industry 4.0 is changing how manufacturing companies work together, shaping a new world that will carefully associate people, frameworks, and hardware through mechanization. As conventional models of assembling keep on being disturbed by patterns, such as Artificial Intelligence (AI), organizations are at risk for falling behind because of the absence of crucial arranging outfitted towards authoritative change, digital challenges, and implementation. The premise for this year was mastering the fourth industrial revolution, or in laymen's terms, how we will deal with the obscuring of lines among man and machine. Each past industrial revolution – marked by the advent of mechanical creation, the development of power, and the rise of the computer – represented a tremendous advance in human progression. The fourth industrial revolution marks the next stage in this movement, and driving organizations have just started to adjust their business approach for the digital age.

9.2 The Effect of Finance 4.0 in a Nutshell

Innovation has been changing how business organizations work, and it's the same in the services industry like the finance industry. Innovation could bring that the budgetary foundations need to comprehend just not benefits of executing a specific innovation yet besides how it will affect their businesses. As the new technology or cutting edge innovations such as IoT, Artificial Intelligence, and robotics process automation are driving the next industrial revolution – alluded to as the next version of the industry. These innovations can change the finance industry with Finance 4.0. With such many sorts of innovations available, it is hard to determine which ones will be the most appropriate to your finance department. Past seeing how a piece of technology works, organizations need to remember the effect of innovation comparable to the guidelines governing the finance industry.

9.2.1 Data Revolution

Industry 4.0 has seen data supplant capital as the primary resource of driving how finance operates, with data at the focal point of plans of action. Amidst the data revolution, associations rely upon organized, sorted out data that isn't just available. Finance has been creating fastidiously organized information for registering frameworks for a considerable length of time, as evidenced by protocols such as double-entry bookkeeping. Organized data has consistently been an essential piece

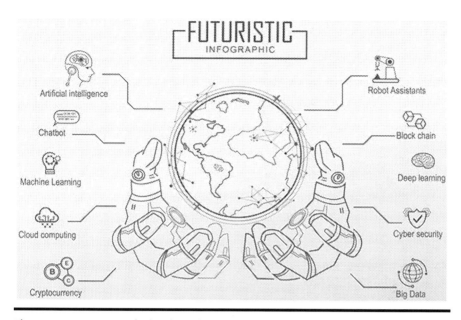

FUTURISTIC
INFOGRAPHIC

Artificial intelligence

Chatbot

Machine Learning

Cloud computing

Cryptocurrency

Robot Assistants

Block chain

Deep learning

Cyber security

Big Data

Figure 9.1 Data revolution in Industry 4.0.

of finance. In any case, digital transformation and globalization have forced organizations to accomplish more with less, with many now adopting a data-driven approach, retaking a gander at empowering innovation that underpins granular details and integrated analytics (Figure 9.1).

Data is nowadays not only the liability of each business but it is also a business-wide accountability as well. First, industrial revolution changed the nature of work forever by bringing people under the same roof, the fourth industrial revolution leads to inclination away from in-office functioning to further assert the 21st-century chestnut of café-working and beyond. Data-driven decision making and knowledge will lead to leaner, more efficient organizations.

Without frameworks like enterprise resource planning (ERP), numerous associations are compelled to utilize different programmers across departments. ERP frameworks separate these data silos, helping businesses analyze data to utilize assets more adequately and productively, accordingly, bringing significant business value and understanding. Along these lines, much like Industry 4.0, finance is data driven, so it would be exceptional if the benefits of this new era did not carry over into the world of finance.

9.2.2 What Does Finance 4.0 Mean?

Detach Finance 4.0 from the previous version is the onset of blockchain or disseminated ledger tools. The perfect approach to reflect on the subject is the structural design of the two different frameworks. Finance 3.0 and previous structure were about hierarchical ledger structure, related to a pyramid, in which barter and arrangements between two parties are matured over a higher testimony. It is called "shadow banking" frame that money-connected controllers and central banks or financial service providers beneficially point the finger at on their incapability to observe or discontinue the most recent worldwide monetary disaster.

9.2.3 The Revolution of Finance Industry

Intellectual technology, such as the Internet of Things (IoT), Artificial Intelligence (AI), and other cutting-edge innovations, are propelling the global economy into a new digital era following the computer age. In this "transformative age," industry disturbance is normal, and change to turn into a wise venture is the road to business endurance. The request for the day in this revolution is versatility. However, like never before, being nimble as a venture implies empowering readiness across organizational units in a manner that makes versatility, understanding, and cost-effective operation. All lines of business need to meet up and work pair to convey the sorts of encounters that customers expect in the digital economy.

9.2.4 Embrace Industry 4.0 in Finance Industry

Industry 4.0 has impacted a scope of enterprises and with the digitization of industrial worth chains, many disregard finance, which has possibly contacted a glimpse of something larger with regards to utilizing innovations. Disruptive technologies are pushing the worldwide economy into the new digital era.

9.2.5 Banking and Big Data

9.2.5.1 Easy to Customer Segment Identification

Customer segmentation has become common in the financial services industry, allowing depository and credit unions to separate their clients into perfect classifications by segmentation. However, basic segmentation results in a lack of granularity, which these institutions need to comprehend their clients' needs and requirements truly. Rather, these organizations must employ technology to advance to the next echelon by constructing point-by-point customer reports.

This outline should include a variety of elements, such as:

a. The segmentation of the customer
b. How numerous records they have
c. Which items they at present have
d. The deals they've previously turned down
e. Which product they're most likely to purchase in the future
f. Their relationships with various clients

g. Their attitude toward their bank and financial services in general

h. Behavioral designs

9.2.5.2 Adopt the Customized Familiarity

Almost a third of clients expect the companies for which they operate to know personal information about them; in reality, a third of clients who ended a business relationship a year ago did so because of a lack of personalization in the service they received. For those banks and credit unions who want to stay in business: However, if you want to succeed, you'll need a banking investigation that's set up to travel in the background and a personalised client experience.

9.2.5.3 Client Behavioral Approach

Practically, the big data in the financial sector is created by customers, during dealings, or by contacts between sales groups and administration delegates. Despite the fact that all forms of client data are valuable, information gathered through exchanges provides banks with a clear picture of their customers' buying habits and, over time, broader behavioural models.

9.2.5.4 Profit-Sharing Possibilities

The company could offer the 60–70% bound to availed clients after that the possibilities, which means strategically pitching and up selling at hand simple open doors for the service providers or financial institutions to expand their income share and opportunities made significantly simpler with the analytics of big data in the financial sector.

9.2.5.5 Deduction of Deceitful Performance

Personality extortion is one of the most prevalent and rapidly growing forms of data misrepresentation. In 2017, the total number of causalities is 16.7 million compared to last year that the causalities followed a record high in 2016. The bank or financial services providers could monitor the customer spending designs and distinguish unusual behavior as one method of using Big Data to prevent misrepresentation and make consumers feel safer about their experience.

9.3 Big Data in the Banking Industry

In today's information-rich environment, data plays a significant role. Knowledge is used to make important basic decisions such as policymaking, budget report investigation, and banking rules and guidelines. We obtain data for analysis from a variety of sources, some of which are mentioned below:

a. Personal information about the customer
b. Account information
c. Transactions with customers
d. Feedback and service requests from customers
e. Feeds from social media
f. Market attitude
g. Product efficiency, and so on

Big Data analytics is helping banks overcome major business problems such as gainfulness, execution, and risk availability. It also aids banks in lowering client acquisition costs, predicting contract default risk, and, most significantly, finding genuine clients.

9.3.1 Four V's of Big Data

Volume, variety, veracity, and velocity are the four V's of big data. Confronting expanding rivalry, administrative requirements, and client needs, monetary foundations look for better approaches to use innovation to pick up proficiency. Contingent upon the business, organizations can take advantage of specific aspects of Big Data to achieve a competitive advantage. The four V's of Big Data that can be used in the banking industry are:

a. **Variety:** Different information types are needed to store various types of data. Banks generate various types of data, such as customer data, value-based data, transactional data, financial assessments, credit ratings, loan descriptions, and so on.
b. **Velocity:** It has to do with how quickly new information is applied to the bank's database.
c. **Veracity**: It refers to the unfairness, clamor, and irregularity in data or data analytics. The data is being stored, mined in meaningful to the problem being analyzed. The reality in data analytics is the biggest confront when contrast to the effects of quantity and speed.
d. **Volume**: It is the amount of space needed to store this data. Every day, massive budgetary organisations like the Bombay Stock Exchange generate terabytes of data.

Big data may be classified as either unstructured or structured data.

Data that is sloppy and does not fit into a predetermined model would be classified as unstructured data. This includes knowledge gathered from social media outlets, which aids organisations in gathering information on client requirements. Data previously supervised by the company in social databases and spreadsheets makes up organized material. As a result, different types of data must be carefully controlled in order to educate informed business decisions.

The growing volume of market data is putting financial institutions to the test. Banking and capital markets must efficiently manage ticker information in addition to large amounts of historical data. Similarly, investment banks and resource management companies depend on a wealth of data to make sound business decisions. For competitive hazard management, insurance and retirement companies may access historical approach and claims data.

9.3.2 Arrangement of Big Data

Every day, 3.5 quintillion bytes of data are generated, and not all of it fits into a single classification. Large information can be exemplified in three ways:

a. **Organized:** This type of data is incredibly well crafted and exists in a predefined format, such as a CSV file.
b. **Unorganized:** There is no predefined information in this type of data, and the design is not fair. Messages may be a blueprint. It is very hard to access information.
c. **Partially Organized:** While semi-organized can appear unstructured at first glance, keywords are used in the preparation process.

Large amounts of data are easily accessible, necessitating advanced preparation methods to translate them into meaningful, noteworthy information.

The most powerful way to channel through a wide variety of Big Data is to use the best available business resources.

9.3.3 Big Data Analysis in Banking

The financial industry has had a significant impact on how clients' knowledge has changed as a result of innovation. Clients will also be able to use their cell phone to verify their deposit number, account deposit, and money transfer, eliminating the need to go to the bank. These self-administration features are fantastic for clients; one of the primary advantages is that it allows them to manage their own finances rationales that established banks attempt to rival comparative organizations and online-just budgetary foundations.

Because most client movement now takes place online, it's important to keep up with client needs. This is why having access to Big Data techniques and tools is so important for the financial sector. Banks can develop a 360° view of their customers by combining person and value-based data to:

a. Keep track of client spending patterns

b. Segmented clients based on their profiles

c. Put chance administration forms in place

d. Make item donations more personal

e. Make maintenance techniques a part of your plan

f. Gather, analyze, and react to client feedback

9.3.4 Leveraging Big Data Analysis

The following are the primary benefits of using Big Data analytics in the financial services industry.

9.3.4.1 Improved Deception Revealing

With Big Data, it could create a client summary that empowers to monitor value-based practices on an individualized level surrounded by the Big Data.

9.3.4.2 Greater Risk Appraisal

The Big Data, while associated with business intellect tools by way of prescient abilities, can trigger warnings on client summary to facilitate be elevated exposure than others.

9.3.4.3 Enlarged Customer Continued Possession

By way of complete information about the customer readily available, the information is simpler to fabricate more grounded, longer-enduring client associations on the force the customer continued possession.

9.3.4.4 Service or Product Individuality

Express the responsibility to see every client through emergent services or products, administrations, and the different contributions customized to the particular desires.

9.3.4.5 Efficient Client Criticism

Keep on answering the client queries, remarks, and doubts through utilizing big data to figure out criticism, besides, to react conveniently.

9.3.5 Significant Role of Big Data in Banking and Finance

Today, the terms "Big Data," "information analytics," and "data visualization" are widely used.

They are terms that you may hear daily in relation to business growth and digital transformation. Every business today is based on data. For settling on powerful choices, information investigation and bits of knowledge are fundamental. Regardless of how big or small the decision is, a business needs to have the right information to make the right decision. The above is critical in the banking and the finance industry today.

Banks and other monetary institutions need to use Big Data appropriately as per their consistent necessities and elevated levels of security measures and standards. Remembering the above-mentioned, banks and financial institutions today are utilizing the information they have to improve their degrees of administrations to their customers. They are making strides toward this path so that fraud can be extortion and forestalled.

In the finance sector, the usage of Big Data tools is increasing. On account of the closeness of Big Data, noteworthy enhancements are presently being made to the banking sector and financial services over the world. Big Data analytics do include a great deal of significant worth, and this post will take a gander at the ways utilizing which Big Data is getting positive change and incentives in the financial and banking industry over the globe.

9.3.6 Prospect of Big Data in Finance Sector

Big Data analytics is occupied in different financial sectors every day with hi-tech innovative products or services. For example, machine learning and Artificial Intelligence (AI) may help banks better target clients in credit selection. These technologies will search a bank's customer record regularly, highlight recurring data points like credit score and family earnings, and demographics and identify key influencers behind a customer's choice and identify the best players within their teams.

9.3.7 The Banking Industry's Big Data Analytics Potential

9.3.7.1 Preventing Frauds

Big Data analytics can help to monitor deceptive activities dramatically (Figure 9.2).

9.3.7.2 Identifying and Acquiring Customers

Client security is more expensive for banks than keeping old ones. Clients can require various services, including purchase discounts, better home purchasing, personalised services, data and alerts, and so on. Traditional data processing methods are insufficient for a wide variety of decision making. As a result, banks are effectively using data analytics to improve client satisfaction.

Millions of dealings occur every day in the banking industry. This transactional data requirement are to be appropriately assessed, inspected, and leveraged for the

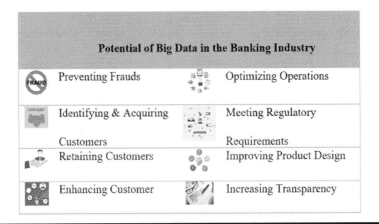

Figure 9.2 Potential of Big Data in the banking industry.

advantage of the banks and their customers. The big data analytics helps to draw significant business impending to enlarge customer fulfillment and faithfulness.

9.3.7.3 Retaining Customers

In this day and age of technological innovation, there isn't much cooperation between clients and financiers, in any event, to guarantee that the current customer is all around happy with their administrations to hold them.

9.3.7.4 Enhancing Customer Experience

Big Data analytics aid in enhancing customer engagement and retaining customers in specific service companies or financial institutions.

9.3.7.5 Optimizing Operations

Big Data analytics can settle on choices identified with branch and ATM areas. Banks might want to open a branch where they can gratify more clients. Opening a bank branch in the prime area can essentially build the client base.

9.3.7.6 Meeting Regulatory Requirements and Dealing with Setbacks in Real Time

Financial and fiscal policies are changed as much as possible in banking and financial institutions.Big data analytics can help you make informed decisions based on cutting-edge methods. Big data analytics can be used to break down different predictions based on different information sources accurately.

9.3.7.7 Optimizing the Overall Product Portfolio/Improving Product Design

Banks can prepare a variety of products based on client socioeconomics and banking proclivities. Big Data analytics can assist in predicting the profitability of goods based on projected clients. We can also use Big Data analytics to predict item requests.

9.3.7.8 Increasing Transparency

Keeping a close eye on deceptive transactions and fraudulent accounts would improve the financial system's transparency. Big Data analytics will aid in the detection of all of these nefarious practices, alerting experts.

9.3.8 Advantages of Big Data in Financial Sectors

Lot of data can be depicted as immense quantities of organized or unorganized data that need for authorizing a business to make a tactical conclusion. Appropriate comprehension of Big Data all the way through enlightening can assist in dealing with gaining critical ground and increasingly effective choices in the domain of the system, economics, client services, and manpower capital. The valuable bring into a play of Big Data can help organizations to overcome rivalry and progress to the subsequently on a further stage.

The advantages of Big Data to businesses and leaders are progressively objecting to the value of information and investigation rather than the quantity of unrefined data. The following are some uses or rewards of uncooked data in the economic sectors.

9.3.8.1 Identification of Innovative Services

The financial service providers like the banks, micro-level money lenders could increase depth approaching into creating the design of services or products. The players could create the services or products as mentioned by the clients' needs, progressively engaged, and could bring about the elevated accomplishment of bigger transactions quantity.

9.3.8.2 Minimize the Deception Movement

The banking and finance drag in various swindle endeavors in this highly regulated sector. The Big Data could be critical to this fragment from the time when the investigation of pertinent information sets can create it possible in the direction of encompassing better deception discovery and evasion. Huge advances to facilitate include be through in analytics and machine learning infer that deception finding specialists and the groups be able to recognize hazard issues quicker and significantly added exactly.

9.3.8.3 Enhanced Maneuvers

The banks, controllers, and other players who are played in the financial sector can get better management by appropriate analysis, intellectual capacity, as well as the practice of the consequences of the analysis. For example, a financial institution can make use of its swap over paperwork to categorize the busiest business time of the day or week and even months, coordinate to have most extreme employees conveyed, supplementary client spaces, and further required administrations. The financial institutions could arrange for the time at work, employ additional personal, or develop their frameworks for continuous as well as faster administrations.

9.3.8.4 Improved Operations

Banks, controllers, and financial sectors can progress their administrations by the appropriate investigation, comprehension, and usage of the consequences of the study. Using the exchange records, the bank can make use of its demanding time of the day, months, and orchestrate to comprise most extreme clients and other required administrations. They may perhaps work more period and employ additional staff to perk up their frameworks for continuous and quick administrations.

9.3.8.5 Identifying and Analyzing Potential Issue

The important problem is a perfect understanding of the potential issue in the financial sector among the players like banks and insurance agencies. The insurance agencies are required to contain the most important intensity of that the understanding of how much exposure they are captivating on as they insure clientele. The lenders in addition to realize the amount, they are discovering themselves when giving advances or hold on to any credit products. Through the appliances of Big Data, the process of the analysis of risk is possible in an earlier and progressively exact manner in the way of astounding client care, the decreased unfavorable encounters among the players of financial division.

9.3.8.6 A Greater Understanding of Market Conditions

Finance companies be capable of examining client buying conduct and become acquainted with what items are more sought after, in this way improving their contribution of the equivalent for a healthier return. They can distinguish on the way out deals for different items and explore the reason, accordingly delightful essential activities to alter the items. Such information on economic situations is pivotal to withstand rivalry and make huge deals.

9.3.8.7 Better Customer Service

The finance industry can utilize Big Data analytics in different vicinity, for example, client traffic, favored items, and input from different stages to improve their client assistance. They can build the number of clerks, candy machines, and sitting space, just as enhance different regions that the customers have given better feedback. The thought is to comprise a client-based approach to deal with numerous dedicated clients to be successful others through transfer from the fulfilled ones.

9.3.8.8 Endeavour to Accomplish a High Growth

Big Data analytics are recognized as prospective emergent areas for areas like banks, insurance agencies, and another financial analysis. They may make use of area-based reactions or criticisms, in the way of other information and it will show a marvelous centralization of commercial or personality clientele in a geographical locale. They can prefer someplace to unlock the new branches, appoint the number of consultants, or establish computerized equipment in the identified place or functional area among the availed data science in the corporate.

9.3.8.9 Marketing Plan and Tactics

The Big Data analytics on dissimilar effects on the level that clients use to post the feedback confirm the most excellent way to arrive at the corporate. The majority of clients use social media platforms, which would be smarter to provide them criticism about the information of marketing or promotional strategy used by the corporate.

9.3.8.10 Designed Constructive Approach in Decrease Costs

The financial corporate players can dispense with certain wasteful aspects among the application of Big Data tools, select the better channels of promoting the products or services, formulate earlier, and clear perfect decisions among the measurement of cost reduction. The usefulness of Big Data in this industry is plentiful, i.e. incorporate the enhanced user support, improved tricks, an elevated stage of deception revealing, legitimate hazard examination, better choice on product or service extension, or innovative product or service enlargement.

9.4 Big Data Analytics in Finance Industry

The finance industry is profoundly a competitive space. It faces a new generation of upsetting banks and guidelines. It's an industry that necessities to use Big Data to drive personalization, security, and fuel ordinary venture choices. The financial services administrations have consistently been at the forefront of technical innovation. The accessibility of new datasets has given an incredible method to get conduct and offers new headings for the financial industry to be prescient. Big Data application in money-related administrations goes past predicting share costs.

9.4.1 Finance Analysis in Cloud

At present the world is "Everything-is-Connected," the span of digital goes way beyond information technology. Gradually, the effective advanced changes require an encompassing digital methodology that connects with the whole business, not simply the information technology, and spotlights on something other than chance alleviation, consistency, and the cost of a breach. Today's business pioneers are finding that the more important job of digital is to help secure and advance their endeavor's development and development goals with a "digital all over" approach. Be that as it may, numerous organizations have yet to embrace this broader perspective.

9.4.2 Finance Team Needs Big Data Experts: How to Find Them

You may prepare to stun the Big Data experts for IT, however, many bookkeeping and finance departments put "successfully breaking down a company's business intelligence" at the highest point of their lists of things to get. Utilizing Big Data can yield incredible bits of knowledge into the firm's operations and customer trends. Making Big Data valuable for your finance team relies upon your capacity to recognize individuals with the correct activity abilities to assist you with disentangling it. It's a well-known fact that this is a hotly debated issue in innovation. "Big data is additionally one of the fastest-developing tech zones, with business hustling to capitalize on its potential."

9.4.3 Data Science in Banking and Finance

The intervention of technological advancement in banking and finance has a tacit primary role nowadays. Banks are operated and have fully changed with trend-setting innovation. This has made it easier and simpler for the consumer and banking officers. At this point, let us discuss the finding of the online stock exchange, internet banking, and so forth. There is a large amount of information in and around us from web-based business, e-mail, and mobile usage that has behavioral data and much more. To acquire the decision making in finance matter through a large number of complex computations on Big Data application by encouraging the latest innovations in data analytics research. Structured and unorganized information led to huge volumes which big data has portrayed. Hidden knowledge can be extracted from big data where unpredictability requires new methods, algorithms, and analysis. Through social media and online banking transactions were enormous data is retrieved through big data. About 5 million gigabytes of data are created by mankind that measures the generation of data. At present, the global production of data is about 3.5 quintillion bytes of data consistently. This has grown periodically and rapidly in this data production by handling the right tools and techniques.

To prevent fraud from utilizing the data helps to improve the customer's experience where numerous enterprises with the banking sector. As pointed out by research, 37% of the client has the same opinion that financial sector understands the needs and fondness. In every finance sector, they begin to apply Big Data analytics and get advantages of applying it.

Big Data guarantees a huge impact on banking and financial services through this strategy, which will propel it into the 21st century. In addition, Big Data analytics has become increasingly important in making business decisions and gaining a competitive advantage. It will examine the most important Big Data applications in the banking and finance sector now and in the future (Figure 9.3).

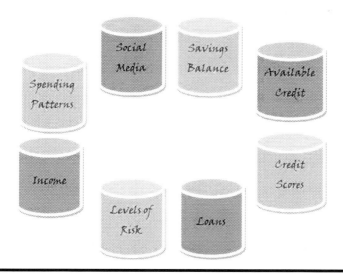

Figure 9.3   Data Science in banking and finance.

Banks are now utilizing the data science to proactively become aware of deception and endow with clientele with a high level of security. This is done by keep an eye on and examine user's banking behavior and to hit upon every apprehensive or malevolent patterns.

9.4.4 Big Data Analysis to Improve Finance Industry

Data analytics, Artificial Intelligence, machine learning, blockchain, and robotic process automation can all be taken for granted in future accounting work. Four key gears should be to be had for organizations hoping to turn out to be in a sequence determined, i.e. technology-based people, data excellence, featured tools, and a compassionate organizational ethnicity. Bookkeepers understand information knowledge and analytics to improve their business efficiency, influencing the knowledge to advance their data dominance and inquiry capabilities. Bookkeepers should keep on building up the essential abilities to stay rapidity with modernism and proceed as planned dealing associates at their corporations or business. The organizations are sending Big Data is significantly more noteworthy than several extra advances. Companies utilizing driving edge analytics be able to contain a vital benefit contrasted with corporate rivals. Among the advancement of analytical tools, every business is paying little mind to measure and needs to begin going down the analytics street to stay serious.

Industries perceive data as a necessary commodity and stimulate. It whips uncooked information into a significant product and uses it to draw insight for healthier execution of the industry. Financial institutions were among the most primitive customers and lead the way of data analytics. Data science is broadly used in areas like risk analytics, customer management, fraud detection, and algorithmic trading (Figure 9.4).

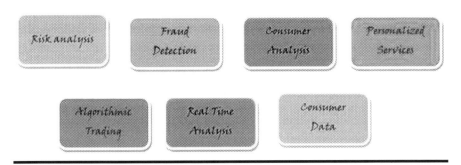

Figure 9.4 Roles of Big Data analytics in banking and finance.

a. **Fraud Detection**: This is probably the most serious issue every financial diligence has been confronting. In this expansion in a virtual business deal, the episodes of extortion have expanded as well. Strategic distance from misrepresentation, the financial sector utilizes Big Data technology that causes to comprehend the pecuniary narration along with the spending prototype of the client and adds to safety on each irregular business deal. It would assist with mitigating every fake movement ahead of it breeds larger.

b. **Customer Segmentation**: Customer segmentation is characterizing the client based on age, gender, behavior, propensities, and so on. The financial service sector has concurred its client upholding is input to the organization's achievement and are turning out to be extra client oriented through the assistance of information innovation. The data analysis assists the monetary administrations to dissect the cash outflow style of a being client which helps to suggest administrations on the clients' time. And also lend hands in distinguishing an important client, one who went through a sound number currency. Furthermore, throughout this analysis, it gives clients better monetary ideas to build their experience more priceless. It eventually would prompt augmented consumer loyalty.

9.4.5 Big Data Analysis in Finance: Pros and Cons

The master's side of Big Data in finance include:

1. **On the Pros Side**
   a. Models are improving the capacity to manage unstructured information
   b. Machine learning is particularly appropriate for nonlinear information forms
   c. Models can "learn" and "adjust"
2. **On the Cons Side**
   a. Interpretation in some cases is hard
   b. Low sign to clamor proportion all in all
   c. Overfitting is a major issue for a fake account as well as traditional quantitative finance

9.5 Sector of Finance Data Science

In the financial sector, data expertise is required to establish a risk analytics routine in order to arrive at a tactical conclusion for the company. Similarly, the financial organization uses machine learning for prognostic analytics and profound knowledge as a separation of data science that brings into plays numerical forms to the issue conclusion.

9.5.1 Data Science for the Internet Age

Data science can be utilized by advertisers and sales people to show website traffic and merchandise purchases in computerized form. Utilizing paraphernalia like Google Analytics, these experts can accumulate information from past, present, and even future customer interactions to give key estimations and indicators to the board. This innovation can be utilized to dig online networking for patterns in client practices and responses. Even though this may appear to be worthwhile for organizations, there are limitations on copyright and client security that must be thought of. Those associations scratching the web also profoundly can be gotten and rebuffed by government agencies.

9.5.2 Modernize Data Science in Finance Industry

It is the right occasion to refurbish economics plans by supporting information knowledge, machine learning and deep learning. Finance has all the time concerning the information. Information knowledge and finance set off person to person. Still, before the expression data science was developed, business was applying it. The banks and finance industries are to be used on computerized risk analytics and the information knowledge toward the mission. Finance diligence perceives data as a vital service and energy. It shakes uncooked information into a momentous creation and employs it to illustrate the approach for superior execution of the sector. The financial sector was a creative abuser and pioneered the use of data analytics. Risk analytics, customer retention, fraud prevention, and algorithmic trading are all fields where data science is commonly used (Figure 9.5).

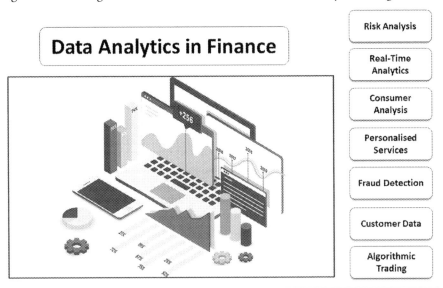

Figure 9.5 Modernize Data Science in finance industry.

The institutions in the finance industry for all time have repugnance toward advanced technology owing to its security anxiety. In actuality, the finance industry is mainly empowered by forward-looking advancements. At the same time as machine learning can make loan procedures precise by declining deception, AI-powered applications can offer improved recommendations to users.

9.5.3 The Financial Sector Needs Data Science

The avalanche of financial data has triggered the detonation of velocity, variety, and volume. Social media commotion, mobile communications, customer overhaul account, transaction data, and information from on-hand databases. To erect a sense of these massive data sets, businesses are more and more whirling to data scientists for answers.

- Incarcerate and scrutinize new foundation of information, constructive foretelling fashion, and running reside mock-up of events
- Using tools such as Hadoop, NoSQL, and nontraditional data sets amalgamate them with more traditional numbers
- Pronouncement and accumulate progressively more sundry acts in its unrefined form for future analysis

There might be an urgent need for refined analytical tools which assist in developing cloud-based data storage.

9.5.4 Machine Learning in Finance Information

Machine learning in finance may do something amazing, even though there is no enchantment behind it. The accomplishment of a machine learning venture relies more upon building an efficient framework, gathering logical datasets that can be implemented by precise algorithms that make critical advances in the financial sector. Finance sectors should keep in mind to actualize with Artificial Intelligence and machine learning algorithms that can be used in the business industry.

9.5.5 Sentiment Analysis in Finance or Service Sector

Sentiment analysis is a technique by which we can find out what the persons think. Nowadays, this kind of approach can be done by using text analysis and computational linguistics to find out what the person's think. Some statistics revelry is even acting as mediators, accumulating, and promoting opinion pointer to trade sponsor.
Professional believes it to:

a. Fabricate algorithms in the region of sentiment data (Twitter) to miniature the marketplace when catastrophe takes place.

b. Instead of novel harvest, pathway developments proceed in response to the subject and get better by and large trademark observation.
c. Investigate amorphous voice footage from various centers through phone conversation and insist on traditions to shrink customers' trouble and identify fraud.

We subdivide this as:

a. Using predictive analytics to pick up on the minuscule discrepancy in business to create their legitimacy
b. Utilizing predictive analysis one can select on the minuscule discrepancy in business to create their legitimacy in fraud detection and positive reduction
c. Using the latest technologies the banks can find out the nonpayer of money overdue to escape from credit card fraud risks

9.5.6 Predictive Analytics in Service or Finance Sector

The predictive analytics in the financial industry on any company could also reduce the risk like the fix on certain consumers in the way to pay off their credit cards and use the technology developed by the leading banks. Alike updating the technology or changing patterns has been one of the forecasting market behaviors. In the past, growing activity in trading or the rapid trade of securities was hugely beneficial. With antagonism came a drop in profits and the need for a new strategy exists. In this view, predictive analytics as point out like

a. Deception Finding and Fake Optimistic Reduction: Through this analytics to easy to choose on the diminutive divergence in the activity to establish their authenticity
b. Credit Card Risk Management: The default payment rate in credit cards may happen more when the cardholder does not pay back their amount overdue
c. Lifetime Value Customer Model: A prophecy of the net profit accredited to complete prospect affiliation with a client and financial institutions

9.5.7 Social Media Insights for Finance Industry

Data analysis is the same old thing for companionship in the financial industry, yet societal media information presents a new confrontation. As opposed to breaking down figures to look forward to future economic movements or grow new financial products, companies can make a group and investigate online discussions. Societal data intelligence not just gathers this data in a single spot yet utilizes top-to-bottom analytics to arrive at data-driven insights of knowledge. This would, in turn helps to coordinate decisions that foresee future financial developments just as a contextual analysis on the move towards versatile and web-based banking.

9.5.8 Analytics Tools for Finance Data

The following are some of the most widely used open-source data analytics methods in the finance industry:

1. R: R is now the most fashionable analytics tool in the industry.
2. Python: Python is a favorite for programmers in the long run.
3. Apache Spark: Spark is one more open source processing engine for analytics.
4. Apache Storm: Storm is the Big Data tool for information drawn closer in a continuous stream.
5. PIG and HIVE: PIG and HIVE are fundamental tools in the Hadoop environment that lessen the intricacy of writing.

Commercial Analytics Tools: Most popular paid analytics tools include:

1. SAS: SAS prolong to be extensively worn in the industry.
2. Tableau: Tableau is an effortless learning tool for creating visualizations and dashboards.
3. Excel: Excel is of the way the most broadly worn analytics tool in the world.
4. Splunk: Splunk is trendier than the Cloud era and Horton works.

9.5.9 Finance Sector and Its Upcoming Role of Data Analysis

Data science will continue developing as the advantages of this innovation are seen by more industry sectors and companies. Those with a passion for numbers and data will flourish utilizing these applications to make openings and financial rewards for businesses and the experts that work with them. Financial establishments are not resident to the computerized landscape and have needed to undertake a lengthy procedure of transformation that has required behavioral and scientific change. In the previous years, Big Data in finance has prompted noteworthy technological advancements that have empowered helpful, customized, and secure solutions for the industry. Thus, Big Data analytics has figured out only individual business forms as the entire financial services sector.

9.6 Conclusion

Digitalization is stimulating the finance sector using Artificial Intelligence, cloud computing, and machine learning techniques. Consumer needs can be enforced by technological tools, strengthening profit and loss in the business sector. The finance sector has stored information that can hoard new and priceless data. In this scenario, every financial overhaul is technical leniency that specifies as circulation of blood. This armada is persuading by escalating customer satisfaction and income generation by improving purchasing and controlling the growth. Big Data analysis has shown significant data privacy and control issues and some significant issues in the quality of data. Still, the research is going on in Big Data which the finance sector has attained its peak stage every second.

Acknowledgments

I would like to express my most profound appreciation to all the people behind me in completing this chapter work. First and foremost, I proffer my sincere gratitude to the Honourable Vice-Chancellor **Prof. Dr. P. Kaliraj** on his excellent leadership for instilling confidence in me during the pursuit of the paper and despite the fact that allowed me work in my own way and contribute the level of my work to encouragement in the book of perspectives of management in education 4.0. I express gratitude to **Dr. K. Murugan**, The Registrari/c, Bharathiar University for the academic support provided to carry out the research work. I show appreciation to **Prof. Dr. T. Devi,** Co-ordinator, and everyone involved in completing the book. I put forward my sincere thanks to **Dr. Rupa Gunasealan,** The Director i/c., and the faculty of Bharathiar School of Management and Entrepreneur Development (BSMED) for providing the background designed for enrichment of this chapter on finance in management discipline.

References

Hariharasudan, A., Kot, S. (2018). A scoping review on digital English and Education 4.0 for Industry 4.0. *Social Sciences, 7,* 227.

Hussin, A. A. (2018, July). Education 4.0 made simple: Ideas for teaching. *International Journal of Education and Literacy Studies, 6*(3), 92.

Lawrence R., Ching L. F., & Abdullah H. Strengths and Weaknesses of Education 4.0 in the Higher Education Institution. *International Journal of Innovative Technology and Exploring Engineering (IJITEE),* 9(2S3). Retrieved from https://prezi.com/i/f_6nqbbm11gw/strengths-and-weaknesses-of-education-40-in-the-higher-education-institution/

Linh, P. K. (2019, June). Education in Industry 4.0. *International Journal of Engineering Science Invention (IJESI), 8*(06), Series. I, 09–13.

Lopez-Garcia, T. J., et al. (2019). Review of trends in the educational model of distance education in Mexico, towards an Education 4.0. *Computer Reviews Journal, 3.* ISSN: 2581-6640.

Morabito, V. (2015). *Big data and analytics: Strategic and organizational impacts.* New York: Springer

Mourtzisa, D., Vlachoua, E., Dimitrakopoulosa, G., & Zogopoulos, V. (2018). Cyber-physical systems and education 4.0 – The teaching factory 4.0 concept. *Procedia Manufacturing, 23,* 129–134.

O'Riáin, S., Curry, E., & Harth, A. (2012). XBRL and open data for global financial ecosystems: A linked data approach. *International Journal of Accounting Information Systems, 13,* 141–162.

Pence, H. E. (2014). What is Big Data and why is it important? *Journal of Educational Technology Systems, 43*(2), 159–171.

Shahroom, A. A., & Hussin, N. (2018). Industrial revolution 4.0 and education. *International Journal of Academic Research in Business and Social Sciences, 8*(9), 314–319.

Sharma, P. (2019, December). Digital revolution of Education 4.0. *International Journal of Engineering and Advanced Technology (IJEAT), 9*(2), 314–319.

Tandon R., & Tandon S. (2020, February). Education 4.0: A new paradigm in transforming the future of education in India. *International Journal of Innovative Science, Engineering & Technology, 7*(2). ISSN (Online): 2348–7968.

Technavio. (2013). Global Big Data market in the financial services sector 2012–2016. Retrieved from https://inkwoodresearch.com/reports/big-data-market/

Tsai, B.-H. (2014). Examination of ex-dividend day trading using Big Data of American depositary receipts. *Proc. 2nd Int'l Conf. Advanced Cloud and Big Data (CBD),* pp. 34–38.

Wang, Y., Li, S., & Lin, Z. (2013). Revealing key non-financial factors for online credit-scoring in e-financing. *Proc. 10th Int'l Conf. Service Systems and Service Management (ICSSSM),* pp. 547–552.

Chapter 10

Role of Big Data Analytics in the Education Domain

C. Sivamathi and S. Vijayarani

Department of Computer Science, Bharathiar University, Coimbatore, India

Contents

DOI: 10.1201/9781003175889-10

10.1 Introduction

10.1.1 Industry 4.0

Education 4.0 is a recent emerging, attractive, and famed phrase in the education domain. It is the result of Industry Revolution 4.0 (IR 4.0) (Admiraal et al, 2019; Alexander et al, 2019; Ameen, 2019). An industrial revolution refers to the changes in industries by which some handmade works are replaced by machinery. The changes here refer to developments in manufacturing, social, economic, chemical, and textile organization that results in the development of concerned industries. Industries play a significant part of our daily life by covering all aspects. It has a major influence on the income, lifestyle, and population of the society (Samans, 2019). The economists believe that the force of the industrial revolution stimulus the standard of living, and it started to increase consistently in history (Altbach et al, 2009; Bates et al., 2019; Boulton, 2017; Cheng et al, 2018). Table 10.1 shows the revolution in the industry.

Table 10.1   Industry Revolution

S.No	Industry Revolution	Time Period	Technology Adopted
1	IR 1.0	1760–1820	Manual and handmade works
2	IR 2.0	1870–1914	Electricity, power machines were introduced
3	IR 3.0	Late 20th century	Web 2.0, Internet
4	IR 4.0	After 2011	IoT, Cyber Security

10.1.1.1 First Industrial Revolution (IR 1.0)

The first industrial revolution period was between the late 1700s and early 1800s. This revolution introduced the use of water and steam-powered engines in the industry. Before that, the industry uses manual labour people for all its work (Schwab, 2016).

10.1.1.2 Second Industrial Revolution (IR 2.0)

The industry met the next revolution in the early part of the 20th century. The revolution introduced steel and electricity to the industries. This introduction made the industrialist achieve high production efficiency. During this phase, the mass production concept like assembly line was introduced.

10.1.1.3 Third Industrial Revolution (IR 3.0)

In the late 20th century, with the introduction of computers, the third industrial revolution started to emerge. The industrialist started to implement computer technologies and more electronic powers into their factories. This revolution shifted analog and mechanical technology into digital and automation software (Figure 10.1).

10.1.1.4 Fourth Industrial Revolution (IR 4.0)

In recent years Industrial Revolution 4.0 has emerged, with the introduction of the cyber-physical systems and Internet of Things. It offers a highly interlinked and holistic approach to industries. IR 4.0 made all industries use information technology that resulted in disruptive effects on the economy, business, governments, countries, and society.

10.1.2 Revolution of Education

Similar to the industry revolution, the education domain can also be narrated (Davies, 2019; JISC, 2018; JISC, 2019) as Education 1.0, 2.0, 3.0, 4.0 as shown in

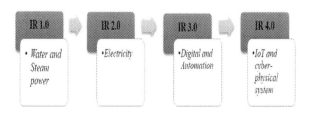

Figure 10.1   Evolution of Industry 4.0.

Table 10.2 Education Revolutions

S.No	Revolution	Time Period	Knowledge Resource	Location
1	Education 1.0	1960–1990	Teachers only	Only within classrooms, within a time period
2	Education 2.0	1991–2004	Teachers and students	Outside classroom, in same time period
3	Education 3.0	2004–2011	Teachers, students, and any online resource person	Anywhere, in the same time period
4	Education 4.0	Beyond 2011	Any person with knowledge	Anywhere anytime

Table 10.2. In Education 1.0, learning is taking place only in a classroom and not outside it. Here, only teachers are knowledge-source and the students are knowledge-receivers. In this generation, the students receive knowledge without any interactions (Feldman, 2018; Fisk, 2017). Hence, the entire learning process purely depends on the teacher's knowledge and their delivery method. This type of education is known as instructivism. The next generation, Education 2.0 was evolved with the introduction of Web 2.0 (Golembiewski, 2019; Gallagher, 2019). This generation has introduced more interactions. Here the teachers are not only the knowledge-source but also the students. This is possible with the usage of the Internet by the students. Hence the knowledge is transferred from student to student also. Now we are in the third revolution, i.e. Education 3.0 (Figure 10.2). In this revolution, the latest technology was introduced in teaching. Hence not only the teachers or students but everyone with the teaching resource will act as a knowledge source.

10.1.3 Education 4.0

In Education 4.0, humans and computers form a partnership with new technologies and results in smart teaching and learning. Education 4.0, as explained in Hussin (2018) and Heaven (2017), is the customized learning process in which learners can frame their learning path and approach achieving their own goals by their choices. In

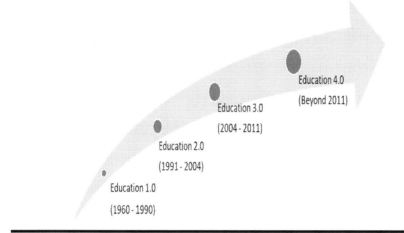

Figure 10.2   History of Education 4.0.

Education 4.0, learning is built around learners to learn wherever and whenever through data-based customization. They learn together and from each other, with their professors as facilitators in their learning (Berners-Lee et al., 2001).

Education 4.0 views education in different dimensions because of the usage of the latest technology-based tools and resources (McGregor & Hamilton, 2019; Ehlers & Kellermann, 2019). Here the students acquire knowledge not only from textbooks and from Professors as in standard classrooms. Moreover, in Education 4.0, remote students can aquire knowledge through the Internet through online courses, live chats, or calls through video/voice. Thus, Education 4.0 acts as more real-time and personalized learning to improve the understanding and exposure in learning methods. Research has also proved that the personalised education in Education 4.0 has improved learners' knowledge and learning skills. Hence, Education 4.0 is a more realistic and practical approach and results in an excessively skilled student community (Salmon & Asgari, 2019). Some of the technologies used in Education 4.0 are:

- Big Data analytics
- Internet of Things
- Sensor networks
- Robotics
- Artificial intelligence
- Three-dimensional technologies
- Augmented reality
- Virtual reality
- Quantum computing
- Smart spaces

10.1.3.1 5 I's of Learning in Education 4.0

ParagDiwan, Chief Executive officer at Paradigm Consultants and Resource defines five essential I's in education as shown in Figure 10.3. They are listed and defined as follows:

1. **Imbibing**: In Education 4.0, the students can easily adopt basic concepts compared to previous generations.
2. **Iterating**: This means that the students can practice basic skills again and again.
3. **Interpreting**: It refers to taking knowledge from studies and implementing those facts to other real-time situations with some modification.
4. **Interest**: It develops more interest among students, as it offers a curriculum based on their interests.
5. **Innovating**: In Education 4.0, the student can explore their own knowledge, so that they can develop innovative products and services.

Education 4.0 incorporates technological advancements in the education domain to enhance the skills of teachers and learners. Also, the novel technologies ease the students to have more interest and concentration towards learning. Hence, Education 4.0 teaches the students about the latest technology in the curriculum and utilizes it to improve their knowledge and skills (Vlachopoulos, 2018). The technologies (Barrow et al. 2019; Bakhshi et al. 2017) of Education 4.0 include Big Data analytics, IoT, Artificial Intelligence, biometrics, cyber security, 3D printing, augmented reality, virtual reality, hologram, multi-touch LCD screen, and robotics.

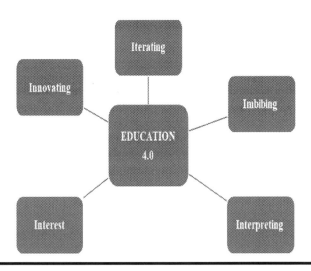

Figure 10.3   Five I's of Education 4.0.

10.1.4 Big Data Analytics

Any characters, numbers, or symbols on which the computer performs some operations and is stored and transmitted as electrical signals are termed as data. As the name says, Big Data is data with huge size. The term Big Data describes a huge collection of data with vast volume and grows exponentially with time. In 2005, Roger Mougalas of O'Reilly Media introduced the term Big Data. The size of data started to grow as Zetta Byte, Yotta Byte, etc. Some real-time datasets are few terabytes to petabytes in size. The introduction of Web 2.0 resulted in more social networks so that more and more data is created daily. Today in every minute, 200 million emails are sent and over millions of questions are searched in Google. 68 hours of new YouTube videos are shared and Facebook shares more than 684,000 bits of content in a minute. Almost 100,000 tweets are created and 5,600 newly added photos shared on Instagram in a minute. Big Data can be applied in various fields like banking, agriculture, biochemistry, finance, marketing, stocks, healthcare, etc. The huge size, high speed, and heterogeneous nature of Big Data cannot deal with traditional technologies.

Big Data analytics refers to the process of analyzing huge bulk data and uncovers hidden patterns, correlations, or any other meaningful insights. Big Data analytics has been used by various organizations like supermarkets, e-commerce, social media, healthcare, banking, education institution, entertainment industries, etc. These organizations apply analytics to understand their business trends, predict future business, analyzing customer vision, etc. In Big Data analytics, it is difficult to design a statistical model. As data is very huge, a large amount of work is needed just for cleaning the data. There is no unique methodology to follow in real large-scale applications. Generally, the business problem is defined first, and then a methodology based on the business problem is designed. The common steps in Big Data analytics are shown in Figure 10.4 and are explained below:

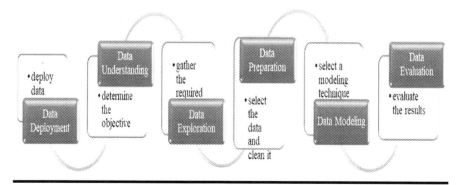

Figure 10.4   Steps in Big Data analytics.

Data Deployment: In this step, the analytics has to plan the deployment, monitoring, and maintenance and review the project.

Data Understanding: This step determines the objective, considers the situation, and defines data mining goals. It also gives the project plan based on the requirement.

Data Exploration: Initial data are gathered, described, and explored. Data are collected from various sources and hence there may be many flaws in the quality of collected data.

Data Preparation: After data exploration, the data was cleaned and constructed, to get useful information.

Data Modelling: In data modeling, a suitable modeling technique was selected and the model was built.

Data Evaluation: Here, we evaluate the results from the last step.

10.2 Need for Big Data Analytics in Education

In the education domain, the application of Big Data is highly substantial. It offers enormous rewards to students, teachers, and institutions. The institutions can monitor things in a much better way with the help of Big Data (Ruiz-Palmero et al., 2020). Education 4.0 aims to provide personalized learning for all students. Personalized learning through Education 4.0 results in fast and depth understanding and extensive learning of diverse materials that make the students more interested in learning. For this personalized learning, each student must be analyzed thoroughly to retrieve his interest, capability, etc. Each student has different characters and abilities. Hence the student data is crucial for their development in their career (Johansson, 2017; Dobozy & Cameron, 2018; Daniel, 2018). There is five major analytics required for data analysis in the education domain as given in Figure 10.5. They are learning analytics, predictive analytics, academic analytics, text analytics, and visual analytics.

10.2.1 Learning Analytics

Traditional data mining tools could not analyze student data much efficiently. Hence learning analytics tools in Big Data analytics are used to perform this kind of analysis and help in the analysis of student data and retrieve personalized skill of students. Learning analytics refers to the quantity, gathering, study, and reports of learner data. Learning analytics can be used to access learning behavior, improve learning materials and tools, provide individualized learning, predict student performance, visualize learning activities, etc. Hence there is a need for Big Data analytics so that the learning process can be enhanced and evaluate efficiency. It also improves feedback and enriches the learning experience.

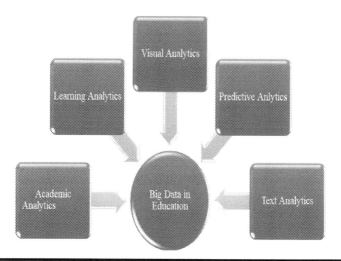

Figure 10.5 Big Data analytics in education.

10.2.2 Predictive Analytics

Once the student skills are identified, the teachers can shape a student's career based on the parameters such as interests and skills. Hence data analytics helps the teachers to trace the learning process and take targeted actions to progress the education process of the students. With data analytics reports, the instructors can pay extra concentration to the students who are lagging behind. It also helps the instructor to obtain detailed analytics from online course students and to detect fraud from students in a much effectively.

10.2.3 Academic Analytics

Other than students and staff, the management of the universities is also in need of Big Data analytics. Such analytics is termed academic analytics. Academic analytics is the process of evaluating and analyzing student data received from the university for better decision making and reporting. Academic analytics embraces analysis, modeling, reporting, admission, advising, financing, academic counseling, enrolment, administration, and decision support regarding university and campus services.

10.2.4 Text Analytics

The process of converting a huge volume of unstructured Big Data text into numerical data to discover hidden patterns is termed as text analytics. This can be applied in education to analyze student data, course details, and staff details. By analyzing student data, it is easy to predict student skills and their interest. Based on this, a personalized curriculum can be designed in education 4.0. Course details can be analyzed to discover information like how many students are enrolled each year, how many students are completing the course, and how many are not completing the course. By this analytics, the reason for incompletion can be identified, which is used to narrate the most trending course. This reflects the decision to improve their instructional schemes and study materials and results in a most optimal learning experience for the students. Text analytics is also used to analyze student feedback to retrieve knowledge about the faculty and course.

10.2.5 Visual Analytics

Visual analytics is the process of analyzing data and produce various interactive visual interfaces. Visual analytics helps decision makers to make well-informed decisions in complex situations. Visual analytics is the combination of visualization, human factors, and data analysis. Visual analytics helps education institutions to take strategic decisions like attaining good student admission, retaining talented and experienced faculty, monitoring expenses and revenues.

10.3 Applications of Big Data Analytics in Education

Big Data analytics can be applied in various parts of the education domain. It has a varied range of applications for students, staff, and educational institutions. Big Data applications in the education system are shown in Figure 10.6 that improved the education system in a modern and better way (Jongbloed, 2015; John, 2019).

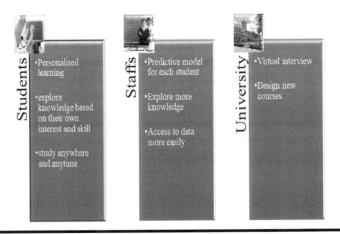

Figure 10.6 Applications of Big Data in education.

10.3.1 Creating Predictive Model

Data analytics tools can build predictive models for learners. A predictive model is the process of building a model, which is used to predict future outcomes. It plays a major role in predictive analytics. In education, with these models, the staff can identify poor learners to provide intervention to assist learners in achieving success.

10.3.2 Personalized Curriculum

Each student has their own skills and ability. With more student data, the analyst can develop more curricula based on individual student skills.

10.3.3 Adaptive Learning

The content is not only adaptive but also the learning itself adaptive. The learners can learn from anywhere and at any time.

10.3.4 Personalized Resources

It provides the learners, more personalized resources, based on their profile and learning goals. It can provide learners with insights into their own learning habits and can give recommendations for improvement.

10.3.5 Data-Driven Decision-Making Culture

With data analytics, there are various statistics models available to back up the decisions. Hence there is no need to depend upon blind truth to make decisions.

10.3.6 Access Data Easier

Data analytics tools depend on Big Data infrastructure to capture, store and organize information, so it is easy to find the required data. It also reduces the search time of data, since data locates in one place; there is no need to search through dozens of files and folders.

10.3.7 Virtual Interview

Big Data analytics helps the organization to conduct interviews virtually. This interview copycats exactly like the real interview, using Artificial Intelligence tools (Luckin, 2019). This reduces travel time and organization of interviews in a building etc.

10.3.8 Design a New Course

A key challenge for universities is to understand industry requirements and design a curriculum to meet those demands. Big Data analytics can be used to recognize industry and employment trends so that a new trendy curriculum can be framed.

10.4 Advantages of Big Data in Education

- E-Learning tools facilitate students to learn anywhere, from anyone, and at any time. Classrooms are exploded and hence students can learn from outside the classrooms.
- Students are classified based on their skills and ability and will learn with their own customized study materials. Below-average students will get the opportunity to practice. This results in positive learning experiences for all kinds of students.
- Students will have an open choice to learn. Based on their own preference, they can choose their own device, program and technique. It includes E-Learning, BYOD (bring your own device) concept.
- Students can adapt to project-based learning, rather than theory-based learning. This turns memorization of the work to project work.
- As each student is having personalized learning, they got in-depth knowledge in their own areas. Here the students are trained instead of taught.
- The curriculum becomes more contemporary, realistic, up-to-date, and useful.
- It makes teachers understand the capability of each student so that they can monitor and mentor the students more efficiently.

10.5 Challenges in Implementing Big Data in Education

Today many institutions want Big Data for their analysis since Big Data help institutions to identify their areas for improvement. There are many practical difficulties and some challenges in implementing Big Data in education. It is not so easy to process, organize, and present large amounts of data in useful ways (Anirban, 2014; Xing, 2019; McGregor & Hamilton, 2019; Ciechanowski et al., 2019).

- Educational Big Data includes both structured data and unstructured data. Before analyzing a variety of Big Data, it must be appropriately integrated. This is an important issue in Big Data.
- Big Data is a recently emerging technology, so there is a lack of highly skilled and experienced staff. More training has to be given to both educators and learners for better understanding.
- Big Data are not well-organized data always, i.e it may have some irrelevant data. Such data must be removed using filtering techniques before processing. It was not that much easy with Big Data.

- Discovering high-quality data from a very large collections of data is difficult and nature of Big Data is tedious.
- It is also difficult to implement visual and text analytics in Big Data. So there is a need to apply enormous parallelization algorithms.
- The cost of memory in Big Data is highly expensive and complex.
- Big Data always has a risk in data placement and its security.

10.6 Education 4.0 in India

Our nation's education system is at a pivotal stage to adopt Education 4.0. For this, Indian education system should have a curriculum that matches the job requirements. In Education 4.0, the students are not taught, rather they should be trained (OECD, 2018; Navitas Ventures, 2017; McVitty, 2019). The Indian education system has been guided to change from Education 3.0 to Education 4.0. The Ministry of Human Resource Development (MHRD) must take the necessary step for this adoption. It has to develop appropriate academic programs and curriculum to focus on dynamic skills and knowledge for students. The current study is a descriptive research design of academicians and students (Connor et al., 2015).

10.7 Case Study: Big Data Analytics in E-Learning

E-Learning refers to the learning process through electronic technologies, in which the educational curriculum moves beyond the traditional classroom. E in E-Learning stands for electronic and the learning can be a course or program or degree acquired completely online. Here, learning is more interactive as in the classrooms, and E-Learning is not learning delivered through CDs or DVDs. Nowadays, E-Learning is conducted as a live program, so that the student can interact in real-time. E-Learning can meaningfully diminish the learning time of a student, as the students can access the material online whenever they have free time. Also, the students don't want to follow in a group, they can move at their own rapid speed, depending upon their skill. They can even skip some lessons, if they already know, and concentrate more on what they need. Cost reduction is another significant advantage of E-Learning, as it reduces traveling cost, learning material cost, trainers cost, etc. The E-Learning materials provide interactive multimedia content to learn and improve their skills and perform quickly. Moreover, E-Learning software provides essential collaboration tools that improve student knowledge and builds a strong collaborative workforce. Hence, it is clear that E-Learning is mandatory in today's fast-moving education world. Some of the E-Learning tools are:

- Elucidat
- Adobe Captivate
- Articulate Storyline

- Articulate Rise
- Gomo
- Lectora
- Adapt
- DominKnow
- Easygenerator
- iSpring Suite

Though Figure 10.7 shows the advantages, E-Learning also has some drawbacks, and they are listed below:

- E-Learning creates social isolation.
- It is not suitable for students with no self-motivation and time management skills.
- Need active internet connection.
- Must have prior knowledge about using computers.
- There are no communicational skill developments among students.
- Cheating prevention during online assessments is expected.
- It is limited to certain disciplines.
- It entirely depends on technology a lot.
- Lack of accreditation and quality assurance in online education.
- Some traditional courses are difficult to simulate.
- The feedback of a student is not sufficient.
- An instructor may not always be available.
- Copyright problems for materials have to be monitored.
- It has adverse effects on health.

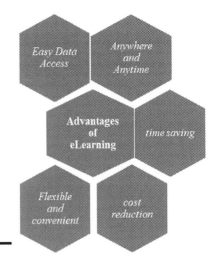

Figure 10.7   Advantages of E-Learning.

In the E-Learning industry, Big Data analytics can be implemented despite its significant rewards. Keen integration of Big Data analytics and E-Learning will help us to make more personalized decisions. For this analysis, we have to collect feedback, reports and analyze the E-Learning data for a long period. Moreover, E-Learning is constantly evolving and changing. Hence it is essential to implement Big Data in E-Learning for efficient analysis. When harvested effectively, this analysis can result in many new possibilities in E-Learning that will empower and enhance E-Learning.

Big Data analytics provides new possibilities in E-Learning. Many E-Learning organizations have already started to implement Big Data for their learning analytics. Big Data analytics allows collecting, analyze and report online learning for better decisions. The data here refers to student data, course data, and faculty data. By analyzing student data, we can obtain meaningful knowledge about the learner. It helps to make study materials, courses based on their skill. From learner data, we can also predict the performance and behaviours (Figure 10.8). Other than this dropping out risk rates and absences tracking can also be predicted.

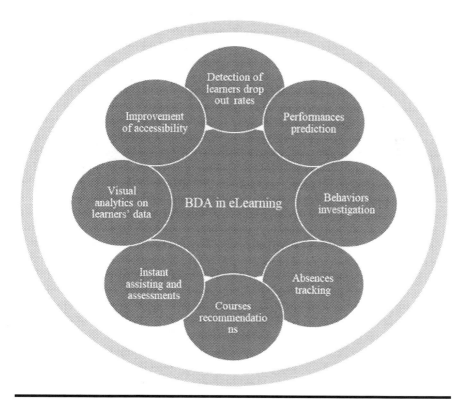

Figure 10.8 Big Data analytics in E-Learning.

Clustering analysis can be adopted in E-Learning, so that the students are divided into different clusters like high, average and low activity learners, using classification and clustering techniques. This helps staff to train the students based on their ability. Predictive analytics of E-Learning includes predictions about student progress in future exams, what new E-Learning courses can be introduced, how many learners may be admitted to each course, etc. For all the above analytics, we need the following data:

- Course period
- Students strength in all courses
- Students dropped-out from a course before completion
- Time spent on entire course period
- Performance grade of the student in course
- Most enrolled courses
- Least enrolled courses
- Number of attempts to complete the course
- Individual quiz/assessments performance

10.7.1 E-Learning Platforms

E-Learning platforms are defined as learning through online services that integrate all online learning processes in a single portal. It provides resource materials and tools to the staff, students, and others involved in education. E-Learning platform services include administration, atomisation, content management, communication among teachers, and trainers. Some of the popular E-Learning platforms are listed in Table 10.3. A good E-Learning platform must have the following characteristics:

- An efficient control on students, staff, and administrators
- Creates and manages resource material and subjects in a simple and intuitive way
- Can access information more easily
- The content must be updatable
- Must include multimedia contents in study materials
- Creates personalized detailed reports of students and courses
- Monitor the attendance of students and staff
- If it is a paid platform then it must able to manage the fees status of students

10.8 Conclusion

The future of our nation highly depends on our education system. It has to be framed accordingly so that the student's learning and teacher's teaching will be revolutionized. Education 4.0 is a recent buzzword in the education domain that

Table 10.3   Popular E-Learning Platforms

S.No	Platform	Description	URL
1	Coursera	It includes free courses from top universities. It is suitable for those users who want to study different courses from different universities.	https://www.coursera.org/
2	Khan Academy	It is a free tool for both learners and teachers. It includes lessons from kindergarten to college.	https://www.khanacademy.org/
3	Udemy	It has both free and paid content and offers users to build custom courses from lessons.	https://www.udemy.com/
4	Edx	Founded by Harvard and MIT, has more than 20 million learners and approximately 2,400 courses from various universities.	https://www.edx.org/
5	Alison	It offers business, technology, and health-related courses only. It also provides certificates for courses.	https://alison.com/
6	NPTEL (National Programme on Technology Enhanced Learning)	Many courses are offered by seven Indian Institutes of Technology i.e IIT Bombay, Delhi, Guwahati, Kanpur, Kharagpur, Madras and Roorkee, and Indian Institute of Science (IISc)	https://nptel.ac.in/
7	Codeacademy	It teaches how to code in different programming languages. There are 45 million learners.	https://www.codecademy.com/

(Continued)

Table 10.3 (Continued)   Popular E-Learning Platforms

S.No	Platform	Description	URL
8	TED-Ed	Other than courses, it includes supplemental materials and quizzes.	https://ed.ted.com/
9	Memrise	It is offered both as a desktop and as an app. It is most famous for studying a language.	https://www.memrise.com/
10	Moodle	It is a safe and cohesive system to make personalized learning atmospheres for both students and staff.	https://moodle.com/

makes education a flexible and customized one for the students. Big Data is deployed in the education system to rebuild and transform future education. Big Data advances the trends of education by its expertise at all levels, like teaching, retention, learning, administration, and reporting. The purpose of this chapter is to describe the use of Big Data analytics in the education domain. The role of Big Data analytics in the education sector is significant. The chapter had explained the need for Big Data analytics in the education domain. Implementation of Big Data analytics in education will provide massive benefits to students, staff, and institutions. This chapter also discussed these advantages in detail. It also listed the practical challenges in implementing Big Data analytics.

References

Admiraal, W., Post, L., Guo, P., Saab, N., Makinen, S., Rainio, O., ... Danford, G. (2019). Students as future workers: Cross-border multidisciplinary learning labs in higher education. *International Journal of Technology in Education and Science*, 3(2), 85–94. Retrieved from https://www.learntechlib.org/p/207262/

Alexander, B., Ashford-Rowe, K., Barajas-Murph, N., Dobbin, G., Knott, J., McCormack, ... Weber, N. (2019). Horizon report 2019 higher education edition. EDU19. Retrieved from https://www.learntechlib.org/p/208644/

Altbach, P. G., Reisberg, L., & Rumbley, L. E. (2009). Trends in global higher education: Tracking an academic revolution in global perspectives on Higher Education. UNESCO Report, from the World Conference on Higher Education. Retrieved from http://www.cep.edu.rs/public/Altbach,_Reisberg,_Rumbley_Tracking_an_Academic_Revolution,_UNESCO_2009.pdf

Ameen, N. (2019). What robots and AI may mean for university lecturers and students? Retrieved from http://theconversation.com/what-robots-and-ai-may-mean-for-university-lecturers-and-students-114383

Anirban, S. (2014). Big data analytics in the education sector: needs, opportunities, and challenges. *International Journal of Research in Computer and Communication Technology (IJRCCT)*, *3*(11), 2278–5841.

Bakhshi, H., Downing, J., Osborne, M., & Schneider, P. (2017). *The future of skills: employment in 2030*. London: Pearson & Nesta. Retrieved from https://media.nesta.org.uk/documents/the_future_of_skills_employment_in_2030_0.pdf

Barrow, J., Forker, C., Sands, A., O'Hare, D., & Hurst, W. (2019). Augmented reality for enhancing life science education. Paper presented at VISUAL 2019 – The Fourth International Conference on Applications and Systems of Visual Paradigms, Rome, Italy.

Bates, G., Rixon, A., Carbone, A., & Pilgrim, C. (2019). Beyond employability skills: Developing professional purpose. *Journal of Teaching and Learning for Graduate Employability*, *10*(1). Retrieved from https://ojs.deakin.edu.au/index.php/jtlge/article/view/794

Berners-Lee, T., Hendler, J., & Lassila, O. (2001). The semantic web. *Scientific American*, *284*(5), 34–43.

Boulton, G. (2017). The digital revolution and the future of science. Retrieved from https://www.timeshighereducation.com/hub/p/jisc-futures-digital-revolution-and-future-science

Cheng, L., Ritzhaupt, A. D., & Antonenko, P. (2018). Effects of the flipped classroom instructional strategy on students' learning outcomes: A meta-analysis. *Education Technology Research and Development*, *67*(4). Retrieved from 10.1007/s11423-018-9633-7

Ciechanowski, L., Przegalinska, A., Magnuski, M., & Gloor, P. (2019). In the shades of the uncanny valley: An experimental study of human–chatbot interaction. *Future Generation Computer Systems*, *92*, 539–548. Retrieved from 10.1016/j.future.2018.01.055

Connor, A., Karmokar, S., & Whittington, C. (2015). From STEM to STEAM: Strategies for enhancing engineering technology education. *International Journal of Engineering Pedagogy*, *5*(2), 37–47. Retrieved from https://online-journals.org/index.php/i-jep/article/view/4458

Daniel, J. S. (2018). Open Universities: Old concepts and contemporary challenges. IRRODL Special Issue on the Future of Open Universities. Retrieved from http://sirjohn.ca/wpontent/uploads/2018/11/20180718_IRRODL_RevNov.pdf

Davies, S. (2019). Moving towards Education 4.0. *Blog*. Retrieved from https://www.jisc.ac.uk/blog/member-stories-towards-higher-education-40-15-jan-2019

Dobozy, E., & Cameron, L. (2018). Editorial: Special issue on learning design research: Mapping the terrain. *Australasian Journal of Educational Technology*, *34*(2), i–v. Retrieved from https://ajet.org.au/index.php/AJET/article/view/4390

Ehlers, U. D., & Kellermann, S. A. (2019). Future skills – The future of learning and higher education. Results of the International Future Skills Delphi Survey. Karlsruhe. Retrieved from https://nextskills.files.wordpress.com/2019/03/2019-02-23-delphi-report-final.pdf

Feldman, P. (2018). The potential of 4.0 is huge – UK must take the lead. *Blog*. Retrieved from https://www.jisc.ac.uk/blog/the-potential-of-education-4-is-huge-the-uk-must-take-the-lead-now-12-sep-2018

Fisk, P. (2017). Education 4.0 ... the future of learning will be dramatically different, in school and throughout life. Retrieved from https://www.thegeniusworks.com/2017/01/future-education-young-everyone-taught-together (Also see Video 'The Future of Learning' on this site.)

Gallagher, M. (2019). Learning for the future of work. Retrieved from https://www.swinburne.edu.au/new-workforce (See Website and video.)

Golembiewski, L. (2019). How wearable AI will amplify human intelligence. Harvard Business Review. Retrieved from https://hbr.org/2019/04/how-wearable-ai-will-amplify-human-intelligence

Heaven, D. (Ed). (2017). *Machines that think*. Boston, MA: Nicholas Barley Publishing.

Hussin, A. (2018). Education 4.0 Made simple: Ideas for teaching. *International Journal of Education and LiteracyStudies*, *6*(3), 92–98. Retrieved from http://www.journals.aiac.org.au/index.php/IJELS/article/view/4616

Johansson, F. (2017). *The Medici Effect*. Boston, MA: Harvard Business Review Press.

John, J. (2019). How to create: A broader, fairer and smarter education system. Retrieved from https://www.jisc.ac.uk/blog/how-to-create-a-broader-fairer-and-smarter-education-system-08-mar-2019

JISC. (2018). Digital skills crucial to the success of fourth industrial revolution. Retrieved from https://www.jisc.ac.uk/news/digital-skills-crucial-to-the-success-of-fourth-industrial-revolution-28-jun-2018

JISC. (2019). Preparing for Education 4.0. Retrieved from https://www.timeshighereducation.com/hub/jisc/p/preparing-education-40

Jongbloed, B. (2015). Universities as hybrid organizations: Trends, drivers, and challenges for the European university. *International Studies of Management & Organization*, *45*(3), 207–225.

Luckin, R. (2019). AI and education: The reality and the potential. *The Knowledge Illusion*. Retrieved from https://knowledgeillusion.blog/2019/04/30/ai-and-education-the-reality-and-the-potential/

McGregor, A., & Hamilton, M. (2019). Shaping education for a hyper connected world. *Digifest Magazine*.

McVitty, D. (2019). The more universities are thinking about value for money, the better the sector looks. WONKHEblog. Retrieved from https://tinyurl.com/y5bxhwmz.

Navitas Ventures. (2017). *Digital transformation in higher education, report*. Retrieved from http://www.navitasventures.com/wp-content/uploads/2017/08/HE-Digital-Transformation-_Navitas_Ventures_-EN.pdf

OECD. (2018). A brave new world: Technology & education. *Trends Shaping Education*. Retrieved from https://www.oecd.org/education/ceri/Spotlight-15-A-Brave-New-World-Technology-and-Education.pdf

Ruiz-Palmero, J., Colomo-Magaña, E., Ríos-Ariza, J. M., & Gómez-García, M. (2020). Big Data in education: Perception of training advisors on its use in the educational system. *Social Sciences*, *9*(4), 53.

Salmon, G., & Asgari, S. (2019). Higher education – The last bastion? European Journal of Open, Distance and E-learning. Retrieved from http://www.eurodl.org/?p=current&sp=brief&article=792

Samans, R. (2019). Globalization 4.0 shaping a new global architecture in the age of the Fourth Industrial Revolution: A call for engagement. *World Economic Forum Report*. Retrieved from http://www3.weforum.org/docs/WEF_Globalization_4.0_Call_for_ Engagement.pdf

Schwab, K. (2016). The Fourth Industrial Revolution: What it means, how to respond. Retrieved from https://www.weforum.org/agenda/2016/01/the-fourth-industrial-revolution-what-it-means-and-how-to-respond/

Vlachopoulos, P. (2018). Curriculum digital transformation through learning design: The design, develop, implement methodology. In K. Ntalianis, A. Andreatos, & C. Sgouropoulou (Eds.), *Proceedings of the 17th European Conference on e-Learning* (pp. 585–591). Reading, UK: Academic Conferences and Publishing International.

Xing, B. (2019). Towards a Magic Cube Framework in understanding Higher Education 4.0 for the Fourth Industrial Revolution. In D. B. A. Khosrow-Pou (Ed.), *Handbook of research on challenges and opportunities in launching a technology driven international university* (pp. 107–130). Hershey: IGI Global.

Chapter 11

Social Media Analytics

E. Suganya and S. Vijayarani

Department of Computer Science, Bharathiar University, Coimbatore, India

Contents

DOI: 10.1201/9781003175889-11

217

Objectives

Social media (SM) platform integrates several websites and applications that permit people to share texts, events, photos, videos, opinions, audios, etc. rapidly and powerfully in real time. Popular websites in SM are WhatsApp, Tumblr, Facebook, YouTube, LinkedIn, Snapchat, Instagram, QZone, Twitter, Pinterest, and so on. Lots of data are to be developed from these SM sites that leads to the development of several techniques and algorithms to analyze these data. Social media analytics (SMA) is the collection of SM data and performs analysis from different websites using analytical tools. Significant applications of SMA are sentiment analysis, opinion mining, recommender systems, fake news analysis, etc. To get automatic and accurate data analysis, it is necessary to develop novel techniques and algorithms. The primary objective of this chapter is to discuss how machine and deep learning algorithms are used for analyzing SM data.

11.1 Introduction

SM is a medium for connection among professionals, friends, and family to share opinions, thoughts, sentiments related to the real and current situation. It is also named as "anywhere anytime" accessible information. SM data is the biggest, well-off and ultimate indication of social activities for getting different prospects to figure out the persons, groups, and also society. The professionals and innovative scientists are progressively identifying significant methods for gathering, merging, and examining data automatically (Bogdan Batrinca et al., 2014).

Retail companies are using SM to selling their product, enhancing marketing, improve customer service, and duplicate detection. SM is used in the finance sector to assessing trading news data (Akshi Kumar et al., 2016). It is also used in the biosciences sector for gathering data on populous partners for tackling obesity, smoking, and monitoring the diseases. In the computational social science domain, SM is used for monitoring the people's activities, events, and speeches particularly political comments, SM voting of groups, the primary discovery of developing events, as with Twitter.

SMA is all about gathering data/information made from SM sites such as Wikipedia, Google+, LinkedIn, Pinterest, YouTube, Facebook, WhatsApp, Twitter, Instagram, Snapchat, WeChat, Tumblr, and so on. SM data are normally in the structure of likes, posts, tweets, shares and links, microblogs, geographical data, and locations for retrieving the information from the dataset using SMA which is used to make perfect decisions in business. SMA also contains the development and evaluation tools and also has frameworks to collect, observe, summarize, analyze, and visualize SM data (D. Kavitha, 2017). It is even used for analyzing opinions, sentiment, and behavior of the customer, and it is also useful to obtain the perceptions on product reviews for making improving marketing strategies and enhancing customer service. Microblogging, forums, social networking, and social bookmarking were dedicated to websites and applications; these are the various kinds of SM (Gitanjali Kalia, 2013).

SM data is defined as SM users can share the data publicly that contains metadata like language spoken, biographical data, user location, and also links. It is more important to vendors because they seek customer perceptions which may boost sales of a product or political for winning votes. There are different varieties of SM data: posts on Facebook, tweets from Twitter, posts on Tumblr, check-ins on Foursquare, pins on Pinterest, and so on. The most commonly used advertising products on SM sites are Facebook and Twitter ads to achieve targeted users who are interested in their ads. SM data is the information from social networks that show how users view and share or connect with their content or profiles (Figure 11.1).

11.2 Process of Social Media Analytics

The process includes three stages for analyzing the SM data: capture, understand, and present. This is shown in Figure 11.2. The first stage capture is used to obtain SM data through monitoring or observing from several SM sources and to archive appropriate data for extracting appropriate information from the sources. This

Figure 11.1   Social media data.

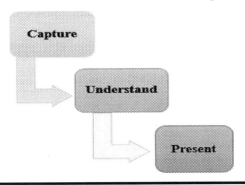

Figure 11.2   Process of social media analytics.

process can be completed by an organization, but all the captured data from the SM will not be useful. Understanding the SM data is the second stage. In this stage, several innovative SM data analytic methods and techniques are used for modeling, removing noisy data, and employing low-quality data. Finally, the last stage presents the data that is used to display and present the findings from the second stage in expressive manner.

11.2.1 Capture Data

This stage permits to find discussion on SM sites that combines its actions and involvement in the business sector (Despoina Antonakaki et al., 2017). This process is finished by gathering enormous volumes of appropriate data across lots of SM sources by APIs, news feeds, or through crawling. Capturing data focuses on the most popular sites, various news sites, and marketing sites. Massive volumes of data are stored to encounter businesses' various requirements.

11.2.2 Understand Data

In a business environment, conversations of the products and operations have to be collected to evaluate their meaning and create methods useful for making the perfect decision. Meanwhile, the first, i.e. capture stage collects data from the sources and users; a large section may contain unnecessary information that is required to remove earlier for extracting meaningful information from SM data. This process offers detail about user's sentiments such as what is the user's opinion about the company and their product (Despoina Antonakaki et al., 2017). Several valuable metrics, trends, interests, covering their backgrounds, network of relationships, and concerns about the users can also be formed in this phase.

11.2.3 Present Data

The present data is the final stage of the process of SMA. This step gives a simple format of several analytics like presentation, analyzation, evaluation, and summarization. Many visualization techniques might be used to display useful and meaningful information. Visualizing the data using the visual dashboard is the most popularly used interface technique that accumulates and displays the information from several sources (Despoina Antonakaki et al., 2017).

11.3 Social Media Analytics

In recent days, the significant domains of SMA are prediction, group/network analysis, and content analysis; this is shown in Figure 11.3.

11.3.1 Content Analysis

It is one of the research approaches, and it is also used for identifying patterns in the recorded communication. In this analysis, automatically gather data from a group of texts that can be oral, written, or visual. It is used to measure the existence of specific phrases, concepts, and words in a group of historical texts. Furthermore, content analysis can able to make qualitative conclusions by analyzing the meaningful words, concepts, and semantic relationship (Chae et al., 2012). It can be implemented in a wide collection of texts, and it is used in a diversity of sectors, containing anthropology, marketing, cognitive science, media studies, psychology, and other social science disciplines (Figure 11.4).

11.3.1.1 Topic Identification

Topic identification is utilized to pick up the most trending topics of chats or conversation on social media sites and classifies the topics based on the content and

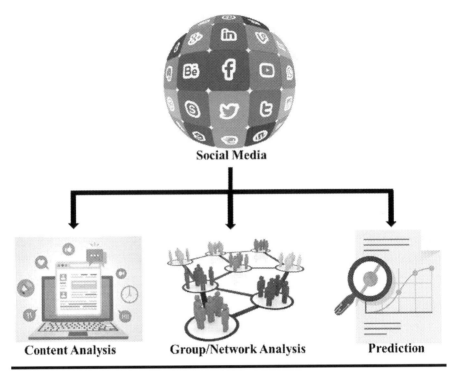

Social Media

Content Analysis   **Group/Network Analysis**   **Prediction**

Figure 11.3   Social media analytics.

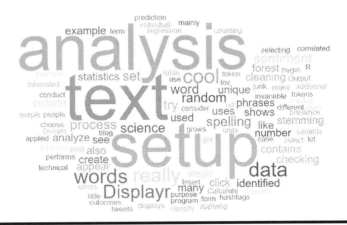

Figure 11.4   Content analysis.

specific areas, brands, and names. Furthermore, the classified and summarized topics from a large SM dataset are to be analyzed, visualize, and interrelate at both topic level and document level for identifying the relationship between topics and documents (Chae et al., 2012). The topic analysis is also an interesting research area that can automatically recognize and identify what kind of issue is stated on a specific site. Consider the given example that helps us to recognize the hidden benefits of topic analysis. For example: "My product hasn't shipped yet" will be labeled as a shipping issue on an online shopping website.

11.3.1.2 Sentiment Analysis

Sentiment analysis that identifies human emotions and sentiments from SM sites is a more complex task, but this process can be done using sentiment analysis for understanding the customer's reactions to the particular product or brand that can make use of business development (Feldman, 2013). The sentiments are mainly divided into three kinds: positive, negative, and neutral that include happy, sad, distressed, humor, surprised, sarcasm, and many others (Ana Mihanovic et al. 2012). Researchers are trying to develop an efficient and capable solution to analyze and visualize the sentiments.

11.3.1.3 Social Multimedia Analysis

Social multimedia includes text, images, videos, maps, and so on. The social multimedia analysis is used to analyze images, speech, video clips, landmarks, and locations and occasionally focuses on content analysis (Cioffi-Revilla, 2010).

11.3.2 Group and Network Analysis

11.3.2.1 Group Identification

SM has two different kinds of groups: primary and secondary. In a primary group, family and friends can chat and share personal things in that group. The secondary group is larger and impersonal when compared to the primary group. Social media analysis helps to find emerging groups (Figure 11.5) and their aims also define the similarity among the social groups. Group identification has detailed relationships like Twitter "followers," a Facebook "friends," and also relationship through a mutual activity like likes, comments, etc. on the SM platform (D. Kavitha, 2017).

11.3.2.2 Relationship Characterization

This method defines identifying the relationship among two groups based on their chats/conversations through SM sites. Relationships are classified based on the conversation. Some research has used SM content to define characteristics of an online community (D. Kavitha, 2017). Some other research used to know about social media user and their character from publicly accessible information from the FB profiles, status updates, photos, etc.

Figure 11.5 Group and network analysis.

11.3.3 Prediction

Prediction is used to predict future indicators in social media and also indicates regular events. Predictive analytics from social media is a grouping of sentiments and influence analysis. Prediction is also recently used in social networks for instance to foretell the cinema revenues and consequence of the civic elections, product-market activities, and financial market.

11.4 Techniques and Algorithms

11.4.1 Techniques

SMA is a developing area that contains a diversity of modeling and analytical techniques from various fields. These are natural language processing (NLP), news analytics, opinion mining, scraping, text analytics, and many others.

11.4.1.1 NLP

NLP interaction between human language, i.e. natural language and computer, is a very tedious task. It can be done by NLP which is commonly used in Artificial Intelligence, computer science, linguistics, and so on. NLP plays an important role in SMA and extracting significant knowledge from human language input and output.

11.4.1.2 News Analytics

News analytics and news sentiment calculations are used by the business trading, market surveillance, and risk management of both buyers and sellers. The news stories are made up of unstructured data that may contain text, images, and also video clips. Automatic text analysis utilizes machine learning and NLP.

11.4.1.3 Opinion Mining

Opinion mining or sentiment mining is a booming research area to identify and analyze human sentiments and their opinion about a particular product, brand in a business environment. It can be used in tweets, movie reviews, message boards, news, weblogs, etc. (Jindal & Liu, 2008). The sentiments and opinions of a particular product using the online customer's reviews can be useful for enhancing online shopping companies. The customer reviews have feedback about a product or a company; however, customer reviews can be categorized into positive, negative, and neutral using opinion mining/sentiment analysis (Malik Khizar Hayat 2012).

11.4.1.4 Scraping

To collect SM data using scraping is also named web data extraction, web harvesting, etc., which is extracting unstructured data and transforming it into a structured format. Scraping is very useful for collecting an enormous quantity of SM data for analysis that is used to make a business decision.

11.4.1.5 Text Analytics

It involves information extraction, information retrieval (IR), pattern recognition, tagging/annotation, lexical analysis to identify word frequency distributions, data mining techniques containing predictive analytics, link analysis, and association of mining and visualization technique.

11.4.2 Machine Learning and Deep Learning Algorithms

Machine learning and deep learning algorithms are used for SMA. The algorithms are as follows.

11.4.2.1 Artificial Neural Network (ANN)

ANN process the information performed based on human nervous systems. The network includes several interconnected layers as like as the connections of neurons in the human brain and information from a single node to many other nodes for disseminating the information in the preliminary layers toward the output layer (Bao & Dawood, 2019).

11.4.2.2 SVM

It is one of the common and popular machine learning algorithms. In this algorithm, every data object is plotted as a factor in n-dimensional space (where n is the variety of facets the users having) with the cost of every character being the value of specific coordinates (Bao & Dawood, 2019).

11.4.2.3 Convolutional Neural Network (CNN)

CNN is involved of several layers by insufficient layers in neural network (NN), and it has a convolutional layer and subsampling layer (Rumelhart et al., 2009). CNN has completely connected networks to produce exact output with minimal cost (Khan et al., 2010).

11.4.2.4 Recurrent Neural Network (RNN)

RNN a classification of ANN has innovative activities. It can utilize to series of inputs unsystematically. RNN founds excellent jobs, i.e. speech to textual content transformation (Khan et al., 2010).

11.4.2.5 Auto-Encoder (AE)

AE is similarly named as auto-associator and Diabolo network due to its structure and it is aimed to examine and encode the data (Bao & Dawood, 2019). AE is an unsupervised learning method having encoder and decoder elements (Rumelhart et al., 2009).

11.4.2.6 Deep Belief Network (DBN)

DBN is a classification of DNN as an alternative propagative model involved quite many hidden layers with implicit variables (Rumelhart et al., 2009).

11.5 Tools

In this section, extracting, transforming, preprocessing, programming, and analyzing the social media analysis tools are discussed, as given in Table 11.1 (Weiguo Fan Michael D.Gordon, 2014).

11.6 Research Challenges

Many research issues in the social network platform are discussed below:

- There are lots and lots of hyperlinks are available on SM sites. The hyperlinks are interconnected with each other. Hence extracting and analyzing the hyperlinks using link analysis is a complex task (Umar, 2014).

Table 11.1 Significant Tools

Tools	Examples
Extraction tools	■ Web Scraping ■ FMiner ■ Parsehub ■ Spinn3r ■ Octoparse ■ Google Trends ■ Social mention ■ Twitter Scraper
Transformation tools	■ Informatica PowerCenter ■ Microsoft SQL Server Integration Services ■ Talend ■ Panoply ■ Alooma ■ Logstash ■ Heka ■ Google Fusion Tables ■ Zoho Reports
Data cleaning tools	■ Google Refine ■ Data Wrangler ■ Drake ■ TIBCO Clarity ■ Winpure ■ DataMatch ■ Quadient Data Cleaner ■ Cloudingo ■ Reifier
Scientific programming tools	■ R Programming ■ MATLAB® ■ Python
Commercial toolkits for business	■ SAS Sentiment Analysis Manager ■ Rapid Miner ■ IBM SPSS
Monitoring tools	■ Trackur ■ FeedBurner ■ PRTG Network Monitor ■ WhatsUp Gold (WUG) ■ Keyhole ■ Hootsuite ■ Twitter Counter ■ Digimind

(Continued)

Table 11.1 (Continued)   Significant Tools

Tools	Examples
	■ TweetReach ■ Sprout Social ■ Klout ■ Simply Measured ■ Buffer
Tools for text analysis	■ OpenAmplify and Jodange ■ Python NLTK— Natural Language Toolkit ■ STATISTICA Text Miner ■ WordStat. ■ Discover Text ■ Google Cloud Natural Language API ■ LexalyticsSaliance ■ IBM SPSS Text Analytics ■ Expert System ■ Meaning Cloud ■ indico
Data visualization tools	■ Tableau ■ Grafana ■ Chartist. Js ■ FusionCharts ■ Datawrapper ■ Infogram ■ Google Charts ■ Chartio

■ Dynamic network analysis is a challenging task in SMA; for example YouTube, Instagram, and Facebook SM sites are dynamically changing at every minute (Chae et al., 2012).

■ Data cleansing, preprocess valuable from the SM dataset consume more time because it has unstructured data (Kularathne et al., 2017).

■ In SM sites, people are chatting with colloquial and private elements in their language. Hence, it is very hard to understand automatic sentiment analysis programs (Bright & Margetts, 2014).

■ The number of likes on a particular product or a brand doesn't perfectly reproduce real conversions. But still, it is difficult to analyze and increase the page likes of SM profiles (Praveena & Lakshmi, 2017).

■ SM sites have fake and duplicate profiles and spread fake news that lacks the quality of SM data. More analysis is needed to analyze the fake and duplicate information and to identify the fake profiles. It is also one of the challenging tasks of researchers.

11.7 Case Studies in Social Media Analytics

SMA is the practice of gathering data from blogs and SM websites and analyzing that data to make business decisions.

11.7.1 Barclays

Barclays is also named as PingIt, it was developed for mobile banking. They have done social media analysis in real time to the app for making significant changes. The results of the app were received well, and a low percentage of comments were negative. This app quickly makes public relations crises, and also this app quickly responds to permit 16- and 17-year-old people.

11.7.2 Keen

Keen company is wanted to know their customer reviews about the product. Hence they built an SMA model with several metrics like effect, sentiment, reach, and influence to understand SM campaigns.

11.7.3 Samsung

Samsung wanted to know customer support of their product using social media analysis. This organization asks the customer feedback about their product and then review their feedback and response within 2 months.

11.7.4 TOMS Shoes

TOMS shoes company targeted "one day without shoes" campaign on thousands of people around the world. It is severely monitored in SM with the #Withoutshoes hashtag. They saw the support building about the hashtag throughout the day.

11.7.5 Yale

This organization creates a blog for academic content, i.e. question and answering system. They used Tumblr for analyzing their content. This analysis improves the number of followers by +142% and 1,200 notes with two posts.

11.7.6 Cisco

Cisco is the worldwide leader in IT and networking. It observed recent trends and booming topics to contribute limited objectives. Cisco used social media analysis and obtained nearer targeted clients.

11.7.7 Kmart

Kmart evaluated SM feedbacks from a specific advertisement launched throughout distinctive networks over online and television at time duration.

11.8 Conclusion

Social media analytics is offering massive opportunities to recognize trends development in SM. The significant aspect of SMA is gathering and handling SM data, and this process is very difficult. A huge quantity of data is available in the SM platform. This chapter mentioned a brief introduction to SMA. Three stages of the process of SMA are discussed. Various kinds of social media data are given in this chapter. Significant applications of social media, fundamental techniques, machine learning, and deep learning algorithms are also presented. Various techniques in SMA and tools are discussed. Finally, research challenges and case studies of SMA is given. SMA is widely applied in business and academic applications to make the right decision.

References

Antonakaki, D., Spiliotopoulos, D., Samaras, C. V., Pratikakis, P., Ioannidis, S., & Fragopoulou, P. (2017, October 31). Social media analysis during political turbulence. *PloS One, 12*(10), e0186836.

Bao, Y., & Dawood, H. (2019). Towards deep learning prospects: Insights for social media analytics. Retrieved from http://www.ieee.org/publications_standards/publications/rights/index.html

Batrinca, B., & Treleaven, P. C. (2014). Social media analytics: A survey of techniques. Tools and platforms, Published online: 26 July. This article is published with open access at Springerlink.com

Bengio, Y. (2009). *Learning deep architectures for AI*. Retrieved from http://www.iro.umontreal.ca/bengioy

Bright, J., & Margetts, H. (2014). Scott Hale and TahaYasseri. The Use of Social Media for Research and Analysis: A Feasibility Study DWP ad hoc research report no. 13, Oxford Internet Institute on behalf of the Department for Work and Pensions. ISBN 978-1-78425-407-0.

Chae, J., Thomy, D., Boschy, H., Sejong, Y. J., Maciejewsk, R., Ebert, D. S., & Ertl, T. (2012). Spatiotemporal social media analytics for abnormal event detection and examination using seasonal-trend decomposition. Visual Analytics Science and Technology (VAST), 2012 IEEE Conference.

Cioffi-Revilla, C. (2010). Computational social science. *WIREs Computational Statistics.* doi:10.1002/wics.95

Feldman, R. (2013). Techniques and applications for sentiment analysis. *Communications of the ACM, 56*(4), 82–89.

Gastelum, Z. N., & Whattam, K. M. (2013). State-of-the arts of social media analytics research Pacific Northwest National Laboratory Richland. Washington 99352. PNNL-22171.

Jindal, N., & Liu, B. (2008). Opinion spam and analysis. In Proceedings of the 2008 International Conference on, Web Search and Data Mining, WSDM '08, 219–230. ACM, New York, NY.

Kalia, G. (2013). *A research paper on social media: An innovative educational tool.* Punjab: Chitkara University.

Kavitha, D. (2017). Survey of data mining techniques for social networking websites. *International Journal of Computer Science and Mobile Computing, 6*(4), 418–426.

Khan, A., Baharudin, B., Lee, L. H., & Khan, K. (2010). A review of machine learning algorithms for text-documents classification. *Journal of Advances in Information Technology, 1*(1). Retrieved from http://www.jait.us/uploadfile/2014/1223/20141223050800532.pdf

Kularathne, S. D., Dissanayake, R.B., Samarasinghe, N.D., Premalal, L.P.G., & Premaratne, S. C. (2017). Customer behavior analysis for social media. *International Journal of Advanced Engineering. Management and Science (IJAEMS), 3*(1). ISSN: 2454–1311.

Kumar, A., Khorwal, R., & Chaudhary, S. (2016). A survey on sentiment analysis using swarm intelligence. *Indian Journal of Science and Technology, 9*(39), 1–7.

Mihanovic, A., Gabelica, H., & Krstic, Z. (2012). *Big Data and sentiment analysis using Knime: Online reviews vs. social media.* Croatia: MIPRO Opatija.

Mukherjee, A., Liu, B., & Glance, N. (2012). Spotting fake reviewer groups in consumer reviews. In Proceedings of the 21st International Conference on World Wide Web, WWW '12, 191–200. ACM, New York, NY.

Patnaik, S., & Sucharita Barik, S. (2018). Social media analytics using visualization. *International Journal of Scientific Research Engineering & Technology (IJSRET), 7*(4). ISSN 2278–0882.

Praveena, T. L., & Lakshmi, N. V. Muthu. (2017). An overview of social media analytics. *International Journal of Advanced Scientific Technologies. Engineering and Management Sciences, 3*(1). IJASTEMS-ISSN: 2454-356X.

Umar, R. (2014). Social media analytics as a business intelligence practice: Current landscape & future prospects. International Conference on Parallel Processing (ICPP 2014).

Weiguo Fan Michael D.Gordon. (2014). Unveiling the power of social media analytics. Retrieved from https://www.researchgate.net/publication/259148570_The_Power_of_Social_Media_Analytics

https://aurus5.com/blog/cisco/cisco-logo-history-and-evolution/
https://barnraisersllc.com/2015/11/23/7-case-studies-show-social-media-analytics-pay-off/
https://biznology.com/2016/08/12-inspiring-social-media-monitoring-case-studies/
https://en.wikipedia.org/wiki/File:Samsung_Logo.svg
https://internetretailing.net/retail-directory-listing/apparel-and-footwear/lipsy
https://monkeylearn.com/blog/text-analysis-tools/
https://www.businessinsider.com/pizza-hut-brings-back-old-logo-2019-6
https://www.google.com/url?sa=i&url=https%3A%2F%2Fwww.freelogovectors.net%2Fkeen-logo-eps-file%2F&psig=AOvVaw1SkarYBiiiwHoki8-0j7v4&ust=1587628689027000&source=images&cd=vfe&ved=0CAIQjRxqFwoTCKDY-PrH--gCFQAAAAAdAAAAABAM
https://www.google.com/url?sa=i&url=https%3A%2F%2Fen.wikipedia.org%2Fwiki%2FKmart&psig=AOvVaw3dy7zw97LS4EiRnTd6aKfs&ust=1587628790156000&source=images&cd=vfe&ved=0CAIQjRxqFwoTCJCVkanI--gCFQAAAAAdAAAAABAD
https://www.google.com/url?sa=i&url=https%3A%2F%2Fen.wikipedia.org%2Fwiki%2FTV_Land&psig=AOvVaw0WDWd41Nk-1XS10E4AW0yG&ust=158762

8808483000&source=images&cd=vfe&ved=0CAIQjRxqFwoTCOiw57nI--gCFQAAAAAdAAAAABAD

https://www.google.com/url?sa=i&url=https%3A%2F%2Fonjalazbroz.blogspot.com%2F2
018%2F11%2Fmulticulturalism-necessity.html&psig=AOvVaw3Ij4r-4LxXCAkMm
wnjqrQK&ust=1587999174434000&source=images&cd=vfe&ved=0CAIQjRxqFwoTC
KCK_e-shukCFQAAAAAdAAAAABAD

https://www.google.com/url?sa=i&url=https%3A%2F%2Fseeklogo.com%2Fvector-logo
%2F205129%2Fgatorade&psig=AOvVaw350C6Xi2l-6s0AS3yrKiiX&ust=158762
8782314000&source=images&cd=vfe&ved=0CAIQjRxqFwoTCLjguNPI--gCFQAAAAAdAAAAABAH

https://www.google.com/url?sa=i&url=https%3A%2F%2Fblogs.helsinki.fi%2Fquantitative-
communication%2Fmethods%2Fcontent-analysis%2F&psig=AOvVaw0ClNC5ASe4o4
wrn4GxPST-&ust=1587999275197000&source=images&cd=vfe&ved=0CAIQjRxqFwo
TCMDC28CshukCFQAAAAAdAAAAABAM

https://www.google.com/url?sa=i&url=https%3A%2F%2Fwww.fte.org%2Fsite-spotlight-
yale-university%2Fyale-logo%2F&psig=AOvVaw19DjEpMeTZByocZtsYVGZV&
ust=1587628774468000&source=images&cd=vfe&ved=0CAIQjRxqFwoTCPjmuq
HI--gCFQAAAAAdAAAAABAD

https://www.google.com/url?sa=i&url=https%3A%2F%2Fwww.pinterest.com%2Fpin
%2F452963674998706292%2F&psig=AOvVaw2vezEFuc6dUujMj8YejGzI&
ust=1587628798183000&source=images&cd=vfe&ved=0CAIQjRxqFwoTCPCC0a7I--gCFQAAAAAdAAAAABAD

https://www.google.com/url?sa=i&url=https%3A%2F%2Fwww.premierleague.com
%2Fpartners%2Fbarclays&psig=AOvVaw15ndhLVdUXJ1ncuZ7DmVWp&ust=15
87628628488000&source=images&cd=vfe&ved=0CAIQjRxqFwoTCNiV2-TH--gCFQAAAAAdAAAAABAD

https://www.google.com/url?sa=i&url=https%3A%2F%2Fwww.prnewswire.com
%2Fnews-releases%2Fmoneygram-launches-new-online-money-transfer-service-plat-
form-with-walmart-300322812.html&psig=AOvVaw06_Nkd8OzRy5X4oHz0RAzl&
ust=1587628793952000&source=images&cd=vfe&ved=0CAIQjRxqFwoTCNiWza7I--gCFQAAAAAdAAAAABAJ

https://www.predictiveanalyticstoday.com/top-free-software-for-text-analysis-text-mining-
text-analytics/

https://www.predictiveanalyticstoday.com/top-software-for-text-analysis-text-mining-text-
analytics/

https://www.socialmediatoday.com/social-business/12-best-social-media-monitoring-tools-
consider

https://www.softwaretestinghelp.com/data-visualization-tools/

https://www.toptal.com/designers/data-visualization/data-visualization-tools

Chapter 12

Robust Statistics: Methods and Applications

R. Muthukrishnan

Professor, Department of Statistics, Bharathiar University, Coimbatore, India

Contents

DOI: 10.1201/9781003175889-12

Objectives

■ To understand the assumptions/limitations of classical statistical procedures.
■ To explore various robust statistical procedures developed in the recent past by considering the measure of location and scale in the area of data depth, regression, and multivariate analysis.
■ To analyze data using robust statistical methods along with conventional statistical procedures using robust statistical packages in *R* programming.
■ To understand the usage of robust statistical procedures in machine learning tasks.

12.1 Introduction

Decision making in several areas of science depends on statistics. Statistics plays an extremely vital role as an aid in decision making. In the present contemporary state of affairs, statisticians increasingly address the problems and issues that arise out in the analysis of large, voluminous, and multidimensional data. This is made possible due to the advancement of computer technology that largely facilitates the analysis of data of multivariate nature that results from scientific and statistical experiments. In this context, traditional/classical techniques are infeasible for analysis due to the enormity of data, high dimensionality of data, and heterogeneous nature of data. These techniques depend on many assumptions like normality, independence, and homogeneity.

Robust statistics offers efficient methods to estimate location, scale, and regression parameters as an alternative approach to conventional statistical methods. The estimators produced by robust statistics are not in any way affected by minor deviations from the model assumptions. But standard methods are comparatively affected. Robust statistics is a theory that supports stability in statistical procedures. Robust statistics examine deviations of model assumptions systematically, using preexisting methods and make improvements in the existing procedures wherever required. The robust approach to data analysis and model fitting involves developing techniques that result in dependable parameter estimates and related tests, even when data does not follow a given assumption exactly.

This chapter explores the most widely used robust statistical methods and their applications. For understanding purpose, the basic robust statistical procedures along with classical procedures are demonstrated using few examples.

12.2 History of Robust Statistics

The robust statistics began to bloom in the middle of the 20th century with the article titled *a survey of sampling from contaminated distributions* (see Tukey [1960]). This work is considered as a revolution in robust statistics. Later, the foundation of the wide-ranging theory of robust statistics was laid by Huber (1964) and Hampel (1968). The theoretical approach to robust statistics with the notion of maximum likelihood type, M-estimators was first introduced by Huber (1964). In the paper, the author found that the estimator behaves optimally in a minimax sense over the neighborhood of a stochastic model that contains data generated by true distribution. Hampel (1968) developed the characteristics of robust statistics, such as the qualitative, quantitative, and infinitesimal robustness in the form of influence function and breakdown point.

These authors' contributions laid the foundation for the growth of modern robust statistical procedures. The collection of research papers on robust statistics has increased, and it has received greater attention. Nowadays, new branches of applications have been opened up in robust statistics areas by combining conventional procedures, which intensifies computational algorithms.

Research in the robust statistics field is experiencing significant growth in the past few decades. This claim can be verified by the publication of a large number of articles, some of them are as follows: Tukey (1960), Huber (1964), Hampel (1968), Maronna (1976), Donoho (1982), Rousseeuw (1984), Rousseeuw and Yohai (1984), Hampel et al. (1986), Davies (1987), Yohai (1987), Rousseeuw and Croux (1993), Hawkins and Olive (1999), Rousseeuw and Driessen (1999), Tatsuoka and Tyler (2000), Croux et al. (2007), Todorov and Filzmoser (2009), Hubert and Driessen (2004), and Hubert et al. (2012). The works of Huber (1981), Rousseeuw and Leroy (1987), Tiku and Akkaya (2004), Huber and Ronchetti (2009), and Wilcox (2010, 2017) kick-started the current research efforts in this research area.

International Conferences on Robust Statistics (ICORS) are being organized, and the conference proceedings are released every year since 2001. A pioneering institute in statistics, the Indian Statistical Institute, Kolkata, has organized the ICORS in India in the year 2015.

12.3 Classical Statistics vs. Robust Statistics

Statistics involves digging out information that is useful from experimental data. For more than two centuries, parametric stochastic models are used to convey the information in the performance of these models and applications require strict adherence to the assumptions. But it is noted that the practical scenario of data does not act as agreeably as defined by their assumptions. The well-known assumption is normality. The normality can be viewed from Figure 12.1.

The above bell-shaped symmetric curve follows a standard normal distribution. It describes the features of data distribution. Almost all conventional

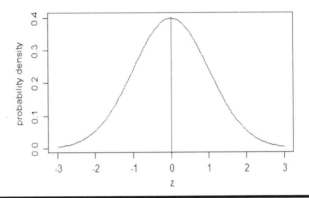

Figure 12.1   Standard normal distribution.

statistical procedures rely on the behavior of this distributional assumption. Classical statistical procedures work well for the data if it is distributed normally. Moreover, the existing procedures are ideal only under a series of assumptions such as linearity, normality, symmetry, independence, or finite moments. These assumptions, which were made in the theory of statistics two centuries ago, formed the framework for developing all the classical procedures. However, the underlying assumptions are rarely met when analyzing the experimental or observable data. Deviations from the distributional and other assumptions, without fail, nullify the optimality seriously. Further, the conventional procedures are mostly based on maximum likelihood theory and are very sensitive to the data, particularly when data deviate from the model assumptions. Hence, in situations involving heavy-tailed/non-normal distributions, the results produced by classical procedures are unrealistic.

Robust statistics is resistant to errors in the results, i.e. it has reasonable efficiency and small bias even if met with the required assumptions approximately. A robust procedure is nearly as good as the conventional procedure for a normal distribution but is substantially more effective for non-normal situations. In the past few decades, various robust alternatives were developed. The main objective of such a robust approach is to fit a model with good data points and to detect the extremes well in advance and it can experiment further if preferred.

Few *limitations* of robust statistical procedures are mentioned below:

Robust measures of location and scale estimates are obtained by considering only the subset of data points, whereas the conventional measures are based on all data points.

The computational aspects of many robust procedures are established by considering the subset of data points. Construction of subsets and selection of best subset would require more time, more storage space, and high-speed computers.

Further, the robust procedures may discard the extreme observations and/or by assigning the least weight to the extreme data points/outliers (inconsistent data points) to compute the robust statistical measures.

12.4 Robust Statistical Measures

Statistical measures, specifically measure of location and scale, play a vibrant part in statistical analyses. The computation of such good measures lays the foundation for almost all statistical methods. Measures of location are defined as finding a good data point in a dataset that represents almost all the data points. Finding the deviations between each point and identified location is referred to as a measure of variation. The mean and variance derived from a set of sample data are, respectively, used as good estimates for the unknown location and scale parameters.

Similarly, when one deals with multidimensional data, the mean vector, which denotes a point in the multidimensional space, collectively represents the location parameters of the variable, and the variance–covariance matrix represents the scattering of data points. The estimation of the location vector and the covariance matrix in the multivariate setup is very monotonous when dealing with a huge volume of data and/or contaminated data. The classical method of estimating the multivariate location and scatter is used for all variables and cases in the given dataset, but it never gives consistent results, if the dataset has outliers. Many robust alternatives are proposed to estimate the multivariate location and scatter. Most robust procedures use only good data points. For example, h out of n observations is used to estimate these parameters in p-dimensional data, where h = (n+p+1)/2.

Many robust alternatives are proposed to estimate location and scale in a univariate and multivariate context. An estimator that is fairly good for a wide variety of distributions is called a robust estimator. The quality of robustness of the estimators has been measured by basic tools such as breakdown point and influence function, which are defined below:

Breakdown Point: It is a threshold value above which the estimators start producing arbitrary results. It indicates the number of incorrect observations that can be handled by an estimator before generating inappropriate results at random.

Influence Function: It is a function that measures the infinitesimal effect of impurity on the estimator. It describes how an estimator acts when there is a small change in a sample.

For example, the median is preferred as a robust measure of the location to mean, because the breakdown value of the median is 0.5 while it is 0.0 for the mean. That is, a single observation can make the results unreliable. Robust statistical measures of dispersion, namely, median absolute deviation and interquartile range, are the viable alternatives to the classical measures such as standard deviation and range.

In general, trimmed and winsorized estimators (see Tukey [1960]) are the robust methods in statistics but the basic class of robust statistics is M-estimators (see Huber [1964]). A simple way of defining a conventional measure of location is to minimize the expected squared difference between the point, x, and some constant a, i.e. $E(x-a)^2$. The resulting value of a gets affected by the extremities of x, i.e. x deviates from a when $(x-a)^2$ increases rapidly. The value of a gets pulled into the tail of the distribution when extremes exist in the case of non-normal distribution. M-measure of location uses the same approach but it allocates less weight to extreme values by replacing $(x–a)^2$ with some other weight function. In this context, the usage of Andrew's, Hampel's, and Tukey's weight functions are referred to as redescending M-estimators. Moreover, Mallows (1975) extended this, by applying suitable weights that reduce the influence function of the gross values of x, called as GM-estimator.

In multivariate analysis, the sample means vector and variance–covariance matrix are the maximum likelihood estimates for the measures of location and scatter. These are reliable estimates in the context of multivariate normal models. But they are very sensitive to non-normal models. Hence, the basic problem is to create robust equivariant estimates as alternatives to the conventional sample mean vector and variance–covariance matrix.

In the context of multivariate setting, multivariate M-estimates were introduced by Maronna (1976). They deal with the measures, namely weighted mean and covariance. The computational steps of these estimators comprise an iterative procedure that corresponds to the weighted estimator in the multivariate version. The initial estimates of the mean vector and variance–covariance matrix are calculated by conventional procedures and then squared Mahalanobis distances are calculated. After that, the distances were sorted and assigned weights by considering the largest distance that receives smaller weights. The extreme observations of the distance have weights very close or equal to zero. The iteration process stops on reaching the final solution when the function gives minimum covariance. The breakdown value of the multivariate M-estimator is not exceeding $1/(p+1)$, where, p denotes the number of variables. The high breakdown robust estimators, such as minimum volume ellipsoid estimator (MVE), minimum covariance determinant estimator (MCD), S-estimators, and MM-estimators, are established in the past few decades.

The minimum volume ellipsoid estimator is a multivariate estimator, which was proposed by Rousseeuw (1985). The estimator tries to find the ellipsoid of minimum volume in such a way to cover h observations (here, h may be at least half of the observations) from n observations in a dataset. The measure of location, which is the geometrical center of an ellipsoid of minimum volume, and variance–covariance matrix are computed based on the data points that cover the ellipsoid of minimum volume. In other words, the subsets of around half of the observations are analyzed to discover the subset that would minimize the volume of ellipsoid occupied by data. The data which covers the ellipsoid of minimum volume is used to compute the covariance matrix. The Mahalanobis distances to all the data points are computed to determine how far away a data point is from the center of the data. A suitable cutoff point is measured and observations having distances that surpass the cutoff are confirmed as outliers. Rousseeuw (1985) has introduced a minimum covariance determinant estimator (MCD) as another robust estimator. In the computational procedure, the first step is to create more subsets that contain at least 50% of observations from a given dataset. Then the next step is to find the determinant of all the subset matrices. The final step is to compute the estimates for location vector and variance–covariance matrix by considering the subset matrix's data points, which has the minimum determinant value.

Davies (1987) proposed an S-estimator, which is defined by minimizing the determinant of a variance–covariance matrix with the constraint on the magnitude of corresponding Mahalanobis distances. Utilization of the differences rather than the residuals have the benefit of an increase in statistical efficacy, while the strength of estimators, computed by their breakdown points, does not change. The highest proportion of outliers that an estimator can tolerate is called a breakdown value. While working with residual differences, it is conceivable to attain the highest breakdown value, 50% or more. MVE is generally viewed as a special case and it can be within the class of S-estimators. Tatsuoka and Tyler (2000) proposed a high efficient and high breakdown value estimator, called MM-estimator, as an extension of the S-estimator for multivariate normal distribution.

Many algorithms were proposed to simplify the computing steps and get more efficiency. Many authors have proposed and studied various algorithmic techniques, such as iterative computation of the robust multivariate MVE, feasible solution algorithm (FSA), improved FSA, fast algorithm for MCD (FAST-MCD), a deterministic algorithm, etc., to enhance the efficiency of robust estimators for location and scatter parameters in the multivariate set up. These algorithmic techniques were developed by Cook et al. (1993), Hawkins (1994a, 1994b), Rousseeuw and Driessen (1999), Hawkins and Olive (1999), Todorov and Pires (2007), Todorov and Filzmoser (2009), Hubert et al. (2012), Filzmoser et al. (2012), Filzmoser and Todorov (2013).

Example 12.1: Computation of measure of location and scale

Consider a company working with 15 employees. Their annual salary (in lakhs) is given below: **3.0, 4.0, 3.2, 4.5, 4.1, 3.5, 3.6, 3.7, 2.4, 4.5, 2.2, 4.9, 2.5, 70.0,** and **100.0**.

The most widely used measure of location is the mean, which is computed as 14.4 lakhs from the above data. Among the 15 observations, 13 of them are below this location and two of them are above the estimated location. This measure of location doesn't represent any one of the above employee's salary or as a whole. It is noted that the mean provides a reliable estimate of the center only when the variable is normally distributed, if not, it gets affected very extensively, i.e. it is not a good representative of the given dataset when extremes are present in the data.

Similarly, in the context of measure of dispersion, the standard deviation is most widely used. The standard deviation of the above data is **29.2** lakhs. The computational part of this measure of scale is also based on the above measure of location, arithmetic mean. It also gets affected when the data follow the non-normality and/or contains outliers.

Many robust alternatives are available for mean such as median, trimmed mean, and winsorized mean. The location measure, the median, can be computed by selecting a data point in the middle position in a dataset after sorting data or averaging the two middle data points. Another method of computing a measure of central tendency is trimmed mean, which uses the concept of mean but eliminates a small proportion of the highest and lowest values. The winsorized mean is similar to the trimmed mean, but the lowest and highest values are not removed but replaced by the lowest and highest untrimmed score.

The median and the trimmed mean of the above data are **3.7** and **3.8**, respectively. These location measures represent nearly nine of the above employee's salary. Apart from this, the basic robust statistical measure of location and scale is computed based on the concept of Huber's M-estimator. The robust measure of location is **3.82**, and the corresponding measure of scale is **1.19** lakhs. The visualization of the above dataset is presented in the form of a boxplot (Figure 12.2).

From this plot, one can observe the extremes values **70.0** and **100.0** and give special attention to those data points. If discarding the extremes from the above data, then the measure of location and scale remains the same in the context of conventional methods (mean and the standard deviation is **3.5** and **0.86** lakhs) and robust method (Huber's location and scale are **3.5** and **0.89**).

A significant point made by the example is that sample mean is profoundly influenced by at least one extreme called *outliers*. Care must be taken when utilizing the sample mean since its value can be profoundly atypical and hence possibly deceptive. Outliers and long-tailed distributions are cause for serious concern in real-world problems since they blow up the standard error of sample mean. A robust statistical measure is a well-defined one that is about as productive as efficient as the conventional measure in a normal distribution. However, it is extensively more efficient in non-normal cases.

Example 12.2: Computation of measure of location vector and scatter matrix

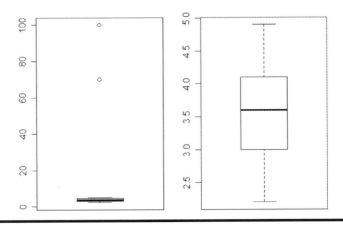

Figure 12.2   Boxplots (with/without outliers).

Consider the following artificial bivariate data, which contains 20 cases of two variables.

X1: {50,51,58,64,69,65,63,68,61,60,59,58,52,95,98,57,63,58,64,53}
X2: {30,31,34,34,36,34,33,34,31,35,33,32,32,30,31,32,34,31,32,32}

For the above data, compute the measure of location vector and scatter matrix under classical and a robust procedure. The computed conventional measure of location, mean vector is (63.30, 32.55) and the covariance matrix is $\begin{pmatrix} 157.27 & -2.12 \\ -2.12 & 2.79 \end{pmatrix}$ by considering all the observations and giving equal weights.

The robust measure of the mean vector and covariance matrix are (59.61, 32.78) and $\begin{pmatrix} 31.43 & 6.44 \\ 6.44 & 2.54 \end{pmatrix}$, respectively. By comparing the covariance matrix estimated under these two procedures, the variance–covariance matrix shows a large variation in X1, i.e. 157.27 and 31.43 under classical and robust procedures, respectively. Similarly, one can see the large variation in the covariance between X1 and X2 under the classical procedure and robust procedure are −2.12 and 6.44, respectively.

The variation in the covariance matrix is due to the extremes observations present in the data. To find the extremes in multivariate data, one can visualize the data in a graph, namely distance–distance (DD) plot by computing robust and Mahalanobis distance. The DD plot (Figure 12.3) shows that there are two points as extremes in the dataset. Suppose if the two extremes are discarded, then the computed conventional covariance matrix is $\begin{pmatrix} 31.42 & 6.44 \\ 6.44 & 2.53 \end{pmatrix}$ and the location vector is (59.61, 32.78), which is similar to the result produced by the robust procedure. It is established that the conventional variance–covariance matrix gets affected even a single extreme is present in the data.

It is known that an extreme point can affect the estimate of the location vector and scatter matrix. To view the extremes (outliers) many graphical procedures have been established. For a bivariate study, a simple visualization of bivariate data is a scatter plot, which is a graph that shows the relationship between two variables. The data is plotted for two different variables on one set of axes. The points that lie at a great distance from core data distribution are referred to as outlier.

The variance–covariance matrix determines multivariate data shape and size. Mahalanobis distance is the broadly realized distance measure that considers the concern of covariance matrix. The observations that have the large squared Mahalanobis distance are defined as multivariate outliers. The Mahalanobis distances are to be computed by following a robust procedure to give solid measures for identifying the outliers. The distance measure gets affected when data departs from the main data cloud because location parameters and covariance matrix are usually

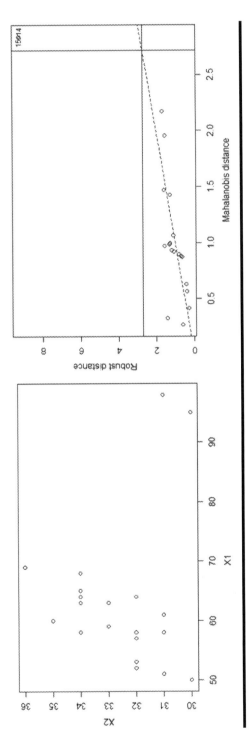

Figure 12.3   Scatter and distance–distance plots.

estimated in a nonrobust manner. The most frequently used robust estimator is the Minimum Covariance Determinant (MCD) estimator. Robust distance is achieved by replacing the estimates, location, and scatter in the distance formula. Rousseeuw and Zomeren (1991) used the robust distance for the detection of multivariate outliers. The corresponding covariance plot is namely distance–distance plot. The tolerance ellipse plot is only suitable to find extreme cases in bivariate data. For more than three variables, a distance–distance plot is more suitable to locate the extremes observations.

12.5 Robust Regression Procedures

The regression analysis has an essential part in model fitting under the study of response and predictor variables. It deals with two main categories, namely, parameter estimation and variable selection. For the estimation of regression parameters, the least square method is being used traditionally. This method mainly relies upon specific assumptions, including the normality of the error distribution. Another part of the regression analysis is to identify the significant variables, namely feature selection. More number of regressors in a model can reduce modeling biases. But, it leads to less accurate predictions and also reduces the efficiency of the estimates. Hence, the selection of relevant variables is vital. When the extremes are available in the data, the least square estimation brings about parameter estimates that don't give valuable information to most of the data.

Regression models with traditional procedures require various assumptions on independent/predictor variables, dependent/response variables, and relationships. The regression analysis is associated with the terms such as linearity, homo-scedasticity, multicollinearity, independence of errors, etc. Various extensions have been advanced, allowing every one of these assumptions to be relaxed and excluded completely in some cases. A few techniques are general enough that they can relax numerous assumptions at once, and in other cases, this can be accomplished by consolidating various extensions. These extensions make the estimation technique increasingly unpredictable and tedious and may likewise require more data to deliver a similarly exact model.

Beyond the assumptions, a few other statistical properties of the data empha-tically impact the performance of various estimation strategies. The statistical connection between the error terms and the regressors assumes a significant job in deciding if an estimation method has necessary sampling properties, for example unbiasedness and consistency. The probability distribution of the independent variables has impacted the accuracy of estimates of regression coefficients.

Conventional statistical procedures attempt to fit better by considering all data points. The standard criterion of the least-squares procedure is to minimize the sum of squared residuals to estimate the regression parameters. In the event of data containing outliers, the parameter estimation may go astray firmly from the clean data. For example, outliers can pull the regression line. Since all data points acquire similar weights in the least-squares principle, huge deviations are conveyed over all the residuals, frequently making them difficult to detect. Robust statistics objective is to minimize outliers' effect on the estimation of regression coefficients. Robust methods attempt to fit the majority of data by assuming that the good data points outnumber the outliers. Outliers would then able to be recognized by observing the residuals, which are enormous in the robust statistical analysis. A significant task thereafter is to ask for the causes of occurrence of outliers, however, they should not be ignored, but have to be examined and inferred.

Many problems may occur while fitting a linear regression model such as non-linearity of data, correlation of errors, assumptions on the variance of error terms, outliers, high leverage points, and collinearity. The least-square sensitivity to outliers is caused by two factors. The first is, the error term is processed using squared residuals. Any residual with a high value will have an extremely huge error term comparative with the others. The subsequent one is that using the mean as a measure of location which is not robust, any large square will have an extremely solid effect on the criterion, bringing about the extreme data point affecting the fit. The two common solutions for these issues are: First, the error term can be estimated in another manner, by supplanting the squared residuals by another function of squared residuals which safely mirrors the residual size. M-estimation idea is derived from this notion (see Huber, 1981). Second, a robust location measure, for example, a median or a trimmed mean is utilized rather than the conventional mean. Regression methods dependent on this notion incorporated on least median of squares (LMS) and least trimmed squares (LTS) (see Rousseeuw, 1984; Rousseeuw and Leroy, 1987). Rousseeuw and Yohai (1984) achieved robustness by minimizing the scale of residuals.

Robust regression analysis delivers a substitute for least squares regression analysis which fails to fulfill the fundamental assumptions due to data characteristics. Sometimes, by applying suitable transformation of a variable to validate the assumptions. However, it affects the parameter estimates significantly when extremes are present in the dataset. Robust regression procedures can tolerate a certain amount of extremes and reliable regression parameters are estimated. Among the robust estimators, the M-estimator (see Huber, 1964), least median squares estimator (LMS), and least trimmed squares estimator (LTS) (see Rousseeuw, 1984) are considered as popular methods. LMS uses the concept of minimizing the median of residuals, while LTS uses minimizing the trimmed squared residuals. Minimizing the function of residuals is considered in M-estimation procedures.

Many works that have been published in the area of model fitting are available in the literature for reference. In the least-squares procedure, least absolute deviation estimation, and comprehensive M-estimation, distant observations sometimes firmly impact the estimation result, veiling a significant and intriguing relationship existing in most of the observations. The class of S-estimator is used in this scenario, which is smoothly down weighing the outliers in fitting the regression model to the data. It uses the concept of minimizing the scale value (see Rousseeuw and Yohai, 1984). The class of MM-estimators was introduced by Yohai (1987) in the context of fitting linear regression. Such estimates are fascinating as they join high proficiency and high breakdown value straightforwardly and instinctively. Regularly, one first begins with a robust regression estimator, normally an S-estimator, and continues with scale-dependent on this preliminary fit alongside a superior tuned function to acquire an increasingly efficient M-estimator of the regression parameter.

Example 12.3: Fitting of simple regression and robust regression model

Consider the data given below for fitting a simple regression model, $Y = \beta_0 + \beta_1 X + \varepsilon$.

X: {50,51,58,64,69,65,63,68,61,60,59,58,52,95,98,57,63,58,64,53}
Y: {30,31,34,34,36,34,33,34,31,35,33,32,32,30,31,32,34,31,32,32}

First, find some descriptive measures, such as mean, covariance matrix, correlation, and regression coefficients. Compare these measures by computing using classical and robust procedures. The measures mean and covariance matrix was already computed and discussed in Example 4.2. The computed correlation coefficients of the data under the conventional and robust procedures are –0.101 and 0.721, respectively. The computed correlation coefficient under conventional procedure indicates the negative correlation exists between variables X and Y. But robust procedures show a positive correlation among these variables. The scatter plot, distance–distance plot, fitted models with and without outliers are shown in Figure 12.4.

The vast difference is due to extreme observations in the dataset. The computed regression coefficients under the least square procedure and robust regression procedure are (33.404, –0.013) and (22.342, 0.176), respectively. Suppose, let us assume that extremes are discarded, then the computed correlation coefficients are 0.721 and 0.865 under classical and robust procedure respectively. Both the procedures show the results very close to each other and also indicate a positive correlation among the variables. The regression coefficients under conventional and robust procedures almost produce similar results, i.e. (20.567, 0.205) and (22.983, 0.167), respectively. It shows that extreme observations affect the fitting of simple regression models. In general, data with extremes can have an impact on fitting models and leads to unreliable predictions and decision making. Many robust procedures are established to fit any regression model with reliable estimates along with predictions. It shows that the researcher can use robust methods for model fitting when extremes are present in the data.

The following section describes one of the nonparametric approaches to compute robust measures of location and scale – data depth procedures.

12.6 Data Depth Procedures

In statistics, the measure of location is a vital aspect in the context of univariate/multivariate data analysis techniques. The conventional sample mean (vector) is

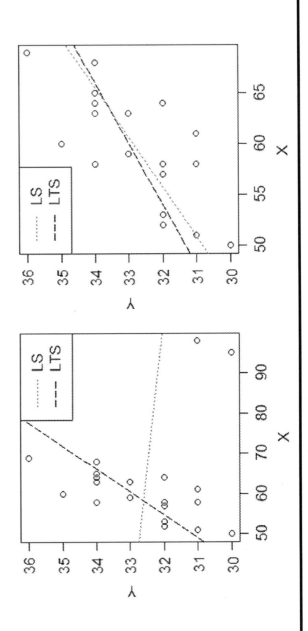

Figure 12.4 Fitted models under classical and robust procedure (with/without outliers).

very sensitive when the data contains extremes and thus gives an unreliable esti-mate of the population mean. For the past few decades, there has been substantial growth in statistics, especially, the concept of robust-based statistics, depth-based robust statistics, etc. in the context of estimation of the measure of location. The concept of depth-based statistics attracts the researchers because it gives reliable estimates of location in a given data cloud and it is a method that uses a non-parametric approach.

Depth is an integer assigned to a particular candidate fit relative to a dataset. This points to outside-inward/center-outward ordering of the sample points. The usual order statistics are different from depth order statistics. In usual order sta-tistics, data are ordered from smallest to largest, while the depth order statistics start from the middle sample point and move towards the outside in all directions. Data depth is defined as the position of the data point concerning entire data points in a data cloud. In a given data cloud the depth of a point is relative to the deepest point. Center-outward ordering of points in any dimension is provided by the data depth concept. This leads to a multivariate statistical analysis which is non-parametrical in nature and wherein no distributional assumptions are needed. Data depth can be used to measure the depth of a given point in an entire mul-tivariate data cloud. This concept is essential for center outward ordering of data points in any dimension rather than usual ranking from smallest to largest. It means ordering starts from the center and moves in all directions.

Multivariate location and scatter are determined by using the depth value of each data point. Interestingly, non-parametric depth functions have geometrical characteristics of data in an affine invariant way. Many graphical and quantitative methods are well established for analyzing the depth measures such as location, scale, and shape as well as comparing inference methods, outlier detection, or-dering of multivariate data, and classification of in-depth machinery. The point that has the highest depth value is considered as the deepest point and the lowest depth value as an outlier. When more than one data point has the same depth value, then their average is considered as the deepest point. The concept of data depth project of multidimensional to single-dimensional as well as projection pursuit is an emerging research field in recent days.

The selection of data depth is mainly based on computational complexity, dis-persion of data, asymmetric shapes, and robustness. Classical multivariate analysis is directly solved by component-wise, distribution-based, and moment-based. If sam-ples are mutually dependent in component-wise analysis and perform badly, then existence moments need to be used in the moment-based analysis. But, depth-based methods are independent of the moment and it is not component-wise.

Mahalanobis (1936) established the distance between the points, namely Mahalanobis distance, and is used to formulate Mahalanobis depth. It is primarily concerned with the conventional estimates namely, the sample means vector and variance-covariance matrix. But, these estimates are very sensitive when the data contains outliers/extremes.

Tukey (1975) introduced the concept of picturing data to formalize the models. It paved the way to establish Halfspace depth and to proceed to formulate the other modern data depth procedures. The quality of depth notions has been measured by the basic tools (Zuo and Serfling, 2000), which are affine invariance, maximality at the center, monotonicity relative to the deepest point, and vanishing at infinity are furnished below:

The depth of a point $x \in R^d$ must does not depend on the fundamental coordinate system or, in particular, on the scales of the underlying measurements.

The depth function should reach a maximum value at the center, a distribution having a uniquely well-defined center.

As a point, $x \in R^d$ drifts away from the deepest point along any fixed ray through the center, the depth at x should decrease monotonically.

The depth of a point x should approach zero as $||x||$ approaches infinity.

Several depth notions have been proposed in the past few decades. Some of the celebrated data depth procedures are as follows: Simplicial Volume Depth (Oja, 1983), Simplicial Depth (Liu, 1990), Zonoid Depth (Koshevoy and Mosler, 1997), Spatial Depth (Vardi and Zhang, 2000), and Projection Depth (Zuo, 2003).

The application aspects of robust procedures are explored briefly in the next section, specifically in the context of statistical learning. These methods are categorized as supervised and unsupervised machine learning techniques.

12.7 Statistical Learning

One of the most remarkable fields of study considered by the researchers to understand data in the current state of affairs is statistical learning. Statistical learning consists of a toolset for understanding data. These tools can be extensively categorized as supervised and unsupervised learning techniques in the area of machine learning. Supervised learning techniques include regression, discriminant analysis, decision tree, etc., that comprises a target variable (dependent variable) which is to be anticipated from a given collection of predictors. On the contrary, unsupervised learning techniques namely as principal component analysis, cluster analysis, factor analysis, etc., do not have any target to predict/estimate. These techniques generally require that the data should be appropriately scaled but it is not so in the case of supervised learning techniques.

In statistics, most of these learning techniques inclusive of principal component analysis, factor analysis, cluster analysis, discriminant analysis, etc., comes under multivariate statistics. Looking for the structure in the data is the major role of multivariate statistics. It is simple to find the structure of a dataset, but the actual task is to find the general structure that can be used to apply it to different datasets. The objectives of multivariate statistical techniques are to find structure by inspecting the data and then divide the cases into groups by assuming a given structure. Almost all classical multivariate techniques rely on the measure of mean vector and covariance matrix/correlation matrix. However, these measures are affected by extreme observations/noise in the data that yields unreliable results. Robust alternatives overcome these limitations, but it is still a tedious task to extract thorough information from the data with or without noise.

12.7.1 *Principal Component Analysis*

This analysis finds a modest number of linear combinations of variables to capture most data variation as a whole. That is, to combine multiple predictor variables into a reduced set of variables, which are weighted linear combinations of the original dataset. The weights are the relative contributions of the original variables to the new principal components. Finally, a set of principal components can be utilized in the place of original predictors for further analysis by reducing dimensionality. PCA comes under unsupervised learning techniques.

This method works with classical mean vectors and scatters matrix with the least square procedure. It is extensively used as a data analytics tool for dimensionality reduction. However, the grossly corrupted entries often put validation at risk. These errors usually happen in modern applications, for example data analysis, bioinformatics, and image processing, where some measurements are randomly adulterated by a sensor failure, or occlusions, malicious tampering, or irrelevant to the low-dimensional data.

In reality, specifically in computer vision applications, the exact position of the noise in the images is not known. The conventional PCA is extremely sensitive to non-Gaussian noise which may degrade the results of image recognition and visual learning. On the other hand, the robust alternatives make the results remain stable even in the presence of various types of noise/outliers. For that, based on various types of robust estimators, many principal component analysis methods are being developed by the researchers. Some of the approaches include random sampling, influence function, multivariate trimming, and weighted function (see Fischler and Bolles, 1981; Huber, 1981; Skocaj et al., 2002; Torre and Black, 2003; Croux et al., 2007). The fast-incremental robust principal component analysis (FRPCA) approach was proposed by Hakim and Saban (2012) to combat the problem of time efficiency for scalable data.

12.7.2 *Factor Analysis*

It is one of the multivariate techniques used for data reduction and summarization. In a study of high-dimensional data, i.e. a huge number of variables, the majority of which are correlated and are diminished to a reasonable level. The objective of the factor analysis is to examine the relations amongst several interrelated variables and is characterized in the form of few underlying factors. The primary objective of the principal component analysis and factor analysis is considered of reducing dimensionality. Even though the objectives of both techniques are the same, they have distinct features, i.e. the variables are expressed as the linear functions of the factors in factor analysis, but in the case of principal component analysis, the principal components are expressed as linear functions the variables. Moreover, PCA explains the total variation of the variables, whereas FA attempts to explain covariance or correlations among the variables.

The analytical process is mainly based on the correlation matrix. The conventional technique begins by calculating the standard sample covariance matrix or correlation matrix, trailed by a second step that decays this matrix as indicated by the model. This methodology isn't robust enough to the outliers in the data, since they already have a heavy impact on the first step. The conventional covariance matrix/correlation matrix can be influenced by the outliers that prompt unseemly outcomes. Alternatively, a robust measure of variance-covariance matrix/correlation matrix can be used. Therefore, in building a robust factor analysis technique, first compute an exceptionally resistant scatter/correlation matrix employing any of the robust methods such as MCD estimator, MVE estimator, S-estimator, and M-estimator (see Maronna, 1976; Huber, 1981; Rousseeuwand Yohai, 1984; Rousseeuw, 1985; Hampel et al., 1986; Davies, 1987; Rousseeuw and Leroy, 1987; Tyler, 1987; Lopuhaa, 1989; Lopuhaa and Rousseeuw, 1991; Kent and Tyler, 1996).

12.7.3 Discriminant Analysis

This analysis is a suitable statistical technique for classifying objects when the response variable is classification type and predictor variables are by nature interval or continuous. It creates the most discrimination among groups by constructing discriminant functions using predictor variables. Furthermore, new observations are categorized into one of the known groups by utilizing this function. The maximum ratio of variation among between-group and within-group for the discriminant scores, the coefficients or loadings are measured so that the groups contrast however much as could be expected on the estimates of the discriminant function. Combinations of variables that are linear that separate groups are called discriminant functions. These are computed using covariance matrix and are used to distinguish objects of one group from another.

Fisher's linear discriminant method is a straightforward and well-known approach in discriminant analysis. In the course of the most recent decade numerous sophisticated discrimination methods, for example support vector machines and random forests were proposed and used currently. However, Fisher's method is most frequently utilized and achieves expected results in numerous applications. In this approach, in the beginning, the measure of location and scatter matrix of each group should be computed, which is normally done employing sample mean vectors and sample variance-covariance matrices. However, sample mean vector and variance-covariance matrices are not robust, and extremities in the dataset may have an excessively huge impact on the conventional Fisher's linear discriminant criterion. This method's robust version is a module comprising robust estimates of location and covariance which uses computing the discriminant function as opposed to usage of conventional location and covariance. Chork and Rousseeuw (1992) utilized such a module approach for getting a robust discriminant analysis, Hawkins and McLachen (1997) and Hubert and Driessen (2004) utilized the minimum covariance determinant estimator, He and Fung (2000) and Croux and Dehon (2001) applied the concept of S-estimators to compute robust version of location and covariance matrix.

12.7.4 Cluster Analysis

It is concerned with methods for searching homogenous groups, i.e. for arranging objects/cases into comparatively similar groups. Cluster analysis involves various algorithms and techniques for grouping objects of a comparable kind into particular categories. A common issue confronting the researchers in numerous fields of inquiry is how to sort out observed data into meaningful structures. Objects having a place with the same groups are similar in nature and with different groups, they are dissimilar in nature. It is fact that both cluster analysis and discriminant analysis are classification methodologies. No prior information about group membership for any objects is required in cluster analysis, however, in discriminant analysis, prior knowledge of group membership for each object is required. To start with the analysis, several decisions must be made on the aspects such as the characteristics, the variables of interest in the analysis, the measurements on the distance between objects, the criterion to group the objects, etc. The selection of variables for any cluster analysis is important since the exclusion of important variables will provide poor or misleading findings. The classical clustering techniques can be broadly classified into hierarchical and non-hierarchical which are mainly based on the assumption of normality of multivariate distribution and distance matrix.

Almost all conventional statistical methods depend on assumptions such as sample observations are independent and distributed identically, and its distribution is normal. In some situations, the first assumption may not be idealistic, but from a practical sense, the second assumption is somewhat unreasonable. Classical methods do not produce an efficient result when these assumptions are violated. Commonly used robust clustering techniques are Trimmed K Mean, Trimmed Cluster, Gallegos, Gallegos, and Ritter. The procedure based on trimmed k-means, discussed in Cuesta-Albertos et al. (1997), Garcia-Escudero and Gordaliza (1999), and Garcia-Escudero et al. (2008), revealed that impartial trimming delivers better results regarding its robustness than consideration of various penalty functions in the k-means technique. The method of trimmed k-means is used for robust clustering in functional datasets. For instance, Garcia-Escudero and Gordalizaa (2005) employed these measures for the projection of functional data onto a lower-dimensional subspace.

Various clusters have different means, since physical guidelines overseeing the procedure remain the same, covariance structures have common features. To improve performance monitoring, using the unaltered physical base, a statistical model connecting several normal distributions with a typical variance-covariance matrix is required to be constructed. Gallegos and Ritter (2005) proposed the robust clustering method that can be used thence. A pooled covariance matrix is considered a common covariance matrix that shares all the clusters. Besides, while categorizing the clusters, these techniques can adapt to potential contaminated data. This establishes a significant advantage considering that contaminated data is unavoidable when monitoring genuine procedures.

Multivariate statistical methods mostly rest on model assumptions and also on estimating the variance-covariance/correlation matrix from a given dataset. Such estimates are exceptionally affected by outliers and become inapt when extremes are present in the dataset. Subsequently, the conventional methodologies are exceptionally complex to datasets with disregarded model assumptions and yield unreliable outcomes. To overcome such problems, robust alternatives are explored and applied, to make the dataset a methodically improved one and to eliminate sensitivity by clearly incorporating the model. The robust covariance matrix/correlation matrix is used instead of conventional estimates of covariance/correlation matrix in the computational aspects of the multivariate techniques. It is to be noted that many robust procedures have been established in the past few decades. One can use robust procedures to perform machine learning techniques, for example principal component analysis, factor analysis classification, clustering, etc., and get reliable results.

12.8 Robust Statistics in R

From the year 2005, a group of scientists has continuously put effort to synchronize various developments and made robust statistical packages in R, such as *robustbase* including other packages, which extends the necessary functionality to certain models. Before R, these robust statistical procedures were available in S during the 1980s. The important functionality has been made available in recommended package *MASS*. This package includes computational aspects of robust regression models and robust multivariate scatter and covariance matrix. *R* offers multiple packages for data analysis and provides interfacing with other tools for data analysis. Further, *S-PLUS*, a robust library version, is now accessible as *robust* in R. The core packages to perform robust statistical analysis are *MASS*, *robust*, *robustbase*, and *rrcov*. The packages *robust* and *rrcov* builds on *robustbase.*

The package *robust* associated with *robustbase* offers appropriate procedures for the common user. A wide range of robust models and their primary functions are available in *robustbase*. The **rrcov** package provides more methods for estimating robust multivariate variance–covariance matrix and for performing robust principal component analyses. The packages *depth*, *depthproc*, and *ddalpha* give the various notions of statistical depth functions for computing depth of data points in a data cloud in the context of a non-parametric approach. Further, depth-based classification and its inference implementations for multivariate data are provided.

Many more robust statistical methods have been developed and the corresponding functionalities are made available in the form of packages in R. Researcher can view and download these packages through completely free and open-source software, named as "Comprehensive R Archive Network (CRAN)." It is completely free and open-source software. Every advanced robust statistical method developed as of late, just as every classical method, is effectively applied in R. One feature that makes R exceptionally important from a research viewpoint is that a group of scholastics do an outstanding job of continually including and refreshing the routines planner for applying modern techniques. A wide scope of modern methods can be applied utilizing the basic package. Various dedicated procedures are accessible through packages available at the R website.

12.9 Summary

Statistics is a science of the art of mining valuable information from observational data. The field of statistics is continually challenged by the issues that science and industry bring to its entryway. These issues regularly emerged from agricultural and industrial experiments and were moderately little in scope in the early days. With the arrival of computers and the data age, statistical problems have detonated both in size and complexity. A voluminous amount of data is being produced in numerous research areas, and it is the researcher's responsibility to identify significant patterns and trends and comprehend what the data says in the form of statistical learning.

The robust statistics field is growing nowadays, because of the exponential increase in the computing speed of the computer. The programming scripts of the existing robust procedures are easily available as packages in script-based software like R, Python, etc. It is also possible to download packages with source code, which one can modify, based on their requirement and do further research/development on more robust statistical methods.

Statistical learning consists of supervised and unsupervised learning techniques. The robust alternatives to conventional methods of classification, regression, and clustering techniques are developed in the recent past. Hence, the researchers can use robust statistical procedures instead of conventional statistical learning techniques when data deviates from the modeling assumptions. These procedures can be beneficial to researchers, who work on machine learning techniques by considering the factors such as noise, computational time, ease algorithm approach, and high dimensionality. These procedures can be applied in almost all multivariate data analysis techniques, and in turn, it would be beneficial to the research communities in the field of machine learning. Fortunately, computers with increasing processing power and larger memory are available now, which is proving highly beneficial for the researcher who concentrates on the work in the domain of robust statistics.

References

Campbell, N., Lopuhaa, H. P., & Rousseeuw, P. J. (1998). On the calculation of a robust S-estimator of a covariance matrix. *Statistics in Medicine, 17*(23), 2685–2695.

Cook, R. D., Hawkins, D. M., & Weisberg, S. (1993). Exact iterative computation of the robust multivariate minimum volume ellipsoid estimator. *Statistics and Probability Letters, 16*, 213–218.

Chork, C., & Rousseeuw, P. J. (1992). Integrating a high-breakdown option into discriminant analysis in exploration geochemistry. *Journal of Geochemical Exploration, 43*(3), 191–203.

Crawley, M. J. (2007): *The R book*. New York: John Wiley and Sons, Limited.

Croux, C., & Dehon, C. (2001). Robust linear discriminant analysis using s-estimators. *Canadian Journal of Statistics, 29*, 473–493.

Croux, C., Filzmoser, P., & Oliveira, M. R. (2007). Algorithms for projection-pursuit robust principal component analysis. *Chemometrics and Intelligent Laboratory Systems, 87*, 218–225.

Cuesta-Albertos, J., Gordaliza, A., & Matran, C. (1997). Trimmed k-means: An attempt to robustify quantizers. *The Annals of Statistics, 25*(2), 553–576.

Davies, P. L. (1987). Asymptotic behavior of S-estimates of multivariate location parameters and dispersion matrices. *The Annals of Statistics, 15*(3), 1269–1292.

Donoho, D. L. (1982). *Breakdown properties of multivariate location estimators*. Ph.D. qualifying paper. Cambridge: Harvard University.

Filzmoser, P., Hron, K., & Templ, M. (2012). Discriminant analysis for compositional data and robust parameter estimation. *Computational Statistics, 27*(4), 585–604.

Filzmoser, P., & Todorov, V. (2013). Robust tools for the imperfect world. *Information Sciences, 245*, 4–20.

Fischler, M. A., & Bolles, R. C. (1981). Random sample consensus: A paradigm for model fitting with applications to image analysis and automated cartography, commun. *ACM, 24*(6), 381–395.

Gallegos, M. T., and Ritter, G. (2005). A robust method for cluster analysis. *The Annals of Statistics, 33*(1), 347–380.

Garcia-Escudero, L. A., & Gordaliza, A. (1999). Robustness properties of k-means and trimmed k-means. *Journal of Americal Statistical Association, 94*, 956–969.

Garcia-Escudero, L. A., & Gordaliza, A. (2005). A proposal for robust curve clustering. *Journal of Classification, 22*, 185–201.

Garcia-Escudero, L. A., Gordaliza, A., Matran, C., & Mayo-Iscar, A. (2008). A general trimming approach to robust cluster analysis. *Annals of Statistics, 36*, 1324–1345.

Garcia-Escudero, L. A. Gordaliza, A., Matran, C., & Mayo-Iscar, A. (2010). A review of robust clustering methods. *Advances in Data Analysis and Classification, 4*(2–3), 89–109.

Hakim, A. E., & Saban, M. (2012). FRPCA: Fast robust principal component analysis for online observations. 21st International Conference on Pattern Recognition, 413–416.

Hampel, F. R. (1968). *Contributions to the theory of robust estimation*, Ph.D. Thesis, University of California, Berkeley.

Hampel, F. R. (1974). The influence curve and its role in robust estimation. *Journal of the American Statistical Association, 69*, 383–393.

Hampel, F. R., Ronchetti, E. M., Rousseeuw, P. J., & Stahel, W. A. (1986). *Robust statistics: The approach based on influence functions*. New York: Wiley.

Hawkins D. M. (1993). The feasible set algorithm for least median of squares regression. *Computational Statistics and Data Analysis, 16*, 81–101.

Hawkins, D. M. (1994a). The feasible solution algorithm for least trimmed squares regression. *Computational Statistics and Data Analysis, 17*, 185–196.

Hawkins D. M. (1994b). The feasible solution algorithm for the minimum covariance determinant estimator in multivariate data. *Computational Statistics and Data Analysis, 17*, 197–210.

Hawkins, D. M., & McLachen, G. (1997). High-breakdown linear discriminant analysis. *Journal of the American Statistical Association, 92*, 136–143.

Hawkins, D. M., & Olive, D. J. (1999). Improved feasible solution algorithms for high breakdown estimation. *Computational Statistics and Data Analysis, 30*, 1–11.

He, X., & Fung, W. K. (2000). High breakdown estimation for multiple populations with applications to discriminant analysis. *Journal of Multivariate Analysis, 72*, 151–162.

Huber, P. J. (1964). Robust estimation of location parameters. *Annals of Mathematical Statistics, 35*, 73–101.

Huber, P. J. (1981). *Robust statistics.* New York: Wiley.

Huber, P. J., & Ronchetti, E. M. (2009). *Robust statistics.* New York: John Wiley & Sons.

Hubert, M., & Driessen, V. K. (2004). Fast and robust discriminant analysis. *Computational Statistics & Data Analysis, 45*(2), 301–320.

Hubert, M., Rousseeuw, P. J., & Verdonck, T. (2012). A deterministic algorithm for robust location and scatter. *Journal of Computational and Graphical Statistics, 21*, 618–637.

James, G., Witten, D., Hastie, T., & Tibshirani, R. (2013). *An introduction to statistical learning with applications in R.* New York: Springer.

Kent, J. T., & Tyler, D. E. (1996). Constrained M-estimation for multivariate location and scatter. *The Annals of Statistics, 24*(3), 1346–1370.

Koshevoy, G., & Mosler, K. (1997). Zonoid trimming for multivariate distributions. *Annals of Statistics, 25*, 49–69.

Lopuhaa, H. P. (1989). On the relation between S-estimators and m-estimators of multivariate location and covariance. *The Annals of Statistics, 17*(4), 1662–1683.

Lopuhaa, H. P., & Rousseeuw, P. J. (1991). Breakdown points of affine equivariant estimators of multivariate location and covariance matrices. *The Annals of Statistics, 19*(1), 229–248.

Liu, R. Y. (1990). On a notion of data depth based on random simplices. *Annals of Statistics, 18*, 405–414.

Mahalanobis, P. C. (1936). On the generalized distance in statistics. *Proceedings of National Institute of Sciences, 12*, 49–55.

Mallows, C. L. (1975). *On some topics in robustness, technical memorandum.* Murray Hill, NJ: Bell Telephone Laboratories.

Maronna, R. A. (1976). Robust M-estimators of multivariate location and scatter. *The Annals of Statistics, 4*(1), 51–67.

Muthukrishnan, R., Boobalan, E. D., & Mathaiyan, R. (2014). MCD based principal component analysis in computer vision. *International Journal of Computer Science and Information Technologies, 5*(6), 8293–8296.

Muthukrishnan, R., & Udaya Prakash, N. (2019). Performance of classification techniques along with support vector machines. *International Journal of Innovative Technology and Exploring Engineering, 9*(2), 4366–4369.

Oja, H. (1983). Descriptive statistics for multivariate distributions. *Statistics and Probability Letter*, *1*, 327–332.

R Core Team. (2019). R: A language and environment for statistical computing. *R Foundation for Statistical Computing*, Vienna, Austria. Retrieved from https://www.R-project.org/

Rousseeuw, P. J. (1984). Least median of squares regression. *Journal of the American Statistical Association*, *79*, 871–880.

Rousseeuw, P. J. (1985). Multivariate estimation with high breakdown point. *Mathematical Statistics and Applications*, *8*, 283–297.

Rousseeuw, P. J., & Croux, C. (1993). Alternatives to the median absolute deviation. *Journal of the American Statistical Association*, *88*, 1273–1283.

Rousseeuw, P. J., & Driessen, V. K. (1999). A fast algorithm for the minimum covariance determinant estimator. *Technometrics*, *41*, 212–223.

Rousseeuw, P. J., & Leroy, A. M. (1987). Robust regression and outlier detection. Wiley series in probability and mathematical statistics. In *Applied probability and statistics*. New York: Wiley.

Rousseeuw, P. J., & Yohai, V. J. (1984). Robust regression by means of S-estimators. In robust and nonlinear time series analysis. *Lecture Notes in Statistics*, *26*, 256–276.

Rousseeuw, P. J., & Zomeren, B. C. (1991). *Robust distances: Simulations and cutoff values, directions in robust statistics and diagnostics* (pp. 195–203). New York: Springer.

Sirkia,S., Taskinen, S., & Oja, H. (2007). Symmetrized M-estimators of multivariate scatter. *Journal of Multivariate Analysis*, *98*, 1611–1629.

Skocaj, D., Bischof, H., and Leonardis, A. (2002). A robust PCA algorithm for building representations from panoramic images. In European Conference Computer Vision, 761–775.

Tatsuoka, K. S., & Tyler, D. E. (2000). On the uniqueness of S-functionals and M-functionals under nonelliptical distributions. *The Annals of Statistics*, *28*(4), 1219–1243.

Tiku, M. L., & Akkaya, A. D. (2004). *Robust estimation and hypothesis testing*. New Delhi: New Age International Limited.

Todorov, V., & Filzmoser, P. (2009). An object-oriented framework for robust multivariate analysis. *Journal of Statistical Software*, *32*(3), 1–47.

Todorov, V., & Pires, A. M. (2007). Comparative performance of several robust linear discriminant analysis. *REVSTAT Statistical Journal*, *5*(1), 63–83.

Torre, F. D., & Black, M. J. (2003). A framework for robust subspace learning. *International Journal of Computer Vision*, *54*, 117–142.

Tukey, J. W. (1960). *A survey of sampling from contaminated distributions. Contributions to probability and statistics* (I. Olkin, Ed.). Stanford, CA: Stanford University Press.

Tukey, J. W. (1962). The future of data analysis. *The Annals of Mathematical Statistics*, *33*, 1–67.

Tukey, J. W. (1975). Mathematics and picturing data, In Proceedings of the International Congress on Mathematics, R. D. James (ed.). *Canadian Mathematics Congress*, *2*, 523–531.

Tyler, D. E. (1987). A distribution-free m-estimator of multivariate scatter. *The Annals Statistics*, *15*, 234–251.

Vardi, Y., & Zhang, C. H. (2000). The multivariate L1-median and associated data depth. *Proceedings of the National Academy of Sciences, USA*, *97*, 1423–1426.

Wilcox, R. (2010). *Fundamentals of modern statistical methods*. New York: Springer.

Wilcox, R. (2017). *Introduction to robust estimation and hypothesis testing*. San Diego, CA: Elsevier.

Yohai, V. J. (1987). High breakdown-point and high-efficiency robust estimates for regression. *The Annals of Statistics, 15*(2), 642–656.

Zuo, Y. (2003). Projection-based depth functions and associated medians. *Annals of Statistics, 31*, 1460–1490.

Zuo, Y., & Serfling, R. (2000). General notions of statistical depth function. *Annals of Statistics, 28*, 461–482.

Chapter 13

Big Data in Tribal Healthcare and Biomedical Research

Dhivya Venkatesan[1], Abilash Valsala Gopalakrishnan[2],
Narayanasamy Arul[3], Chhakchhuak Lalchhandama[4],
Balachandar Vellingiri[1], and N. Senthil Kumar[5]
[1]Department of Human Genetics and Molecular Biology, Bharathiar University,
Coimbatore, India
[2]Department of Biomedical Sciences, School of Biosciences and Technology,
Vellore Institute of Technology, VIT, Vellore, India
[3]Department of Zoology, Bharathiar University, Coimbatore, India
[4]Department of Pathology, Civil Hospital Aizawl, Aizawl, India
[5]Department of Biotechnology, Mizoram University, Aizawl, India

Contents

DOI: 10.1201/9781003175889-13

13.1 Introduction

Big Data performs with analysis, extracting information from large datasets that are usually laborious to process when performed using traditional data-processing software. Key concepts that govern Big Data analysis are volume, velocity, and variety (Boyd & Crawford, 2012). It is concerned with the vast computing resources required to manage the rising volume and complexity of data from many platforms, including the Internet and remote sensor networks (Benke & Benke, 2018). There could also be empirical inconsistencies during Big Data pipelines and impeding decisions by humans and computers, including data corruption, data errors, duplicate records, missing records, and incomplete digital records related to general variables (Benke & Benke, 2018). Big Data comprise the Internet of

Things (IoT), cyber-physical systems, and cloud computing, where these massive data processing could involve process automation.

The inception of the current Big Data era has been utilized in a range of fields, including physics, mathematics, bioinformatics, sociology, and economics, to name a few. Other sectors to utilize these data are genetic sequencing, social media communications, health reports, phone registries, government registries, and other digital networks. But these advancements have led to the emergence of various questions regarding Big Data analysis. Will it lead to designing better tools, assistance, and public welfares or will it commence with privacy invasions and exploitive retailing? Will Big Data aid us in learning about online platforms and political campaigns or to pursue protesters and repress speech? Will it lead to advancements in human communication and culture or make people isolated. Pursuing Big Data in terms of the socio-technical phenomenon requires thorough interrogation and suppression of biases (Boyd & Crawford, 2012). By claiming that Big Data is involved in a wide classical and reflective shift does not suggest that it is liable. There are an extensive management and manufacturing initiative toward gathering and extracting maximal benefit from the obtained data, which could be in the form of information that guides the targeted promotion, product configuration, traffic outlining, or criminal policing. But there are severe and wide-ranging associations for the execution of Big Data and its embroilment with ever-growing research agendas. Hence questioning Big Data applications is mandatory.

In the era of Big Data, the tribal population still relies on incomplete or inadequate data about their habitat (Rodriguez-Lonebear, 2016). This lack of specific strategy data is just one sign of a deficit in Indian country's data. Tribal Epidemiology Centers, established the Indian Health Care Improvement Act to collect, analyze, and monitor health data on tribal and urban organizations to report the data gaps. Many tribes are attentive in conducting their evaluations for local planning and governance. By the time, the number of tribal-based data projects has increased from the wide range of tribal surveys to tribal research review boards and data repositories, which are not currently much into practice.

In 2016, we received the project entitled "Screening and create the data registry of disease pattern in Tribal communities and provide the Health Care Strategies, Genetic Counselling and create the awareness camp to schedule Tribes population in Tamil Nadu" sanctioned by Natural Resources Data Management System (NRDMS-DST), New Delhi, Government of India for a period of 3 years. The project focused on assessing the socioeconomic status, lifestyle factors, hereditary diseases, and rare genetic disorders in tribal communities.

13.1.1 Photographs Were Taken During the NRDMS Project Data Survey

Based on the survey, we conducted awareness camps, provided genetic counseling and skill development program to the tribes in the districts of Nilgiris, Valparai, Thiruvallur, Coimbatore, Dharmapuri, Gummidipoondi (Chennai), and Salem. All the villages were given genetic counseling and provided with a nutritional supplement chart to enrich the blood count in the people. Maximum people were observed with anemia, gastro-intestinal problem, and undiagnosed diseases. The reasons for these issues were unknown due to insufficient information. The common reasons found in these tribes were con-sanguineous marriages, work stress, improper diet, and more intake of beetle leaves. From the survey, we identified that females are affected psychologically during pregnancy and males were found to with stress due to work that makes them to a daily habit of smoking and drinking. Nutrition status of individuals and general health condition indicates the socioeconomic condition prevalent the society. The project continued with the aim of implementing training sessions in previously analyzed tribal communities. Training on skill development programs such as vermicomposting, tailoring, and fish-eries were given to the tribal people to enhance their income for their daily living. It was assessed as Human Developmental Index (HDI). The obtained data were created as a data registry on the website www.nrdms-bu.edu.in that helps the healthcare professionals for their survey in the Tamil Nadu tribal population.

13.1.2 NRDMS Project-Based Website (www.nrdms-bu.edu.in)

Here, the chapter approaches the Big Data applications to change the health needs of tribal communities. The chapter confers Big Data approaches, Big Data in socioeconomic status, Big Data in genomic research mainly focusing on NGS and Metagenomics, and the software and databases used in analyzing genomic and clinical data. Also, we aim at discussing the Big Data on the healthcare repository, its analytics, and challenges in data retrieval. Finally, we conclude with the re-quisite healthcare data for the tribal population.

13.1.3 Big Data Approaches

Big Data technologies made a huge revolution that has received great attention by handling more data when compared to traditional methods. The features in Big Data handle prognostic model design and mining tools that agree to a better choice of applicable information. Big Data can achieve by batch processing and stream processing (Shahrivari, 2014). The batch process aims at more data volume by gathering and storing data to be analyzed for results. MapReduce depicts in batch computing that divides data into small to acquire transitional results (Dean & Ghemawat, 2008). Trying to advance computational assets use, MapReduce apportions handling assignments to hubs near the information area. This approach has experienced a great deal of accomplishment in numerous applications, particularly in bioinformatics and medicinal services. The cluster preparing structure has numerous attributes; for example, the capacity to get to all information and perform numerous unpredictable calculation tasks. Its inertness is estimated by minutes or more.

13.2 Data Lifecycle

Computerized information has numerous points of interest, for example, being anything but difficult to share, repeat, and recombine, which results possibly reusable. In any case, to misuse all the advantages of advanced information, it should be appropriately gathered, prepared, and protected. Information misfortune or harm may infer financial expenses just as lost possibilities. The motivation behind why funding operators are progressively requesting establishments to report and run information the board plans considering the entire lifecycle of information (Clifford, 2008). Consequently, it is fundamental to characterize what stages and procedures the lifecycle to actualize strong and adaptable models to oversee information with regards to the digital time.

The information cycle is the arrangement of phases that follows from a framework to the deleted framework (Simonet et al., 2015). Amid the information passageway and exit, information experience various stages, which may contrast contingent upon the kind of information and reason to accomplish as archived in the accumulation of exemplary information lifecycle. The Knowledge Discovery in Databases process is the main proposition model to oversee computerized information (Fayyad et al., 1996). It alludes to the entire procedure of extricating information from information and incorporates five principal stages: information determination, information preprocessing, information change, information mining, and translation. As databases began to develop in size and multifaceted nature, the need for a more extensive plan to properly deal with this information was featured, particularly by the business (Chapman et al., 2000).

Till date, eight phases are included: the initial four phases (arranging, information assortment, information quality control, and examination) relate to overseeing information in a customary venture, which is new. It proceeds with extra information disclosure, information reconciliation, finally, the investigation. Rüegg et al. (2014) refer to information reuse as a task where prevailing information is utilized, including a few stages inside this lifecycle. Also, to finish every information lifecycle, this work incorporates two additional means: information documentation and information chronicling in an open storehouse, which we think about essential for safeguarding and distributing information. The audit of these references permitted coordination and complete the various phases of a full information life cycle regarding monetary and social investigations. Its point is to institutionalize the information life cycle and fill in

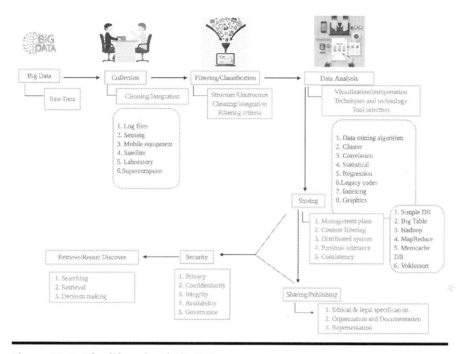

Figure 13.1 The lifecycle of Big Data.

as structure with regards to planning appropriate information board design right now. Our proposition for an information lifecycle had delineated in Figure 13.1.

The stages are described as follows:

1. **Preparation:** This stage comprises structuring the examination or business undertaking to accomplish the ideal objectives of funders or administrators. When each investigation characterizes, it is important to arrange for what systems to treat information will be applied.

2. **Data Collection:** Comprises in getting to the sources and gathering introductory or crude information. Contingent upon the field of information and the information required for building up the undertaking, exercises, for example, perception, experimentation, recording, re-enacting, scratching, and haggling with outsider information suppliers.

3. **Data Documentation and Quality:** This comprises recording the gained information and its quality. The information securing procedure ought to be recorded by partner information to the metadata. The metadata incorporates data identified with the wellspring of source, information group, and specialized subtleties on the recovery procedure and getting to dates, among others, in this way, empowering its reuse and rights. Second, information quality and legitimacy ought to guarantee. It is essential to confirm the dependency of the information sources to control any information irregularities.

4. **Data Incorporation:** This stage comprises combining information acquired from various information sources with an intelligent and homogeneous structure, which assists with making information discernible and simpler to get to and control in progressive ventures. Information coordination should likewise consolidate protection requirements to abstain from revealing some private data in the incorporated information. It is a significant concern since rich coordinated information may encourage finding some close-to-home subtleties in any case mysterious.

5. **Data Preparation:** This stage comprises changing information to meet the organization's necessities of the examination devices and strategies that will be applied. It incorporates interpreting, digitizing, introducing, setting up an unthinkable configuration in the informational index and determining new information by working with the current information.

6. **Data Analysis:** This comprises investigating information, getting, and deciphering results. An enormous scope of measurable strategies and computational apparatuses calls to utilize right now. The last choice of the most proper strategies will rely upon the sort of information examined and look into goals.

7. **Publishing and Sharing:** This distributes the results and information examination, or produces informational indexes. The yields of this stage expect to encourage the dynamic procedure of chiefs or strategy creators to spread information and take care of organizations' programmed frameworks with data of importance to enable the staff to settle on choices. Other related exercises right now are setting up the copyright of information and results, composing productions, referring to information sources, circulating information, and controlling information.

8. **Storage and Maintenance:** This comprises chronicling and enlisting all the information assembled, prepared, and broke down for permitting extended information safeguarding and reuse. Activities such as information in explicit archives or computational frameworks move to different stages of medium backing up the information delivering related metadata, protecting the documentation during the entire procedure, controlling information security, and eradicating information whenever required by legitimate guidelines.

9. **Data Reuse:** This comprises information to reuse that has recently been assembled, prepared, and broken down. The activity started for a wide range of purposes, for example, testing new speculations identified with a similar task for which information gathers, sharing or offering information to organizations, directing new undertakings for which existing information can be helpful, and utilizing information with education.

13.2.1 Big Data in Socioeconomic Status

When employed in socioeconomic policy construction, Big Data analysis serves the benefits of the larger community when feasible. Further, it must aid in contributing to enhance the quality of the subjects. Various Big Data studies are built, tested with an algorithm for assisting administrations based on compiling massive data sets of socioeconomic reports based on the policies of the economy and treating within network analysis. Algorithms are intensive in developing an operation that aids higher professionals as well as common masses, who are distinct in their representativeness (Polyakova et al., 2019). Hence, Big Data is also associated with socio-political initiatives. Planning and estimating network bonds and connections using Big Data has evolved into a tool for generating operations of strategic devising. Further, spatial planning related to Big Data and studying the network outcomes in spatial commerce are upcoming. Thriving applications in this sector exist and have empirically proven the feasibility of implementing network analysis for spatial interactions to recognize spatial stations, hubs, and barriers vital for handling spatial communications.

Polyakova et al. (2019) further stated that methodical advancements based on network analysis tools for the requirements of diplomatic evolution superintendence. Blazquez and Domenech (2018) described the novel Big Data structure that estimates the individual parameters of economic and social analysis in the current digital age. Their work highlights the importance of a Big Data design with the particularities grounded on the data cycle strategy for data administration. It further implements various technologies such as computing models and scientific software based on the obligations and objectives of every single appropriate case. By achieving this, an industry could make the most of all accessible resources. The construction of authorizations and their association with Big Data analytical tools for present and future socioeconomic variables is beneficial. An individual lifestyle, work, and other factors have a profound effect on a patient's well-being, and identifying the impact of these factors can help to develop treatment plans. Development in preventive care and reduction in disparities can be organized based on complete and accurate socioeconomic data.

The Big Data paradigm highlights and imposes modifying and promoting research methods that estimate the future precisely (Jin et al., 2015). As betterment with proposed challenges, the Big Data architecture has designs for casting variables of interest. Conversely, no specific planning is available for social and economic variables; hence, this arises as an important factor in assessing human behaviour and predicting the changes in economic and social conditions. The Big Data could indicate improving economic conditions such as unemployment and favor policymakers to monitor and implement policies and grants (Vicente et al., 2015; Blazquez & Domenech, 2018).

13.3 Big Data in Genomic Research

The advancement of next-generation sequencing techniques has increased data generation. Hence, contemporary biology faces new hurdles in data administration and investigation. Human DNA containing about 3 billion base pairs with an individual genome expressing roughly 100 gigabytes of data, makes the use of Big Data analysis tools mandatory (O'Driscoll et al., 2013). Marking the accomplishments of the Human Genome Project (HGP), there has been an unusual generation of genomic data. Leading to the outcome that biomedical invention will depend on processing and investigating the efficiency of current researchers using extensive genomic data sets has a rapidly increasing rate due to decreased sequencing price. During these times, tools of Big Data present a summary of cloud computing. Especially, the Apache Hadoop project, provides a divided and equivalent data analysis in petabyte-scale data (O'Driscoll et al., 2013).

Life science has provided a comprehensive platform for cloud computing and Big Data technologies as a high throughput analytic expedite of enormous data sets. One such technology, suited for batch processing purposes is Hadoop. It has been highly suitable in tremendous areas, such as metagenomics, personalized medicine, protein functional analysis, and composition prediction, to name a few. To increase the magnitude of this application, it has also been employed in metagenomics. Unique genes encoding novel and yet uncharacterized proteins whose composition and function have yet to discover could use Big Data as a reliable means of investigation (O'Driscoll et al., 2013). Big Data have also been useful in genomics, integrated with neuroscience, in brain research through advancing innovative neurotechnologies platform from 2013. Through this, mapping brain circuits, measurement of electrical and chemical motions, and cognitive function assessment are achieved. As part of the HGP, this initiative has been dubbed as the "Higgs boson of the brain."

Data distributing in neuroscience involves confronting concerns related to subject privacy, which the researchers failed to maintain. Neuroscience organizations have been developing the most suitable systems and regulated ethics for neuroimaging experiments aimed to respond to researchers regarding the dearth of ethical strategies for distributing individual data (Choudhury et al., 2014). Genomics and fields such as transcriptomics, metagenomics, and OMICS have generated massive datasets. They were considering that heatmaps represent a colored palette composed of a network of cells, indicating the efficacy and activity to be significant in the method of transforming data into graphics. Such fields involve the use of the "shiny heatmap" tool. It is known to be a user-friendly Big Data analysis software accessible using a web browser (Khomtchouk et al., 2017).

13.3.1 Hadoop

Stacking a lot of information into the memory is not an effective method to work with vast knowledge. Hadoop actualizes MapReduce calculation for handling and creating massive datasets. MapReduce utilizes an outline to delineate legitimate record in the contribution to a lot of middle key or esteem matches, and decrease the activity of all the qualities that characterize a similar key (Dean & Ghemawat, 2008). It parallelizes the calculation, handles discontents, and organizes machine correspondence across huge scope bunches of machines. Hadoop Distributed File

System (HDFS) is the document framework that gives an adaptable, practical, and imitation-based information stockpiling at different hubs that structure a piece of a group (Shvachko et al., 2010).

13.3.2 Apache Spark

Apache Spark is another open-source option that bound together motor for disseminated information that incorporates more elevated level libraries for supporting Sparkle SQL, Spark Streaming, MLlib, and GraphX (Zaharia et al., 2016). These libraries help in expanding engineer profitability since programming requires lesser coding endeavours and flawlessly consolidates more kinds of complex calculations. The handling of vast information with Apache Spark would require an enormous measure of memory. The degree of genomic information has increased, making it difficult to use information in the clinical field without preprocessing (Andreu-Perez et al., 2015; West et al., 2006). Along these lines, genomic data may look simple to deal with as far as its volume; however, it requires a serious entangled procedure because of the multifaceted nature, heterogeneity, and hybridity of its qualities. The primary objective in genomics is to group genomes of all living animals to break down and comprehend the rest of the insider facts of the human body and make it conceivable to identify reasons for a few hereditary illnesses. Numerous difficulties are noticed in genomic information that requires building a solid model for the prehandling step. There are chiefly six feature selection types; the first three methods are:

- **Filters:** Filter methods are a preprocessing step that is free of ensuing learning algorithms.
- **Wrappers:** Wrappers assess a subset of qualities by the exactness of a proactive model prepared alongside them.
- **Embedded**: The above two stages were found to be in the combined version.

Other types have also been mentioned below.

- **Hybrid**: Methods that relate numerous primary feature selection methods sequentially (Naseriparsa et al., 2014).
- **Ensemble**: Use a combined feature subset of various base classifiers with a diverse feature subset (Tsymbal et al., 2005).
- **Integrative:** Integrate external information for feature selection (Grasnick et al., 2018).

13.3.3 NGS Read Alignment

NGS breaks down DNA into fragments known as a 'read'. Because of predispositions in test handling, library planning, sequencing-stage science, and bioinformatics techniques for genomic arrangement and gathering conveyance length of reads over the genome can be lopsided (Sims et al., 2014). Along these lines, some genomic areas secure with more reads. Read profundity indicates the average number of times each base has read. In RNAseq, read profundity has assigned a huge number of reads. Read arrangement includes arranging the succession reads to a reference grouping to permit arrangement information from an example sequenced with the reference genome (Church, 2015). Various arrangement devices, such as CloudBurst, Crossbow, and SEAL, have been created on Big Data foundations (Schatz, 2009; Langmead et al., 2009; Pireddu et al., 2011). Table 13.1 shows the next-generation sequencing platform.

A few strategies are intended for specific sequencing innovations, while others are progressively broad. Some essentially address effectiveness, though others address versatility, exactness, or interpretability. The fundamental objective in mapping genomic DNA is to decide grouping variety. Tumour DNA sequencing has been possible through the enormous decrease in sequencing price. It is currently conceivable to deliver information from a couple of DNA nanograms. The typical encompassing tissue or a different solid example from a similar individual is as often as possible used to separate somatic from germline variety. A few applications can be performed fundamentally quicker whenever means of particular arrangement programs. For example, DNA sections from ChIP-seq tests should be adjusted to a reference genome.

The epigenomic investigation requires particular arrangement calculations because the set of nucleotides must be reached out to consider the methylation alterations. As a glaring difference, the standard example readiness strategy of bisulfite treatment of DNA delivers diminished multifaceted nucleotides in order.

13.3.4 Variation Calling

Variation calling is progressively dependable with higher profundity, which is particularly important for distinguishing uncommon hereditary variations with higher certainty. The read profundity required for precisely calling variations depends on different variables, including nearness of dull genomic districts, blunder pace of the sequencing stage, and calculation utilized for collecting adds something extra to a genomic arrangement. In germline variation calling SAMtools, GATK, FreeBayes, and Atlas2 were incorporated. SAMtools include various utilities for controlling adjusted succession reads and calling single nucleotide variation (SNV) or potentially INDEL variations. GATK is intended to distinguish SNVs and INDELs information. It also utilizes a MapReduce foundation to quicken the technique for preparing a lot of succession-adjusted reads. Presently, it has extended to incorporate substantial variation calling apparatuses by joining MuTect and handling CNVs and basic varieties (SVs). SAMtools utilizes defined channels while GATK takes the channels from the information. FreeBayes detect SNVs, INDELs, multiallelic destinations, and CNVs. Atlas2 can utilize to examine

Table 13.1 List of Major Next Generation Sequencing Platform

Technology (Company)	Amplification	Chemistry	Sequencing Method	Yield (Gb/run)	Highest Average Read Length	Error Rate	Output File	Disadvantage	Advantage	Website
SOLiD (Life Technologies)	Emulsion PCR	Sequencing by ligation (SBL)	Fluorescent short linkers	3	75bp (paired end sequencing)	>0.06	Fastq (Phred +33)	Short read assembly	Accuracy	www.applied-biosystems.com
454 (Roche)	Emulsion PCR	Pyrosequencing (seq-by synthesis)	Incorporation of normal nucleotides	0.7	700bp	1	SFF, fasta, fastq	Error rate with polybase more than 6, high cost, low throughput	Read length fast	www.454.com
Ion Torrent (Life Technology)	N/A	Proton detection (seq by synthesis)	Measuring pH change	1	400bp (bidirectional sequencing)	1	Fastq (Phred +33)	lags behind in total data output	read lengths of around 200 bp; multiple runs in a short time for generation of more data	www.iontorrent.com
Illumina	Bridge amplification	Reversible dye terminator (seq-by-synthesis)	Incorporation of fluorescent nucleotides	1–60	300bp (overlapping paired-end-sequencing)	≥0.1	Fastq (Phred +64 & 33, Illumina +1.8)	Expensive	Simple, scalable, high yield	www.illumina.com
SMAT (Pacific bio)	N/A (single nucleotide)	Single Molecule Real Time (SMRT™)	Incorporation of fluorescent nucleotides	0.3–0.5	Can reach read up to 60,000bp	16	Fastq (Phred +33)	Low yield of high-quality sequences	Fast and informative data	www.pacific-bio.com

Source: De Mandal et al., 2015.

information produced by the SOLiDTM stage using calculated relapse models prepared on approved WES information to recognize SNVs and INDELs. This instrument can likewise dissect information created by the Illumina stage utilizing setback models for INDELs, a blend of strategic relapse, and a Bayesian model for SNVs. For assessing different projects or devices, 13 variation calling programs utilizing the highest quality level, individual exome variations have been analyzed.

13.3.5 Variant Annotation

NGS is creating a lot of grouping information. For mentioning useful variations, numerous explanation programs have been created. Commonly utilized comment programs, such as ANNOVAR on SNVs, INDELs, and CNVs investigate the results on qualities, cytogenetic groups, and revealing natural capacities and different utilitarian scores, including PolyPhen-2 score, Sorting Intolerant From Tolerant (SIFT) score, Combined Annotation Dependent Depletion (CADD) score, etc. Besides, ANNOVAR can utilize databases from the UCSC Genome Browser or some other information assets fitting in with Generic Feature Format adaptation 3 (GFF3). Furthermore, variation explanation relies upon natural information to provide data on the identified or possible effect of variations on quality guidelines and protein work.

13.3.6 Metagenomics

Microorganisms present in natural environments depict a significant reservoir of unknown biodiversity. They can occupy varied habitats from sea to atmosphere (Nichols et al., 2002; Torsvik & Øvreås, 2011). Most microbes are uncultivable by a standard protocol; hence their function and ecology are elusive, and the microbial composition is undeveloped. Though some studies had tried to culture uncultivable microbes where the technique is time-consuming and arduous; hence alternative methods are needed to analyze them. DNA sequence methods that isolate the genetic material from cells are called "metagenomics." The study involves uncultivable microorganisms from samples such as soil, seawater, groundwater, etc. (Uchiyama et al., 2005; Voget et al., 2006; Waschkowitz et al., 2009). Metagenomics is also called environmental genomics and community genomics. It results in various microorganisms, metabolic pathway identification and determining enzyme candidates (Elend et al., 2006; Handelsman, 2005; Vakhlu et al., 2008). In 2007, the structure for Human Microbiome Project was put forth. This was an immediate result of the HGP neglecting to represent the absolute capacity found to exist inside the human body (Turnbaugh et al., 2007). Due to the undeniable test of the metagenome, there are expanding patterns towards evaluating the genomic content in animal categories that are looking at unique metagenomes (Oulas et al., 2015). The entirety of this presents a fascinating computational test that must tend to push ahead. The computational difficulties are a prime case of enormous information investigations in the organic sciences.

16S gene shows 80% of total bacterial RNA that contains independent domains. 16S rRNA consists of scattered with variable regions for PCR and sequencing. Many studies have been performed with 16S rRNA used as a phylogenetic marker with varied hypervariable regions parted by conserved gene segments (De Mandal et al., 2015). A new period of metagenomics piloted in 16S rRNA of microbial taxonomy. By entering a microbial genome brings the cost of sequencing drastically down (Pace, 1997). Denaturing Gradient Gel Electrophoresis (DGGE) or Terminal Restriction Fragment Length Polymorphism (T-RFLP) has been established to identify the uncultivable microbes in various surroundings (Cancilla et al., 1992; Muyzer et al., 1993). The methods differentiate gene molecules based on reduced electrophoresis motion. The Sanger sequencing methods reveal to be over-priced and could not detect rare microbes (Sheffield et al., 1992). Shotgun metagenomics provides the benefit of species- and strain-level ordering of bacteria.

Moreover, it allows investigators to inspect the efficiency between hosts and bacteria by identifying the functional effect of samples (Walsh et al., 2018). It will enable the unknown microbial lifecycle that might continue the unclassifiable way (Rinke et al., 2013). Figure 13.2 represents the workflow of the analysis of metagenomic data.

The methodologies can partition into two classifications: read-based and gathering-based (Breitwieser et al., 2019). Read-based investigates network profiling and distinguishes proofs, particularly if significant references are accessible. MetaPhlAn2 distinguishes clade-explicit marker qualities for proof of the related clade nearness (Truong et al., 2015). Most metagenomic order devices coordinate reads or contigs to distinguish the taxon of each succession. A few goals ordered profilers were as of late created (Albanese & Donati, 2017; Truong et al., 2015).

There are not many programming instruments giving the factual techniques and artificial intelligence modules to infer microbiome phenotype relationships alongside metagenomics-based expectations utilizing ordered profiling. For instance, MetAML was produced for evaluating the quality of the microbiome phenotype (Pasolli et al., 2016). Reiman et al. (2017) investigated the convolutional neural system to anticipate the phenotype dependent on its microbial ordered bounty profile. Meta-omics approaches have gained notoriety for being a definitive device to disentangle the full metabolic capability of any microbial network since they permit the investigation of network piece and usefulness all in all and dodge any potential development predisposition. Since the field has developed, there is a general agreement that metagenomic ought to connect with the bacteria that endeavors to decipher and approve microbiome-based perceptions. Moreover, genomic, biochemical, practical, and applied microbiology can profit a piece of huge information to guide and target the investigation of bacterial nature and to evaluate the effect of the discoveries on a network level. The software and databases used in genomic research are represented in Table 13.2 and 13.3.

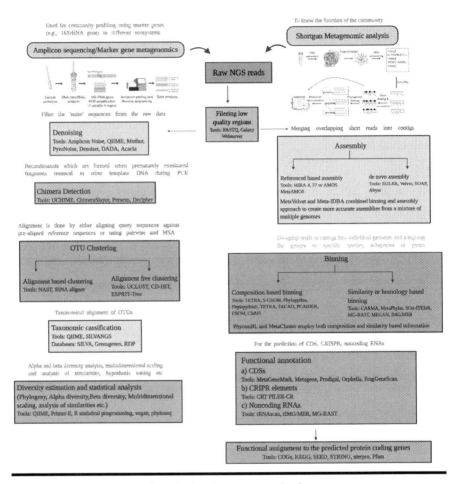

Figure 13.2 Workflow of analysis of metagenomic data.

13.4 Big Data in Biomedical Research

Understanding various constituents and biological systems, the experiment gathers data, and it shows the best understanding of biological processes with more data. NGS-based data were unreachable and took the new setup to a different aspect. It also records the biological process linked to diseases. The "*omics*" has significant development of studying from a single "*gene*" to the whole "*genome*" within a short duration of time. Likewise, all the gene expressions under "*transcriptomics*" studies can be analyzed. Each experiment generates large data with more information. But, this complexity and determination be inadequate to provide the particulars to clarify a specific pathway.

To perform whole-exome analysis to characterize the landscape of genetic alterations, fresh tumour tissue, as well as adjacent normal tissue, can be collected for DNA

Table 13.2   List of Software's Used in Genomic Research

Software	Purpose
FastQC 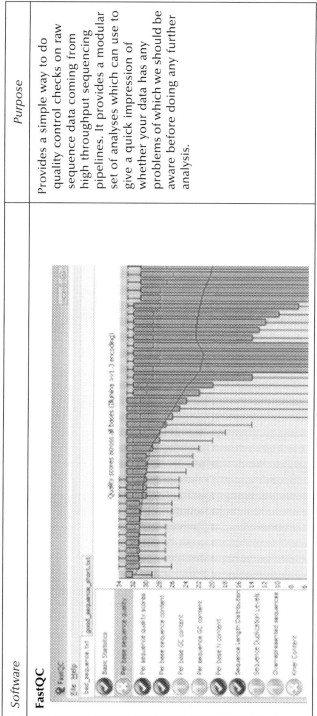	Provides a simple way to do quality control checks on raw sequence data coming from high throughput sequencing pipelines. It provides a modular set of analyses which can use to give a quick impression of whether your data has any problems of which we should be aware before doing any further analysis.

(Continued)

Table 13.2 (Continued)   List of Software's Used in Genomic Research

Software		Purpose
Trimmomatic		Trimmomatic includes processing steps for read trimming and filtering, but the main algorithm is related to finding the adapter sequences and quality filtering.

(Continued)

Table 13.2 (Continued)   List of Software's Used in Genomic Research

Software		Purpose
Stampy	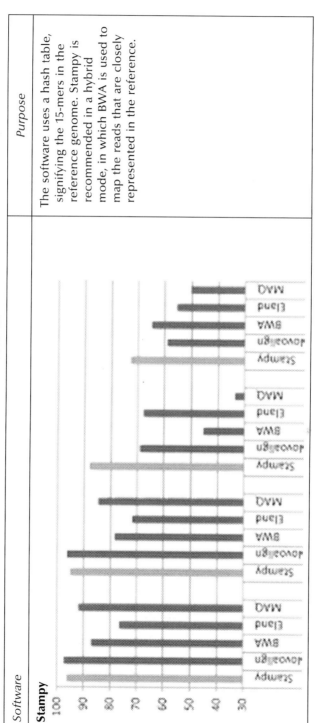	The software uses a hash table, signifying the 15-mers in the reference genome. Stampy is recommended in a hybrid mode, in which BWA is used to map the reads that are closely represented in the reference.

(Continued)

Table 13.2 (Continued)   List of Software's Used in Genomic Research

Software		Purpose
Samtools		It is a set of utilities that manipulate alignments in BAM format. It imports and export to the SAM format and it does sorting, merging and indexing, and finally retrieve reads in any regions.

(Continued)

Table 13.2 (Continued) List of Software's Used in Genomic Research

Software		Purpose
BWA		It is a software package that maps low-divergent sequences against a large sequence.

(Continued)

Table 13.2 (Continued) List of Software's Used in Genomic Research

Software		Purpose
Picard, GATK, and Integrated Genome Viewer	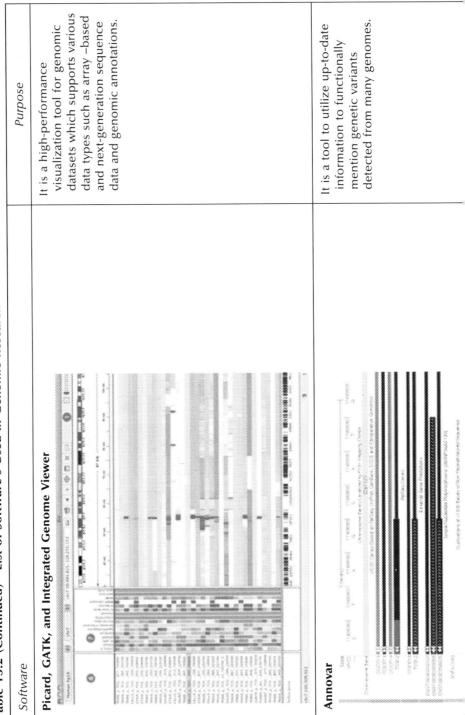	It is a high-performance visualization tool for genomic datasets which supports various data types such as array –based and next-generation sequence data and genomic annotations.
Annovar		It is a tool to utilize up-to-date information to functionally mention genetic variants detected from many genomes.

Table 13.3   List of Databases Used in Genomic Research

Database	Purpose
refGen 	The database specifies human protein-coding and non-protein coding genes that are retrieved from the NCBI RNA reference sequence.
1000g2015aug_all	It is the largest public catalogue of human variation and genotype data.

(Continued)

Table 13.3 (Continued) List of Databases Used in Genomic Research

Database		Purpose
ExAc03 or GnoMAD_exome		Genome Aggregation Database (gnomAD) seek to aggregate and harmonize exome and genome sequencing data from large-scale sequencing projects.
Avsnp150		Annotate variants with dbSNP identifiers.
Esp6500siv2_all		To examine the frequency of variants in whole-exome data.

(Continued)

Table 13.3 (Continued) List of Databases Used in Genomic Research

Database		Purpose
ClinVar	ClinVar Genomic variation as it relates to human health About Access Submit Stats FTP Help Advanced sear NM_000059.3(BRCA2):c.3909C>A (p.Gly1303=) Interpretation: Likely benign Review status: ★★★☆ reviewed by expert panel Submissions: 2 (Most recent: Jun 29, 2017) Last evaluated: Jun 29, 2017 Accession: VCV000051559.2 Variation ID: 51559 Description: single nucleotide variant FEEDBACK	It is an archive for declarations of clinical significance made the submitters. If multiple groups have reported different results for the same variant, then there is a conflict and report all the results submitted for clinical significance.

(Continued)

Table 13.3 (Continued)   List of Databases Used in Genomic Research

Database	Purpose
OMIM **OMIM Database** 	It is a comprehensive and authoritative collection of human genes and phenotypes that is freely available and updated every day.

isolation. DNA can be isolated from the tissue by using a QIAamp DNA Mini Kit with some modifications as per the manufacturer's protocol. DNA library can be prepared using Illumina v4 TruSeq Exome library prep as per the manufacturer's protocol. The whole-exome sequence data analysis can involve the preprocessing of the sequence file. The quality of the raw read FASTQ files can be checked before trimming the adapter sequence, and the low-quality reads can be removed by Trimmomatic software (AVG = Q30, MINLENGHT = 50) using FastQC. Processed FASTQ files can be mapped on human reference sequence using BWA followed by variant calling using GATK. Annotation of the variants can be performed with Annovar using databases such as refGene, bSNP, 1000 Genomes (1000 Genomes Project Consortium, 2015) for testing the previously reported variants. Gene function prediction tools like SIFT, Polyphen2, PROVEAN, and Mutation Taster can be used to predict the effect of the variants using the LJB database. The variants can also be matched with the CIVic database for describing the somatic variants (Griffith et al., 2017). Further analysis of the variants can be done through ClinVar for studying the relationships among medically important variants and phenotypes and COSMIC database of acquired mutations found in human cancers (Forbes et al., 2010; Landrum et al., 2014). Figure 13.3 shows the flowchart of exome analysis.

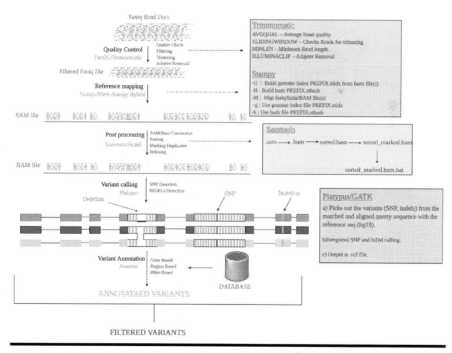

Figure 13.3   Overview of exome analysis.

13.5 Healthcare as a Big Data Repository

The major purpose of healthcare is to ascertain for prevention, diagnosis, and treatment of human beings. The healthcare system has lots of components that include health professionals; also, it is categorized depending on their mode of operation, such as clinics, hospitals, and institutions. Depending on the urgency, healthcare professionals will work on different levels to serve themselves. Primary health centers serve as the first point of consultation, followed by a medical expert, medical investigation, and treatment. All the above professionals hold various levels of responsibility, such as patient's medical history documentation, medical and clinical data, and other medical data. Initially, the documents of patients have been prepared and protected with handwritten papers and files. Even the professional's exam data are being registered and filed in a paper format. Electronic health records (EHR) are a computerized medical record that has all the information of a patient, which gradually monitored. It captures, transmits, receives, store, recover, connect, and alter the data for the primary purpose (Reisman, 2017).

13.5.1 Electronic Health Records (EHR)

One of the main advantages of EHRs is that medical professionals can use the whole medical history of a patient. From previous test results, we can start absorbing and treating the patient without any delay also. We do not need to get any confusion or worry about any additional examination as it makes better coordination between healthcare providers. Web or online-based electronic platforms improve the reputation of healthcare professionals in many ways, such as automatic reminders regarding vaccinations, strange laboratory results, cancer tests, and others.

13.5.2 Digital Information about Healthcare and Big Data

An electronic medical record (EMR) stores patient's medical and clinical data. Healthcare data has been increasing the dependency on information technology. So, the rapid growth in the development and usage of this information can be advanced to signals and share health-related data by launching a monitoring system. These devices need enormous data to analyze clinical or medical care (Shameer et al., 2017). Big Data made a revolution in the medical sector, health outcomes, and costs. The Big Data for healthcare is depicted in Figure 13.4.

13.6 Management of Big Data

The information assembled from different sources requires upgrading purchaser benefits rather than shopper utilization. The significant test with enormous information is how to deal with this huge volume of data. For making it

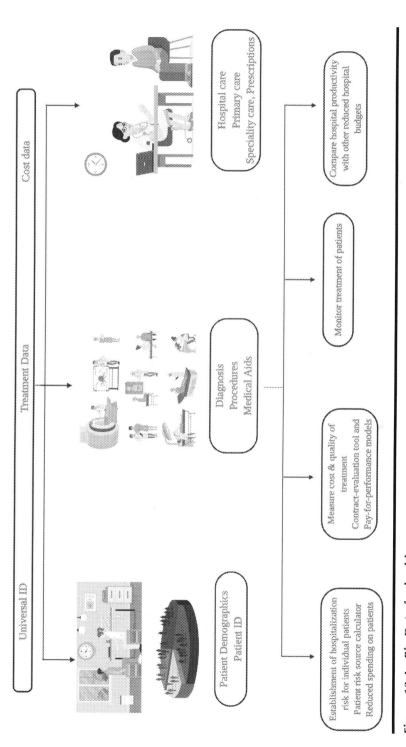

Figure 13.4 Big Data for healthcare.

accessible for the academic network, the information required to be put away in a document group that is effectively available and understandable for a proficient examination. In the setting of medicinal services information, another significant test is the usage of top of the line registering devices, conventions, and top of the line equipment in the clinical setting. Specialists from science, data innovation, measurements, and arithmetic, are required to cooperate to accomplish this objective. The information gathered utilizing devices can be accessible with pre-introduced programming apparatuses created by explanatory device engineers. These devices have information mining and capacities created by artificial intelligence specialists to change the data information. Upon execution, it would improve the productivity of securing, examining, and representation of enormous information from human services. The fundamental assignment is to comment on, incorporate, and present this intricate information in a proper way for superior comprehension.

13.7 Challenges in Healthcare Data

Big Data administration and analysis are expanded along with visualization solutions that can assimilate to utilize EMRs with healthcare. The availability of EHR commodities, with many clinical terms, technical conditions, and operative capacities, has met with challenges in the distribution of data. Presently, the foremost intention is to collect large numbers of EMR data. Here, a few challenges were discussed below.

13.7.1 Storage

Storing more data is a challenge; nonetheless, it has various benefits like security and access. It seems that lowering costs and legitimacy. The cloud-based warehouse is a more desirable choice that has been opted by many healthcare industries.

13.7.2 Data Cleansing

The data needs to clean to assure accuracy, exactness, appropriateness, relevancy, furthermore purity after the purchase. The cleansing process might be by logical rules that guarantee high levels of certainty and uprightness. More tools use to lessen time and costs to arrest unclean data from crashing Big Data projects.

13.7.3 Combined Format

Subjects with a large data size are not simple with a conventional EHR setup. It is excessively challenging to manage Big Data, particularly with healthcare providers. Classifying all the appropriate data is essential.

13.7.4 Accuracy

Few studies have the patient data in EHR and EMR, which is not reliable yet, because of the complexity and lower EHR with a faulty perception. All these can affect the quality results for Big Data. The EHRs enhance the feature and data transfer in clinical workflows; however, records show disparities in specific perspectives. The documentation might improve with self-report patient surveys.

13.7.5 Image Preprocessing

Researchers witnessed several environmental factors that alter data quality and errors from prevailing therapeutic records (Belle et al., 2015). Medical photographs often undergo technical limitations that involve various sorts of sound and artefacts. Inappropriate handling of photos can also cause damaging images. Decreasing noise, removing artefacts, sharpening the contrast of collected photographs and image quality are some of the steps that can be implemented to serve one purpose.

13.7.6 Security

Several security breaches remain a preference for healthcare institutions. Due to vulnerabilities, technical protection has been developed for protected health information. Well-known security measures like antivirus software, firewalls, etc. can elude a lot of trouble.

13.7.7 Metadata

For having a data governance strategy, it is necessary to have comprehensive, precise, and up-to-date metadata about the collected data. Metadata has a purpose and an individual accountable for the data. They would permit to replicate queries and support scientific researches with accuracy.

13.7.8 Querying

Metadata is easier for companies to query data with solutions. Despite the lack of proper compatibility, the query tools may not find a data repository. Similarly, various elements of a dataset should be connected and attainable.

13.7.9 Visualization

Clear and attractive data visualization using heat maps, charts, and histograms with conflicting images and accurate information can make it simpler to consume information and use it competently.

13.7.10 Data Distribution

Subjects may or may not obtain care at various locations. Sometimes both providers and patients would deliberately restrict the information between different EHR systems. Healthcare providers need to thrive and generate a Big Data exchange that delivers honest, appropriate, and significant information by combining all the caring members.

13.8 Tribal Research in India

As of the 2011 census, the tribal population in India was 104 million, which consists of some 705 different ethnic groups scattered across 30 states and Union Territories with diverse cultural and life practices. The tribal population primarily the most susceptible and marginalized people of society. Moreover, they lag from social beings, health aspects and other development. Child malnutrition is higher, along with poverty, which is more common in tribes than in other populations. In a study in Maharashtra, three-fourths (76.6%) of the 2926 under-5 children found to be moderate or severely malnourished. In most tribal populations, undernutrition found to be worrisome. According to NFHS-4 data, 94.7% of children and 83.2% of women were affected with anaemia. Health services in tribal areas remain under-developed and less accessible. Limited data on tribal health conditions and disease profiles due to environmental, cultural practice and social factors have been assessed (Basu, 2000). Health problems in primitive tribes are challenging, and diseases such as malaria, tuberculosis, haemoglobinopathies, thalassemia, and G6PD deficiency along with the prevalence of diabetes, hypertension, and cancer noticed throughout India. These diseases are caused due to tobacco usage, lack of physical activity, and an unhealthy diet. Tribes were found to have a low level of awareness and knowledge and health-seeking behaviour (Singh & Reddy, 2015). Through political commitment and concerted efforts, the lives of the tribal population can be changed (Narain et al., 2015).

13.8.1 Indigenous Data

The data from the indigenous population are inconsistent, inaccurate, and irrelevant, lack of funding for data organization and insufficient data describing lifestyle and behaviour (Rainie et al., 2017; Rodriguez-Lonebear, 2016). Indigenous data dominance disrupts the current pattern, thereby causing a realization of indigenous goals and visions. At present, an increase in research funding for tribes has been opened particularly in the field of Big Data as it corresponds with better data through tribal people, researchers, and community stakeholders (Rainie et al., 2017; Rodriguez-Lonebear, 2016). To empower families and well-being, the tribal people have sought data plans through government policies also. For indigenous data systems, an individual's acquisition and transmission of knowledge are essential to support the data collection. Indigenous data systems are based on the way of being, knowing, and doing, which carried from one generation to the next. Tribal data comprise information about their environment, cultures, community, and interests (Nickerson, 2017). Hence the data information can be both collective and individual data. which are yet to be assessed in the Indian tribal population.

13.9 Conclusion

Tribal health is a concern due to the traditional health care system. At present, growing interests in Big Data analytics and precision medicine can use in tribal population health by enhancing large population datasets to attain a better understanding of health and its inequities, and second, to impulse complex data that reflects a person's framework from social, economic, and biological viewpoints. By recommending the following priorities for Big Data initiative about health can assure of producing health insights that can lead to promoting health interventions and policies in a population.

13.9.1 Priorities

1. Socioeconomic data must be linked to health services that help with the Big Data plan.
2. We should accelerate from ecological studies at an individual level that examines at varying levels, such as occupational and community-level exposures to pollution.
3. Collaborations with researchers and public health decision-makers to ensure the research questions and findings make an impact on health.
4. Reasonable efforts must protect privacy.

Acknowledgments

The authors would like to thank the authorities of the Natural Resources Data Management System (NRDMS – grant no. NRDMS/SC/ST/033/16), New Delhi, for granting us the fund to conduct the project on a tribal survey of Tamil Nadu. The authors wish to thank VIT for providing the necessary infrastructure facility and ICMR [F.No.5/7/482/2010-RBMH&CH] for funding the National Task Force Project on hemoglobinopathies and G6PD deficiency studies of Vellore hills, Tamil Nadu. The authors thank the Department of Biotechnology (DBT), New Delhi, for the Bioinformatics Infrastructural Facility (BIF-BTISNeT) at Mizoram University.

References

1000 Genomes Project Consortium. (2015). A global reference for human genetic variation. *Nature*, *526*, 68–74.

Albanese, D., & Donati, C. (2017). Strain profiling and epidemiology of bacterial species from metagenomic sequencing. *Nature Communications, 8*, 1–14.

Andreu-Perez, J., Poon, C. C., Merrifield, R. D., Wong, S. T., & Yang, G.-Z. (2015). Big data for health. *IEEE Journal of Biomedical and Health Informatics, 19*, 1193–1208.

Basu, S. (2000). Dimensions of tribal health in India. *Health and Population Perspectives and Issues, 23*, 61–70.

Belle, A., Thiagarajan, R., Soroushmehr, S., Navidi, F., Beard, D. A., & Najarian, K. (2015). Big data analytics in healthcare. *BioMed Research International*, 2015: 370194.

Benke, K., & Benke, G. (2018). Artificial intelligence and big data in public health. *International Journal of Environmental Research and Public Health, 15*, 2796.

Blazquez, D., & Domenech, J. (2018). Big Data sources and methods for social and economic analyses. *Technological Forecasting and Social Change, 130*, 99–113.

Boyd, D., & Crawford, K. (2012). Critical questions for big data: Provocations for a cultural, technological, and scholarly phenomenon. *Information, Communication & Society, 15*, 662–679.

Breitwieser, F. P., Lu, J., & Salzberg, S. L. (2019). A review of methods and databases for metagenomic classification and assembly. *Briefings in Bioinformatics, 20*, 1125–1136.

Cancilla, M., Powell, I., Hillier, A., & Davidson, B. (1992). Rapid genomic fingerprinting of Lactococcus lactis strains by arbitrarily primed polymerase chain reaction with 32P and fluorescent labels. *Applied and Environmental Microbiology, 58*, 1772–1775.

Chapman, P., Clinton, J., Kerber, R., Khabaza, T., Reinartz, T., Shearer, C., & Wirth, R. (2000). CRISP-DM 1.0: Step-by-step data mining guide. *SPSS Inc, 9*, 13.

Choudhury, S., Fishman, J. R., McGowan, M. L., & Juengst, E. T. (2014). Big data, open science and the brain: Lessons learned from genomics. *Frontiers in Human Neuroscience, 8*, 239.

Church, D. (2015). Schneider V a, Steinberg K, Schatz MC, Quinlan AR, Chin CS, et al. Extending reference assembly models. *Genome Biology, 16*, 13.

Clifford, L. (2008). Big Data: How do your data grow. *Nature, 455*, 28–29.

De Mandal, S., Panda, A., Bisht, S., & Kumar, N. (2015). Microbial ecology in the era of next generation sequencing. *Next Generation Sequencing and Applications, 1*, 2.

Dean, J., & Ghemawat, S. (2008). MapReduce: Simplified data processing on large clusters. *Communications of the ACM, 51*, 107–113.

Elend, C., Schmeisser, C., Leggewie, C., Babiak, P., Carballeira, J. D., Steele, H., Reymond, J.-L., Jaeger, K.-E., & Streit, W. (2006). Isolation and biochemical characterization of two novel metagenome-derived esterases. *Applied and Environmental Microbiology, 72*, 3637–3645.

Fayyad, U., Piatetsky-Shapiro, G., & Smyth, P. (1996). The KDD process for extracting useful knowledge from volumes of data. *Communications of the ACM, 39*, 27–34.

Forbes, S. A., Bindal, N., Bamford, S., Cole, C., Kok, C. Y., Beare, D., Jia, M., Shepherd, R., Leung, K., & Menzies, A. (2010). COSMIC: Mining complete cancer genomes in the Catalogue of Somatic Mutations in Cancer. *Nucleic Acids Research, 39*, D945–D950.

Grasnick, B., Perscheid, C., & Uflacker, M. (2018). A framework for the automatic combination and evaluation of gene selection methods. Presented at the International Conference on Practical Applications of Computational Biology & Bioinformatics, Springer, pp. 166–174.

Griffith, M., Spies, N. C., Krysiak, K., McMichael, J. F., Coffman, A. C., Danos, A. M., Ainscough, B. J., Ramirez, C. A., Rieke, D. T., & Kujan, L. (2017). CIViC is a community knowledgebase for expert crowdsourcing the clinical interpretation of variants in cancer. *Nature Genetics, 49,* 170.

Handelsman, J. (2005). Metagenomics: Application of genomics to uncultured microorganisms. *Microbiology and Molecular Biology Reviews, 69,* 195–195.

Jin, X., Wah, B. W., Cheng, X., & Wang, Y. (2015). Significance and challenges of big data research. *Big Data Research, 2,* 59–64.

Khomtchouk, B. B., Hennessy, J. R., & Wahlestedt, C. (2017). shinyheatmap: Ultra fast low memory heatmap web interface for big data genomics. *PloS One, 12*(5), e0176334.

Landrum, M. J., Lee, J. M., Riley, G. R., Jang, W., Rubinstein, W. S., Church, D. M., & Maglott, D. R. (2014). ClinVar: Public archive of relationships among sequence variation and human phenotype. *Nucleic Acids Research, 42,* D980–D985.

Langmead, B., Schatz, M. C., Lin, J., Pop, M., & Salzberg, S. L. (2009). Searching for SNPs with cloud computing. *Genome Biology, 10,* R134.

Muyzer, G., De Waal, E. C., & Uitterlinden, A. G. (1993). Profiling of complex microbial populations by denaturing gradient gel electrophoresis analysis of polymerase chain reaction-amplified genes coding for 16S rRNA. *Applied and Environmental Microbiology, 59,* 695–700.

Narain, J. P., Jain, S., Bora, D., & Venkatesh, S. (2015). Eradicating successfully yaws from India: The strategy & global lessons. *The Indian Journal of Medical Research, 141,* 608.

Naseriparsa, M., Bidgoli, A.-M., & Varaee, T. (2014). A hybrid feature selection method to improve performance of a group of classification algorithms. arXiv preprint arXiv:1403.2372.

Nichols, D. S., Sanderson, K., Buia, A., Van De Kamp, J., Holloway, P., Bowman, J. P., Smith, M., Mancuso Nichols, C., Nichols, P., & McMeekin, T. (2002). Bioprospecting and biotechnology in Antarctica. The Antarctic: past, present and future, Antarctic CRC research report 28.

Nickerson, M. (2017). *Characteristics of a nation-to-nation relationship.* Ottawa: Institute on Governance.

O'Driscoll, A., Daugelaite, J., & Sleator, R. D. (2013). "Big data," Hadoop and cloud computing in genomics. *Journal of Biomedical Informatics, 46,* 774–781.

Oulas, A., Pavloudi, C., Polymenakou, P., Pavlopoulos, G. A., Papanikolaou, N., Kotoulas, G., Arvanitidis, C., & Iliopoulos, I. (2015). Metagenomics: Tools and Insights for Analyzing Next-Generation Sequencing Data Derived from Biodiversity Studies. *Bioinformatics and Biology Insights, 9,* 75-88

Pace, N. R. (1997). A molecular view of microbial diversity and the biosphere. *Science, 276,* 734–740.

Pasolli, E., Truong, D. T., Malik, F., Waldron, L., & Segata, N. (2016). Machine learning meta-analysis of large metagenomic datasets: Tools and biological insights. *PLoS Computational Biology, 12.* doi:10.1371/journal.pcbi.1004977

Pireddu, L., Leo, S., & Zanetti, G. (2011). SEAL: A distributed short read mapping and duplicate removal tool. *Bioinformatics, 27,* 2159–2160.

Polyakova, A. G., Loginov, M. P., Serebrennikova, A. I., & Thalassinos, E. (2019). Design of a socio-economic processes monitoring system based on network analysis and big data. *International Journal of Economics and Business Administration, VII*(1), 130–139.

Rainie, S. C., Schultz, J. L., Briggs, E., Riggs, P., & Palmanteer-Holder, N. L. (2017). Data as a strategic resource: Self-determination, governance, and the data challenge for Indigenous nations in the United States. *International Indigenous Policy Journal*, 8(2). doi:10.18584/iipj.2017.8.2.1

Reiman, D., Metwally, A., & Dai, Y. (2017). Using convolutional neural networks to explore the microbiome. Presented at the 2017 39th annual international conference of the IEEE engineering in medicine and biology society (EMBC), IEEE, pp. 4269–4272.

Reisman, M. (2017). EHRs: The challenge of making electronic data usable and interoperable. *Pharmacy and Therapeutics*, 42, 572.

Rinke, C., Schwientek, P., Sczyrba, A., Ivanova, N. N., Anderson, I. J., Cheng, J.-F., Darling, A., Malfatti, S., Swan, B. K., & Gies, E. A. (2013). Insights into the phylogeny and coding potential of microbial dark matter. *Nature*, 499, 431–437.

Rodriguez-Lonebear, D. (2016). Building a data revolution in Indian country. In Tahu Kukutai & Taylor John (Eds.), *Indigenous data sovereignty: Toward an agenda* (pp. 253–272). Australia: Australian National University Press.

Ruegg, J., Gries, C., Bond-Lamberty, B., Bowen, G. J., Felzer, B. S., McIntyre, N. E., Soranno, P. A., Vanderbilt, K. L., & Weathers, K. C. (2014). Completing the data life cycle: Using information management in macrosystems ecology research. *Frontiers in Ecology and the Environment*, 12, 24–30.

Schatz, M. C. (2009). CloudBurst: Highly sensitive read mapping with MapReduce. *Bioinformatics*, 25, 1363–1369.

Shahrivari, S. (2014). Beyond batch processing: towards real-time and streaming big data. *Computers*, 3, 117–129.

Shameer, K., Badgeley, M. A., Miotto, R., Glicksberg, B. S., Morgan, J. W., & Dudley, J. T. (2017). Translational bioinformatics in the era of real-time biomedical, health care and wellness data streams. *Briefings in Bioinformatics*, 18, 105–124.

Sheffield, V., Beck, J., Stone, E., & Myers, R. (1992). A simple and efficient method for attachment of a 40-base pair, GC-rich sequence to PCR-amplified DNA. *BioTechniques*, 12, 386–388.

Shvachko, K., Kuang, H., Radia, S., & Chansler, R. (2010). The hadoop distributed file system. Presented at the 2010 IEEE 26th symposium on mass storage systems and technologies (MSST), Ieee, pp. 1–10.

Simonet, A., Fedak, G., & Ripeanu, M. (2015). Active data: A programming model to manage data life cycle across heterogeneous systems and infrastructures. *Future Generation Computer Systems*, 53, 25–42.

Sims, D., Sudbery, I., Ilott, N. E., Heger, A., & Ponting, C. P. (2014). Sequencing depth and coverage: Key considerations in genomic analyses. *Nature Reviews Genetics*, 15, 121.

Singh, D., & Reddy, C. K. (2015). A survey on platforms for big data analytics. *Journal of Big Data*, 2, 8.

Torsvik, V. L., & Øvreås, L. (2011). DNA reassociation yields broad-scale information on metagenome complexity and microbial diversity. In *Handbook of Molecular Microbial Ecology I: Metagenomics and Complementary Approaches* (pp. 3–16). New York: Wiley-Blackwell.

Truong, D. T., Franzosa, E. A., Tickle, T. L., Scholz, M., Weingart, G., Pasolli, E., Tett, A., Huttenhower, C., & Segata, N. (2015). MetaPhlAn2 for enhanced metagenomic taxonomic profiling. *Nature Methods*, 12, 902–903.

Tsymbal, A., Pechenizkiy, M., & Cunningham, P. (2005). Diversity in search strategies for ensemble feature selection. *Information Fusion, 6*, 83–98.

Turnbaugh, P. J., Ley, R. E., Hamady, M., Fraser-Liggett, C. M., Knight, R., & Gordon, J. I. (2007). The human microbiome project. *Nature, 449*, 804–810.

Uchiyama, T., Abe, T., Ikemura, T., & Watanabe, K. (2005). Substrate-induced gene-expression screening of environmental metagenome libraries for isolation of catabolic genes. *Nature Biotechnology 23*, 88–93.

Vakhlu, J., Sudan, A. K., & Johri, B. (2008). Metagenomics: future of microbial gene mining. *Indian Journal of Microbiology, 48*, 202–215.

Vicente, M. R., López-Menéndez, A. J., & Pérez, R. (2015). Forecasting unemployment with internet search data: Does it help to improve predictions when job destruction is skyrocketing? *Technological Forecasting and Social Change, 92*, 132–139.

Voget, S., Steele, H., & Streit, W. (2006). Characterization of a metagenome-derived halotolerant cellulase. *Journal of Biotechnology, 126*, 26–36.

Walsh, A. M., Crispie, F., O'Sullivan, O., Finnegan, L., Claesson, M. J., & Cotter, P. D. (2018). Species classifier choice is a key consideration when analysing low-complexity food microbiome data. *Microbiome, 6*, 50.

Waschkowitz, T., Rockstroh, S., & Daniel, R. (2009). Isolation and characterization of metalloproteases with a novel domain structure by construction and screening of metagenomic libraries. *Applied and Environmental Microbiology, 75*, 2506–2516.

West, M., Ginsburg, G. S., Huang, A. T., & Nevins, J. R. (2006). Embracing the complexity of genomic data for personalized medicine. *Genome Research, 16*, 559–566.

Zaharia, M., Xin, R. S., Wendell, P., Das, T., Armbrust, M., Dave, A., Meng, X., Rosen, J., Venkataraman, S., & Franklin, M. J. (2016). Apache spark: A unified engine for big data processing. *Communications of the ACM, 59*, 56–65.

Chapter 14

PySpark toward Data Analytics

J. Ramsingh

Department of Computer Applications, Bharathiar University, Coimbatore, India

Contents

DOI: 10.1201/9781003175889-14

14.1 Introduction

14.1.1 Apache Spark

Apache Spark is a real-time lightning-fast cluster computing framework for large-scale data processing. Apache Spark is developed to overcome the drawbacks of Apache Hadoop MapReduce since Hadoop works only on batch processing and lacks real-time processing features. It is formulated based on Hadoop MapReduce, Spark extends the MapReduce model for its interactive queries and stream processing. Spark supports in-memory cluster computing that increases the processing speed of the application.

Apache Spark has its own cluster manager for faster general data processing and to host its application. It uses Apache Hadoop for both storage and processing. It uses HDFS (Hadoop Distributed File system) for storage and YARN (Yet Another Resource Negotiator) to run its applications. It provides high-level APIs in Java, Scala, and Python and supports a rich set of higher-level tools including Spark SQL, MLlib, GraphX.

14.1.1.1 Spark Architecture

Apache Spark has a layered architecture where all the spark components and layers are loosely coupled. The architecture is further integrated with various extensions and libraries. Apache Spark Architecture is based on three main abstractions. Figure 14.1 illustrates the cluster management of Apache Spark using its components.

- **Resilient Distributed Dataset (RDD)**
- **Directed Acyclic Graph (DAG)**
- **Spark context**

I Resilient Distributed Datasets (RDD)

RDDs are the collection of data items that are split into partitions and can be stored in memory on workers nodes of the spark cluster. In terms of datasets, apache spark supports two types of RDDs – Hadoop Datasets created from the files stored on HDFS and parallelized collections based on existing Scala collections. Spark RDDs support two different types of operations – Transformations and Actions.

II Directed Acyclic Graph (DAG)

DAG is a sequence of computations performed on data where each node is an RDD partition and edge is a transformation on top of data. The DAG abstraction helps eliminate the Hadoop MapReduce multistage execution model and provides performance enhancements over Hadoop.

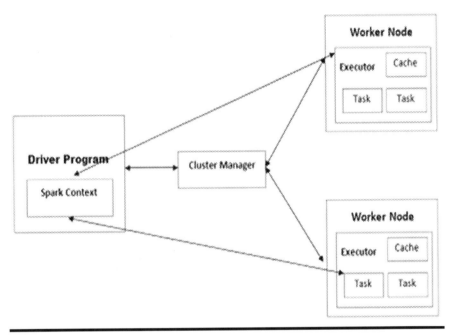

Figure 14.1   Apache Spark cluster mode.

Direct - Transformation is an action which transitions data partition state from A to B.

Acyclic -Transformation cannot return to the older partition

III Spark Context (SC)

Spark Context is the internal engine that allows the connections with the clusters. If you want to run an operation, you need a SparkContext.

14.1.2 PySpark

PySpark is a Python API for Apache Spark released by the Spark community to support Python with Spark. PySpark can work and integrate with RDD easily using Python language. The library **Py4j** in Python helps to achieve this feature. PySpark shares Spark Shell to link Python API to the spark core and to initializes the Spark context.

There are several features of the PySpark framework:

- Faster processing frameworks
- Real-time computations and low latency due to in-memory processing
- Polyglot [integrating several languages like Java, Python, Scala, and R]

- Powerful caching and efficient disk persistence
- Deployment can be performed by Hadoop through Yarn

14.1.2.1 Prerequisites to PySpark

Before learning PySpark, the readers should have basic knowledge about the python programming language as well as its frameworks. The reader should have a sound understanding of Spark, Hadoop, Scala Programming Language, and HDFS. A comparison of PySpark and Scala is shown in Table 14.1.

14.1.2.2 PySpark - Environment Setup

Note: To install Apache Spark, Java and Scala should be installed in your system.

Table 14.1 PySpark vs. Scala

Criteria	Python with Spark	Scala with Spark
Performance Speed	Python is slower than Scala when it is used with Spark, but Python provides an easier interface to programmers.	Scala is faster than Python since Spark is developed using Scala integration with Spark is easier when compared to Python
Learning Curve	Python is a high-level language easier to learn and has simple syntax for implementation.	Scala has a mysterious syntax making it hard to learn.
Data Science Libraries	Python API supports many Data Science libraries. We can easily import the core libraries of R to Python.	Scala lacks Data Science libraries and tools.
Readability of Code	Readability and maintenance of code are easy in Python API	Readability and maintenance of code in Scala API is easy since Spark is written in Scala
Complexity	Implementing Machine Learning algorithms in Python is comparatively straightforward since it has many ML libraries.	Implementing Machine Learning in Scala is more complex when compared with Python

Step 1. To download the latest version of Apache Spark, go to the official Apache Spark website. In this tutorial, we are using **spark-2.1.0-bin-hadoop2.7**.

Step 2. Extract the downloaded Spark tar file.

```
Sudo tar -xvf User/Downloads/spark-2.1.0-bin-hado-
op2.7.tgz
```

Step 3. To start PySpark, you need to set the environments to set the Spark and the **Py4j** path in**.bashrc file, sudo vi ~/.bashrc**.

```
export SPARK_HOME = user/home/spark-2.1.0-bin-
hadoop2.7
export PATH = $PATH: user/home/spark-2.1.0-bin-
hadoop2.7/bin
export PYTHONPATH = $SPARK_HOME/python:$SPARK_HOME/
python/lib/py4j-0.10.4-src.zip:$PYTHONPATH
export PATH = $SPARK_HOME/python:$PATH
```

Step 4. Save the.bashrc file using the following command
```
source.bashrc
```

Step 5. Start your PySpark shell.
```
./bin/pyspark
```

Step 6. Check the execution
```
Jps
```

14.2 PySpark: SparkContext

SparkContext is the entry point to every spark functionality. The Spark driver application is used to generate SparkContext. It allows your Spark Application to

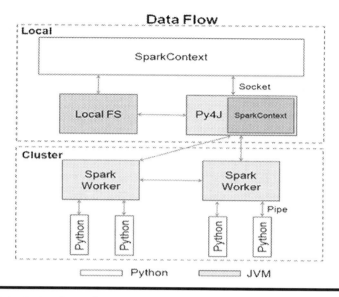

Figure 14.2 PySpark spark context (SC) data flow overview.

access Spark Cluster with the help of the Resource Manager. Three resource managers Spark Standalone, YARN, Apache Mesos is available for Spark. From the three anyone can be the Resource Manager. SparkContext uses the Py4J library to launch a **JVM** and **Java SparkContext**. Figure 14.2 shows the flow of data in the Apache spark cluster using SparkContext.

14.2.1 SparkContext Parameters

SparkContext has some of the following parameters:

- **Master:** The SparkContext cluster URL.
- **AppName:** The application name of the current job we have created.
- **SparkHome:** The home directory of the Spark.
- **PyFiles:** The.py files send to the cluster and then added to PYTHONPATH.
- **Environment:** environment variables for the worker node.
- **BatchSize:** The number of Python objects for representation.
- **Serializer:** RDD serializer invoked in executors.
- **Conf:** An object to set all Spark properties.
- **profiler_cls:** Custom class profilers for profiling.
- **JSC:** The JavaSparkContext instance.

The **Master** and **AppName** are the most widely used parameters. The initial code for any PySpark application is:

```
-----------------------------BU_APP.py------------
--------------------------------------------------

from pyspark import SparkContext
sc = SparkContext('local', 'BU App')

--------------------------------------------------
--------------------------------------------------
```

14.2.2 SparkContext Example

Input

```
-----------------------------BU_APP.py------------
--------------------------------------------------

from pyspark import SparkContext
Attendance= 'file:///user/home/Desktop/ Attend.csv'
sc = SparkContext('local', 'BU_APP')
Data = sc.textFile(Attendance).cache()
Percentage = Attendance.filter (lambda s: '60' in s).count()
Percentage2 = Attendance.filter(lambda s: '80' in s).count()
print ('Students with 60 %i, Students with 80: %i' %
(Percentage, Percentage2))

--------------------------------------------------
--------------------------------------------------
```

Output

```
--------------------------------------------------
--------------------------------------------------

$SPARK_HOME/bin/spark-submit BU_APP.py
Students with 60 22, Students with 80: 18

--------------------------------------------------
--------------------------------------------------
```

In the above example, we calculate the student percentage count with 60 and 80 percent. The file attendance.csv holds the students' attendance data.

14.3 PySpark Shared Variables

Apache Spark uses shared variables for parallel processing. Shared variables are the variables that are required to be used by many functions & methods in parallel. Spark segregates the job into the smallest possible operation running on different nodes on the cluster and each node having a copy of all the variables of the Spark job. Any changes made to these variables don't affect the driver program and to overcome the limitation Spark provides a different type of shared variables – **Broadcast Variables and Accumulators**.

14.3.1 Broadcast Variables

A broadcast variable is one of the shared variables which is used to save a copy of the data across all nodes. It helps the programmer to cache read-only variables on all the machines rather than transporting a copy of it with all the jobs. In Spark to distribute broadcast variables with minimum communication cost, it allows using different efficient algorithms. For PySpark, the following syntax shows the use of the Broadcast variable. It has an attribute called value which stores the data and is used to return a broadcast value.

```
-----------------------------------------------------
-----------------------------------------------------

class pyspark.Broadcast (sc = None, value = None, pickle_
registry = None, path = None)
```

14.3.1 Accumulators

The accumulator variables are used to combine the information through associative and commutative operations. As an example, for a sum operation or counters (in MapReduce), we can use an accumulator. Besides, we can use Accumulators in any Spark APIs.

```
-----------------------------------------------------
-----------------------------------------------------

class pyspark.Accumulator(aid, value, accum_param)

-----------------------------------------------------
-----------------------------------------------------
```

14.4 PySpark: RDD (Resilient Distributed Dataset)

- **Resilient:** Fault-tolerant and handling data failure
- **Distributed:** Distributed data in multiple cluster node
- **Dataset:** Collection of partitioned data

RDDs are the building blocks of the Spark application. RDD is the elements that run and operate on multiple nodes to do parallel processing on a cluster. It is immutable in nature and follows lazy transformations for quick processing. RDDs are fault-tolerant in nature so the lost data are recovered automatically.

RDDs are the backbone of PySpark by their simple functionalities and their schema-less data structure that can handle both structured and unstructured data. The in-memory data sharing in RDDs help to share the network and disk faster.

The data in RDD is split into multiple chunks based on a key generated in RDDs. RDDs are highly resilient in nature ie., they can recover quickly from any network communication issues or data loss issues. This allows performing our functional calculations very quickly and easily.

Two types of operations can be performed using RDD:

14.4.1 Transformations

Transformations are the process that is used to create a new RDD in PySpark. It follows the principle of Lazy Evaluations to create the new RDD. The sample transformation function are listed below

- Map
- flatMap
- filter
- distinct
- reduceByKey
- mapPartitions
- sortBy

14.4.2 Actions

Actions are used in RDD to instruct Apache Spark to do computation and return the result to the driver. Sample action functions are listed below

- collect
- collectAsMap
- reduce
- countByKey/countByValue
- take
- first

The dataset in RDDs is divided into logical partitions, which help to compute on different nodes of the cluster. Due to the logical partitions, we can perform transformations or actions parallel to the data. The distributions of data are taking place automatically by Spark. Figure 14.3 illustrates the RDD workflow in PySpark.

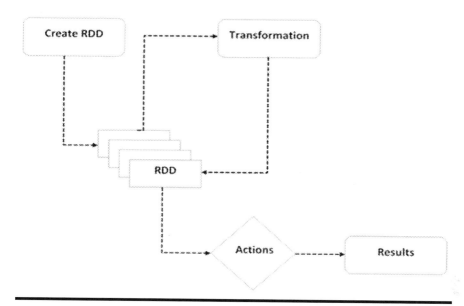

Figure 14.3   Work flow of RDD in PySpark.

14.4.3 Features of PySpark RDDs

14.4.3.1 In-Memory Computations

PySpark provides the facility of in-memory computation which helps improve the performance by order of magnitudes. PySpark stored the Computed results in distributed memory (RAM) instead of stable storage (disk).

14.4.3.2 Lazy Evaluation

All transformations in RDDs are lazy. When we call some operation in RDD for transformation, it does not execute immediately until an action is triggered. Lazy Evolution plays an important role in saving calculation overhead. It provides optimization by reducing the number of queries.

14.4.3.3 Fault-Tolerant

RDDs track data processing history to recover the lost Data automatically. If a failure occurs in any partition of RDDs, then that particular lost partition can be recovered automatically from the original fault-tolerant input dataset.

14.4.3.4 Immutability

Data in PySpark are immutable in nature. Once if the Data is created or retrieved, its value can't be changed.

14.4.3.5 Partitioning

PySpark RDDs are the collection of various data items that are huge in volume so they cannot be fit into a single node and it must be partitioned across various nodes

14.4.3.6 Persistence

PySpark RDDs can be reused and a user can choose a storage strategy. It is an optimization technique where we can save the result of RDDs evaluation. It stores the intermediate result so we can reuse the data. It reduces the computation complexity.

14.4.3.7 Coarse-Grained Operations

The coarse-grained operation means that we can transform the whole dataset but not the individual element on the dataset. On the other hand, fine-grained means we can transform individual elements in the dataset.

14.4.4 Creating RDD

PySpark provides two different methods to create RDDs: one is distributing a set of collection of objects or loading an external dataset. We can create RDDs using the parallelize() function which creates a collection in the program and pass the same to the Spark Context. It is the simplest way to create RDDs.

Input

----------------------Sparkpar.py------------------------

```
from pyspark import SparkConf, SparkContext
sc = SparkContext('local', 'count_app')
words   =   sc.parallelize   (['Spark','PySpark','RDD','
SparkContext'])
words.show()
```


Output


```
$SPARK_HOME/bin/spark-submit Sparkpar.py
+-----+-------+----+-----------+
|col1 |col2 |col3| col4 |
+-----+-------+----+-----------+
```

```
|Spark|PySpark|RDD |SparkContext|
+-----+-------+----+------------+
-----------------------------------------------------
-----------------------------------------------------
```

14.4.3 *Operations in RDD*

COUNT()

The count() function returns the number of items present in the RDD. In the following example, we are calculating the count of items present in the list.

Input

--------------------Sparkcount.py------------------------

```
from pyspark import SparkContext
sc = SparkContext('local', 'count_app')
words  =  sc.parallelize  (['Spark','PySpark','RDD','
SparkContext'])
counts = words.count()
print ('Number of items in RDD: %i' % (counts))
```


Output


```
$SPARK_HOME/bin/spark-submit Sparkcount.py
Number of items in RDD: 4
```


COLLECT()

To lists all the items in the RDD the collect () operation is used.

Input

------------------Sparkcollect.py------------------------
```
from pyspark import SparkContext
sc = SparkContext('local', 'count_app')
words  =  sc.parallelize  (['Spark','PySpark','RDD','
SparkContext'])
collect = words.collect()
```

```
print (' items in RDD: %s' % (collect))
```


Output


```
$SPARK_HOME/bin/spark-submit Sparkcollect.py
items in RDD: ['Spark','PySpark','RDD','SparkContext']
```

----

filter()
A new RDD is returns the element which satisfies the function inside the filter. In the following example, we filter out the strings containing "spark'.

Input
------------------------Sparkfilter.py------------------
```
from PySpark import SparkContext
sc = SparkContext('local', 'count_app')
words   =   sc.parallelize   (['Spark','PySpark','RDD','
SparkContext'])
filter_words = words.filter(lambda i: 'Spark' in words)
fill = filter_words.collect()
print (' Filtered words: %s' % (fill))
```


Output


```
$SPARK_HOME/bin/spark-submit Sparkfilter.py
Filtered words: ['Spark','PySpark','SparkContext']
```

----

foreach(f)
The foreach(f) function returns only those elements which match the condition of the function inside foreach. In the following example, we call a print function in foreach, which prints all the elements in the RDD.

Input
```
-----------------------Sparkforeach.py-----------------
from pyspark import SparkContext
sc = SparkContext('local', 'count_app')
words   =   sc.parallelize   (['Spark','PySpark','RDD','
SparkContext'])
def f(x):
print(x)
for_each= words.foreach(f)
```


Output


```
$SPARK_HOME/bin/spark-submitSparkforeach.py
Spark
PySpark
RDD
SparkContext
```

----

map()
A Mapped value is returned as a new RDD by applying a map function to each element of the RDD. Spark map itself is a transformation function that accepts a function as an argument and returns only one value. In the following example, the word Apache is mapped with the list of items.

Input
```
----------------------Sparkmap.py----------------------
from pyspark import SparkContext
sc = SparkContext('local', 'count_app')
words   =   sc.parallelize   (['Spark','PySpark','RDD','
SparkContext'])
map_word = words.map(lambda x: (x, 'Apache'))
map_len= words.map(lambda x: (x,len(x)))
mymap = map_word.collect()
mylen = map_len.collect()
print ('My word mapping: %s'%(mymap))
print (' key val based on length: %i'%(mylen))
```



```
$SPARK_HOME/bin/spark-submit Sparkmap.py
My word mapping:
[('Spark','Apache'),
('PySpark','Apache'),
('RDD','Apache'),
('SparkContext','Apache')]
key val based on length:
[('Spark','5'), ('PySpark', '7'), ('RDD', '3'),
('SparkContext','12')]
```

---

flatMap()

PySpark flatMap is a transformation operation of RDD, flatMap function is Similar to map, which returns a new RDD by flattening the results. In the following example we differentiate map and flatmap function. The result of map operation will return Array of Arrays and flatMap operation will return Array of words.

```
------------------------Sparkflatmap.py------------------
from pyspark import SparkContext
sc = SparkContext('local', 'count_app')
words    =    sc.parallelize    (['Spark    PySpark    RDD'],
['SparkContext map'])
map_words= words.map(lambda x: words.split(' '))
mymap = map_words.collect()
flatmap_words= words.flatmap(lambda x: words.split(' '))
myflatmap = flatmap_words.collect()
print ' my map:%s'% (mymap)
print ' my flatmap: %s'% (myflatmap)
```


Output


```
$SPARK_HOME/bin/spark-submit Sparkflatmap.py
my map: [['Spark', 'PySpark', 'RDD'],['SparkContext',
'map']]
my flatmap: ['Spark', 'PySpark', 'RDD','SparkContext',
'map']
```

---

reduce()

The specified commutative and associative binary operator is used in the reduce function to reduce the items of RDD. PySpark reduces operation is an action-based operation that triggers all lazy instructions. In the following example, a list of 10 values is created and the values 1 to 10 are reduced by adding them.

```
------------------------Sparkreduce.py------------------
from pyspark import SparkContext
sc = SparkContext('local', 'count_app')
x = sc.parallelize([10,20,30,40,50,60,70,80,90,100])
reduceSum = x.reduce(lambda a, n: a + n)
print ('reduced sum:' %i%(reducedSum))
```


Output


```
$SPARK_HOME/bin/spark-submit Sparkreduce.py
Reduced sum: 550
```

---

join()

PySpark join returns RDD with a pair of elements, the matching keys with their values in a paired form. We will get two different RDDs for two pairs of the element. In the following example, there are two pair of elements in two different RDDs. After joining these two RDDs, we get an RDD with elements having matching keys and their values.

```
----------------------Sparkjoin.py----------------------
from pyspark import SparkContext
sc = Spark Context('local', 'count_app')
li1   =   sc.parallelize  ([[('Spark',2),('PySpark',3),
('RDD',1)])
```

```
li2  =  sc.parallelize  ([('Spark',5),('PySpark',3),
('RDD',2)])
li_join = li1.join(li2)
map_join= li_join.collect()
print('joined elements: %s'%(map_join))
```


Output


```
$SPARK_HOME/bin/spark-submit Sparkjoin.py
joined elements:
[('Spark',(2,5)),('PySpark',(3,3)),('RDD',(1,2))]
```

----

groupBy()
PySpark RDD groupBy function returns a group of RDD items. The groupBy function will return a new RDD with a KEY (which is a group) and a list of items (in a form of an Iterator).

```
-----------------------Sparkgroupby.py-----------------
from pyspark import SparkContext
sc = Spark Context (local', 'count_app')
li1 = sc.parallelize
(['Ram','Raja','John','Thomas','Kavin','Kumar'])
ligroup = li1.groupBy()
print('Grouped elements: %s'%(ligroup))
```


Output


```
$SPARK_HOME/bin/spark-submit Sparkgroup.py
Grouped elements:(['John']) (['Kavin','Kumar']
(['Thomas'])
(['Ram','Raja'])
```


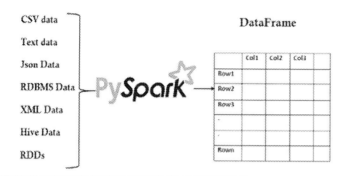

Figure 14.4 Dataframe in PySpark.

14.5 PySpark DataFrames

DataFrames is a two-dimensional data structure, which is tabular in nature similar to an SQL table or a spreadsheet. It represents Rows and columns, each of which consists of several observations. Rows can have Heterogeneous data, whereas a column can have Homogeneous data. Figure 14.4 shows the conversion of different data set into common PySpark Dataframes.

14.5.1 Need of DataFrames

14.5.1.1 Processing Heterogeneous Data

Dataframes are designed to process a large collection of Heterogeneous (structured and Semi-Structured) data. Spark DataFrame is an organized structure that helps to understand the schema data and to optimize the execution plan.

14.5.1.2 Slicing and Dicing

Data frame supports different data slicing and dicing operations like 'selecting' rows, columns, and cells by name or by row index, filtering out rows, etc. Statistical Data is usually very messy and contains lots of missing and wrong values and range violations data frames help to manage the messy data.

14.5.2 Features of DataFrame

  a. Distributed
     DataFrames are distributed in nature, which makes it a fault-tolerant and highly available data structure.
  b. Lazy evaluation
     Lazy evaluation is an evaluation strategy that holds the evaluation of an expression until its value is triggered.

c. Immutable

The DataFrames are immutable in nature and the object states cannot be modified.

14.5.3 PySpark DataFrames

A DataFrame can be accepted as a distributed and tabulated collection of titled columns which is similar to a two-dimensional table in a relational database. A DataFrame in Apache Spark can be created in multiple ways:

1. Creating data from Existing RDD.
2. DataFrames can be created by reading TEXT, CSV, JSON, and PARQUET file formats.
3. Programmatically specifying schema

14.5.4 Creating DataFrame from RDD

The DataFrame is created using RDDs in PySpark. In the following example, a list of tuples is created with name and age. A DataFrame is created by using createDataFrame() function on RDD with the help of sqlContext().

Input

```
------------------------Sparkdgf.py---------------------
from pyspark import SparkContext
from pyspark.sql import Row
sc = SparkContext('local', 'dfapp')
personal_info  =  [('Ram',21),('Raja',20),('John',22),
('Thomas',22),('Kavin',21),('Kumar',20]
rdd = sc.parallelize(personal_info)
personal_info = rdd.map(lambda x: Row(name=x[0], age=int
(x[1])))
personal= sqlContext.createDataFrame(personal_info)
type(personal)


------------------------------------------------------
------------------------------------------------------
```

Output

```
------------------------------------------------------
------------------------------------------------------

$SPARK_HOME/bin/spark-submit Sparkdf.py
<class 'pyspark.sql.dataframe.DataFrame'>
------------------------------------------------------
------------------------------------------------------
```

14.5.5 *Creating the DataFrame from CSV, JSON and Text Files*

The DataFrame is created in PySpark by loading the CSV, JSON, or Text file using the spark.read.csv () function in PySpark. In the following example a movie dataset in csv format is loaded using spark.read.csv () and spark.read.load().

```
------------------------Sparkdgf.py----------------------
from pyspark.sql import Row
sc = SparkContext('local', 'dfapp')
Data_movie=  spark.read.csv('/home/hduser/Desktop/IMDB-
Movie-Data.csv')
Data_movie2=spark.read.load('/home/hduser/Desktop/
IMDB-Movie-Data.csv', format='csv', header='true')
type(Data_movie)
type(Data_movie2)
```


Output


```
$SPARK_HOME/bin/spark-submit Sparkdf.py
<class 'pyspark.sql.dataframe.DataFrame'>
<class 'pyspark.sql.dataframe.DataFrame'>
```


In the following example, Tamilnadu state land data in JSON format data is loaded.

```
------------------------Sparkdgf.py----------------------
from pyspark.sql import Row
sc = SparkContext('local', 'dfapp')
Data_Land=  spark.read.  json('/home/hduser/Desktop/
TNLAND. json')
type(Data_Land)
```


Output


```
$SPARK_HOME/bin/spark-submit Sparkdf.py
<class 'pyspark.sql.dataframe.DataFrame'>
```


In the following example, the same Tamilnadu state land data in text format is loaded using the Spark.read. text.

```
------------------------Sparkdgf.py--------------------
from pyspark.sql import Row
sc = SparkContext('local', 'dfapp')
Data_Land=  spark.read.  text('/home/hduser/Desktop/
TNLAND. txt')
type(Data_Land)
```


Output


```
$SPARK_HOME/bin/spark-submit Sparkdf.py
<class 'pyspark.sql.dataframe.DataFrame'>
```


14.5.6 DataFrame Manipulations

We can manipulate the data loaded using different PySpark functions.

14.5.6.1 How to Retrieve the Datatype of Columns in Our Dataset?

To view the data types of the columns in DataFrame, we can use the printSchema, dtypes methods that help show our data frame's schema. In this example, we are applying printSchema() on personal data frame created using RDD, the same printSchema() can be applied to all formats (csv, text, json) of data.

Input

```
------------------------Sparkdgf.py---------------------
from pyspark.sql import Row
```

```
sc = SparkContext('local', 'dfapp')
personal_info  =  [('Ram',21),('Raja',20),('John',22),
('Thomas',22),('Kavin',21),('Kumar',20]
rdd = sc.parallelize(personal_info)
personal_info = rdd.map(lambda x: Row(name=x[0], age=int
(x[1])))
personal= sqlContext.createDataFrame(personal_info)
personal.printSchema()
```


Output


```
$SPARK_HOME/bin/spark-submit Sparkdf.py
root
|-- age: long (nullable = true)
|-- name: string (nullable = true)
```


14.5.6.2 *How to View the First n Observation?*

The head() function is used to view the first n observation in our dataframe. The head () operation in PySpark is similar to head() operation in Pandas.

Input

------------------------Sparkdgf.py----------------------
```
personal.head(3)
```


Output


```
$SPARK_HOME/bin/spark-submit Sparkdf.py
[Row(age=21, name=u'Ram'), Row(age=20, name=u'Raja'),
Row(age=22, name=u'John')]
```

The result from the head() function will be in compressed row format, to view the result in interactive format show() function can be used.

Input
----------------------Sparkdgf.py----------------------
```
personal.show()
```

Output

```
$SPARK_HOME/bin/spark-submit Sparkdf.py
+---+------+
|age| name|
+---+------+
| 21| Ram|
| 20| Raja|
| 22| John|
| 22| Thomas|
| 21| Kavin|
| 20| Kumar|
+---+------+
```

14.5.6.3 How to Get the Statistics Summary of Numerical Columns in a DataFrame (Standard Deviance, Mean, Max, Count, Min)?

The statistical summary of the numerical column in the DataFrame can be calculated using describe() function. The argument of the function is optional; generally by default it will calculate summary statistics for all numerical columns present in DataFrame.

Input
----------------------Sparkdgf.py----------------------
```
personal.describe().show()
```

Output

```
$SPARK_HOME/bin/spark-submit Sparkdf.py
+-------+------------------+
|summary| age|
+-------+------------------+
| count| 6|
| mean| 21.0|
| stddev|0.8944271909999159|
| min| 20|
| max| 22|
+-------+------------------+
```

14.5.6.4 How to Find the Distinct Data and Remove Duplicate Values?

The distinct () function is used to calculate the number of distinct rows in the DataFrame and the dropDuplicates() is used to drop the duplicate values in our DataFrame.

Input

```
-------------------Sparkdgf.py-------------------------
personal.select('Name'). distinct().show()
personal.select('Age').dropDuplicates().show()
```

Output

```
$SPARK_HOME/bin/spark-submit Sparkdf.py
+-------+
| name |
+-------+
```

```
| Ram |
| Kumar |
| Raja |
| John |
| Kavin |
| Thomas|
+-------+
+---+
|age|
+---+
| 21|
| 20|
| 22|
+---+
```

14.5.6.5 Removing and Filling Null Values from Data Frames

The dropna() operation is used to drop the null values from the DataFrame and.fillna() operation is used to fill the missing values in a DataFrame

Input

```
----------------------Sparkdgf.py----------------------
personal. dropna() .count ()
personal. fillna(1) .show ()
```

Output

```
$SPARK_HOME/bin/spark-submit Sparkdf.py
Output:
6
```

Note:

We can use groupby, orderby, filter, aggregate functions, etc.,to manipulate the data.

14.6 PySpark MLlib (Machine Learning Libraries)

PySpark MLlib is a machine-learning package wrapper over PySpark Core to perform data analysis using machine-learning algorithms. Machine Learning in PySpark is easy to use and scalable. It works on distributed and lazy evaluation systems. You can use various techniques with Machine Learning algorithms such as classification, clustering etc., using the PySpark MLlib.

14.6.1 Various Tools Provided by MLlib

a. **ML Algorithms:** collaborative filtering, classification, and clustering
b. **Featurization:** feature extraction, dimensionality reduction, transformation, and selection
c. **Pipelines:** Evaluation, construction, and tuning ML Pipelines

14.6.1.1 Why PySpark MLlib

scikit-learn is a popular Python library for data mining and machine learning algorithms only work for small datasets on a single machine. PySpark's MLlib algorithms are designed for parallel processing on a cluster, Provides a high-level API to build machine learning pipelines

14.6.2 PySpark MLlib Algorithms

14.6.2.1 Classification Using PySpark MLlib

Classification (Binary and Multiclass) is a supervised machine learning algorithm for sorting the input data into different categories. The PySpark supports Linear SVMs, decision trees, random forests, naive Bayes, linear least squares.
  Example:

14.6.2.2 Logistic Regression

Logistic Regression predicts a binary response based on some variables The Logistic regression is done by importing the following library in PySpark.

-----------------------Import mllib----------------------

```
from  pyspark.mllib.classification  import  Logistic-
Regression With LBFGS
```

LabelledPoint()
A LabeledPoint is a wrapper for input features and to predict value. For binary classification in Logistic Regression, a label can be either 0 (negative) or 1 (positive).

Input

```
---------------------mllib_class-------------------
from pyspark import SparkContext
from   pyspark.mllib.classification   import   Logistic-
RegressionWith LBFGS
sc = SparkContext('local', 'ml_app')
positive = LabeledPoint(1.0, [1.0, 0.0, 3.0])
negative = LabeledPoint(0.0, [2.0, 1.0, 1.0])
print(positive)
print(negative)
```

Output

```
LabeledPoint(1.0, [1.0,0.0,3.0])
LabeledPoint(0.0, [2.0,1.0,1.0])
```

HashingTF()
HashingTF() algorithm is used to map feature value to indices in the feature vector

Input

```
---------------------mllib_class-------------------
from pyspark import SparkContext
from pyspark.mllib.feature import HashingTF
sc = SparkContext('local', 'ml_app')
sentence = 'hello hello world'
words = sentence.split()
tf = HashingTF(10000)
tf.transform(words)
```


Output


```
SparseVector(10000, {3065: 1.0, 6861: 2.0})
```


14.6.2.3 Logistic Regression Using Logistic Regression With LBFGS

Logistic Regression using PySpark MLlib is achieved using Logistic Regression With LBFGS class

Input

```
-------------------- mllib_class------------------
from pyspark import SparkContext
from pyspark.mllib.classification import Logistic-
RegressionWith LBFGS
sc = SparkContext('local', 'ml_app')
data = [LabeledPoint(0.0, [0.0, 1.0]), LabeledPoint(1.0,
[1.0, 0.0])]
RDD = sc.parallelize (data)
lrm = LogisticRegressionWithLBFGS. train (RDD)
lrm.predict ([1.0, 0.0])
lrm.predict ([0.0, 1.0])
```


Output


```
1
0
```


14.6.2.4 Collaborative Filtering

Collaborative filtering is done based on collecting and analyzing a large volume of information based on user's behaviour, activities, or preferences and prediction based on their similarity to other users. Collaborative filtering is commonly used for recommender systems. Alternating least squares (ALS) library is used in PySpark for Collaborative filtering.

```
-------------------Import mllib--------------------
from pyspark.mllib.recommendation import ALS

---------------------------------------------------
---------------------------------------------------
```

14.6.2.5 Rating Class in `pyspark.mllib.recommendation`

The Rating class is a wrapper around tuple (user, product and rating) Useful for parsing the RDD and creating a tuple

Input

```
----------------------------- mllib--------------
----------
from pyspark import SparkContext
from pyspark.mllib.recommendation import Rating
sc = SparkContext('local', 'ml_app')
r = Rating(user = 1, product = 2, rating = 5.0)
print(r[0], r[1], r[2])

---------------------------------------------------
---------------------------------------------------
```

Output

```
---------------------------------------------------
---------------------------------------------------
(1, 2, 5.0)

---------------------------------------------------
---------------------------------------------------
```

randomSplit()
Splitting data into training and testing sets is important for evaluating predictive modeling. PySpark's randomSplit() method is used to split randomly with the provided weights and returns multiple RDDs.

Input

```
----------------------- mllib--------------------
from pyspark import SparkContext
sc = SparkContext('local', 'ml_app')
data = sc.parallelize([1, 2, 3, 4, 5, 6, 7, 8, 9, 10])
training, test=data.randomSplit([0.6, 0.4])
training.collect()
textcoll = test.collect()
print(' test data:%s'(textcoll))

-----------------------------------------------------------
-----------------------------------------------------------
```

Output

```
-----------------------------------------------------------
-----------------------------------------------------------

Test data
[1, 2, 5, 6, 9, 10]
[3, 4, 7, 8]

-----------------------------------------------------------
-----------------------------------------------------------
```

14.6.2.6 Alternating Least Squares (ALS)

PySpark provide Alternating Least Squares (ALS) in mllib for collaborative filtering.

Input

```
----------------------- mllib----------------------
from pyspark import SparkContext
sc = SparkContext('local', 'ml_app')
r1 = Rating(1, 1, 1.0)
r2 = Rating(1, 2, 2.0)
r3 = Rating(2, 1, 2.0)
ratings = sc.parallelize([r1, r2, r3])
ratings.collect()
[Rating(user=1, product=1, rating=1.0),
Rating(user=1, product=2, rating=2.0),
Rating(user=2, product=1, rating=2.0)]
model = ALS.train(ratings, rank=10, iterations=10)
```

---

predictAll()

The predictAll() method returns a list of predicted ratings. The method takes in an RDD without ratings to generate the ratings

Input

```
---------------------- mllib ----------------------
from pyspark import SparkContext
sc = SparkContext('local', 'ml_app')
unrated_RDD = sc.parallelize([(1, 2), (1, 1)])
predictions = model.predictAll(unrated_RDD)
predictions.collect()
---------------------------------------------------
---------------------------------------------------
```

Output

```
---------------------------------------------------
---------------------------------------------------

[Rating(user=1, product=1, rating=1.0000278574351853),
Rating(user=1, product=2, rating=1.9890355703778122)]

---------------------------------------------------
---------------------------------------------------
```

14.6.2.7 Model Evaluation Using MSE

The MSE is the average value of the square of (actual rating - predicted rating)

Input

```
---------------------- mllib----------------------
from pyspark import SparkContext
sc = SparkContext('local', 'ml_app')
rates = ratings.map(lambda x: ((x[0], x[1]), x[2]))
rates.collect()
[((1, 1), 1.0), ((1, 2), 2.0), ((2, 1), 2.0)]
preds = predictions.map(lambda x: ((x[0], x[1]), x[2]))
preds.collect()
rates_preds = rates.join(preds)
rates_preds.collect()
```


Output


```
[((1, 1), 1.0000278574351853), ((1, 2), 1.989035570377-
8122)]
[((1, 2), (2.0, 1.9890355703778122)), ((1, 1), (1.0,
1.0000278574351853))]
```


14.6.2.8 Clustering

Clustering is the unsupervised learning method to organize a collection of data in a group. PySpark MLlib library currently supports K-means, Bisecting k-means, Streaming k-means, Gaussian mixture, Power iteration clustering (PIC).

Example: K-means algorithm
K-means algorithm is an iterative algorithm that helps to partition the dataset into pre-defined K distinct non-overlapping subgroups.

Input

```
-------------------Import mllib-------------------
from pyspark import SparkContext
sc = SparkContext('local', 'ml_app')
from pyspark.mllib.clustering import KMeans
data = sc.textFile('Data.csv').map(lambda x: x.split
(',')).
map(lambda x: [float(x[0]), float(x[1])])
data.take(5)
kmodel = KMeans.train(data, k = 2, maxIterations = 10)
kmodel.clusterCenters()
```


Output


```
[[14.23, 2.43], [13.2, 2.14], [13.16, 2.67], [14.37,
2.5], [13.24, 2.87]]
[array([12.25573171, 2.28939024]), array([13.636875,
2.43239583])]
```


Chapter 15

How to Implement Data Lake for Large Enterprises

Ragavendran Chandrasekaran

Senthil Nagar, Vandalur, Chennai, India

Contents

DOI: 10.1201/9781003175889-15

Objectives

This chapter focusses on implementation of the Data Lake (DL) in cloud and the significance of Data Lake where the pre-existence of a Data Warehouse (DW) helps businesses to take decisions. In general, Data Lake is not a replacement of existing data warehouse applications but there is a high need for modernizing the data platform architecture in the industry to sustain and stabilize the growing consumer needs. This chapter provides an overview on data warehouse, basics of DW, benefits of DW, date lake, architecture of data lake, need for data lake, components and design of data lake in the cloud and data lake storages, data transformation and data security.

15.1 What Is a Data Warehouse?

A data warehouse (DW) is a centralized data storage system where a large volume of information can be stored and analyzed to bring more insights from data. Data in large enterprises come from various sources (Figure 15.1) like transactional processing systems, master data applications, communication systems, customer interactions and third party systems. In recent years, there is a growing need to organize and archive them for late analytical purposes.

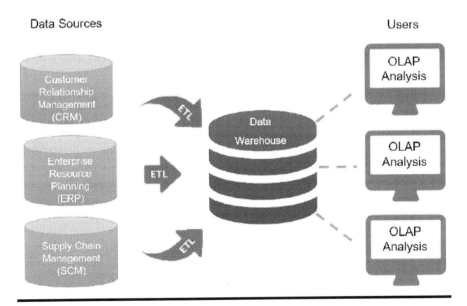

Figure 15.1 Sources of data in an organization.

Data gets added to data warehouse from the various applications including high-performance transactional system which handling hundreds to millions of transactions in a regular cadence. Processing the data in same systems becomes very expensive, time consuming, and heterogeneous forms of data sources limits organizations to make better decisions. DW often referenced as a processed data layer where business knows exactly what data is consumed and stored in the system. Use case would be identified before the data is added to the system. Data model is well designed prior to data movement into the data warehouse storage layer and key performance indexes are identified.

15.1.1 Roles of Data Warehouse for Industries

Data warehouse for industries such as Banking and Financial Services, Healthcare, Retail, e-commerce, Agriculture, Hospitality and Quick Service Restaurants plays a major role in curating the complex data, organize the data from various sources, enables systematic approach in making decisions, durable and reliable for processing large volume of data in batch mode.

Major role of data warehouse is to integrate the corporate data sources to provide users with rich information to operationalize and improvise the business standards from the generated data. DW also the primary component in persisting the Source of Records (SORs) from various business modules in an organization. It provides various framework to store massive volume of data efficiently.

- **Business Intelligence** tools such as SAP BOBJ, Tableau, QlikSense and others uses the data warehouse application as main source to represent the valuable insights. It makes it easy for business teams and data analysts to experience the holistic view of their business performance/ progress in a single place. Key performance indexes delivered to the industry experts are cleaner, easy to access, accurate and reliable data points makes it easy to take impactful decisions.
- **Data Quality** (DQ) is an integral part of data warehouse which helps users to apply rules to perform pre-processing techniques to cleanse the data before it gets stored into the DW system. DQ captures the accepted, rejected and erroneous of data that's getting inserted into the DW and the data team works on the rejected and data errors to make it right before it gets added to the DW storage layer. DQ process helps to understand the data from multi sources and analyse to determine the final form of data stored in the DW, this process is called Data Profiling. Data team identifies the data inconsistent data formats or layouts such as valid/ in valid values, date format, verifying the address information, and so on.
- **Data Integration** is an important feature for the DW teams to integrate similar data from various entities. It helps to standardize the data to form a meaningful and consistent reference to any fields which are used differently in multiple systems in the same organizations. It acts as a data movement tool from various systems into the DW while applying all the standardization and cleansing techniques.

15.2 What Is a Data Lake?

In the last decade, the nature of data is not just structured data which is well known for the business. In fact, about 80% of the data we have today are generated in less than a decade and it is very important to store, analyze and make decisions on unknown data for every large organization.

A data lake (DL) is a centralized repository for storing structured and unstructured data at the scale of peta-byte or more. It allows users to store the data as raw without having the metadata and its kind. DL provides a unified way of gathering known and unknown data and enables users to run analytics, build dashboard and framework to run computation in parallel on big data and components to perform real-time analytics on massive datasets (Figure 15.2).

15.3 Why Do We Need Data Lake?

Organizations that heavily invested on data platform requires a secure, highly scalable, cost efficient and fault tolerant solutions to ingest, store, and analyze massive datasets to achieve best business value from their data. Enterprises who implemented a data lake are outperforming over 10% in organic revenue growth when compared with others who do not have data lake in their data strategy. New era of analytics highly leverages machine learning over new data sources like log files, click-streams, social media, and IoT devices stored in the data lake. Early prediction of business demand, customer 360 analytics, behavioral analytics, and trend analysis are some popular use cases opened up by incorporating the data lake solutions in the large organizations.

Empowering the data engineering team to design cost-effective and standardized data layer helps to improve the solution delivery by 40% when compared to the legacy storage and data warehouse strategies. In cloud, data lake takes advantage of endless storage elasticity feature and pay per use costing principles helps business to build solutions instantly whereas in legacy architecture extension of resources and licenses takes months to fulfil the needs of the data engineering team with respect to hardware and software procurements. Centralized data repository in cloud helps security practice to control and protect the data much more ease than the traditional approach. Adaption of shared server/storage model not only reduces the cost of implementing the data lake and also enables security tightly lockdown as per organizations security policies. Data lakes in cloud provides seamless integrations to many existing business applications and products which makes it easy to connect and continue the pre-existing tools in place.

15.4 Overview of Data Lake in Cloud

Data lake in cloud is a game-changing, cost-effective and scalable solutions that enables easy to start and provision any organization with a high grade and well-suited

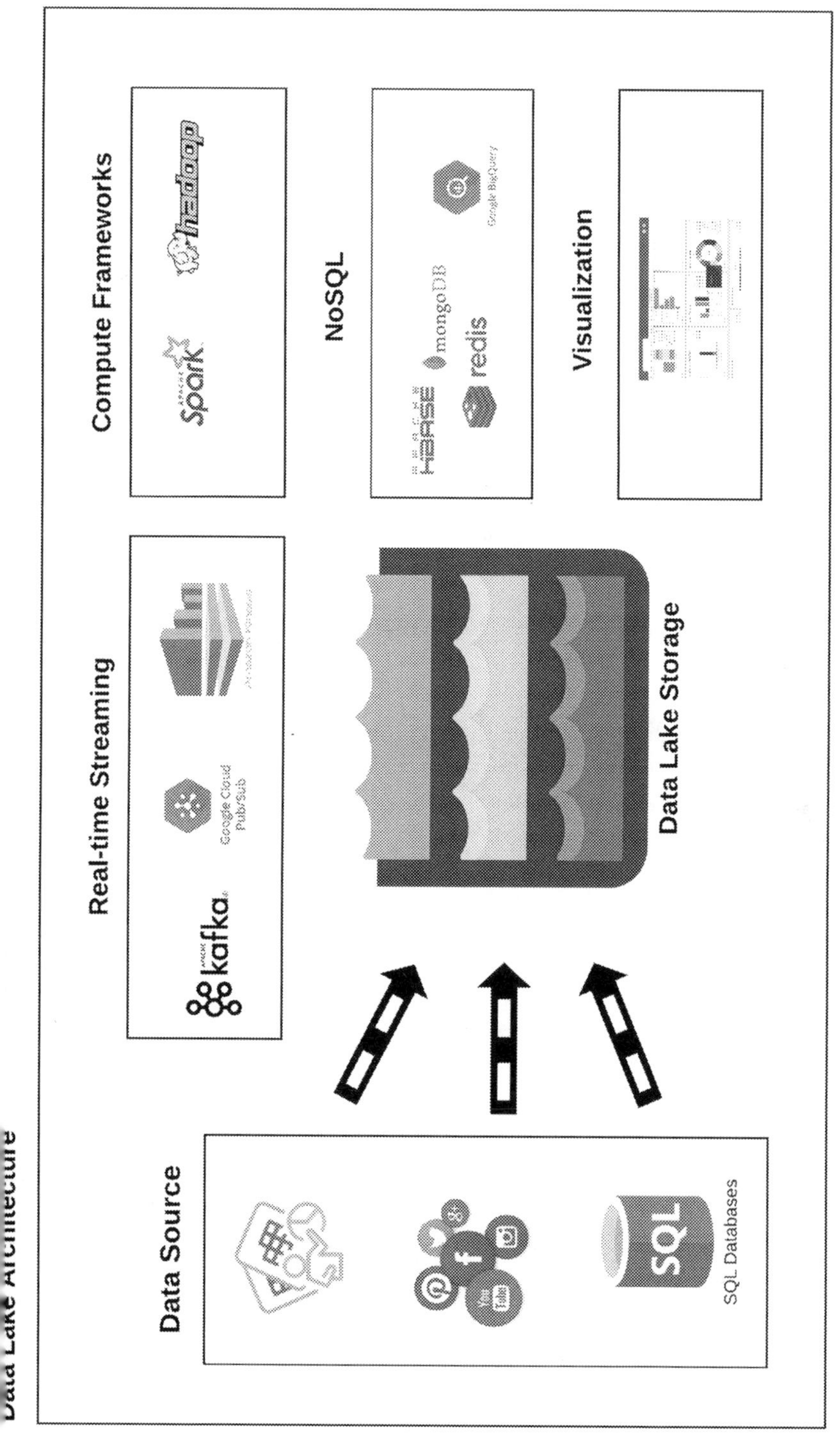

Figure 15.2   Data lake architecture.

Source: https://aws.amazon.com/big-data/datalakes-and-analytics
https://cloud.google.com/solutions/smart-analytics

solutions for most of the existing data platforms. Building data lake with the awareness of store without purpose brings more ideas to the business results and at the same time features of storing them organized for later usage. Data lake in cloud comes with many benefits in using robust services such as Big Data compute applications, Machine Learning services, and massively distributed storage layer which stores peta-bytes of data and trillions of objects.

In general terms data lake is referred as a stream of water flowing from various parts and finally stored in to a lake which has mixed water properties that can be stored in mass and leverages when needed. Likewise, data lake provides user with multiple data sources integration into unique standardized layer for storing structured and un-structured data formats, analyse the data when needed. Data movement in/out of the data lake has various options and in cloud variety of data sources and downstream applications makes it easier to implement rather than in on-premises architecture. Modern database architecture comes with the super-fast compute framework such as Apache Spark/Hadoop and the massively distributed file storage systems like HDFS. Concept of distributed data storage makes the data locality and process of compute where the data resides accelerates the processing speed and enabled more room for in-memory computation techniques. Traditional data warehouse applications heavily consume the data transfers between the storage and the processing layers since the data has to be fetched to some extend to the system that performs the computations. Whereas the distributed storage and processing framework makes it easier, when data lakes built on top of such best performing and optimized storage architecture smooths the usage and produces quick results for the business users.

Cloud services are fully decoupled in a way that enables organization to choose services according to their needs. Any services that helps them to achieve the results then it's easy to productionize the solutions in matter of days. In recent years another advantage of building data lake in cloud is the evolution of hybrid, and multi-cloud enablement which makes an organization to choose many services from different cloud providers. According to the latest survey more organizations are moving to-wards the cloud and hybrid architecture for minimizing the procurement and maintenance overheads. Cloud also provides various serverless capability for data lakes in the form of Code as a Service, or Function as a Service. Auto scale up/out and scale down/in features helps data teams to increase or decrease data usage on the go without commitment of the required resources.

15.5 Key Considerations for Data Lake Architecture

Building a data lake is an imperial process of shifting the pyramid towards modern data storage capabilities. During this process having the right team with good experience in digesting the form of data your business handles and right skill set to craft the platform of your choice. There are some understanding to be made about what you would be expecting to do in the new solutions.

- Expect the data may be of many forms
- Data is not going to clean like before
- Advanced analytics might need more than one way to the problem
- Building quick solutions and meeting the failure is normal

Identify the applications that you need to focus to migrate to new architecture, prioritize them accordingly to your demands. Initial data lake you build should be simple enough to see if the framework covers all your data aspects by just adding basic data store feature, enabling the security and governance principles to the infrastructure. Ingestion framework to handle structured and unstructured data and secure them in the storage (Figure 15.3). Data protection at scale is a major element to be considered since the volume, variety, and velocity going to be more than ever before. Selecting the data cleaning, processing, aggregating and reduced redundancy would be another area to be carefully selected.

Advanced analytical tools and machine learning work bench are very essential elements while building new data lake solutions. Data lineage and metadata management should be made available to users to easily search for the data points that are stored in the data lake. Source of record for each data object need to be identified to make sure the data that comes in must follow certain standard and shall be notified for any changes/ use case/ conversion applied to the data sources (Figure 15.4). Data security shall be configured in an advanced way with some Single Sign On feature and enabling Multi Factor Authorization (MFA) components.

15.6 Phases of Data Lake Implementation

Implementing the data lake to a large organization needs multi-phase execution and it highly critical white board the end-to-end solution. As discussed in the key consideration section we will focus deeper into each segment. Before deep dive into the phases of data lake, this section explains the components and design of data lake in the cloud using Amazon Web Services Cloud, Google Cloud and Azure

15.6.1 Data Lake Architecture on Amazon Web Services

Amazon Simple Storage Service is an object storage to store and retrieve any volume of data from anywhere. AWS S3 offer users with scalable, secure, durable and highly available storage solutions. S3 has a lifecycle policy which helps users to define and select various pricing options based on storage and access requirements.

AWS Lambda allows users to write code as functions and deploy them to AWS Lambda (Figure 15.5 Ingestion) without worrying about the servers and the infrastructures. Users will pay only for the consumed compute time.

AWS Elastic Cloud Compute is a cloud service, which offers compute instances based on user's requirements. EC2 interface simple web interface helps

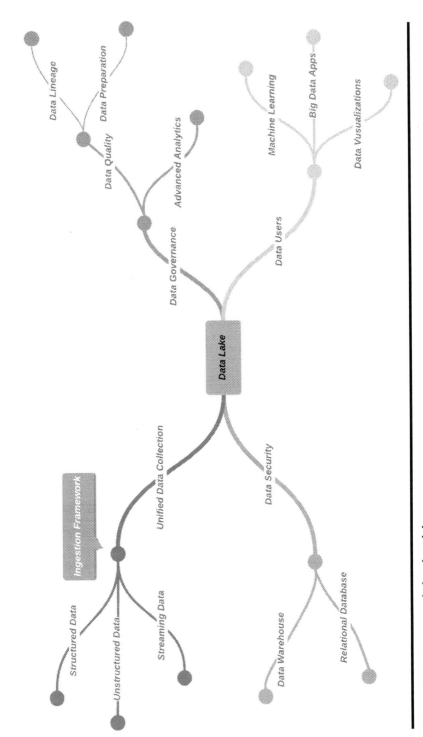

Figure 15.3   Framework for data lake.

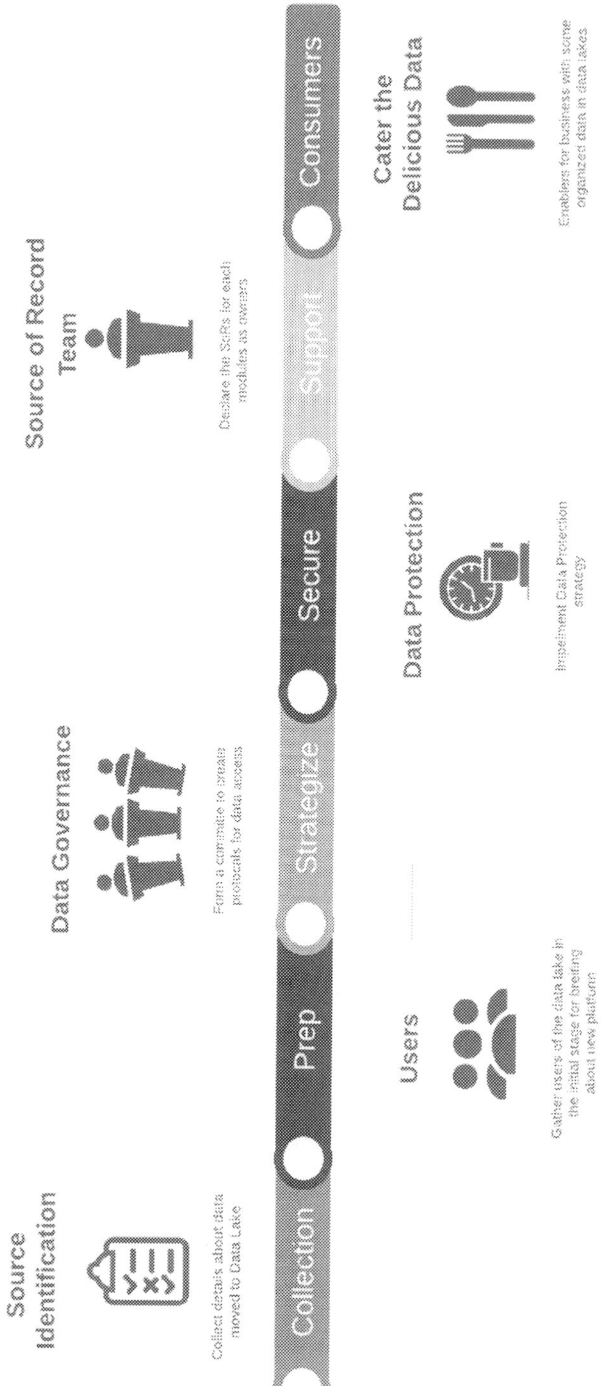

Figure 15.4 Process of building data lake solution.

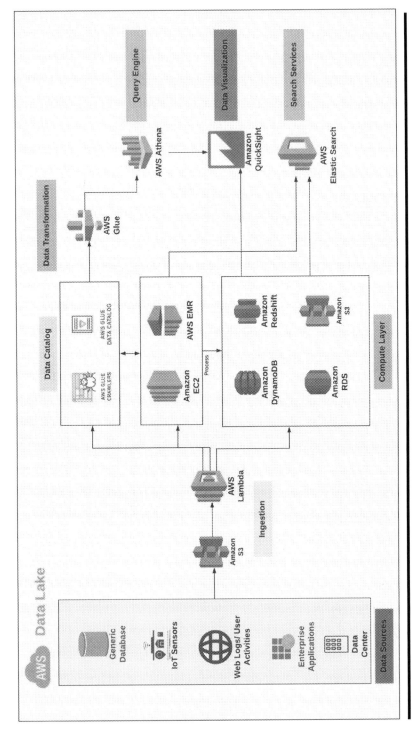

Figure 15.5   AWS data lake architecture.

Source: https://aws.amazon.com/big-data/datalakes-and-analytics/

users to select and configure the instance for their scale and spins up within few minutes.

AWS Elastic Map Reduce *service* is a cloud big data platform (Figure 15.5, Compute Layer) that enables users to run and scale Apache Spark, Hive, HBase, and so on. Also has highly available clusters and auto-scaling policies to make data platform more stable.

15.6.2 Data Lake Architecture on Google Cloud Platform

Cloud Storage is a unified, scalable, and highly durable object storage for developers and enterprises. It allows user to store media, files and application data.

Cloud DataProc is a managed Spark and Hadoop service that allows users to perform batch processing, querying, streaming, and machine learning. Dataproc (Figure 15.6) automation helps user to create clusters quickly, manage them easily, and close the instances when it is not used.

BigQuery is a Server less, highly scalable, and cost-effective cloud data warehouse that can analyze Petabytes of data using ANSI SQL model. Greater results found for real-time and predictive analytics.

Cloud DataFlow is a fully managed unified streaming and batch data processing engine. Serverless app which provides automatic provisioning and management of the resources. This service provides higher reliability and fault-tolerant in nature.

Cloud Bigtable is a fully managed NoSQL database for large analytical and processing workloads. Organized data lake formats often require such NoSQL for personalization, Digital contents and Internet of Things applications.

Cloud DataLab tool is mainly used for exploratory data analysis on Google cloud to perform any machine learning and transformation using any languages such as Python, SQL from Jupyter notebooks.

Cloud Functions offers your code to be deployed in Google platform and execute when needed. Users will pay as they use the resources without any server procurement or management.

15.6.3 Azure Cloud Data Lake

Below architecture of data lake from Azure integrates heterogeneous sources like click-stream data, censor data, traditional data sources such as databases and event based real-time data pipelines. Azure supports data lake storage (Figure 15.7) with the power of HDInsights for high processing framework which extends the utilization of Spark and its core services.

15.7 What to Load into Your Data Lake?

Organizations claims to use a data lake approach to load and analyze data and content that would not go into a traditional data warehouse, such as web server

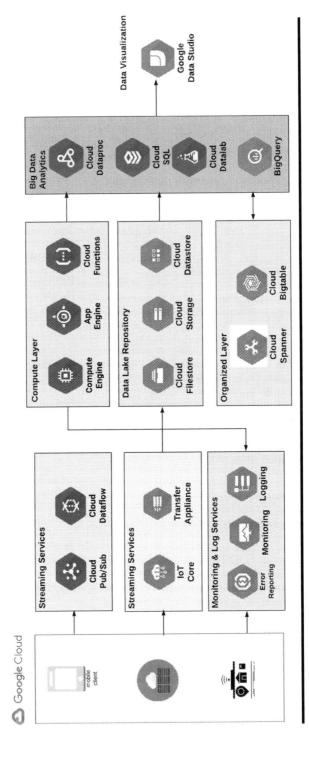

Figure 15.6 Google Cloud data lake architecture.

Source: https://cloud.google.com/solutions/smart-analytics

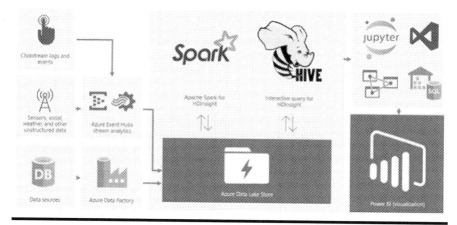

Figure 15.7 Azure data lake architecture.

Source: https://azure.microsoft.com/en-in/services/data-lake-analytics

logs or sensor logs, social media content, IoT feeds or image files and associated metadata. Data lake analytics can therefore encompass any historical data or content from which you may be able to derive business insights. But a data lake can play a key role in harvesting conventional structured data as well. Data that you offload from your data warehouse in order to control the costs and improve the performance of the warehouse.

Other key strategy to be taken would be on offloading traditional data warehouse into data lake and the data pipeline to move the data using any standard extract transform and load interface. ETL frameworks does supports data movements for full data loads, change data captures and slowly changing dimensions. Incremental loads are so popular for any large and growing datasets which are transactional in nature.

15.8 A Cloud Data Lake Journey

This session have been focus more into cloud technologies and top providers in the markets as you have seen Gartner's cloud infrastructure provides: Amazon Web Services, Google Cloud, and Microsoft Azure. Discuss phases along with the service offerings from different provides.

15.8.1 Cloud Infrastructures

Building a data lake in cloud brings lot of advantages, mainly fully managed services offers an organization to focus on their data needs rather than the maintenance of physical hardware and licensing. Below are the important benefits of using Cloud solutions for your data lake:

- **Storage Capacity:** In cloud you can storage start with small files and it provides elasticity to grow your data into data lake to Exa-byte size. This helps your organization to focus on data strategy without worrying about the storage servers.
- **Cost Efficiency:** Cloud providers has various options in storing and processing your data applications and also has various pricing options such as pay for your usage, fixed standard pricing, and long-term pricing which gives like 60–75% of cost savings. Most of the service providers allow for multiple storage classes and pricing options. This enables companies to only pay for as much as they need, instead of planning for an assumed cost and capacity, which is required when building a data lake locally.
- **Central Repository:** A centralized location for all object stores and data access means the setup is the same for every team in an organization. This improves efficiency and now engineers can focus on more critical items.
- **Data Security:** All companies have a responsibility to protect their data; with data lakes designed to store all types of data, including sensitive information like financial records or customer details, security becomes even more important. Cloud providers guarantee security of data as defined by the shared responsibility model.
- **Auto-Scaling:** Modern cloud services are designed to provide immediate scaling functionality, so businesses don't have to worry about expanding capacity when necessary or paying for hardware that they don't need. Auto-scaling can be done in horizontal scale out/ in or vertical up/ down based on the business needs.

15.8.2 Data Lake Storage

In this section, we can see options available for data storage. Collecting data from various sources has various kinds and types, most of the modern data applications has heterogeneous sources and has veracity in nature.

Data movements from on-premises data warehouse into cloud data lake has different types; lift and shift, Database migration, and processed loads. Depends on the applications need and the priority of the business. The following sources of data is common across the cloud data lake and the services and tools used to ingest the data only differs: Databases, Files (csv, xls, pdfs, and logs), IoT device feeds, Apps data. We will be seeing various ways to capture the data into data lake from top cloud providers and open source engines.

- **Google Cloud Platform – Storage**

Cloud Storage, you can start with a few small files and grow your data lake to Exabyte in size. Cloud Storage (Figure 15.8) supports high-volume ingestion of new data and high-volume consumption of stored data in combination with

Figure 15.8   GCP storage.

Source: https://aws.amazon.com/big-data/datalakes-and-analytics/

other services such as Pub/Sub. Cloud storage also promises durability of 99.999999999% annual durability. Google cloud provides various ingest options. Pub/Sub is an option to ingest real-time or near real-time data into GC. Storage Transfer Service offers moving data from online or from on-premises such as data centre to cloud seamlessly and quickly. gsutil (Google Store) an option if you want one-time or scheduled frequency file transfers into Google Storage.

■ **Amazon Web Services**

AWS S3 acts as a primary drop location for the data lake solutions (Figure 15.9), once the file is placed into a bucket (a folder in cloud) using an ETL engine there are various ways to process them. S3 provides 99.999999999% durability and 99.99% availability of objects over a given year with endless storage so customers no need to worry about the growing data storage needs. Once the data is place inside the S3 buckets it can trigger consecutive actions based on the type of data ingested. Migrating a data base can be done using Database Migration Service which helps to migrate data quickly and securely. With no downtime to the existing databases. DMS can support homogeneous migrations like Oracle to Oracle.

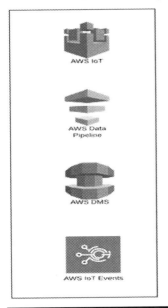

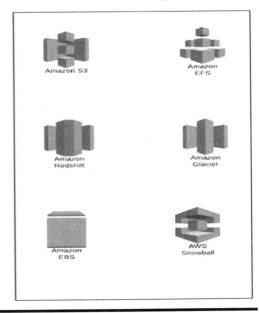

Figure 15.9   AWS storage.

Source: https://aws.amazon.com/big-data/datalakes-and-analytics/

SQL Server to SQL Server and also heterogenous migrations like Oracle or Microsoft SQL Server to AWS Aurora database.

■ **Microsoft Azure**

Azure storage service is a MS cloud storage solution, it's a massively scalable object store. Storage comes with various data services such as Azure Blobs, Files, Queues, Tables, and Disks (Figure 15.10). Copy Data service from Azure offers data ingestion from 70+ data sources on premises or cloud. An easy graphical user interface driven ingestion process allows users to select 1,000 of tables and databases, and it automates the data pipeline instances based on the options user has selected.

15.8.3 Data Transformation

Building a modern data platform requires a flexible and efficient transformation tools to perform the data transformations. Since the data lake brings an ability to store raw data with no oversight on the contents. In traditional data warehouse we saw the is a high need for intermediate storage or database such as data marts whereas in data lake there should be no excessive use of database and pre-

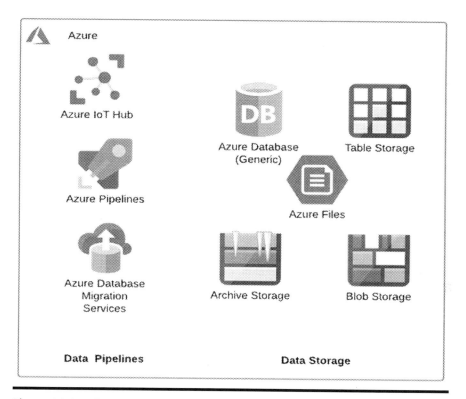

Figure 15.10 Azure storage.

Source: https://azure.microsoft.com/en-in/services/data-lake-analytics

processing methods. Data lake architecture completely decouples the complexity and reduces cost by enabling stateful operations in-memory and supports all kinds of complex transformations and aggregations without any database. The process of schema-on-read is also formally referred as Extract–Load–Transform and it is mainly applicable in data lake platforms.

Accessing data with no schema is a major challenge in selecting the any ETL and data lakes are typically used as repositories for raw data in structured or semi-structured formats.

15.8.4 Data Security

Organizations stepping into cloud and data platform solutions always tend to build a strong data governance and security strategies. In the current cloud industry, every provider focus more on security layers since most of the cost effective and preferred solutions on cloud ends with shared hardware infrastructures. Below are some standards followed across all the cloud data storage provides in the industry.

- Cloud native key management services
- Customer owned private/public key managements
- Encryption based key management services

15.9 Conclusion

There are various options available for building a data lake solution in the market and that are available in matter of hours to operate. Serverless and fully managed solutions providers lead the customer engagements with high availability and secured platform integrations.

References

AWS Services. Retrieved April 15, 2021, from https://aws.amazon.com/big-data/datalakes-and-analytics/

Azure Cloud Services. Retrieved April 10, 2021, from https://azure.microsoft.com/en-in/services/data-lake-analytics

Google Cloud. Retrieved April 12, 2021, from https://cloud.google.com/solutions/smart-analytics

Chapter 16

A Novel Application of Data Mining Techniques for Satellite Performance Analysis

S.A. Kannan[1] and T. Devi[2]

[1]*U R Rao Satellite Centre, Bangalore, India*
[2]*Professor and Head, Department of Computer Applications, Bharathiar University, Coimbatore, India*

Contents

DOI: 10.1201/9781003175889-16

16.1 Introduction

Artificial satellites have opened up a new industry ever since the first satellite Sputnik started going around the earth in 1957. The myriad of applications developed and launched in many new fields have made the satellite technology industry an essential part of human civilization's present-day socioeconomic, cultural, industrial, and commercial fabric. Despite the high cost of access to space, satellites have become the mainstay in essential areas like global communication, mapping of the earth, weather monitoring, navigational needs for terrestrial-based services, atmospheric studies including climate modeling and pollution monitoring, and as a platform for space research and exploration. Space platform is the most accurate and capable method for most scientific research concerning earth surface and environment studies as it enables studying the entire globe and its atmosphere (Maini & Agrawal, 2007).

Many countries have launched several satellites to meet the application needs in various fields like communication, navigation, remote sensing, and scientific research. According to the Union of Concerned Scientists, 548 satellites orbit the earth in geostationary orbits and 1186 satellites orbit in low earth as of April 2018. Orbits like the geostationary orbit are sought after by satellite fleet operators for parking their satellites and offering premium communications service continuously to a wide variety of customers.

When satellites develop anomalies and do not provide the intended mission performance, disrupting service to the customer requirements, it causes all round losses in finance, customer-base, and technology integrity. In addition to ending up as premature junk in space, these satellites pose a danger to new satellites by increasing chances of collision since they keep traveling at speeds more than 6 km/sec. Hence, the ground stations monitoring satellites in orbit must have a system of analyzing its entire health data exhaustively and generating a complete knowledge base about its health.

An artificial satellite in orbit sends information containing its health parameters to the ground station in telemetry data. "Telemetry" refers to the information content beamed by satellites from their orbit to the ground station. During the entire mission life of a satellite in orbit, a large volume of telemetry data is collected and archived by the concerned ground stations. Analysis of this data gives an understanding of the performance of the satellite. But the sheer volume of data and the number of parametric attributes pose a big challenge for conventional statistical analysis. Dynamic changes in thermal, mechanical, and electrical loads during the various on-orbit events undergone by the satellite lead to nonlinear and unexpected interactions between the various subsystems of a satellite. The outcome of these interactions is hidden in the corresponding telemetry data received on the ground. Conventional statistical analysis does not potentially bring out such hidden relationships between the parametric attributes of health parameters from different subsystems of the satellite.

This research work deals with the application of data mining techniques for analyzing a pilot set of satellite on-orbit telemetry data. In this research, standard data mining techniques and algorithms developed on this basis have been applied to analyze a set of onboard telemetry data collected from a mars bound satellite. The results obtained show that brute-force modified rule induction algorithm has the maximum potential in uncovering hitherto unknown hidden relationships among the satellite on-orbit telemetry parameters. Such new knowledge can help in the systematic understanding of the satellite on-orbit performance, prevention of potential fault conditions and further help in configuration refinement and finalization of future satellite systems.

16.2 Data Generation and Analysis

In the present era of technological excellence that is successfully translated into commercial applications, business corporates, organizations, governments and almost all entities in many of the organized sector generate and accumulate data at an enormous rate. Data generation is from various sources such as customer transactions, employee information databases, credit card transactions, news and weather information, bank withdrawals and credits. The growth in technology leading to very high computing power has resulted in an explosion in the use of databases for various applications such as e-governance, scientific research, engineering production, business, and commerce.

Each of these entities maintains a bank of relational database servers built to store such massive quantities of data. Specifically designed online transactional processing systems based on customized business processes are employed to route such data into database servers to streamline the conduct of business. Every transaction that is carried out every instance of time in the industry, such as sale orders, purchase orders, and other processes involving capital management and other resources management, finds its way into the online transactional processing systems that store all the transactional data into the database. Fast decision-making is enabled at the top-level management based on facts provided by online analytical processing systems such as data warehouses. The vast amount of data recorded in the transactional processing systems are pushed to the analytical processing systems for such decision-making and reporting purposes.

In medical applications, the patient history, diagnosis and treatment details are created in the hospital database and continuously accessed by the doctors to monitor the health of the patients. Latest information on critical areas like medicines, drugs, surgical procedures, referral reports, super-specialist surgeons, and consultant doctors are also maintained at a level commensurate with the standing of the hospital. Such data is continuously updated and made available for all concerned users within the medical fraternity so that timely actions are taken up in providing the best available treatment to patients. In scientific applications related to pure and applied sciences areas, a huge amount of data gets generated because of the tremendous computing power made available by the latest computer systems. Access to such data repositories and systematic analysis of the data gives impetus to discoveries and inventions.

Whichever field one is concerned about, data available, generated and archived in that field is the mainstay of the processes that define the field. It is a matter of fact that data itself is critical to the growth of organizations, institutions of commercial and noncommercial nature, business corporates, and concerned stakeholders. It contains nuggets of knowledge that can lead to important decisions that can raise the business to the next level or lead to a better outreach of the organization. But when the vast amount of generated data is not tracked continuously and analyzed but just examined in a superficial manner, it becomes a case of data-rich but knowledge poor society. The explosive growth in data and databases has generated the important need for new techniques and tools that can intelligently, automatically transform the available processed data into useful information and thereafter as immediately usable knowledge. As a consequence, Data mining has become a research and applications area that has gained increasing importance (UM Fayyad et al., 1996).

16.3 Data Mining

Data mining is the core area of Knowledge Discovery from Databases (KDD), which involves diverse fields such as artificial intelligence, information retrieval, and pattern recognition (Arun K Poojari, 2003). Analyzing a given data set by simple statistical techniques or by highly evolved algorithms depends on the complexity of information content embedded within the data that is expected to be brought out for benefit of the user. The main task of data mining is to extract intelligent information or patterns embedded or hidden within the data which exercise is not possible by conventional methods of statistical analysis.

Data mining is to be differentiated from knowledge discovery from data (KDD). The latter term refers to the total process through which data is collected, prepared, and then analyzed. On the other hand, data mining is an essential and important step in the knowledge discovery process, as it helps uncover hidden patterns or information. Generally, the term data mining is quite often used as a synonym of knowledge discovery process but which in fact it is not. Therefore it becomes imperative to emphasize the difference between the two terms. Data mining is the process of discovering hidden relationships between entities in large data sets that can reveal important and interesting patterns or information that lay hidden in the database. Sources of data include databases, warehouses or other content repositories, etc. Irrespective of the source of data, the aim and task carried out are in general the same. Though data mining is the core activity in this process of new knowledge extraction, there are sequences of processes along with it that prepare the data in a form amenable for analysis, and after mining is completed, present the results in a form that is required or easily understood by the end user. These other processes include data cleansing, data integration, data transformation in the premining part, and data presentation in the postmining part. Each of these processes plays a vital role in the ultimate mining activity, and taken individually. They have a high degree of influence on the accuracy of the outcome.

Sources from where data is generated could be either a single point or a multitude of points. And it could be either the same type of data or different types that are even unrelated to one another. Again it may be simple text or numeric data without any conversion or it may be coded, converted data that cannot be directly handled for any general data processing purposes but needs to be decoded and de-converted beforehand.

As mentioned above, data mining is essentially the central part of the knowledge discovery in data (KDD) process. It comprises of the following broad steps: (a) Data comes in different formats and from a variety of sources and is archived into a single target datastore, (b) Data is then pre-processed and transformed into a common standard format, and (c) Data mining algorithms analyze the data and provide the output in the form of patterns or rules. Figure 16.1 shows these different steps of the whole process. Domain experts interpret the patterns and rules extracted from the data and the new knowledge or information is applied for decision-making processes or trouble-shootings. The ultimate goal of the data mining process is to find the patterns that are hidden among the huge sets of data and interpret them to useful knowledge and information that can aid in important decision-making processes concerning the main activities of the application area.

16.4 Artificial Satellites and Data Mining

Data mining algorithms can be used for improving the on-orbit performance of satellites similar to its application in other domains. The basic idea is to analyze the health data from a satellite and uncover parametric interrelationships in it. This involves the development of an algorithm that can handle all the intricacies embedded in the data set and at the same time handle the huge volume of data. After

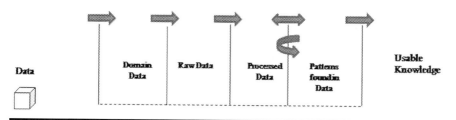

Figure 16.1   Knowledge deduction process from data.

an artificial satellite is launched into orbit, it sends information containing its health parameters to the ground station in the form of telemetry data. This telemetry data contains all the information related to the functioning of the different subsystems of the satellite like an onboard computer, power subsystem, thermal subsystem, sensors, attitude control subsystem, structure and payload. The information is essentially made up of parametric values of attributes related to voltage, current, temperature, pressure, error, and on/off status of the different units that make up the subsystem packages. During the entire mission life of a satellite in orbit, a large volume of this telemetry data is collected and archived by the concerned ground stations. A detailed analysis of this data gives an understanding of the functional status of the different subsystems and thereby the overall performance of the satellite. But the sheer volume of data and the number of parametric attributes pose a big challenge for conventional statistical analysis.

The need for mining the satellite data arises from the fact that there are about a thousand health keeping (H-K) parameters in a typical satellite that need to be monitored continuously to ensure that the satellite is fully operational after it is launched in space and starts providing the required mission services to the users. During the satellite's development phase, all these parameters are monitored by the ground checkout teams during the various tests carried out on the satellite. When any anomalous conditions are observed, required corrective actions are immediately carried out in the concerned subsystems by the satellite designers and integration teams. But after the launch of the satellite into orbit, the telemetry information containing the instantaneous values of the various attributes of the different parameters received from the satellite by the ground station and analyzed by the mission controllers is the only link with the satellite. Any anomalies in the performance of the satellite can be observed only from this telemetry data and therefore analysis of this data by all possible means and extracting as much information or knowledge becomes important. As mentioned earlier, data mining techniques offer different pliant methods for analyzing the telemetry data in such a manner as to be compatible with the nature of the parameter (such as temperature, voltage, current, on/off status, etc.). This facility of customization of an algorithm for the target data is woefully inadequate for conventional statistical methods.

16.5 Statistical Techniques for Satellite Data Analysis

Various researches have been conducted for analyzing the telemetry parameters of satellites for fault detection and prediction (Yu Gao et al., 2012; Takehisa Yairi et al., 2006; Tianshe Yang et al., 2013). Many of these researches have been focused on taking selected telemetry attributes, checking their limits and searching for outliers. Outliers are those values that are beyond the expected range. Even inter-relationships among health parameters have been used in a few of these researches only to address the fault detection and prediction conditions.

Starting with the conventional limit checking, there are many statistical methods available for the analysis of satellite data like those applications in many other domains. Statistical analysis of data is a field of mathematical operations where a given data set is subjected to organization and analysis so that different types of inferences and conclusions can be drawn about the nature of the data set. Where the population of the data set is very large and presents difficulty in going through the entire set for drawing observations, statistical methods of estimation and tests of hypothesis can be applied to make inferences or generalizations (Mehmed Kantardzic, 2003). The advantage is that the entire data set does not have to be analyzed to find out the characteristics, rather small samples are taken for classification and prediction exercises. Statistical averages like mean, median, and mode are the most commonly applied techniques used to find the characteristics of a set of data. When such techniques are applied to satellite telemetry data, each parameter in the data has to be individually analyzed over a train of values for inferring its weight. But when it is needed to correlate the performance of a given parameter to that of another randomly selected parameter, the techniques fall short in giving a meaningful outcome. Dynamic changes in thermal, mechanical and electrical loads of the different satellite subsystems during various on-orbit events undergone by the satellite lead to non-linear and unexpected interactions between the different parameters. These unpredictable relationships cannot be addressed by conventional methods due to the very nature of their unpredictability.

If a structured method of defining all possible outcomes and further learning from these results can be built in an intelligent algorithm, then the outcome of these interactions can be found by analyzing the behavior of the various concerned telemetry attributes of the parameters. This information would be hidden in the corresponding telemetry data received on the ground. Also, with conventional statistical analysis, it is possible only to analyze a limited set of telemetry parameter attributes that too against the limits set for them. It is quite difficult to ferret out non-linear relationships between the attributes with the help of statistical methods. This is so essential because random analysis against undefined logics that look for previously unknown patterns from very large sets of databases defies the standard methods of conventional statistics. Therefore it does not have the potential to bring out such hidden relationships.

16.6 Novel Application

In the current research, the nature of the satellite telemetry data in the categorical and numerical domains have been studied and three data mining techniques have been identified as being suitable, compliant in sifting through the mass of data. As a first step, a database has been created from a set of onboard telemetry data collected from a mars bound satellite. Subsequently, a set of parametric attributes have been selected as the candidate domain in which the hidden patterns of inter-relationships between the attributes are to be brought out. Algorithms developed based on three data mining techniques are separately applied to the data obtained during five on-orbit operations of the satellite. The results obtained are found to be promising in uncovering hitherto unknown hidden relationships among the telemetry parameters. This can help in better understanding of the satellite on-orbit performance, prevention of potential fault conditions and further help in configuration finalization of future satellite systems.

The satellite on-orbit telemetry data is a hex-coded information stream that is modulated in the S-band Radio Frequency carrier wave and beamed down to the ground station. The data consists of a continuous stream of values corresponding to various attributes of the parameters associated with different subsystems of the satellite. Values of the same set of parameters are collected by the telemetry subsystem at fixed intervals of time, then digitized, hex-coded and multiplexed before feeding to the radio frequency subsystem. Here the data is modulated with the carrier wave and beamed down as signals to the ground station. The values of the parameters are time-tagged with reference to the onboard computer. Any abnormal change in the values can be identified as an outlier with respect to the values before and after that change. The main requirement is to look for the correlation of this change in value with values of other parameters that do not bear a direct functional relationship to the parameter under consideration. The following criteria are set to identify the hidden patterns among the satellite telemetry parameters that throws light on correlation through unintended functional inter-relationships:

1. The nature of the signal given by the source of the parameter could be voltage, current, pressure, temperature, servo/position error or parameter status like on/off. The signals are beamed to the ground station in two different streams called Analog telemetry and Digital telemetry multiplexed and later modulated with the carrier wave.
2. The attributes of a given parameter can be different though the source subsystem of the satellite is the same. For example, the voltage of a DC–DC converter has different class attributes called primary voltage, secondary voltage, ripple voltage, etc.
3. The sensor which is the origin of information for a given parameter could be close to the sensors of other parameters.
4. There is no direct functional relationship between the attributes of a given parameter and the attributes of other parameters.

16.7 Selection of an Appropriate Data Mining Technique

One of the fundamental tasks in the application of data mining to real-world problems is related to characterizing the methodology for the selection of candidate data mining techniques and algorithms that can be used to effectively analyze the data and bring out the hidden patterns of information in the particular application domain. Features and processes that are amenable for handling multivariate, multi-dimensional data and extracting the hidden knowledge vary from application to application. Though a common data mining technique may be used for different applications, still depending on the characteristic features of the domain and data, different algorithms may perform the task differently in trying to meet the same objective (Ma et al., 2012). Similarly, different data mining techniques may seemingly be working on the same lines though the result may be altogether different. A comparison of the processes and requirements for different data mining techniques is done for the present research while selecting the candidates as shown in Table 16.1. The various features of algorithms are analyzed to arrive at a desirable framework that can address the requirements of the domain application. The inputs provided to an algorithm are the first feature that can aid in deciding the kind of algorithm framework needed. Generally, a slight difference in the input can result in the analyzing capability of the algorithm, and naturally, the output can change in a significant manner. Some problems can be solved by several algorithms with the approach being different and the objective being the same. Though many variations of a popular algorithm may be available, still customization maybe needed to address some unique properties in the data or the knowledge that is to be extracted (Liu & Motoda, 2000). As an example, when an application calls for using association rule mining, the classic algorithm that is generally selected is the Apriori algorithm. But many variations of this algorithm are available like discovering associations through weights or fuzzy associations and indirect or rare associations. The kind of data to be mined and the outcome desired or sought to decide if an already existing algorithm is sufficient to meet the ultimate task or a modification is needed.

The next important feature to be looked at is the strategy used by the algorithm. There are different problem-solving approaches such as divide-and-conquer, greedy, brute-force, depth- or breadth-first search, recursive operation, or a linear operation (Ramaswamy et al., 2000). This decides how many times the database has to be scanned for mining the data and the required memory for the application (Liu & Motoda, 2001). In this context, the data structure also plays an important role in terms of execution time and memory but in the present research there is not any standard followed and hence this factor does not have a major contribution (Khalid & Abdelwahab, 2016). The exactness of the algorithm is assessed when numerical and/or categorical data from the database and the mining task leads to definitive solutions or outcomes if definite processes are used in the algorithm (Liu, 1998). If the algorithm does not return a correct solution then it may be an approximate algorithm that may not always guarantee a correct answer (Pham & Afify, 2005).

Another feature of the algorithm is its ability to give the same result when it is run multiple times on the same data (Weiss & Indurkhya, 1998). If it returns

Table 16.1 Comparison of Processes for Different Data Mining Techniques

Process	Association Mining	Clustering Technique	Neural Networks	Genetic Algorithm	Decision Tree	Rule Induction
Multi-format data conversion	Needed	Needed	Not needed	Not needed	Not needed	Not needed
Data preprocessing	Needed	Needed	Needed	Needed	Needed	Not needed
Dimensionality reduction	Preferable	Not required	Not required	Not required	Not required	Not required
Database multiple scans	Required	Not required	Not required	Not required	Required	Not required
Mining inter-relationships between attributes of the parameter(s)	Not possible	Not possible	Not possible	Not possible	Possible to a limited extent	Possible for the entire database
Sequential / Parallel mining	Sequential	Sequential	Parallel	Parallel	Sequential	Parallel

different results even if the difference is either minor or major then it may be using a random generator process in its strategy (Mitchell, 1997). An incremental algorithm has an inbuilt process to take care of new data as and when it comes without having to recompute from zero. The incremental algorithm possesses a sub-process that allows the user to influence the processes of the algorithm even during the run-time of the algorithm.

To assess the performance of an algorithm, it has to be compared with the performance of another algorithm for the same application. For this exercise, appropriate metrics like memory usage, execution time, accuracy, recall, and scalability of an algorithm are generally used (Dzeroski S et al., 2001). The kind of data used also determines the performance of the algorithm. Using more than one dataset and usage of datasets with various characteristics ensure that the algorithm's efficiency in returning the required result is tested. While evaluating association mining algorithms both sparse and dense datasets are to be used since all algorithms may not be able to perform equally well with both. Also, using real datasets is preferable to artificial datasets because data integrity can change the performance of the algorithm (Liu et al., 2008). If parallel processing on distributed systems is possible then scalability of the algorithm is ensured which reduces the run-time and adds computational power. At the same time, complexity analysis would help in finding if the cost of using the algorithm where performance is assessed based on the actual datasets (Barua et al., 2011). Resources for implementation and accessibility for making changes along with the availability of open-source implementations are other important features that identify algorithms as preferable for any given application.

In the current research, an attempt has been made to develop and apply three data mining algorithms for assessing the attributes of different telemetry parameters obtained from the telemetry data of a Mars-bound satellite. Subsequently, this has been carried forward in developing an algorithm to improve the effectiveness of analysis with respect to the satellite on-orbit performance and thereby the parametric interdependency identification.

16.8 Satellite Telemetry Data: Association Mining

Association mining is one of the common techniques of data mining that is used for local pattern discovery in unsupervised learning systems. A market-basket analysis is a common form of expression for this technique that denotes a collection of items purchased by a customer in a single transaction. The exercise is to analyze the transactions database and find a set of items, called *itemsets*, that appear together in many transactions. For example, a supermarket can find out how many customers buy butter along with bread and how many buy jam along with bread. Such information or knowledge of the patterns can be used by the end-user in improving the business strategy. It can be used in improving the placement of these items in the store or in improving the layout of web pages. Support for an itemset is a metric expressed as a percentage of transactions that contain the given itemset. When the support for an itemset is higher than a user-specified minimum percentage then such item set is said to be frequent. Finding a frequent itemset is treated as a nontrivial problem because the number of transactions can be very large and the potential number of frequent itemsets could be exponential in number to the number of different items. The algorithm should possess scalability property and should discern between frequent and infrequent itemsets with the capability to ignore the latter. Inter-relationships among satellite telemetry parameters are analogous to associations in a market-basket type of analysis. The methodology used here needs to retrieve all possible patterns in the database and the usability of the output has to be assessed separately.

16.9 Satellite Telemetry Data: Decision Tree Technique

A decision tree is a classifier mechanism where the instance space is subjected to a recursive partition based on certain criteria drawn for each stage of the partition. This is much like a flow diagram used to describe a given process. A candidate data item is subjected to a condition leading to a "yes" or "no" type of classification. By this classification, the data item is mapped into a predefined class. The input for algorithms based on inductive learning and using classification consists of a dataset with attribute values and a corresponding class. In the model, a classifier is created that can predict the class for some entity with the values of available attributes of the input. Basically, classification identifies the class label to an unlabeled record. The classifier is a model that predicts the attribute-class of a sample when other attributes are known. Classification methods in data mining applications are generally used for identifying the behavior of stocks and shares in the financial market and finding out objects in large databases. In the present research, classification is considered since anomalies as a class has a unique identity, and tuples that go by certain fault criteria would readily be identified as having an anomalous behavior.

Based on this classification process, a decision tree consists of nodes that form a tree with a root node that does not have an incoming edge and all other nodes having one incoming edge. The node with outgoing edges is the test node and the other nodes are the leaf nodes. Each test node splits the instance space into two or more subspaces as per the discrete function of the input attribute values. Each of the leaf nodes is identified with one class which shows the most appropriate target value to which the sample points finally reach. Instances of space are classified by following them from the root of the tree down to a leaf node as per the outcome of the tests along the path (Maimon & Rokach, 2005). The decision tree is a predictive model where the target variable takes a finite set of values that leads to classification trees.

In the decision tree structure, each internal node represents a test on an attribute with each branch representing the test outcome and each leaf node representing a class label (Maimon & Rokach, 2005). Paths from the root node to leaf nodes represent classification rules and the complexity of the decision trees gets decided by decision-making criteria and the type of pruning used. The path of the root node to each of the leaf nodes represents a rule by combining the tests performed along the path which form the antecedent part and the class decision made at the leaf being treated as the class value. In this manner decision tree closely resembles rule induction (Maimon & Rokach, 2005). But the major difference is that rule induction can combine any number of antecedents while decision tree has to individually treat each of them. A decision tree creates a model that predicts the value of a target variable attribute based on several input variables.

16.10 Satellite Telemetry Data: A Modified Brute-Force Rule-Induction Algorithm

Rule induction technique has been widely used for mining data in different fields of application. In the current research, the proposed algorithm under this technique has a simple structure and gives results in a short duration during implementation. It also possesses the advantage of generating models that are easy to understand and which are accurate. Rule induction algorithm possesses a logic structure that can classify without building a decision tree and without the need for repeated scans of the database. Other methods like instanced-based learning, neural networks, and support vector machines do not generally give outputs that bring out hidden knowledge in a straightforward fashion. Knowledge extraction through the 'if/then' rules breaks down complex data in a manner amenable for easy processing, leading to outputs that can be easily understood and interpreted.

The search mechanism in a rule induction algorithm is generally structured into three kinds of search strategies, the bottom-up, top-down, and bidirectional strategy. In the first strategy, the search starts with a specific rule and is iteratively generalized. In the top-down strategy, the search starts with a general rule and iteratively goes into specific instances. A bi-directional search is a combination of both these strategies. In the present research, a bi-directional search strategy is adopted. The reason is that satellite design requirements define some specific functions but in the operational environment some unintended functional operations that are general are likely to take place. The search is aimed at uncovering rules that address these unintended functional operations and which can be thereby extended to different operational conditions.

In rule induction algorithms, the generation of different concepts for a target class is made possible since the governing rule IF (condition) THEN (class) can easily accommodate any attributes of tuples to identify the class which by itself can be of multiple descriptions (Ömer, 2013). A tuple is defined as a data structure consisting of multiple parts. In a relational database, it refers to an ordered set of data constituting a record.

The tuples coming under the IF condition are termed the antecedent and those coming under the class part are the consequent.

Unlike the Decision tree structure, in rule induction methods it is possible to concatenate (join together) more than one attribute that can lead to a unique consequence. Sequential covering rule induction algorithms like the AQ family of algorithms are based on this principle of sweeping through the conditional rule across all possible antecedents. For a given set of attributes if the condition shows truly it means that the rule antecedent has been satisfied and the given rule covers the attributes of tuples. The fraction of tuples that get covered in this way by the rule to the total number of tuples gives a measure of the coverage of the rule. The accuracy of the rule is given by the ratio of the correctly classified tuples to the total number of tuples. The class generalization process ends when new rules cannot be generated or the rule condition is exhausted. The extracted decision rules from training datasets are used to classify the attributes in the test dataset.

In the present research, the rule induction method is modified to accommodate the various kinds of categorical attributes and the parameters they represent along with the numerical values. These form the data chain acquired by the satellite telemetry subsystem during each sampling period and then subsequently telemetered to the ground station. A second modification is carried out to concatenate the attributes and the values under the condition part of the rule and the consequent class is opened for generalization in such a manner that any combination of categorical attributes with corresponding numerical values would certainly lead to a certain classification. When such a rule is tested on the actual data, it brings out patterns that do not surface under normal classification. This amounts to a brute force application of abstract logic on the tuples that is a specialty in this particular application and research.

16.11 Methodology

A sample data set with multi-dimensions has been created with telemetry data from a satellite functioning on-orbit. The data pertains to events when the LAM (Liquid Apogee Motor) engine was fired during three earth burn phases, trans mars injection, and Mars orbit insertion events of the mission. The selected window covers an equal interval of time during which the LAM engine is made on. Values of temperature, current, voltage, angle, speed, and error changes of a randomly selected number of parametric attributes in LAM Engine "ON" condition during all these events form the primary database. A rule-set is generated based on the domain expertise giving the relation between different sets of related parameters. The design of the algorithm is such that it learns the relationship between these parameters, scans through the multi-dimensional database and generates a series of relationships hitherto unknown among various parameters within the same event set and between the two event sets.

The methodology adopted for the application of the above three data mining techniques is unique to each of them since the processes of classification are different. When the data was processed with the Apriori algorithm, the nature of parameters had to be taken to look for similarities. A voltage signal had to be compared with another voltage signal and assessed for change in values of the former with the latter. In the case of the decision tree algorithm, this situation slightly improved since comparison could be carried out irrespective of the nature of the two parameters i.e. a change in voltage could be made as a condition for change in any other parameter other than a voltage parameter. But the process of making decisions had to go through the full cumbersome cycle of inclusions and eliminations. In the rule-induction method, a brute force method of comparison irrespective of the nature of the parameters and inclusion/elimination cycle could offer the simultaneous inclusion of many parameters being compared at the same instant with a baseline parameter. Thus it is seen that analysis of large volumes of data against the performance of any of the parameters within the dataset is achieved with the shortest path effort resulting in meaningful outputs.

16.12 Conclusion

Three data mining algorithms as discussed above have been used in this research to analyze a set of onboard telemetry data collected from a mars bound satellite. Apriori algorithm based on association mining technique, algorithm based on ID3 & C4.5 decision tree technique, and the newly developed modified brute force rule induction algorithm is independently applied on the satellite telemetry database. From this analysis, it has been possible to uncover hidden relationships among the different telemetry parameters that have a significant effect on the on-orbit performance of the satellite. The results obtained as shown in Figure 16.2 are found to be promising in understanding the hitherto unknown and unintended functional relationships among the telemetry parameters.

It is seen that the proposed modified brute force rule induction algorithm has uncovered a maximum number of hidden inter-relationships among the telemetry parameters received from a satellite on its onward journey to planet mars. The algorithm is structured to handle very large databases with a large number of parameters. The hidden knowledge of inter-relationships uncovered by the modified brute force rule induction algorithm from telemetry data pertaining to critical on-orbit events can serve towards optimizing the performance of various satellite subsystems. It can also aid in configuring the autonomy features of an onboard

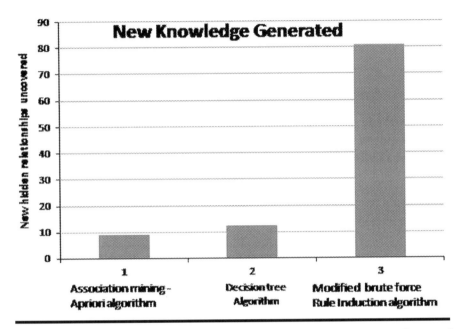

Figure 16.2 Comparison of new hidden inter-relationships among attributes of satellite house-keeping parameters uncovered by the three DM algorithms.

computer when ground intervention is not possible and in enhancing the life of the satellite by minimum manoeuvres, thus conserving precious onboard fuel. This can help in better understanding of the satellite's overall on-orbit performance, in the prevention of potential fault conditions, and, in the long run, help in improving the technical configuration of future satellite systems.

References

Barua, A., & Khorasani, K. (2011). Hierarchical fault diagnosis and health monitoring in satellites formation flight. *IEEE Transactions on Systems, Man, and Cybernetics—Part C:Applications and Reviews*, *41(2)*, 223–239. 10.1109/TSMCC.2010.2049994

Džeroski, S., & Lavrac, N. (2001). Relational Data Mining. Dzeroski, S., & Lavrac, N., Ed. ISBN: 3540422897, September 2001. 10.1007/978-3-662-04599-2

Fayyad, U., Piatetshy-Shapiro, G., Smyth, P., & Uthurusamy, R. (1996). *Advances in knowledge discovery and data mining*. CA, United States: AAAI/MIT Press, 445 Burgess Drive Menlo Park.

Gao, Y., Yang, T., Xing, N., & Xu, M. (2012). Fault Detection and Diagnosis for Spacecraft using Principal Component Analysis and Support Vector Machines, *7th IEEE Conference on Industrial Electronics and Applications (ICIEA)*, 978-1-4577-2119-9/12/$26.00 ©2011 IEEE, pp. 1984–1988.

Gao, Y., Yang, T., Xu, M., & Xing, N. (2012). An Unsupervised Anomaly Detection Approach for Spacecraft Based on Normal Behavior Clustering, *2012 Fifth International Conference* on *Intelligent Computation Technology and Automation*, 978-0-7695-4637-7/12 $26.00 © 2012 IEEE, DOI 10.1109/ICICTA.2012.126, pp. 478–481.

Kantardzic, M. (2003). *Data mining – Concepts, models, methods and algorithms*. New York: Wiley-Interscience, John Wiley & Sons Inc. pp. 91 -193.

Khalid, B., & Abdelwahab, N. 2016. A comparative study of various data mining techniques: Statistics, decision trees and neural networks. *International Journal of Computer Applications Technology and Research*, 5(3), 172–175.

Liu, H., & Motoda, H. (2000). *Feature selection for knowledge discovery and data mining* (2nd Printing). Boston, MA: Kluwer Academic Publisher.

Liu, H., & Motoda, H. (2001). *Instance selection and construction for data mining*. Boston, MA: Kluwer Academic Publishers.

Liu, H. M. (1998). *Feature extraction, construction and selection: A data mining perspective*. Boston, MA: Kluwer Academic Publishers.

Liu, X., Kwan, B. W., & Foo, S. Y. (2008). Time series prediction based on fuzzy principles, *Proc. Huntsville Simulation Conference*, Department of Electrical & Computer Engineering FAMUFSU College of Engineering, Florida State University.

Ma, L., Liu, H., & Feng, Z. (2012). *An equipment failure prediction accuracy improvement method based on the gray GM (1, 1) model, artificial intelligence and computational intelligence* (pp. 294–300). Berlin Heidelberg: Springer.

Maimon, O., & Rokach, L. (2005). Top-down induction of decision trees classifiers—A survey. *IEEE Transactions on Systems, Man and Cybernetics, Part C (Applications and Reviews)*, 35, 476–487. 10.1109/tsmcc.2004.843247

Maimon, O., & Rokach, L. (2009). *Data mining and knowledge discovery handbook* (pp. 165–187, 277–293, 353–373). New Delhi: Springer Science + Business Media Inc.

Maini, A. K., & Agrawal, V. (2007). *Satellite technology – Principles and applications* (pp. 303–466). New York: John Wiley & Sons Ltd.

Mitchell, T. (1997). *Machine learning* (pp. 16–25). New York, NY: McGraw Hill.

Ömer, A. (2013). A rule induction algorithm for knowledge discovery and classification. *Turkish Journal of Electrical Engineering and Computer Sciences*, 1–38. 10.3906/elk-12 02-27

Pham, D. T., & Afify, A. A. (2005). RULES-6: A simple rule induction algorithm for supporting decision-making. *IEEE*. 0-7803-9252-3/05/$20.00.

Poojari, A. K. (2003). *Data mining techniques* (pp. 54–87). Hyderabad: Universities Press.

Ramaswamy, S., Rastogi, R., & Shim, K. (2000). Efficient Algorithms for Mining Outliers from Large Datasets, *Proc. SIGMOD2000*, ACM Press, pp. 162–172.

Takehisa, Y., Kawahara, Y., & Takata, N. (2010). Spacecraft Telemetry Data Monitoring by Dimensionality Reduction Techniques, *SICE Annual Conference 2010 August 18–21, 2010*, Taipei, Taiwan, pp. 1230–1234.

Weiss, S. M., & Indurkhya, N. (1998) Predictive Data Mining: a Practical Guide, *Morgan Kaufman, Sun Francisco*.

Yairi, T., Kawahara, Y., Fujimaki, R., Sato, Y., & Machida, K. (2006). Telemetry-mining: A Machine Learning Approach to Anomaly Detection and Fault Diagnosis for Space Systems, *Proc. of the 2nd IEEE International Conference on Space Mission Challenges for Information Technology (SMC-IT 2006)*, July 17–20, Pasadena, California, USA.

Yang, T., Chen, B., Gao, Y., Feng, J., Zhang, H., & Wang, X. (2013). Data Mining-Based Fault Detection and Prediction Methods for In-Orbit Satellite, *2013 2nd International Conference on Measurement, Information and Control, Harbin, China,978-1-4799-1392-3/13/$31.00 m013 IEEE*, pp.805–808.

Chapter 17

Big Data Analytics: A Text Mining Perspective and Applications in Biomedicine and Healthcare

Jeyakumar Natarajan[1*], Balu Bhasuran[2],
and Gurusamy Murugesan[3]

[1]*Professor and Head, Department of Bioinformatics Bharathiar University, Coimbatore, India*
[2]*Ph.D. Research Scholar, DRDO-BU Center for Life Sciences Bharathiar University Campus, Coimbatore, India*
[3]*Guest Lecturer, Department of Bioinformatics Bharathiar University, Coimbatore, India*

Contents

DOI: 10.1201/9781003175889-17

Objectives

This chapter seeks to lay out the text mining perspective of Big Data analytics, emphasizing applications in biomedicine and healthcare. The chapter aims to understand better areas such as Big Data, Text Mining, Data Mining, Natural Language Processing, Machine Learning, and its inter linkage. The chapter illustrates the phases and task of text mining in the Big Data scope. Finally, the chapter describes the two application areas of biomedicine and healthcare where text mining using Big Data analytics is applied.

17.1 Introduction

17.1.1 Big Data

Today we live in a Big Data era where colossal amounts of data are generated and collected by various industries (Finance, Healthcare, etc.) for current and future innovation, research, and development purposes (Hashem et al., 2015; Herland et al., 2014; Omar, 2015; Sagiroglu & Sinanc, 2013). The word "big" in "Big Data" refers to 5Vs: *velocity, veracity, value, variety*, and *volume*. It represents a collection of data that is massive in volume, dimension and yet so large and complex. It also grows enormously over time, in the current technological advancement scenario on day-to-day basis. Examples of such data are stock exchange, social media, banking transactions, patient details, and so forth (Amado et al., 2018; De Mauro et al., 2015; Hilbert, 2016). So none of the conventional data management tools or systems can store, manage, and process it efficiently. The one-stop solution to this data abundance problem is a Big Data framework.

Since Big Data is generated in various fields/domains and it can be divided into the following three general types

- Structured
- Semi-structured
- Unstructured

Structured Data: It refers to the contents that are already formatted and stored in large databases. Examples of such data are organization employee details, biological databases, marketing data, etc.

Semi-Structured: In this, some unstructured data are stored along with structured data like databases. Some examples are table definitions in databases, XML files that contain both structured and unstructured data.

Unstructured: While structured data accounts for 20% of Big Data already existing, the remaining 80% of Big Data exists in unstructured form. Examples of such data include audio, text, video, social media, mobile data (GPS, sensors, etc.).

These types of data are complex to process and manage using traditional data management techniques, which paved the way for the following data framework architecture.

Some of the Big Data–driven application domains are briefly introduced below:

Finance: One of the highly invested and profited fields of Big Data is the financial sector. In this sector, the data sources mainly comprise banking transactions, financial market and service management, credit service, etc. (Kimball, 2011). The data is generated as billions of data points in the form of online and banking transactions, user account creation and updation, and many other financial operations like credit and debit, social media, and advertisement. Big Data frameworks are using these data for customer preference, market prediction, risk assessment of user credit and loan, recommendation systems, classification of user buying and selling of products and shares, trend prediction, business intelligence, etc., thereby enabling the financial organizations a better understanding of the current financial trend in general.

Media and Entertainment: Media and entertainment are other major fields that extensively apply the Big Data–based business model. In the media and entertainment field, the Big Data–based frameworks are implemented to achieve goals like predicting audience interest, classification of genres, optimization of scheduled streaming, target advertisement, personalized recommendation, new product development, etc. (Rifaie et al., 2008).

Healthcare: A large trove of data is generating in the health care industry daily. Due to the lack of standardization and consolidation of biomedical data, the health care industry initially lagged in the Big Data–based framework architecture. One of the major reasons behind this situation was the semi-structured and unstructured data as the major source of biomedical data in the health care industry (Inmon & Linstedt, 2014). The major sources of biomedical data are from scientific publications, clinical records, discharge summaries, electronic health records, life science patents, drug trial information, health care recommendations, and discussions from social media like Twitter, blogs, and so forth (Akter & Wamba, 2016). A majority of these data represent unstructured data, and some fall into the semi-structured category. Since the traditional enterprise data warehouse (EDW) architectures are developed with domain-specific structured data processing, the biomedical data could not be processed. The new Big Data–based framework architectures solved this issue by integrating a specific subset of data mining approach called text mining into the framework (Pouyanfar et al., 2018).

This chapter emphasis one specific type of Big Data, i.e. unstructured data in the form of text and its analysis in the text mining perspective and applications in biomedical/healthcare data.

17.1.2 Text Mining

Advancement in science and technology paved the way for the rapid accumulation of digital data with unprecedented growth daily. To bring the ultimate potential of the Big Data regardless of disciplines, automated information extraction approaches are sorely needed. Text mining is a highly applied automated approach across academia and industry to tackle this staggering speed of data abundance. Text mining is continuously applied in various sectors like finance and marketing, banking, multimedia, life science, astronomy, etc. In simple terms, Text Mining is the process of deriving highly quality actionable and meaningful information from unstructured data.

In this Big Data era, the amount of unstructured text information is massive, and it's still rapidly growing in various fields. Unstructured text information, which exists in natural language form (e.g. English), can be collected from multiple sources like scientific literature, news, social media, web pages, electronic health records. In this regard, text mining is continuously applied in the following major areas for information mining (Dimitrov, 2016).

- Web mining
- Social media mining
- Opinion mining
- Healthcare/biomedical literature mining

Web Mining: The World Wide Web (WWW) is the largest textual information resource in the form of social media, blogs, emails, and news articles. It is a widely used medium for the published and useful information (Baro et al., 2015). The quantity and complexity of text information are big enough so that traditional methodology cannot analyze this information. Text mining methods and techniques are applied to WWW data for various purposes, such as news articles and spam mail classification, analyzing users' online behaviors, and fraudulent activity in online financial transactions (Raghupathi & Raghupathi, 2014).

Social Media Mining: The prominent rise of social media created a lot of unstructured text data that provides a new opportunity for various domains (e.g. collecting customer opinions for market research). It is a significant data source for Big Data analytics because of the large volume of data generated daily. Social media platforms like Twitter, Facebook creates a perfect opportunity for people to interact as a group or with each other to express their views on a particular product or topic (van Altena et al., 2019). Text mining is widely applied to extract knowledge and information from this social media data for sentiment classification, market research, counter-terrorism, etc.

Opinion Mining: The main concept of opinion mining is to reveal how the text the user has can support or oppose a specific topic (Mirza et al., 2019). Opinion mining also uses social media data and sentiment classification to analyze political text and posts from social media platforms. It is also applied to various other problems like customer feedback on a product and response of audiences to a particular movie etc.

Healthcare/Biomedical Literature Mining: An important emerging field of Big Data analytics is the ever-growing scientific literature data. The vast growing scientific literature is a major source of knowledge for biomedical researchers. Scientific literature's massive growth makes manual analysis complex, costly, and time-consuming. So as an automated solution, text mining is applied to extract useful knowledge such as entity recognition, relation extraction, and pathway construction, etc. (Baro et al., 2015).

17.1.3 Applications in Biomedicine and Healthcare

Several research studies have been addressed on the processing of unstructured textual information available in biomedicine in the form of abstracts and full-text known as biomedical literature mining and healthcare datasets such as clinical records, discharge summaries, electronic health records, etc.

Biomedical Literature Mining: Biomedical Text Mining (BTM) is focused on the identification and extraction of biological entities and their relationships, such as genes, proteins, diseases, drugs, phenotypes, cell type, miRNA, or even more broadly, biologic events and pathways from the scientific text (Cohen & Hersh, 2005; Hearst, 1999). Furthermore, the extracted information has been used for hypothesis generation, knowledge discovery, annotation of specialized databases, tools, and manual curation of biological databases such as infer novel relationships: fish oil and Raynaud disease, magnesium deficiency and migraine, creation of databases CTD, OMIM, DisGeNET, STRING, building sophisticated web servers PubTator, mirCancer, PolySearch, DISEASES, PKDE4J, and formation of discovery platforms such as BEST, DigSee, Beegle, and Implicitome (Aggarwal & Zhai, 2012; Zweigenbaum et al., 2007; Zhu et al., 2013). Thus, BTM has become a vital part of many knowledge discovery systems and tools utilized by a wide audience of researchers and scientists (Tao et al., 2020).

Healthcare Text Mining: The Healthcare industry has a large trove of information in various styles and structures of text like prescriptions, patient visits, physician notes, and more. These details were encapsulated with electronic health records, clinical records, discharge summaries, etc., which provide insights to future research (Akter & Wamba, 2016; Inmon & Linstedt, 2014; Pouyanfar et al., 2018). NER in the healthcare domain is concerned with extracting terms like anatomy, symptoms, disease, drug, dosage from EHRs, and other healthcare text sources. On the other hand, relation extraction focuses on cancer survival, Disease risk, surgery outcome, adverse drug reactions in healthcare information extraction systems. Researchers also developed knowledge discovery platforms, annotation of specialized databases, and tools in healthcare text mining. Some of the well-known systems are cancer Biomedical Informatics Grid (caGRID) Browser, Research electronic data capture (REDCap), i2b2 Hive3, MIMIC Critical Care Database, etc. (Gök et al., 2015).

17.2 Text Mining Overview and Related Fields

17.2.1 Definition and Overview

According to Marti A. Hearst, text mining is the automatic discovery of new, previously unknown information by computer using different unstructured text sources (Hearst, 1999). Text Mining, also known as Text Data Mining (TDM), differs from Data Mining (DM). Text mining handles natural language text, whereas data mining focuses on structured data. TM is the process of generating high-quality information in the form of a novel, relevant and exciting patterns, trends, facts, or hypotheses by shifting through a large volume of unstructured data (Cohen & Hersh, 2005; Zweigenbaum et al., 2007).

To identify and extract hidden patterns and trends, generate a hypothesis, and discover knowledge, text mining integrates a variety of disciplines such as Artificial Intelligence (AI), Data Mining (DM), Computational Linguistics (CL), Natural Language Processing (NLP), Machine Learning (ML), Statistics and act as an interdisciplinary domain (Aggarwal & Zhai, 2012). This section presents a brief overview of three related key fields of Text Mining, namely Data Mining, Natural Language Processing, and Machine Learning.

17.2.2 Data Mining

A large amount of data is generated in many domains and stored in databases in a structured format. This structured data contains information that can be used for various health, research, and business applications ranging from market predictions and analysis to drug target identification (Ferreira-Mello et al., 2019). So the need for computational techniques to extract fruitful knowledge from this data was in high demand. Data mining was proposed as one of the automated solutions to extract the hidden and valuable patterns and information from these databases (Uramoto et al., 2004).

Data Mining is the procedure of identifying and extracting patterns and knowledge from structured text like databases. Data Mining utilizes various computational techniques like machine learning algorithms, association-rule-based approaches, and dictionaries for pattern discovery and knowledge extraction. Some of the most widely explored used data mining techniques are clustering, classification, regression, pattern matching, association, and data visualization (Ferreira-Mello et al., 2019; Uramoto et al., 2004).

Clustering: The clustering process groups the objects based on a certain set of features and assign these objects into a certain category. The main task of clustering is to find the similarity between objects so that similar featured objects moved to the same cluster. The clustering approach is one of the classic examples of un-supervised learning. Some of the widely employed clustering algorithms are k-means, hierarchical, and probabilistic clustering algorithms.

Classification: Classification is the process of training a model/function using a set of representative features and separating new data values into multiple categories using the generated model/function. Classification is considered the best example of a supervised learning approach. A classification model/function is generated using labeled data based on certain conditions or parameters. The model/function is evaluated on its ability to predict the label for unknown data. Some of the famous classification algorithms are Conditional Random Fields (CRF), Decision Trees (DT), Naive Bayes (NB), Support Vector Machines (SVM), and K-Nearest Neighbor (KNN).

Regression: Regression focuses on creating a model/function for differentiating the data into a numeric range or continuous values. Regression focuses on predicting constant real values as the dependent variable based on using multiple independent variables from the training data. Some of the famous regression algorithms are linear regression, multiple regression, polynomial regression, and logistic regression.

Data Visualization: Data visualization visually represents data and information using various graphical elements such as charts, maps, and graphs. The key idea is to represent complex relations with a large trove of information to a more easily readable visual representation. In the era of Big Data, data visualization tools are getting increased attention due to their ability to proceed with larger data sets of multi-omics data, apply various types of data mining algorithms and support discovering novel associations and hidden patterns and trends. Some of the Big Data-supported data visualization tools are Tableau, D3.js, Gephi, and Cytoscape.

With reference to Big Data, classification approaches use vast volumes of an-notated data, especially in image and text classification (single, multiclass) and time series prediction tasks. Supervised models are generated by feeding this bid data corpora. Some of the annotated Big Data corpora are Google's open image (9 million images with 6000+ categories), Amazon reviews (35 million reviews), Google N-gram corpus (1 trillion words), IMDB reviews (25,000 movie reviews), Youtube-8M (Millions of video IDs with 3800+ entities), Plant Image (1 million plant images with 11 species), etc.

In the context of Big Data, clustering approaches are focusing on natural language generation and understanding models (NLU, NLG) and classification and prediction models using unsupervised learning approaches. Deep learning-based unsupervised learning approaches are increasingly developed in the Big Data scenario by feeding massive databases such as entire Wikipedia and biomedical bibliographic database Medline (30 million articles).

Hence, Big Data plays a major role in classical data mining. Some of the widely used Big Data–based data mining applications and tools include Apache Hadoop, IBM Watson Studio, High-Performance Computing Cluster (HPCC), Apache Cassandra, Qubole, RapidMiner, Azure Machine Learning Studio, Tableau Server, Google Cloud AI Platform, Amazon SageMaker, etc.

17.2.3 Natural Language Processing

Natural Language Processing (NLP) is an interdisciplinary domain merging var-ious linguistic processing techniques applied to discover the underlying meaning of data represented in natural language. NLP domain integrates information retrieval, computational linguistics, probability and statistics, and machine learning to achieve extraction, analysis, interpretation, understanding of data represented in the form of natural language (Agerri et al., 2015). The type of the data can be image, speech, or text, and the approaches can be classification, structure extrac-tion, translation, or segmentation of the data.

As discussed in the earlier sections, the unprecedented growth of data (Big Data) in which a majority falls under natural language text. This situation makes NLP one of the important processing techniques in data science (Hirschberg &

Manning, 2015). NLP techniques are continuously applying using Big Data in various tasks such as document summarization, language modeling, question answering systems, named entity recognition, article classification, etc. In the context of a text (semi-structured/ unstructured), the core focus of using NLP is to discover the meaning of that text by analyzing syntax, semantics, and grammatical structures. To find the syntax and semantics, a processing pipeline is generally employed. The processing pipeline consists of sentence tokenization, POS tagging, lemmatization, chunking, and dependency analysis (Agerri et al., 2015; Hirschberg & Manning, 2015).

Sentence tokenization: Tokenization divides the sentences of text into meaningful constituent elements called tokens by detecting word boundaries.

Example 1:

Original sentence: Data innovation has changed how healthcare services are implemented.

Tokenized sentence: ('Data') (innovation') ('has') ('changed') ('the') (manner') ('in') ('which') ('healthcare') ('services') ('are') ('implemented')

POS tagging: part-of-speech (POS) tagging is also known as grammatical tagging, or word-category disambiguation, is the process of categorizing the words and labeling them accordingly. In other words, POS defines a word's lexical class in a grammatical context.

Example 2:

Original sentence: Data innovation has changed how healthcare services are implemented.

After POS: Data/NNP innovation/NN has/VBZ changed/VBN the/DT manner/NN in/IN which/WDT healthcare/NN services/NNS are/VBP implemented/VBN

Lemmatization: Lemmatization applies morphological analysis and vocabulary of words to return the dictionary form or base format of a lemma word by removing inflectional endings. In other words, Lemmatization is the process of converting the tokens to the basic form of the word.

Example 3:

Original sentence: Data innovation has changed how healthcare services are implemented.

After Lemmatization: Data innovation have changed how healthcare service is implemented

Chunking: Chunking is an NLP procedure that generates the grammatical structure (Kang et al., 2011). The process of chunking splits the text into grammatical units, namely noun phrase (NP), verb phrase (VP), or preposition phrase (PP).

Example 4:
Original sentence: Data innovation has changed how healthcare services are implemented.
After Chunking: ('Data/NNP innovation/NN') ('has/VBZ changed/VBN') ('the/DT manner/NN') ('in/IN which/WDT')('healthcare/NN services/NNS') ('are/VBP implemented/VBN')

Dependency analysis: Dependency parsing or syntactic parsing is the process of parsing a sentence to extract grammatical structure. It also defines the relationship between the headwords and other words, such as nouns and verbs. These play a vital role in various tasks like relation extraction. An example of the dependency parsed tree is depicted in Figure 17.1.

Example 5:
Original sentence: Data innovation has changed how healthcare services are implemented.
After Dependency parsing:

To perform these tasks especially using Big Data language processing toolkits giving the state-of-the-art results are required. Some of the widely used Big Data–based NLP tool kits are SpaCy, TextBlob, Stanford's Core NLP, Natural Language Toolkit (NLTK), and Gensim. One of the widely recognized Big Data–based NLP interfaces is the question answering (QA) system, IBM Watson.

17.2.4 Machine Learning

Both DM and NLP use machine learning algorithms or techniques for trend analysis and pattern detection and can play a pivotal role in the development of TM applications. Machine Learning (ML) is the class of learning strategies from Artificial Intelligence (AI), which enables the system to learn automatically and improve the performance using the experience without being programmed explicitly (Yang et al., 2007). A machine learning system (model) is generated by learning the features and patterns from the training data and evaluated using the unknown data from the test set. ML-based approaches aim to enable the model to automatically learn from the experience so that without any human intervention

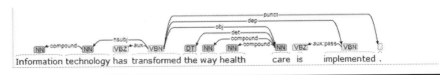

Figure 17.1 Dependency parsed tree of the given sentence.

the system can perform well. ML algorithms used for classification tasks, known as supervised learning and clustering, are known as unsupervised learning (Ye et al., 2016). The various categories of supervised and unsupervised learning algorithms are given in the following Table 17.1.

17.2.5 Text Mining: Big Picture

In general, text mining is considered a subfield within data mining that deals with semi-structured and unstructured data (Zhu et al., 2013). Hence, its related fields, such as Data Mining (DM), Natural Language Processing (NLP), and Machine Learning (ML) which play an active role in the text-based knowledge process, are introduced in this section. Two other disciplines closely related to text mining and its process pipeline includes Information Retrieval (IR) and Information Extraction (IE), are introduced in the next section. Combining all, Figure 17.2 represents a Venn diagram of text mining as a multidisciplinary field.

17.3 Phases and Tasks of Text Mining

The ultimate goal of any text mining study is to derive novel implicit knowledge or generate a new hypothesis that is either hidden or presented as an explicit observation. To do so, text mining integrates a variety of computational technologies such as data mining, natural language processing, machine learning, which are discussed in detail in the previous section. The other two technologies often discussed with TM are Information Retrieval and Information Extraction and part of the TM pipeline. Hence, the process of text mining pipeline consists of,

- ***Information Retrieval (IR)***
- ***Information Extraction (IE)***
- ***Knowledge Discovery & Hypothesis Generation***

In the context of TM, IR focuses on finding relevant natural language text from a set of literature-based databases. Information extraction can be defined as the automatic process of extracting structured information from semi-structured and/or unstructured machine-readable text acquired from the information retrieval phase. Finally, the third phase is knowledge discovery and hypothesis generation. The sole purpose of automated TM is the discovery of new knowledge, generation of new ideas, or hypothesis from literature by applying various statistical and algorithmic techniques (Aggarwal & Zhai, 2012; Cohen & Hersh, 2005;Hassani et al., 2020; Hearst, 1999; Tao et al., 2020; Zweigenbaum et al., 2007). A detailed representation of the text mining pipeline process is illustrated in Figure 17.3.

Table 17.1 Various Categories of ML Algorithms with Task and Representative Reference

Category	Machine Learning Algorithm	Task	Representative Reference
Regression Algorithms	Linear Regression	Classification/Regression	(Tsuruoka et al., 2007)
	Logistic Regression	Classification/Regression	(Yang et al., 2007)
	Polynomial Regression	Classification/Regression	(Toh et al., 2004)
Instance-based Algorithms	k-Nearest Neighbor (kNN)	Classification/Regression	(Deekshatulu & Chandra, 2013)
	Support Vector Machines (SVM)	Classification/Regression	(Gunn, 1998)
	Self-Organizing Map (SOM)	Classification/Regression	(Isa et al., 2009)
Sequence Labelling Algorithms	Hidden Markov Models (HMM)	Classification/Regression	(Kang et al., 2018)
	Conditional random fields (CRFs)	Classification/Regression	(Murugesan et al., 2017b)
Regularization Algorithms	Ridge Regression	Classification/Regression	(Mukherjee & Zhu, 2011)

(Continued)

Table 17.1 (Continued) Various Categories of ML Algorithms with Task and Representative Reference

Category	Machine Learning Algorithm	Task	Representative Reference
	Least-Angle Regression (LARS)	Classification/ Regression	(Fraley & Hesterberg, 2009)
Decision Tree Algorithms	Classification and Regression Tree (CART)	Classification/ Regression	(Fonarow et al., 2005)
	Iterative Dichotomiser 3 (ID3)	Classification/ Regression	(Wang et al., 2017)
	C4.5 and C5.0	Classification/ Regression	(Qiang, 2006)
Bayesian Algorithms	Naive Bayes	Classification/ Regression	(Ye et al., 2016)
	Gaussian Naive Bayes	Classification/ Regression	(Jahromi & Taheri, 2017)
	Bayesian Belief Network (BBN)	Classification/ Regression	(Ayre et al., 2014)
Clustering Algorithms	k-Means	Clustering	(Jing et al., 2005)
	Hierarchical Clustering	Clustering	(Azzag et al., 2006)
	Probabilistic	Clustering	(Larsen et al., 2002)

(Continued)

Table 17.1 (Continued) Various Categories of ML Algorithms with Task and Representative Reference

Category	Machine Learning Algorithm	Task	Representative Reference
Association Rule Learning Algorithms	Apriori algorithm	Classification/Regression	(Abaya, 2012)
	Eclat algorithm	Classification/Regression	(Zhang et al., 2010)
Dimensionality Reduction Algorithms	Principal Component Analysis (PCA)	Feature Extraction	(Uguz, 2011)
	Linear Discriminant Analysis (LDA)	Feature Extraction	(AbuZeina & Al-Anzi, 2018)
Ensemble Algorithms	AdaBoostBootstrapped	Ensemble Learning	(Hanif & Prevost, 2009)
	Aggregation (Bagging)	Ensemble Learning	(Bashir et al., 2015)
	Stacked Generalization (Stacking)	Ensemble Learning	(Bhasuran et al., 2016)
Artificial Neural Network Algorithms	Multilayer Perceptrons (MLP)	Classification/Regression	(Crone & Koeppel, 2014)
	Back-Propagation	Classification/Regression	(Kaur & Rashid, 2016)
Deep Learning Algorithms	Convolutional Neural Network (CNN)	Classification/Regression/Clustering	(Poria et al., 2015)
	Long Short-Term Memory Networks (LSTMs)	Classification/Regression/Clustering	(Palangi et al., 2016)
	Deep Belief Networks (DBN)	Classification/Regression/Clustering	(Jiang et al., 2018)

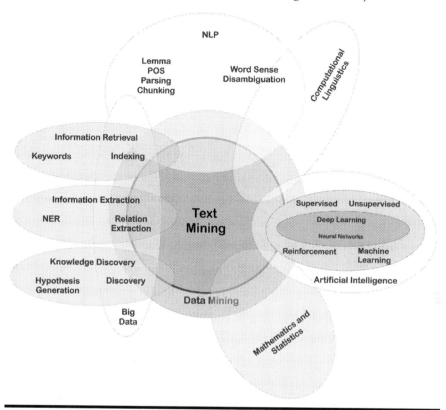

Figure 17.2   Venn diagram of text mining as a multidisciplinary field.

17.3.1 *Information Retrieval*

IR is the process of finding relevant natural language text from a set of literature-based databases (Aggarwal & Zhai, 2012). IE focuses on finding relevant articles in response to a formulated query based on the specific information in demand. IE is the initial step in which the end-user collects all the required information by searching various indexed databases such as PubMed or Google Scholar. Following are the conventional information retrieval related sub-tasks in the text mining pipeline:

   i. Query-based document search
   ii. Text preprocessing
   iii. Text clustering
   iv. Text classification

Query-based document search: The query-based document search focuses on re-trieving information from the indexed database by providing a search input. A

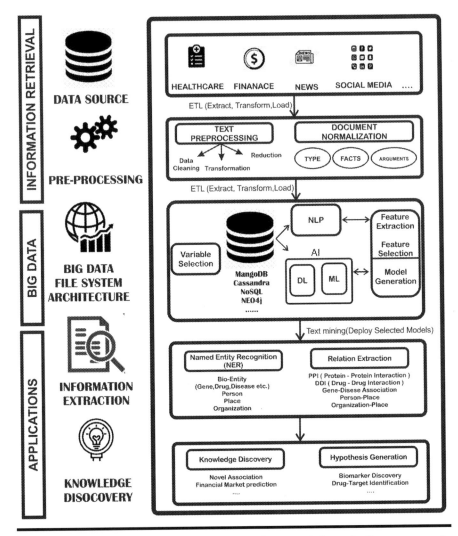

Figure 17.3 The schematic architecture of text mining pipeline process in Big Data.

majority of the IE tools are web-based. The user is expected to form a single or advanced query based on keywords and domain-specific terms representing the information they seek. A majority of the indexed databases are based on query-based document searches. The user is expected to provide some keywords in a simple search scenario or a more detailed search query by indexing additional query words like author name or MeSH term in advanced search scenario (Lu, 2011).

Text preprocessing: After collecting the data from these various sources, a set of text pre-processing and document normalization operations needs to be performed on the collected data. These pre-processing operations include data cleaning, transformation, and reduction (Cohen & Hunter, 2008). Data cleaning is used to tackle problems such as missing and irrelevant data or ASCII format errors. In data cleaning and transformation, these situations are handled by filling NULL or Zero value or other suitable value in the missing data place and transforming the format of text. A set of preprocessing operations such as sentence splitting, tokenization, capitalization, stop word removal, POS tagging, stemming, chunking, and lemmatization will be performed. Finally, data reduction deducing the amount of processing data by various techniques such as dimensionality reduction, subset selection, or cube aggregation. In document normalization, the document type, the represented facts and arguments, and associated information will be identified. These pre-processing techniques are performed to make the available data less noisy, less inconsistent, and easily manageable (ETL to Big Data file system architecture), thereby enabling various data analysis techniques can be performed using it.

Text clustering: Text clustering intuitively focuses on finding heterogeneous documents and summarizing them uniformly by partitioning them into clusters (Aggarwal & Zhai, 2012). Text clustering is achieved by assigning data point vectors in a multi-dimensional space and clustering these data points based on similarity. High dimensionality, Big Data, and complex syntax and semantics are the major challenges in text classification.

Text classification: In general, the text classification procedure of finds an appropriate category for a particular document or sentence. The scope of text classification can be at various levels such as document, abstract, subsection, paragraph, sentence, and sub-sentence levels (Feldman & Sanger, 2007; Abdulkadhar et al., 2020). Text classification is applied on a range of topics and across languages with important applications such as Topic Detection (feedback, review, field of interest), Sentiment Analysis (positive/negative, adverse reactions), language detection (English or French).

17.3.1.1 IR and Big Data

From a Big Data mining perspective, the information retrieval phase consists of identifying and extracting data from various data sources, perform a set of pre-processing operations on the retrieved data for information extraction. A set of operations collectively known as ETL (extract, transform, load) will be performed in between these phases. ETL is the computing procedure of extracting data from source systems and apply a set of operations such as formatting (such as XML or PubTator), concatenation or calculation, and loading the transformed data to the destination system (Baro et al., 2015; Dimitrov, 2016; Hassani et al., 2020; Herland et al., 2014; Mirza et al., 2019; Raghupathi & Raghupathi, 2014; van Altena et al., 2019).

The Big Data era textual corpus comes with larger sizes that the traditional extraction systems cannot manage. Some of the widely explored Big Data textual corpus are Amazon reviews (35 million reviews), Google N-gram corpus (1 trillion words), Medline database (30 million citations), IMDB reviews (25,000 movie reviews), etc.

17.3.1.2 Big Data File System Architecture

With the emergence of Big Data, a major difficulty has emerged as data management and access for various applications. As discussed earlier, traditional enterprise data warehouse (EDW) architectures unable to deliver the goals paved the way for Big Data Warehousing. The generated data is from various sources with different formatting and type, and the data is generated in the terabyte range. A Big Data file system-based framework is necessary to handle all these challenges (Inmon & Linstedt, 2014; Kimball, 2011; Rifaie et al., 2008). The Big Data file system is used to ETL the pre-processed data and is equipped with various other resources like NLP and AI. The big textual data will be stored in a distributional database capable of handling multidimensional literature data.

Some of the most famous databases which support Big Data management are Apache Cassandra (https://cassandra.apache.org/), MongoDB (https://www.mongodb.com/), Neo4j (https://neo4j.com/), Amazon DynamoDB (https://aws.amazon.com/dynamodb/), etc. The Big Data warehouse is connected with the NLP and AI (Machine Learning and Deep Learning) components, which in turn interact with feature selection, extraction, and machine learning model generation (training, development, and testing) components. The Big Data file system architecture phase develops a ready-to-be deployed machine learning/deep learning-based model for the information extraction phase.

17.3.2 Information Extraction

The information extraction technique automatically extracts specific structured information from semi-structured or unstructured natural language text (Hearst, 1999). In text mining, IE is considered a critical process and a widely studied task that focuses on the recognition and extraction of useful information such as names and relations. IE's two major fundamental tasks are Named Entity Recognition (NER) and Relation Extraction (Zhu et al., 2013). The IE phase uses a text-mining deployment of the model from the previous Big Data file system architecture phase and uses it for the tasks. The NER approach automatically identifies the entities that can be mentions of person/organization name or location in the general domain and gene/protein or disease name in the biomedical domain and classify them. Relation Extraction task is the procedure of automatically extracting potential relationships between entities such as person-organization, organization-location, and person-role in the general domain and protein-protein interaction or gene-disease association in the biomedical domain. These two major IE tasks act as a baseline for other text mining application areas such as text summarization, question-answering system, article classification, and more broadly hypothesis generation and knowledge discovery (Zhu et al., 2013). In recent years IE becomes more advanced by integrating new technologies such as ML, AI, or Deep Learning (DL) with NLP and CL (Hassani et al., 2020). In a border sense, IE deals with the automatic extraction of entities, normalization of these entities and attributes, and the various relationships among these entities (Aggarwal & Zhai, 2012; Hassani et al., 2020; Hearst, 1999). The important information extraction sub-tasks in the text mining pipeline are:

- Named Entity Recognition
- Relation Extraction
- Event Extraction

17.3.2.1 Named Entity Recognition

Named Entity Recognition (NER), first introduced in the Message Understanding Conferences (MUC), is the process of automatically recognizing the various entities such as persons, locations, or organizations (Hearst, 1999). NER is the important crucial step in IE, which eventually results in the Knowledge Discovery in Text (KDT) (Zweigenbaum et al., 2007). When NER is applied in BTM, it focuses on various biomedical entities, as mentioned above, and becomes a very challenging and complex task.

NER is applied in the finance domain to identify entities like bank account number, invoice date, invoice number, etc. NER is used in the medical categories domain to identify entity types like a medical condition, anatomy, treatment, procedure, test, and medical condition (Francis et al., 2019). NER is also applied in other domains like social media (Yang et al.2019), multimedia (Arshad et al., 2019; Rim et al., 2019), and oil and gas (Rademaker, 2018).

17.3.2.2 Relation Extraction

Relation extraction can be defined as the method of identifying and extracting semantic relationships, coreference, or negation in nature between entities from the literature (Zhu et al., 2013). In the context of text mining, a relation can be defined as a connection between entities, which can be of different types such as semantic, grammatical, coreference, or negation. The automatic extraction of these semantic connections among entities with high accuracy and efficiency is called relation extraction. In general, most of the relations can be binary; however, ternary or higher-order can also occur, such as events and pathways. The aim is the identification of a specific relation between co-occurring entities mentioned together of a specific relatedness.

Relation extraction is mainly applied in domains like cybersecurity for analyzing vulnerability in web connection (Georgescu, 2020), identifying the relation between medicine concepts (Liu et al., 2017; Lv et al., 2016), and question answering (Chen et al., 2018). Georgescuet al., analyzed the cybersecurity-related documents using the NLP model to identify vulnerability in web connection (Georgescu, 2020). Liuet al., developed a concept recognition approach using the CRF model for clinical relation extraction (Liu et al., 2017).

17.3.2.3 Event Extraction

One of the important tasks in the text mining pipeline is event extraction from unstructured data such as news messages, biomedical text, etc., which extracts domain-specific knowledge from the literature. Event extraction emphasizes the identification and extraction of periodical incidents mentioned in the text, thereby enabling to answer questions like, what happened, how it happened, what the entities involved, and when it happened, etc. Using Event extraction, IE systems can improve and enhance the performance of domain-specific knowledge extraction or generation. Events can be presented in a complex manner of relationships in a text. Few examples for event extraction from text is as follows:

i. General text
   Representation:<company><buy><company>
   Example 1: Facebook buys WhatsApp

ii. Biomedical text
    Representation:<gene1><relation><gene2> and <gene3>
    Example 2: TGF2-beta mediates RUNX induction and FOX3

The above are fewer examples of event extraction in text. It is limited to the entities mentioned above and expands to person, organization, interest, disease, drug, etc. (Agerri et al.2015; Hirschberg & Manning, 2015; Hogenboom et al., 2011; Zhu et al., 2013). The biomedical domain bio-molecular event is defined as the change of state of various biomedical entities such as protein, chemical, or cells. In general, an event is represented as a trigger expression along with bio-entities as its participants. The event representing the change in a single gene or protein is called a simple event. In contrast, events representing multiple bio-entities and another event acting as participants are called complex events. The extraction of the bio-molecular event is a highly focused research area because it can give crucial insight into physiological and pathogenesis mechanisms and can be used for drug target identification and re-purposing (Agerri et al., 2015; Hirschberg and Manning, 2015; Zhu et al., 2013).

17.3.2.4 IE and Big Data

Information extraction in the context of Big Data is performed with large-scale identification and extraction of entities and relations from big corpora (Adnan & Akbar, 2019; Bhasuran & Natarajan, 2019). A supervised named entity recognition model will be generated on 100 to 1000 labeled train data in the traditional information extraction approach. The model will be tested on 50 to 500 test data sets. In Big Bata scenarios, the NER and relation extraction models use millions of data as input, mostly employing an unsupervised or weakly supervised approach based on deep learning architectures for model generation. Even in Big Data scenarios with large-scale data points for training, complex unstructured data poses challenges such as ambiguity, nested entity, domain-specific vocabulary, language variability, noisy and missing data in mining information.

Some of the notable Big Data scale information extraction using unstructured text are, 100 million clinical notes were used to identify arterial blood pressure control on Diabetes Mellitus (Boytcheva et al., 2015). To identify disease-drug pairs Wang et al. employed 27 million medical abstracts from PubMed (Wang et al., 2017).

17.3.3 Knowledge Discovery and Hypothesis Generation

The rapid growth of literature in recent years, especially in the life science and financial domain, causes the problem of missing a large number of important connections between various types of entities (Baro et al., 2015; Dimitrov, 2016;Hassani et al., 2020; Mirza et al., 2019; Raghupathi & Raghupathi, 2014; van Altena et al., 2019). To discover this unnoticed and hidden information, automated text mining procedures are required (Bhasuran et al., 2018; Maroli et al., 2019). The major goal of this text mining sub-field is to formulate a highly confident hypothesis by navigating through and connecting a large number of concepts of disjoint literate sets, which falls under the Knowledge Discovery in Text (KDT) approach. The discovery platforms and literature-wide analysis studies (LWAS) focusing on alleviating these problems are collectively known as Literature-Based Discovery (LBD) in text mining (Hassani et al., 2020; Tao et al., 2020). Knowledge Discovery is sometimes referred to as hypothesis generation. Hypothesis generation is the process of generating unknown facts by utilizing information discovered with the use of IR and IE (Cohen & Hersh, 2005). Generating hypotheses in various fields such as biomedicine, finance, or multimedia is a significant task to gather unknown facts and use them to guide the devise of experiments or market predictions in the future or explain existing experimental or business results (Zweigenbaum et al., 2007). In turn, this helps determine new drug targets or business investment, or new novel interactions between biomedical concepts that are not proved before.

17.3.3.1 TM and Big Data

In Big Data analytics, text mining is escalated as one of the effective tools to exploit the power of the unstructured textual data by identifying existing information and generating new hypotheses and knowledge. Text mining in Big Data analysis focused on data from scientific articles, electronic health records, websites, blogs, and social media, and so forth. Using these data, various text mining tasks like named entity recognition (Francis et al., 2019), relation extraction (Liu et al., 2017), sentiment analysis (Amado et al., 2018), event extraction (Hogenboom et al., 2011; Zhu et al., 2013), knowledge discovery (Ferreira-Mello et al., 2019) are applied to extract the information which is implicit as well as explicit. In general, text mining helps to efficiently exploit the textual Big Data on a wide variety of real-world applications such as decision making, new insights into marketing strategies, generating new and existing knowledge from scientific literature, and insights into treatment methods from HER, etc. In this regard, the next section details the application of text mining in biomedicine Big Data.

17.4 Applications in Biomedicine
17.4.1 Biomedical Text Mining

The significant outcomes and insights of scientific research and clinical study end up in publication or clinical records, an unstructured text. Due to advancements in biomedical research, the growth of published literature is gaining tremendous momentum in recent years. To generate high quality, reliable information from this large collection of continuously increasing unstructured text collection by manual efforts or even using simple data processing using computers is unattainable (Cohen & Hersh, 2005; Hearst, 1999; Zweigenbaum et al., 2007). Scientists and clinical researchers face a big challenge to stay current and extract hidden information from this sheer quantity of millions of published biomedical literature. The potential one-stop automated solution to this problem is biomedical text mining. The researchers and scientists require robust and sophisticated text mining methodologies and tools to cope up with this data abundance. There is a broader acceptance for the fact that refined biomedical text mining systems can play a major role in various areas of biomedicine such as from earlier applications such as gene prioritization, function prediction, and pathway extraction to recent initiatives such as drug repurposing and precision medicine (Aggarwal & Zhai, 2012; Hassani et al., 2020; Tao et al., 2020, 25). An overview of biomedical text mining in Big Data analysis with an application in cancer biology is illustrated in Figure 17.4.

17.4.2 Biomedical Text Mining Resources

Normally IR is performed as query-based or document-based searches for retrieving abstract or full-text from digital libraries or databases (Zhu et al., 2013). Even though the commonly well-known IR systems are search engines like Google or Yahoo, in BTM the major source is life science literature databases such as MEDLINE, PubMed Central, and BioMed Central, etc. The most important resource for scientific literature has been the MEDLINE database, which is the

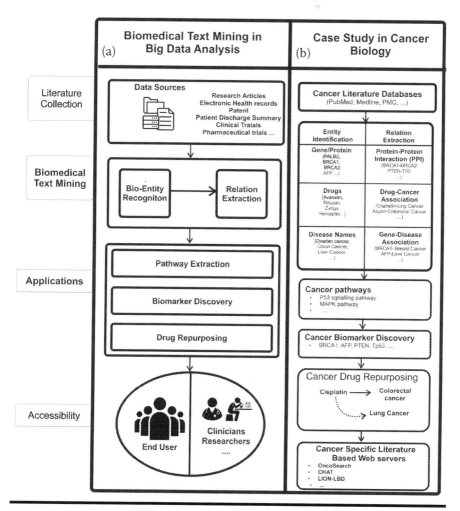

Figure 17.4 (a) Overview of biomedical text mining in Big Data analysis. (b) Illustration of biomedical text mining assisted cancer biology approach.

major bibliographic database developed and managed by the U.S. National Library of Medicine (NLM) which covers over 30 million articles from 5200 articles in the field of life science with a focus on biomedicine (Fiorini et al., 2018). On an average day, PubMed is used by 2.5 million people, resulting in 9 million pageviews from their 3 million search queries. Apart from large indexed databases, various task-specific biomedical corpora are released in BTM. Biomedical corpus plays a major role in the training, development, and testing of the BTM methodologies and tools in terms of performance, reliability, integrity, and robustness. The majority of the widely used corpora comes from a well-known text mining community challenge called BioCreAtIvE. BioCreAtIvE released Corpus like

BioCreative II Gene Mention (GM), BioCreative V CDR (Chemical Disease Relation), CHEMDNER (Chemical entity), ChemProt (Chemical-Protein), and PPI corpus. Other important biomedical text mining corpora are GENIA, NCBI disease, EU-ADR, PolySearch, and AlMed, etc.

17.4.3 Bio-Named Entity Recognition

NER focuses on recognizing and normalizing biomedical entities such as drugs, genes and proteins, diseases, cell type, miRNA, phenotypes, etc. Some of the major NER corpus employed in BTM are CHEMDNER patent (Chemicals, Genes/proteins), BioCreative V CDR (Chemical, Disease), BioCreative II Gene Mention (Genes/proteins), LocText (Species), Gellus (CellLines), etc. The major issues that arise in NER in the context of BTM are due to naming conventions, polysemic words, ambiguity and variability, term synonymy, lexical and typographical variants, heavy use of acronyms, domain-specific terminology, and referring expressions (Jensen et al., 2006; Zweigenbaum et al., 2007). To overcome these complex challenges, a variety of methodologies and tools are proposed in NER which can be generally categorized as rule-based, dictionary-based, machine learning-based, and hybrid approaches (Zhu et al., 2013; Bhasuran et al., 2016; Murugesan et al., 2017a). Even though machine learning and hybrid approaches exhibited a state of the result, recently deep learning-based unsupervised approaches using Big Data show greater significance in performance. One of the well-known deep learning-based Big Data systems is BioBERT which was developed using PubMed Abstracts (4.5B words), PMC Full-text articles (13.5B), Wikipedia (2.5B words), Books Corpus (0.8B words). BioBERT reported significant performance improvement in NER, relation extraction, and the task of question answering (Lee et al., 2020). The below example illustrates the NER process in biomedical text mining.

> *Example 1*: **PubMed ID: 10072428**
> **Original sentence**: We have confirmed that germline mutations in the CDH1 gene cause familial gastric cancer in non-Maori populations
> **Tagged sentence**: We have confirmed that germline mutations in the <gene>***CDH1 gene***</gene> cause <disease>***familial gastric cancer***</disease> in non-Maori populations

17.4.4 Bio-Relation Extraction

Relation Extraction focuses on the extraction of biological associations such as Protein-protein interactions (PPIs), Gene-disease associations, Drug-drug interactions (DDIs), miRNA-gene relation, genotype-phenotype association, etc. between the entities (Zweigenbaum et al., 2007; Murugesan et al., 2017b; Bhasuran, & Natarajan. 2018). Some of the widely employed BTM-based relation extraction corpora are BioInfercorpus (Genes/Proteins, RNAs), DDI corpus (Drug-Drug Interaction), ChemProt (Chemical-Protein), BioCreative V CDR (Chemical Disease Relation), EU-ADR (Gene-Disease). In the context of BTM, relation extraction focuses on extracting pairs or triplets of biomedical entities that are exhibiting certain biological connections between them. In relation to extraction, Big Data models are reporting improved performance with fast performance. SparkText is a Big Data framework built with Apache Spark and Cassandra NoSQL. Information extraction is performed at PubMed scale (28 million abstracts) with a response time of 6 minutes compared to 11 hours from traditional systems (Ye et al., 2016). The below example illustrates the relation extraction process in biomedical text mining.

> ***Example 2*: PubMed ID: 10945637**
> **Original sentence**: Thus, FGF6 is increased in PIN and prostate cancer and can promote the proliferation of the transformed prostatic epithelial cells via paracrine and autocrine mechanisms
> **Tagged sentence**: Thus, <gene>***FGF6***</gene> is <trigger>***increased***</trigger> in PIN and <disease>***prostate cancer***</disease> and can <trigger>***promote***</trigger> the <event>***proliferation***</event> of the transformed prostatic epithelial cells via paracrine and autocrine mechanisms

17.4.5 Event Extraction

Biomolecular event is the dynamic bio-relation with the involvement of one or more participants such as bio-entities (gene/protein) or bio-events (regulation, transcription) and plays a role like a theme and cause of the event. Using text mining, events are identified in two steps, namely trigger detection and argument detection. Event triggers and their types using domain-specific ontologies are identified in trigger detection. Argument detection identifies and extracts the theme of the event. The majority of the event extraction systems are developed through corpora from BioNLP-ST (Biomedical Natural Language Processing Shared Task) which is held in 2009, 2011, 2013, and 2016. Another major corpus that supports event extraction is the GENIA-MK (Meta-knowledge) corpus. One of the notable systems developed for complex event task is TEES (Turku Event Extraction System). Bjorne et al., developed TEES using graph words, dependency, and trigger word matching and evaluated on various corpora (Björne et al., 2011). Van Landeghem et al., developed a large-scale event extraction system using 21.9 million abstracts from PubMed and extracted 40 million bimolecular events (Van Landeghem et al., 2013). The below example illustrates the biomolecular event extraction process in biomedical text mining.

Example 3: **PubMed ID: 10029571**
Original sentence: Interleukin-10 inhibits expression of both interferon alpha- and interferon-gamma- induced genes by suppressing tyrosine phosphorylation of STAT1.
Tagged sentence: <gene>*Interleukin-10*</gene><event>*inhibits*</event><trigger>*expression*</trigger> of both interferon alpha- and interferon gamma- induced genes by <trigger>*suppressing*</trigger><event>*tyrosine phosphorylation*</event> of <gene>*STAT1*</gene>.

17.4.6 Applications

Due to the high performance and robustness, core IE tasks such as NER, Relation extraction, and Event extraction were applied to various applications such as biomedical pathway extraction, biomarker discovery, and drug re-purposing, etc. Pathway Extraction focuses on constructing the biological pathways automatically by identifying various biomedical entities such as protein, chemical, or cells and the extraction of biomolecular events involving these entities from text. Molecular biomarker discovery is an essential task in literature mining using which therapeutic mechanisms can be developed against target disease. The identification of biomarkers can give insight into the phenotypic states of cells or organisms. Finally, Drug repurposing or repositioning is the process of discovering and developing new therapeutic usage for an existing drug, different from the use it was invented for. Extraction of various associations such as disease–gene, gene-drug, and disease–drug relationships and ABC model has been successfully used for drug repurposing in text mining. The example shown below discusses these applications in biomedical text mining.

Example 4(Pathway): **PMC:3201112**
Original sentence: p53 enhances PTEN transcription and represses the expression of p110,145,146 the loss of p53 in cells with constitutively active RTK signaling can further potentiate PI3K pathway activation.
Tagged sentence: <gene>*p53*</gene> enhances <gene>*PTEN*</gene> transcription and represses the expression of p110,145,146 the loss of <gene>*p53*</gene> in cells with constitutively active RTK signaling, can further potentiate <pathway>*PI3K pathway*</pathway>activation.
In the above example, PI3K pathway mention has been recognized.

Example 5(Biomarker): **PMID:20863780 //Use this example//**
Original sentence: XRCC1 194Trp allele significantly increased the risk of gastric cancer and also associated with the risk of gastric cardia carcinoma and promoted distant metastasis of gastric cancer

Tagged sentence: <gene>*XRCC1*</gene> 194Trp allele <re-lw>*significantly increased the risk*<relw> of <disease>*gastric cancer*</disease> and also associated with risk of <disease>*gastric cardi carcinoma*</disease> and promoted distant metastasis of <disease>*gastric cancer*</disease>

In the above examples, XRCC1 significantly increased the risk of gastric cancer, indicating the potential use of XRCC1 as a biomarker target.

Example 6(Drug Repurposing):
PMID: 15383624: <drug>*tazarotene*</drug> acts as an agonist for retinoic acid receptor alpha (RARA)
PMID: 11788593:
Original sentence: These results suggest that RAR ligand-associated down-regulation of EGFR activity reduces cell proliferation by reducing the magnitude and duration of EGF-dependent ERK1/2 activation
Tagged sentence: These results suggest that RAR ligand-associated <event>*down-regulation*</event> of <gene>*EGFR*</gene> activity reduces cell proliferation by reducing the magnitude and duration of EGF-dependent <gene>*ERK1/2*</gene><event>*activation*</event>.
In the above examples, tazarotene activates RARA, which inhibits EGFR, indicating the potential use of tazarotene as an oncology therapy.

17.4.7 Case Studies in Cancer Literature

Cancer occurs when the abnormal cell is growing uncontrollably in masses. In other words, when the body's normal control mechanism stops working. It is one of the most fatal diseases in the present time with the highest death rate of 9.6 million in 2018 globally. According to the American Institute for Cancer Research (AICR), around 18 million cases were reported worldwide in 2018, of which 9.5 million are male and 8.5 million are women. With this concern, numerous treatment methods were developed and published in the form of unstructured scientific texts like EHR, patient summary, and publications. This unstructured information provides valuable information and resources for future researches to uncover essential information's about cancer studies (Hsiao & Lu, 2019; Zhu et al., 2013).

The availability of cancer literature is growing in the masses because of the need for efficient treatment. The PubMed repository search on May 23, 2020, with the keyword 'cancer' resulted in 4,110,932 articles. Manual reading and retrieving useful information from this big literature data are complex and time-consuming tasks. As discussed earlier, as an automated solution for information extraction from unstructured text, text mining can tackle this task. Text Mining helps the researchers in cancer biology in numerous ways like extracting cancer-related concepts (gene/protein, drug, and disease), extracting the relationship between these concepts, building or improving cancer-related pathways, and generating new hypotheses or knowledge based on existing information.

Some of the well-known text mining-based methodological studies are discussed here. Korhonen et al. developed a fully integrated text mining system for knowledge discovery in cancer risk assessment and research (Korhonen et al., 2012). Jurca et al. developed a framework for the identification of breast cancer biomarkers that integrates text mining with social network analysis (Jurca et al., 2016). Dai et al. presented a system named LiverCancerMarkerRIF to extract liver cancer-related summaries and curate supporting evidence from PubMed (Dai et al., 2014). Similarly, another text mining system named TMT-HCC was developed by Seoud et al. for hepatocellular carcinoma (HCC) biomarker identification (Seoud & Mabrouk, 2013). In their study, molecular biomarker genes along with HCC were identified for the diagnosis and prognosis of HCC. It also extracts protein-protein interaction information for HCC. Kawashima et al. applied text mining with a simple K-means clustering algorithm for identifying marker genes of breast cancer (Kawashima et al., 2017).

By incorporating various IE techniques discussed earlier, various benchmarking biomedical text mining-based discovery tools specifically focusing on cancer literature have also been developed. These studies focused on different areas such as identification of drivers, oncogenes and tumor suppressors, Hallmarks of Cancer (HoC) identification, clinically relevant cancer biomarker identification, and identification of genes, drugs, and variants from clinically relevant publications based on a profile of oncological mutation. It is also worthy to be mention that all of these studies were performed on the entire collection of PubMed reported at the time of the study. A detailed representation of these studies is discussed in Table 17.2. To conclude, in this Big Data era text mining researchers are continuously working on delivering systems that can support the research community to a great extend in information extraction, hypothesis generation, and knowledge discovery.

17.5 Applications in Healthcare

A vast number of sectors are befitting from big data, and among them, one of the major sectors is health care. The section discusses the application of Big Data and text mining in health care. We first introduce what healthcare text mining followed by two popular application areas electronic health records mining and health-related social media content mining is.

17.5.1 Healthcare Text Mining

Healthcare is one of the leading and enormously growing industries with medical data generated from patient management, diagnosis treatment and medication, new solutions for deadliest diseases, and efficient treatment techniques for all the

Table 17.2   Benchmarking Biomedical Text Mining–Based Discovery Tools Specifically Focusing on Cancer Literature

Discovery Tool	System Description	Availability
CancerMine	Text mined information on different types of cancer especially providing genes as drivers, oncogenes, and tumor suppressors	http://bionlp.bcgsc.ca/cancermine
Cancer Hallmarks Analytics Tool (CHAT)	Hallmarks of Cancer (HoC) identification using cancer-related references from PubMed into the taxonomy connecting different entities drugs, cancers, genes, and growth factors	http://chat.lionproject.net
OncoSearch	Text mined gene expression information on Cancer especially on up-regulated or down-regulated, progresses or regresses cancer and cancer genes roles	http://oncosearch.bio-pathway.org
miRCancer	microRNA–cancer associations were extracted by identifying microRNA expressions profiles using handcrafted rule matching	http://mircancer.ecu.edu/
DigSee (Cancer Version)	Direct(explicit) gene-disease associations from genes involved in the bio-molecular events with sentence scoring	http://gcancer.org/digsee
LION LBD	Implicit and Explicit associations generation using mapped ontology and concept graph with a special emphasis on Cancer	http://lbd.lionproject.net
BEST	High-speed text annotation tool covering 10 biological entities like genes, diseases, drugs, targets, mutation, miRNAs, transcription factors, etc.	http://best.korea.ac.kr

(Continued)

Table 17.2 (Continued) Benchmarking Biomedical Text Mining–Based Discovery Tools Specifically Focusing on Cancer Literature

Discovery Tool	System Description	Availability
SparkText	Big data framework based biomedical text mining tool demonstrated with various cancer types such as breast, lung, and prostate cancers	https://figshare.com/articles/New_draft_item/3796302
CIViCmine knowledgebase	Text mined clinically relevant biomarkers curated by genomic experts, Clinical Interpretation of Variants in Cancer (CIViC) knowledgebase	http://bionlp.bcgsc.ca/civicmine/
Variant-Information Search Tool for precision oncology(VIST)	Identification of genes, drugs, and variants from clinically relevant publications based on the profile of oncological mutation	https://vist.informatik.hu-berlin.de/

diseases (Baro et al., 2015). In this regard, there are a lot of huge volumes of information is generated in the form of unstructured text in the healthcare industry. Some statistics show that 10 million patient medical transactions are captured by a large medical organization over 10 years and hospital management systems generate roughly 150,000 medical data (Seoudand Mabrouk, 2013). Mining these Big Data can provide immense potential from disease progression prediction, disease comorbidities, diagnosis, medication, patient stratification, recovery rate, adverse drug reactions, drug-drug interactions, etc. (Kawashima et al. 2017). This information exists in the form of prescriptions, patient visits, clinician notes, medical test results, and more. Extracting useful information from these texts is a complex and prolonged process because of the volumes and unstructured nature. Healthcare Text Mining (HTM) is proposed as a solution to transform the unstructured text into structured representation by extracting information like entity recognition, entity linking, and relation extraction. HTM not only transforms the text into the structure format but also used to generate a novel hypothesis and new knowledge. HTM uses various techniques like machine learning, NLP, statistical techniques to extract useful information. HTM has been applied in the healthcare domain in various tasks like identification of patients' obesity status, disease-drug association extraction, and disease-specific classification of clinical discharges, and more (Dai et al., 2014; Hsiao & Lu, 2019; Korhonen et al., 2012; Jurca et al., 2016).

HTM data are existing in the form of EHR, clinical records, drug trial information, scientific literature, and health-related social media interactions (Dimitrov, 2016). EHR is the major source of information for HTM which encapsulated with discharge summaries, medicine prescription, test results, patient visits, etc. Three of the major application areas in heath care text mining such as Electronic Health Records Mining, Clinical Records Mining, and Social Media Mining are discussed in the following section.

17.5.2 Electronic Health Records Mining

Digitization and growth of patient medical data in recent years made EHR one of the sources of health care Big Data. From a research point of you, mining electronic health records provide the opportunity to create a personalized medical profile of a patient thereby consolidating important medical information such as details of genetic variation characterization and genotype-phenotype interactions. It is also worth mentioning that these patient-centric phenotypic profiles support a great deal in personalized precision medicine, case-control, and clinical trials.

Due to these vast potential applications variety of methodologies, data management protocols, and tools were developed for mining EHRs such as Text Analysis and Knowledge Extraction System (cTAKES), Informatics for Integrating Biology and the Bedside (i2b2) HITEX, Medical Language Extraction, and Encoding (MedLEE), cancer Biomedical Informatics Grid (caGRID) Browser, Research electronic data capture (REDCap), i2b2 Hive3, Electronic Medical Records and Genomics Network (eMERGE Network), MIMIC Critical Care Database, Electronic Health Records for Clinical Research(EHR4CR), Intelligent care delivery analytics (ICDA), and Observational health data sciences and informatics (OHDSI), etc. To support the development of these systems and methodologies researchers used numerous health care and clinical ontologies, controlled vocabularies and terminologies, some of them are Unified Medical Language System (UMLS), Systematized Nomenclature of Medicine-Clinical Terms (SNOMED-CT) from International clinical terminology and International Classification of Disease (ICD) from World Health Organization.

EHR comes with a variety of unstructured data in the form of clinical documents such as patient discharge summary, admission note, treatment plan, medication and recovery rate, etc. These clinical documents are heterogeneous in nature and lack proper syntactic and semantic representation and grammar making them computationally difficult to process. Extraction of structured information such as named entities (Drug, Disease, Phenotype, etc), mapping them to various vocabularies (ICD, SNOMED CT, etc), extraction of relations (Drug-Drug Interaction, Genotype-Phenotype Association), extraction of reaction events (Adverse Drug Reaction) and discovery of knowledge (Cancer survival rate), etc. are some of the major tasks in EHR mining. Table 17.3 shows the highly recognized EHR mining systems for various applications.

Table 17.3 Important Electronic Health Record Mining Systems and Applications

System	Description
DeepPatient (Miotto et al., 2016)	Clinical predictive modeling using deep feature learning on EHR data to create general-purpose patient representations for clinical applications such as drug targeting, clinical trial recruitment, disease prediction, patient similarity, personalized prescriptions, etc.
Doctor AI (Choi et al., 2016a)	Recurrent Neural Networks (RNN) based predictive model using large-scale EHR data from 260K patients. A multi-label prediction approach focusing categories like diagnosis and medication of a future visit by feeding the RNN with record information such as diagnosis, medication, or procedure codes
DeepCare (Pham et al., 2016)	Long Short-Term Memory (LSTM) based medical outcome prediction model using information about patient illness memory. The system uses time parameterizations for handling the illness memory and supports prognosis using EHR
Med2Vec (Choi et al., 2016b)	A robust two-layer neural network algorithm handling large scale of medical data and produces interpretable representations for medical codes and hospital visits. The system was demonstrated with training on 30K medical codes with big data of up to 5.5 million visits
i2b2 (Murphy et al., 2010)	National Center for Biomedical Computing (NCBC) developed i2b2 which combines genomic data with medical records and supports end-user for mini-databases creation of specific research projects
iDASH (Ohno-Machado et al., 2012)	iDASH (integrating data for analysis, anonymization, and sharing) is an NCBC system that focuses on sharing of algorithms and tools for Biological Projects spanning from molecule to population levels with an emphasis on biological and clinical data
iHealthExplorer (McAullay et al., 2005)	Electronic health databases web server enables the users for applying a variety of analytic algorithms for knowledge discovery from the queried data
ICDA (Gotz et al., 2012)	Clinical data analysis system based on normalized clinical data and allows the generation of use case-based analytic plugins

17.5.3 Health-Related Social Media Mining

In recent years, social media plays a vital role in healthcare research due to the growth of social media usage and information exchange between the internet communities (Hassani et al., 2020). There is an increasing need for utilizing social media for healthcare research from scientific communities. Nowadays, the Internet is one of the major sources of information for healthcare research because of the information exchanged in online health support communities and social media groups (Yang & Yang, 2013).

Nowadays people use social media platforms like Facebook, Twitter, and Online support groups to express their illness experience, side effects of the treatment, and search for advice from people who suffer from the same condition and clinicians. Therefore, the increased use of utilizing social media data for healthcare research has gained more attention. One of the major benefits of social media platforms is that people share their opinions freely than with healthcare providers. Due to these large volumes of unstructured text data is generating on daily basis. This opens a whole lot of opportunities for healthcare companies and clinicians to learn public and patient opinions on their products or treatment methods. To analyze, these information text mining techniques are effectively utilized.

Social media text analysis is successfully utilized in fields like conduct analysis on disease treatments (He et al., 2019) and drugs (Paul & Dredze, 2014), detecting early drug adverse side effects, drug-drug interactions, and more. Sampathkumar et al. (2014) extracted drug adverse side effects from online healthcare forums using the HMM model. Yates and Goharian (2013) created a framework called ADRTrace to detect unexpected and expected drug adverse reactions from social media using patterns, lexicons, and synonym sets. Yang and Yang (2013) identified the drug-drug interactions from online healthcare communities using associations mining. They used drug bank data as a gold standard for testing their model.

Apart from the above specific studies, social media can be analyzed for patients interested and the most discussed topic from online support groups. For example, He et al. utilized text mining methods to identify patient concerns, treatment issues from online support groups for epilepsy (He et al., 2019). Paul et al. utilized word frequency, lexical analysis and phrase pattern identification to extract patient concerns clinical differences posted by patients in online memories (Paul & Dredze, 2014). In this regard, social text media mining is a major field for healthcare research. Clinicians and researchers use public opinions to learn about treatment methods, product opinions, side effects, etc. A detailed representation of important health-related social media mining systems is given in Table 17.4.

Daily electronic and social media data are generating in the health care domain in the form of clinical records, discharge summaries, electronic health records, life science patents, drug trial information, health care recommendations, as well as discussions from social media like Twitter, Facebook and so forth. This health care Big Data provides immense opportunity to expand our understanding of the

Table 17.4 **Important Healthcare-Related Social Media Mining Systems and Applications**

System	Description
SSEL-ADE (Liu et al., 2018)	A framework was developed to extract adverse drug events from social media which exploit various semantic, lexical and syntactic features along with integrated semi-supervised learning and ensemble learning
Batbaatar & Ryu, 2019	Health-related Twitter corpora based named entity recognition of Disease or Syndrome, Sign or Symptom, and Pharmacological substances. The system used a recurrent neural network (RNN) based deep learning architecture and Unified Medical Language System (UMLS)
Jelodar et al., 2020	Sentiment classification and topic discovery from 563,079 COVID-19 Online Discussions using a deep learning approach. The system used Gibbs sampling, LDA topic model, Ranking, and Visualization. For the deep learning part, they used word embedding and LSTM RNN
McRoy et al., 2018	Text classification approach to identify the unmet needs of breast cancer survivors using random forest-based approach from online MayoConnect (MC) forum
Rong et al., 2019	A deep learning-based framework was developed to extract real-time surveillance data for Australia - pollen allergy from Twitter using deep learning architectures like LSTM, CNN, GRU, RNN.
Paul & Dredze, 2014	A topic modeling framework was developed to detect health topics from Twitter data using Latent Dirichlet Allocation (LDA) and Ailment Topic Aspect Model along.
Edo-Osagie et al., 2019	A semi-supervised approach for the classification of the symptomatic tweet and relevance filtering using features like word classes, positive and negative word counts, denotes laughter, and negative emojis/emoticons. Then using these features various supervised algorithms like Naive Bayes, Decision Trees, Logistic Regression, Support Vector Machines (SVMs), and Multilayer Perceptron (MLP) neural networks. Finally, a semi-supervised approach using the Iterative Labelling Algorithm was trained using the features.

complexity of medical and biological aspects of health care. It is evident that by mining this Big Data it is possible to attain tremendous breakthroughs in various applications ranging from quicker validation of disease diagnosis, treatment optimization, and prevention, drug re-purposing to personalized precision medicine.

17.6 Conclusion

Innovations in science and technology boost-up the generation of an immense volume of digital data in the form of text, audio, video, images and paved the way for a new era called Big Data. A majority of this data is generated in a semi-structured and unstructured format poses a challenge for NLP and text analytics. The volume of this data is getting bigger every day, makes the traditional computational approaches and manual process of managing, understanding, and extracting information from this Big Data unattainable. As an automated solution text mining provides a framework pipeline using which a large volume of text data can be processed thereby increasing the value of information to superlative. In practice, three major components of text mining are Information Retrieval (IR), Information Extraction (IE), and Knowledge Discovery. The biomedicine and health care industry, in particular, pose a great challenge in Big Data management and information extraction due to reasons like lack of standardization and consolidation of both research and clinical data, complexity in entity and relation mentions, term synonymy and homonymy, lexical and typographical variants, data sparseness, heavy use of acronyms, domain-specific terminology, ambiguity, variability and referring expressions, etc. This chapter discussed different systems solving these issues for different tasks such as named entity recognition, relation extraction, event extraction, pathway extraction, biomarker identification, drug repurposing, EHR mining, and health-related social media mining. It is also worthy to mention that the newly developed text mining systems are accessed by their ability to scale up to Big Data platforms.

In summary, text mining systems show immense potential in various applications across industry and academic sectors especially by handling Big Data. Text mining systems are developing as cutting edge technologies by training on billions of word tokens as training data with nearly human-like accuracy using techniques like deep learning, a recent advancement in machine learning. Moreover, data science, in general, is the leading topic of research and development in Big Data. To conclude, text mining can act as an influential elucidation in the Big Data era.

References

Abaya, S. A. (2012). Association rule mining based on Apriori algorithm in minimizing candidate generation. *International Journal of Scientific & Engineering Research*, 3(7), 1–4.

Abdulkadhar, S., Murugesan, G., & Natarajan, J. (2020). Classifying protein-protein interaction articles from biomedical literature using many relevant features and context-free grammar. *Journal of King Saud University-Computer and Information Sciences*, 32(5) 553-560.

AbuZeina, D., & Al-Anzi, F. S. (2018). Employing fisher discriminant analysis for Arabic text classification. *Computers & Electrical Engineering, 66*, 474–486.

Adnan, K., & Akbar, R. (2019). An analytical study of information extraction from unstructured and multidimensional big data. *Journal of Big Data, 6*(1), 91.

Agerri, R., Artola, X., Beloki, Z., Rigau, G., & Soroa, A. (2015). Big data for natural language processing: A streaming approach. *Knowledge-Based Systems, 79*, 36–42.

Aggarwal, C. C., & Cheng, X.Z. (2012). *"A survey of text clustering algorithms." Mining text data* (pp. 77–128). Boston, MA: Springer.

Aggarwal, C. C., & Zhai, C. (2012). An introduction to text mining. In *Mining text data* (pp. 1–10). Boston, MA: Springer.

Akter, S., & Wamba, S. F. (2016). Big data analytics in E-commerce: A systematic review and agenda for future research. *Electronic Markets, 26*(2), 173–194.

Amado, A., Cortez, P., Rita, P., & Moro, S. (2018). Research trends on Big Data in Marketing: A text mining and topic modeling based literature analysis. *European Research on Management and Business Economics, 24*(1), 1–7.

Arshad, O., Gallo, I., Nawaz, S., & Calefati, A. (2019). Aiding intra-text representations with visual context for multimodal named entity recognition. arXiv preprint arXiv:1904.01356.

Ayre, K. K., Caldwell, C. A., Stinson, J., & Landis, W.G. (2014). Analysis of regional scale risk of whirling disease in populations of Colorado and Rio Grande cutthroat trout using a Bayesian belief network model. *Risk Analysis, 34*(9), 1589–1605.

Azzag, H., Guinot, C., & Venturini, G. (2006). Data and text mining with hierarchical clustering ants. In *Swarm intelligence in data mining* (pp. 153–189). Berlin, Heidelberg: Springer.

Baro, E., Degoul, S., Beuscart, R., & Chazard, E. (2015). Toward a literature-driven definition of big data in healthcare. *BioMed Research International*, 1–9. 639021.

Bashir, S., Qamar, U., & Khan, F. H. (2015). BagMOOV: A novel ensemble for heart disease prediction bootstrap aggregation with multi-objective optimized voting. *Australasian Physical & Engineering Sciences in Medicine, 38*(2), 305–323.

Batbaatar, E., & Ryu, K. H. (2019). Ontology-based healthcare named entity recognition from Twitter messages using a recurrent neural network approach. *International Journal of Environmental Research and Public Health, 16*(19), 3628.

Bhasuran, B., Murugesan, G., Abdulkadhar, S., & Natarajan, J. (2016). Stacked ensemble combined with fuzzy matching for biomedical named entity recognition of diseases. *Journal of Biomedical Informatics, 64*, 1–9.

Bhasuran, B., & Natarajan, J. (2018). Automatic extraction of gene-disease associations from literature using joint ensemble learning. *PloS One, 13*(7), e0200699.

Bhasuran, B., & Natarajan, J. (2019). Distant supervision for large-scale extraction of gene–disease associations from literature using DeepDive. In International Conference on Innovative Computing and Communications (pp. 367–374). Springer, Singapore.

Bhasuran, B., Subramanian, D., & Natarajan, J. (2018). Text mining and network analysis to find functional associations of genes in high altitude diseases. *Computational Biology and Chemistry, 75*, 101–110.

Björne, J., Heimonen, J., Ginter, F., Airola, A., Pahikkala, T., & Salakoski, T. (2011). Extracting contextualized complex biological events with rich graph-based feature sets. *Computational Intelligence, 27*(4), 541–557.

Boytcheva, S., Angelova, G., Angelov, Z., & Tcharaktchiev, D. (2015). Text mining and big data analytics for retrospective analysis of clinical texts from outpatient care. *Cybernetics and Information Technologies, 15*(4), 58–77.

Chen, H. C., Chen, Z. Y., Huang, S. Y., Ku, L. W., Chiu, Y. S., & Yang, W. J. (2018, July). Relation extraction in knowledge base question answering: From general-domain to the catering industry. In International Conference on HCI in Business, Government, and Organizations (pp. 26–41). Springer, Cham.

Choi, E., Bahadori, M. T., Schuetz, A., Stewart, W. F., & Sun, J. (2016a, December). Doctor AI: Predicting clinical events via recurrent neural networks. In Machine Learning for Healthcare Conference (pp. 301–318).

Choi, E., Bahadori, M. T., Searles, E., Coffey, C., Thompson, M., Bost, J., Tejedor-Sojo, J., & Sun, J. (2016b, August). Multi-layer representation learning for medical concepts. In Proceedings of the 22nd ACM SIGKDD International Conference on Knowledge Discovery and Data Mining (pp. 1495–1504).

Cohen, A. M., & Hersh, W. R. (2005). A survey of current work in biomedical text mining. *Briefings in Bioinformatics, 6*(1), 57–71.

Cohen, K. B., & Hunter L. (2008). Getting started in text mining. *PloS Comput Biol, 4*, e20.

Crone, S. F., & Koeppel, C. (2014, March). Predicting exchange rates with sentiment indicators: An empirical evaluation using text mining and multilayer perceptrons. In 2014 IEEE Conference on Computational Intelligence for Financial Engineering & Economics (CIFEr) (pp. 114–121). IEEE.

Dai, H. J., Wu, J. C. Y., Lin, W. S., Reyes, A. J. F., Syed-Abdul, S., Tsai, R. T. H., & Hsu, W. L. (2014). LiverCancerMarkerRIF: A liver cancer biomarker interactive curation system combining text mining and expert annotations. *Database*, 2014.

De Mauro, A., Greco, M., & Grimaldi, M. (2015, February). What is big data? A consensual definition and a review of key research topics. In AIP conference proceedings (*Vol. 1644*, No. 1, pp. 97–104). American Institute of Physics.

Deekshatulu, B. L., & Chandra, P. (2013). Classification of heart disease using k-nearest neighbor and genetic algorithm. *Procedia Technology, 10*, 85–94.

Dimitrov, D. V. (2016). Medical internet of things and big data in healthcare. *Healthcare Informatics Research, 22*(3), 156–163.

Edo-Osagie, O., Smith, G., Lake, I., Edeghere, O., & De La Iglesia, B. (2019). Twitter mining using semi-supervised classification for relevance filtering in syndromic surveillance. *PloS One, 14*(7), e0210689.

Feldman, R., & Sanger, J. (2007). *The text mining handbook: Advanced approaches in analyzing unstructured data.* Cambridge: Cambridge University Press.

Ferreira-Mello, R., André, M., Pinheiro, A., Costa, E., & Romero, C. (2019). Text mining in education. *Wiley Interdisciplinary Reviews: Data Mining and Knowledge Discovery, 9*(6), e1332.

Fiorini, N., Leaman, R., Lipman, D. J., & Lu, Z. (2018). How user intelligence is improving PubMed. *Nature Biotechnology, 36*(10), 937–945.

Fonarow, G. C., Adams, K. F., Abraham, W. T., Yancy, C. W., Boscardin, W. J. and ADHERE Scientific Advisory Committee (2005). Risk stratification for in-hospital mortality in acutely decompensated heart failure: Classification and regression tree analysis. *JAMA, 293*(5), 572–580.

Fraley, C., & Hesterberg, T. (2009). Least angle regression and LASSO for large datasets. *Statistical Analysis and Data Mining: The ASA Data Science Journal*, *1*(4), 251–259.

Francis, S., Van Landeghem, J., & Moens, M. F. (2019). Transfer learning for named entity recognition in financial and biomedical documents. *Information*, *10*(8), 248.

Georgescu, T. M. (2020). Natural language processing model for automatic analysis of cybersecurity-related documents. *Symmetry*, *12*(3), 354.

Gök, A., Waterworth, A., & Shapira, P. (2015). Use of web mining in studying innovation. *Scientometrics*, *102*(1), 653–671.

Gotz, D., Stavropoulos, H., Sun, J., & Wang, F. (2012). ICDA: a platform for intelligent care delivery analytics. In AMIA annual symposium proceedings (*Vol. 2012*, p. 264). American Medical Informatics Association.

Gunn, S. R. (1998). Support vector machines for classification and regression. *ISIS Technical Report*, *14*(1), 5–16.

Hanif, S.M., & Prevost, L. (2009, July). Text detection and localization in complex scene images using constrained adaboost algorithm. In 2009 10th international conference on document analysis and recognition (pp. 1–5). IEEE.

Hashem, I. A. T., Yaqoob, I., Anuar, N. B., Mokhtar, S., Gani, A., & Khan, S.U. (2015). The rise of "big data" on cloud computing: Review and open research issues. *Information Systems*, *47*, 98–115.

Hassani, H., Beneki, C., Unger, S., Mazinani, M. T., & Yeganegi, M. R. (2020). Text mining in Big Data analytics. *Big Data and Cognitive Computing*, *4*(1), 1.

He, K., Hong, N., Lapalme-Remis, S., Lan, Y., Huang, M., Li, C., & Yao, L. (2019). Understanding the patient perspective of epilepsy treatment through text mining of online patient support groups. *Epilepsy & Behavior*, *94*, 65–71.

Hearst, M. A. (1999, June). Untangling text data mining. In Proceedings of the 37th annual meeting of the Association for Computational Linguistics on Computational Linguistics (pp. 3–10). Association for Computational Linguistics.

Herland, M., Khoshgoftaar, T. M., & Wald, R. (2014). A review of data mining using big data in health informatics. *Journal of Big Data*, *1*(1), 1–35.

Hilbert, M. (2016). Big data for development: A review of promises and challenges. *Development Policy Review*, *34*(1), 135–174.

Hirschberg, J., & Manning, C.D. (2015). Advances in natural language processing. *Science*, *349*(6245), 261–266.

Hogenboom, F., Frasincar, F., Kaymak, U., & De Jong, F. (2011, October). An overview of event extraction from text. In DeRiVE@ ISWC (pp. 48–57).

Hsiao, Y. W., & Lu, T. P. (2019). Text-mining in cancer research may help identify effective treatments. *Translational Lung Cancer Research*, *8*(Suppl 4), S460.

Inmon, W. H., & Linstedt, D. (2014). *Data architecture: a primer for the data scientist: big data, data warehouse and data vault*. Morgan Kaufmann.

Isa, D., Kallimani, V. P., & Lee, L. H. (2009). Using the self organizing map for clustering of text documents. *Expert Systems with Applications*, *36*(5), 9584–9591.

Jahromi, A. H., & Taheri, M. (2017, October). A non-parametric mixture of Gaussian naive Bayes classifiers based on local independent features. In 2017 Artificial Intelligence and Signal Processing Conference (AISP) (pp. 209–212). IEEE.

Jelodar, H., Wang, Y., Orji, R., & Huang, H. (2020). Deep sentiment classification and topic discovery on novel coronavirus or covid-19 online discussions: Nlp using lstm recurrent neural network approach. arXiv preprint arXiv:2004.11695.

Jensen, L. J., Saric, J., & Bork, P. (2006). Literature mining for the biologist: from information retrieval to biological discovery. *Nature reviews genetics*, *7*(2), 119–129.

Jiang, M., Liang, Y., Feng, X., Fan, X., Pei, Z., Xue, Y., & Guan, R. (2018). Text classification based on deep belief network and softmax regression. *Neural Computing and Applications*, *29*(1), 61–70.

Jing, L., Ng, M. K., Xu, J., & Huang, J. Z. (2005, May). Subspace clustering of text documents with feature weighting k-means algorithm. In Pacific-Asia Conference on Knowledge Discovery and Data Mining (pp. 802–812). Springer, Berlin, Heidelberg.

Jurca, G., Addam, O., Aksac, A., Gao, S., Özyer, T., Demetrick, D., & Alhajj, R. (2016). Integrating text mining, data mining, and network analysis for identifying genetic breast cancer trends. *BMC Research Notes*, *9*(1), 236.

Kang, M., Ahn, J., & Lee, K. (2018). Opinion mining using ensemble text hidden Markov models for text classification. *Expert Systems with Applications*, *94*, 218–227.

Kang, N., van Mulligen, E. M., & Kors, J. A. (2011). Comparing and combining chunkers of biomedical text. *Journal of Biomedical Informatics*, *44*, 354–360.

Kaur, S., & Rashid, E. M. (2016). Web news mining using Back Propagation Neural Network and clustering using K-Means algorithm in big data. *Indian Journal of Science and Technology*, *9*(41), 1–8.

Kawashima, K., Bai, W., & Quan, C. (2017, June). Text mining and pattern clustering for relation extraction of breast cancer and related genes. In 2017 18th IEEE/ACIS International Conference on Software Engineering, Artificial Intelligence, Networking and Parallel/Distributed Computing (SNPD) (pp. 59–63). IEEE.

Kimball, R. (2011). The evolving role of the enterprise data warehouse in the era of big data analytics. Whitepaper, Kimball Group, April.

Korhonen, A., Séaghdha, D. Ó., Silins, I., Sun, L., Högberg, J., & Stenius, U. (2012). Text mining for literature review and knowledge discovery in cancer risk assessment and research. *PloS One*, *7*(4), e33427.

Larsen, J., Szymkowiak, A., & Hansen, L. K. (2002). Probabilistic hierarchical clustering with labeled and unlabeled data. *International Journal of Knowledge Based Intelligent Engineering Systems*, *6*(1), 56–63.

Lee, J., Yoon, W., Kim, S., Kim, D., Kim, S., So, C. H., & Kang, J. (2020). BioBERT: a pre-trained biomedical language representation model for biomedical text mining. *Bioinformatics*, *36*(4), 1234–1240.

Liu, J., Zhao, S., & Wang, G. (2018). SSEL-ADE: a semi-supervised ensemble learning framework for extracting adverse drug events from social media. *Artificial Intelligence in Medicine*, *84*, 34–49.

Liu, M., Jiang, L., & Hu, H. (2017). Automatic extraction and visualization of semantic relations between medical entities from medicine instructions. *Multimedia Tools and Applications*, *76*(8), 10555–10573.

Lu, Z. (2011). PubMed and beyond: a survey of web tools for searching biomedical literature. *Database (Oxford)*; 2011:baq036.

Lv, X., Guan, Y., Yang, J., & Wu, J. (2016). Clinical relation extraction with deep learning. *International Journal of Hybrid Information Technology*, *9*(7), 237–248.

Maroli, N., Kalagatur, N. K., Bhasuran, B., Jayakrishnan, A., Manoharan, R. R., Kolandaivel, P., Natarajan, J., & Kadirvelu, K. (2019). Molecular mechanism of T-2 toxin-induced cerebral edema by aquaporin-4 blocking and permeation. *Journal of Chemical Information and Modeling*, *59*(11), 4942–4958.

McAullay, D., Williams, G., Chen, J., Jin, H., He, H., Sparks, R., & Kelman, C. (2005, January). A delivery framework for health data mining and analytics. In *Proceedings of the Twenty-eighth Australasian conference on Computer Science-Volume 38* (pp. 381–387). Australian Computer Society, Inc.

McRoy, S., Rastegar-Mojarad, M., Wang, Y., Ruddy, K. J., Haddad, T. C., & Liu, H. (2018). Assessing unmet information needs of breast cancer survivors: Exploratory study of online health forums using text classification and retrieval. *JMIR Cancer*, *4*(1), e10.

Miotto, R., Li, L., Kidd, B. A., & Dudley, J. T. (2016). Deep patient: An unsupervised representation to predict the future of patients from the electronic health records. *Scientific Reports*, *6*(1), 1–10.

Mirza, B., Wang, W., Wang, J., Choi, H., Chung, N. C., & Ping, P. (2019). Machine learning and integrative analysis of biomedical big data. *Genes*, *10*(2), 87.

Mukherjee, A., & Zhu, J. (2011). Reduced rank ridge regression and its kernel extensions. *Statistical Analysis and Data Mining: The ASA Data Science Journal*, *4*(6), 612–622.

Murphy, S. N., Weber, G., Mendis, M., Gainer, V., Chueh, H. C., Churchill, S., & Kohane, I. (2010). Serving the enterprise and beyond with informatics for integrating biology and the bedside (i2b2). *Journal of the American Medical Informatics Association*, *17*(2), 124–130.

Murugesan, G., Abdulkadhar, S., Bhasuran, B., & Natarajan, J. (2017a). BCC-NER: bi-directional, contextual clues named entity tagger for gene/protein mention recognition. *EURASIP Journal on Bioinformatics and Systems Biology*, *2017*(1), 7.

Murugesan, G., Abdulkadhar, S., & Natarajan, J. (2017b). Distributed smoothed tree kernel for protein-protein interaction extraction from the biomedical literature. *PLOS One*, 12, e0187379.

Ohno-Machado, L., Bafna, V., Boxwala, A. A., Chapman, B. E., Chapman, W. W., Chaudhuri, K., Day, M. E., Farcas, C., Heintzman, N. D., Jiang, X., & Kim, H. (2012). iDASH: Integrating data for analysis, anonymization, and sharing. *Journal of the American Medical Informatics Association*, *19*(2), 196–201

Omar, Y. (2015). Al-Jarrah, Paul D. Yoo, Sami Muhaidat, George K. Karagiannidis, Kamal Taha, Efficient Machine Learning for Big Data. *Big Data Research*, *2*(3), 87–93.

Palangi, H., Deng, L., Shen, Y., Gao, J., He, X., Chen, J., Song, X., & Ward, R. (2016). Deep sentence embedding using long short-term memory networks: Analysis and application to information retrieval. *IEEE/ACM Transactions on Audio, Speech, and Language Processing*, *24*(4), 694–707.

Paul, M. J., & Dredze, M. (2014). Discovering health topics in social media using topic models. *PloS One*, *9*(8), e103408.

Pham, T., Tran, T., Phung, D., & Venkatesh, S. (2016, April). Deepcare: A deep dynamic memory model for predictive medicine. In *Pacific-Asia Conference on Knowledge Discovery and Data Mining* (pp. 30–41). Springer, Cham.

Poria, S., Cambria, E., & Gelbukh, A. (2015, September). Deep convolutional neural network textual features and multiple kernel learning for utterance-level multimodal sentiment analysis. In *Proceedings of the 2015 conference on empirical methods in natural language processing* (pp. 2539–2544).

Pouyanfar, S., Yang, Y., Chen, S. C., Shyu, M. L., & Iyengar, S. S. (2018). Multimedia big data analytics: A survey. *ACM Computing Surveys (CSUR)*, *51*(1), 1–34.

Qiang, L. I. (2006). A Comparative Study on Algorithms of Constructing Decision Trees——ID3, C4. 5 and C5. 0 (J). *Journal of Gansu Sciences*, *4*, 84–87.

Rademaker, A. (2018). Challenges for Information Extraction in the Oil and Gas Domain. In ONTOBRAS (pp. 11–25).

Raghupathi, W., & Raghupathi, V. (2014). Big data analytics in healthcare: promise and potential. *Health information science and systems*, *2*(1), 3.

Rebholz-Schuhmann, D., Oellrich, A., Hoehndorf, R. (2012). Textmining solutions for biomedical research: enabling integrative biology. *Nat Rev Genet*, *13*, 829–839.

Rifaie, M., Kianmehr, K., Alhajj, R., & Ridley, M. J. (2008, July). Data warehouse architecture and design. In 2008 IEEE International Conference on Information Reuse and Integration (pp. 58–63). IEEE.

Rim, K., Lynch, K., & Pustejovsky, J. (2019, June). Computational Linguistics Applications for Multimedia Services. In Proceedings of the 3rd Joint SIGHUM Workshop on Computational Linguistics for Cultural Heritage, Social Sciences, Humanities and Literature (pp. 91–97).

Rong, J., Michalska, S., Subramani, S., Du, J., & Wang, H. (2019). Deep learning for pollen allergy surveillance from twitter in Australia. *BMC medical informatics and decision making*, *19*(1), 208.

Sagiroglu, S., & Sinanc, D. (2013, May). Big data: A review. In 2013 international conference on collaboration technologies and systems (CTS) (pp. 42–47). IEEE.

Sampathkumar, H., Chen, X. W., & Luo, B. (2014). Mining adverse drug reactions from online healthcare forums using hidden Markov model. *BMC Medical Informatics and Decision Making*, *14*(1), 91.

Seoud, R. A. A., & Mabrouk, M. S. (2013). TMT-HCC: A tool for text mining the biomedical literature for hepatocellular carcinoma (HCC) biomarkers identification. *Computer Methods and Programs in Biomedicine*, *112*(3), 640–648.

Tao, D., Yang, P., & Feng, H. (2020). Utilization of text mining as a big data analysis tool for food science and nutrition. *Comprehensive Reviews in Food Science and Food Safety*, *19*(2), 875–894.

Toh, K. A., Yau, W. Y., & Jiang, X. (2004). A reduced multivariate polynomial model for multimodal biometrics and classifiers fusion. *IEEE Transactions on Circuits and Systems for Video Technology*, *14*(2), 224–233.

Tsuruoka, Y., McNaught, J., Tsujii, J. I. C., & Ananiadou, S. (2007). Learning string similarity measures for gene/protein name dictionary look-up using logistic regression. *Bioinformatics*, *23*(20), 2768–2774.

Uguz, H. (2011). A two-stage feature selection method for text categorization by using information gain, principal component analysis and genetic algorithm. *Knowledge-Based Systems*, *24*(7), 1024–1032.

Uramoto, N., Matsuzawa, H., Nagano, T., Murakami, A., Takeuchi, H., & Takeda, K. (2004). A text-mining system for knowledge discovery from biomedical documents. *IBM Systems Journal*, *43*(3), 516–533.

van Altena, A. J., Moerland, P. D., Zwinderman, A. H., & Delgado Olabarriaga, S. (2019). Usage of the term Big Data in biomedical publications: A text mining approach. *Big Data and Cognitive Computing*, *3*(1), 13.

Van Landeghem, S., Björne, J., Wei, C. H., Hakala, K., Pyysalo, S., Ananiadou, S., Kao, H. Y., Lu, Z., Salakoski, T., Van de Peer, Y., & Ginter, F. (2013). Large-scale event extraction from literature with multi-level gene normalization. *PloS One*, *8*(4).

Wang, P., Hao, T., Yan, J., & Jin, L. (2017). Large-scale extraction of drug-disease pairs from the medical literature. *Journal of the Association for Information Science and Technology*, *68*(11), 2649–2661.

Wang, Y., Li, Y., Song, Y., Rong, X., & Zhang, S. (2017). Improvement of ID3 algorithm based on simplified information entropy and coordination degree. *Algorithms, 10*(4), 124.

Yang, H., & Yang, C. C. (2013, September). Harnessing social media for drug-drug interactions detection. In 2013 IEEE International Conference on Healthcare Informatics (pp. 22–29). IEEE.

Yang, L. C., Tan, I. K., Selvaretnam, B., Howg, E. K., & Kar, L. H. (2019, May). TEXT: Traffic Entity eXtraction from Twitter. In Proceedings of the 2019 5th International Conference on Computing and Data Engineering (pp. 53–59).

Yang, Y. H., Lin, Y. C., Su, Y. F., & Chen, H. H. (2007, July). Music emotion classification: A regression approach. In 2007 IEEE International Conference on Multimedia and Expo (pp. 208–211). IEEE.

Yates, A., & Goharian, N. (2013, March). ADRTrace: detecting expected and unexpected adverse drug reactions from user reviews on social media sites. In European Conference on Information Retrieval (pp. 816–819). Springer, Berlin, Heidelberg.

Ye, Z., Tafti, A. P., He, K. Y., Wang, K., & He, M. M. (2016). Sparktext: Biomedical text mining on big data framework. *PloS One, 11*(9), e0162721.

Zhang, Y. F., Xiong, Z. Y., Geng, X. F., & Chen, J. M. (2010). Analysis and improvement of ECLAT algorithm. *Computer Engineering, 23*, 28–30.

Zhu, F., Patumcharoenpol, P., Zhang, C., Yang, Y., Chan, J., Meechai, A., Vongsangnak, W., & Shen, B. (2013). Biomedical text mining and its applications in cancer research. *Journal of Biomedical Informatics, 46*(2), 200–211.

Zweigenbaum, P., Demner-Fushman, D., Yu, H., & Cohen, K. B. (2007). Frontiers of biomedical text mining: Current progress. *Briefings in Bioinformatics, 8*(5), 358–375.

Index

Note: *Italicized* page numbers refer to figures, **bold** page numbers refer to tables

Printed in the United States
by Baker & Taylor Publisher Services